June Mathis
The Rise and Fall of a
Silent Film Visionary

Thomas J. Slater

UNIVERSITY PRESS OF KENTUCKY

A note to the reader: Some of the quotations printed in this volume include racial slurs and other insensitive language. The book also contains images of an actor wearing theatrical makeup and costuming to portray a character of a different race. The original terminology and imagery are reproduced here for the purpose of historical accuracy. Discretion is advised.

Portions of this book have been adapted from Slater, Thomas J. "June Mathis: A Woman Who Spoke Through Silents." *Griffithiana* 18, no. 53 (1995): 133–169; "June Mathis's *Ben-Hur*: A Tale of Corporate Change and the Decline of Women's Influence in Hollywood." In *Bigger than Ben-Hur: The Book, Its Adaptations, & Their Audiences,* edited by Barbra Ryan and Millette Shamir, 108–124. Syracuse, NY: Syracuse University Press, 2016; "June Mathis's *Classified*: One Woman's Response to Modernism." *Journal of Film and Video* 50, no. 2 (1998): 3–14; "June Mathis's *The Legion of Death* (1918): Melodrama and the Realities of Women in World War I." *Women's Studies* 37, no. 7 (2008): 833–844. https://doi.org/10.1080/00497870802 341541; "June Mathis's Valentino Scripts: Images of Male 'Becoming' after the Great War." *Cinema Journal* 50, no. 1 (2010): 99–120; "The Vision and the Struggle: June Mathis's Work on *Ben-Hur* (1922–24)." *Post Script: Essays in Film and the Humanities* 28, no. 1 (2008): 63–78.

Scholarly publisher for the Commonwealth,
serving Bellarmine University, Berea College, Centre
College of Kentucky, Eastern Kentucky University,
The Filson Historical Society, Georgetown College,
Kentucky Historical Society, Kentucky State University,
Morehead State University, Murray State University,
Northern Kentucky University, Spalding University,
Transylvania University, University of Kentucky,
University of Louisville, University of Pikeville,
and Western Kentucky University.

Editorial and Sales Offices: The University Press of Kentucky
663 South Limestone Street, Lexington, Kentucky 40508-4008
www.kentuckypress.com

Unless otherwise noted, photographs are courtesy of Diane Mathis Madsen.

Cataloging-in-Publication data is available from the Library of Congress.

ISBN 978-1-9859-0192-6 (hardcover: alk. paper)
ISBN 978-1-9859-0194-0 (epub)
ISBN 978-1-9859-0193-3 (pdf)

Member of the Association of University Presses

To Mary Ann, the best writing partner and life partner.
This book would not exist without her.
And to Gretchen and Alli, unmatchable.

Contents

Introduction: The Importance of June Mathis   1

1. June Mathis's Journey from Acting to Writing, 1897–1915   7
2. Success at Metro, 1915–1921   26
3. Metro's Women Writers, 1917–1921   51
4. The Nazimova Films, 1917–1921   58
5. The Valentino Films, 1921   87
6. The Valentino Films, 1922   109
7. Crucial Films and Transitions, 1920–1923   123
8. June Mathis's *Ben-Hur*, 1922–1924   152
9. First National and Freelancing, 1924–1927   183

Acknowledgments   215
Notes   219
Selected Bibliography   259
Index   269

Illustrations follow page 86

Introduction
The Importance of June Mathis

In July 1923, *Photoplay* magazine noted, "Probably the most powerful woman in the motion picture industry today is June Mathis. This well known writer seems to be the head and shoulders of the Goldwyn organization at present, and rumor says her word is law and is final upon every angle of every production being made."[1] Mathis reached the position of editorial director at Goldwyn after six years with Metro Pictures and a few months with Famous Players-Lasky. Her amazing success with Metro's *The Four Horsemen of the Apocalypse* in 1921 brought both actor Rudolph Valentino and director Rex Ingram from obscurity to fame. Thus, on July 15, 1922, Goldwyn's new president, Joe Godsol, hired her to produce and write *Ben-Hur* for which he had just purchased the rights.[2] In December, he put her in charge of all the studio's productions.[3] Fan magazines hailed this promotion, as did Goldwyn vice president Edward Bowes, who told a sales staff convention that "the presence of June Mathis as editorial director fortified the company immeasurably."[4] Two years later, her *Ben-Hur* production collapsed, and Mathis then spent two years as editorial director at First National Pictures and started to freelance in November 1926.[5] On July 26, 1927, her life ended at the age of forty.

Mathis's death came at the end of the silent film era in which more women worked as writers, directors, and production company leaders (several doing all of these simultaneously) than at any time until the end of the century. Mathis's workload during her eleven-and-a-half-year career included writing the screenplays for approximately ninety-nine completed films and numerous other unmade productions, serving as an adviser and editorial director for countless others, and watching on the set to assist actors and directors. Alice Guy Blaché built her own state-of-the-art studio, Solax, where she produced, wrote, and directed.[6] Mary Pickford cofounded United Artists; Lois Weber was a popular producer/writer/director, sometime star, and head of her own company.[7] In the teens, Universal employed several female directors. Nell Shipman performed all of the same duties as Weber at her own studio in Priest Lake, Idaho; Alla Nazimova did likewise at Metro Pictures; Lule Warrenton, Cleo Madison, Ruth Stonehouse, and many others also produced, wrote, and directed.[8]

Although the online Women Film Pioneers Project now makes their achievements abundantly clear, women filmmakers began to disappear from historical records by the 1930s.[9] By the 1970s, women in film scholarship largely assumed that there had been no women directors until their time. In 1992, Patricia Mellencamp commented that only during the previous decade had feminists begun expanding film history. But she does so by asserting the use of "fan magazines, penny novels, and other cheap amusements as evidence."[10] The study of actual films directed or scripts written by women was yet to be pursued. Cari Beauchamp's 1997 book on writer/director Frances Marion placed her in the context of "the Powerful Women of Early Hollywood" by focusing on the stories of her struggles and triumphs within the industry.[11] But in 2003, Kay Armatage noted that "there is still a relative paucity of books that give a broad picture—either historical or contemporary—of women's creative production in film."[12] Armatage's biographical study of Nell Shipman emphasizes the filmmaker as a creative worker whose few successful years were rewarded when she was "driven out of the industry by the rise of the major studios and their monopoly practices."[13] Shelley Stamp's 2015 text on Lois Weber takes a deep look into the director's entanglements with Hollywood's "institutional structures, its celebrity culture, its evolving visual grammar, and its ever more dominant role in American daily life" as well as to define her artistry and ideas.[14] Like Armatage, Stamp concludes with discussing how Weber was also "written out of [the film] industry's history early on."[15]

Like Shipman and Weber, June Mathis's story "also represents in microcosm the history of women's participation in the industry."[16] But her life in film production, which began in the midteens, achieved great heights and outlasted that of most of her female colleagues, has received scant attention. Questions abound about how Mathis, while competing with thousands of other women, was quickly able to gain distinction as a writer in 1915 and achieve great prominence by 1923. Answers lie in exploring how she worked within the early studios to exploit her opportunities, and secondary sources such as fan magazines and books on film history can provide some insights on this topic. But much more fascinating material is available in extant films and film scripts, telegrams and memos, and personal letters that complement published interviews and opinion pieces. This cache of resources helped me pursue answers to the questions that have driven my work: what did June Mathis wish to achieve, what obstacles did she face, and how much was she able to accomplish?

In her essential book on women in the silent film industry, Karen Ward Mahar asks whether "female screenwriters, directors, producers, and editors were able to realize their own vision[.] Did women filmmakers make a difference on the screen."[17] Her answer is that we can "know enough from the primary sources to piece together a history of gender in the early American film industry" but not how much of what is on the screen was the product of women filmmakers' personal goals.[18] Yet, Mathis was an artist whose work was born from her knowledge of filmmaking and ideas based on her experiences and beliefs in relation to crucial issues of the times, something that is recognizable throughout her work.

Mathis's scripts feature a postwar world populated by young men whose fathers are either missing or ineffective. She challenges viewers to recognize the suffering caused by violence and greed and turn their visions toward a spiritual realm. These aspects of her conception of reality are evident in the contrasting endings of her two most prominent screenplays. She sets the conclusion to *The Four Horsemen* in a huge cemetery that would remind viewers of the suffering of war while the final shot of *Ben-Hur* places the light of Christ at the center of the screen. Such skillful inclusions of ideas through narrative and stylistic elements specified in her scripts identify her as an artist whose work reveals much about our ideological heritage.

And yet, as Virginia Wright Wexman states, establishing the case for Mathis as an auteur is problematic.[19] Like most studio writers, she produced numerous scripts for projects assigned to her and her work usually did not appear on the screen as written. Many of her screenplays were adaptations, sometimes written with collaborators and often heavily revised by directors. Her frequent teaming with specific directors through several productions often produced great work impossible to attribute to either artist. But her distinctive ideas and artistry are recognizable by examining her extant scripts in the context of her entire oeuvre, categorizing them, and recognizing her use of genre. Her work on productions over which she possessed nearly total control, at least initially (*The Four Horsemen, Ben-Hur, The Greater Glory*), are especially valuable. Along with her unproduced script for *The Enemy*, these reveal her essential ideas and writing techniques most clearly. Her artistry is also evident through comparing her adaptations with their original sources (i.e., *Blue Jeans, Eye for Eye, The Red Lantern, Camille, The Four Horsemen of the Apocalypse, The Conquering Power, The Idle Rich, Blood and Sand, A Trip to Paradise, Ben-Hur, Classified*); through studying her completely original work (i.e., *The Legion of Death*); through examining her unproduced scripts (*Ben-Hur; The Enemy*); and through revisions of her work by directors (*The Legion of Death, Camille, The Conquering Power, The Idle Rich*).

Wendy Holliday's important dissertation on women writers in silent film states that their generation was modern in the sense that they were ready to move into professional positions where they might gain independence and influence.[20] By 1915, women had spent more than twenty years taking advantage of new opportunities outside the home. They wanted to be out in the exciting industrial/commercial world, but they were not particularly interested in undermining or changing the male hierarchy. These contradictory attitudes were based in ideas centered around the Victorian notion of essential natures of men and women and separate spheres of influence for each. While men were simply assumed to be actors and doers in business, politics, the working world, and all other areas outside the home, women were considered essentially spiritual in nature.[21]

Though thoroughly debunked now, essentialism was capable of providing women with a basis for social criticism. It did not mean that women should always be passive, as the action-oriented serial queens such as Pearl White and Helen Holmes were anything but. Mathis heroines like Junie in *Blue Jeans* (1917) and Marya in *The Legion of Death* (1918) followed in this mold. But mostly, Mathis showed women as spiritual figures who provided guidance at a time when men had failed their societies. Their spirituality might not always be clearly evident. It might be located in their abilities to transcend physical and social boundaries as with Alla Nazimova's characters in *Eye for Eye* (1918) and *The Red Lantern* (1919). It might show through in their articulation of biblical messages as in *Blue Jeans* or in their donning of new roles as with Marguerite in *The Four Horsemen*. They might receive messages through dreams, signs, or mystical figures. Whatever the manifestation of the spiritual might be, it reveals that where aggressive masculinity promotes violence, greed, and war, female spirituality encourages unity, inclusion, and love.[22]

Popular culture has labeled the 1920s as the "Jazz Age" and the "Roaring Twenties," a time of ascendance for aggressive masculinity in industry, architecture, sports, literature, and art. But June Mathis, working through popular melodrama, offers a different view. Melodrama incorporates a spiritual realm that Mathis defined as a part of reality and a source of justice as seen in her scripts for *The Four Horsemen*, *A Trip to Paradise*, and *Ben-Hur*. "Melodrama . . . sides with the powerless," writes Christine Gledhill, "while evil is associated with 'social power and station.'" She continues: "Powerlessness regains moral power in its association with a family or social position that should command protection: that of the child, the daughter or mother, the ageing parent, the labouring poor. Through such 'moral touchstones' the contradictions of capitalism are negotiated: the apparently powerless, who by their persevering endurance win through, defeat the logic of capitalism, for reward comes through 'wholly noncompetitive virtues and interests.'"[23]

Gledhill has argued that melodrama "conceives 'the promise of human life' . . . not as a revolutionary future, but rather as a return to a 'golden past': less how things ought to be than how they should have been."[24] Matthew Buckley, however, significantly revises these assertions with his argument that melodrama is more revolutionary than established histories of the form have allowed. It is "a new kind of form, . . . one produced not by crisis, cataclysm, or collapse, but by convergence, synthesis, and progressive strengthening over time." It "marks not a break with the past but rather its logical outcome and determinate aim: the achievement of a compressive, distillate form for a world of intensified, continual, accelerating change."[25] These simultaneous conservative and subversive qualities suffuse Mathis's work.

Helen Day-Mayer and David Mayer write that melodrama "emerges from societies where things go wrong, where ideas of secular and divine justice and recompense are not always met, where suffering is not always acknowledged, and where the explanations for wrong, injustice, and suffering are not altogether understandable."[26] Mathis's heroes, female and male, respond to these physical and spiritual needs. Through melodrama and essentialism, women perform social criticism because they have an outside perspective from which to judge the secular world. They place restraints on capitalism's violence and greed. In the twenties, the transition from matriarchal to patriarchal cultural dominance, as with all such historical transitions, was neither clear nor uncomplicated. Cultural historian Ann Douglas writes, "The matriarch's authority, however the moderns exaggerated it, was the ascendant cultural force in late-Victorian America, and it did not disappear after the Great War."[27] Thus, Mathis brings her melodramatic heroines into the modern world. They might be spiritual in nature, but they are also soldiers, protesters, nurses, working women, deprived and oppressed mothers, and individuals struggling to keep their lives and families together in the midst of devastation.

Mathis was also a fighter. In 1925, a time when the number of influential creative women in Hollywood was well into steep decline, she argued in *Film Daily* that women were largely responsible for the film industry's economic success. She asserts that there is a "woman's viewpoint," which she defines as the "voice of the home" that gives American films their "magical" qualities, an argument supported by her work.[28]

Many of Mathis's shortcomings are obvious and undeniable, but she was incredibly committed to her profession and believed in the movies as a means for promoting progressive ideals, identifying women as social and spiritual leaders, exposing greed for money, power, and possessions as major evils, and recognizing minorities as part of America.[29] Mathis's work suggests that the masculine qualities celebrated for defining the twenties had troubling aspects as well. In response, she taps into a suppressed set of values and ideas with deep roots in American culture that still challenges leanings toward violence, greed, and war. These values beg for recovery not just as part of film history or women's history, but as part of who we are.

1

June Mathis's Journey from Acting to Writing, 1897–1915

On the night of July 26, 1927, Jean Bart's three-act drama, *The Squall*, about a Hungarian Roma woman, was in performance at New York's Forty-Eighth Street Theater. At that time, Forty-Eighth Street was "the street of hits." Next door, at the Playhouse, "Jane Cowl was starring in Robert Sherwood's first big success, The Road to Rome. At the Cort Theatre across the street, Ethel Barrymore was appearing in Maugham's comedy The Constant Wife."[1] Having opened the previous November 11, *The Squall* would run until the end of the year for a total of 444 performances.[2] This evening was to be the most notable but not for anything that occurred on stage.

During the third act, cast member Blanche Yurka was aware of some disturbance in the audience. She carried on until the end of the show and then asked about what had happened. Mervin Williams, playing her son, went to find out. He returned to tell her, "It's June Mathis, the scenario writer; you know, the one who discovered Valentino. She had a heart attack. They've telephoned the coroner's office; they say she mustn't be moved until they arrive."[3] Near the end of the performance, at 10:50 p.m., Mathis had fallen from her seat and yelled, "Oh, mother, I'm dying!"[4]

The crowd rose in excitement to see what was happening. The actors hesitated, uncertain of what to do. Ushers pushed people back as two doctors and a nurse managed to reach the victim. They carried her outside and laid her on the concrete pavement of an alley on the theater's east side. Exact details of what happened then differ. One report states, "Water and restoratives were pressed upon the gasping young woman, but she died with a gasp as Louis Katz, a taxi driver, worked to revive her."[5] Another states that after laying her down, one of the physicians quickly pronounced her dead. An ambulance surgeon, Dr. Coler, agreed. The police officer on duty kept people away, but the body remained on the pavement for at least an hour. The officer said it could not be moved until viewed by the medical examiner.[6]

Mathis's last words were confusing as her mother had died almost five years prior, in September 1922. It was her grandmother, Emily Hawkes, who had attended the play with her that night. The next day, some accounts referred to her as Mathis's mother.[7] But all agree that Mrs. Hawkes kept insisting that if they would just allow her to take June home with her, she was certain she could revive her granddaughter. Yurka claims that hours passed while she and Williams stayed with the corpse and Mrs. Hawkes, who continued to insist that June would be all right. The coroner was supposedly on the way, but did not arrive until 12:30 (or, according to Yurka, 2:30). At that point, Mrs. Hawkes finally allowed Yurka to take her home.[8]

The *New York Herald Tribune* reported that "at 12:30, Richard Roland [*sic*], president of First National Pictures, took the body to the Campbell Funeral Church."[9] This final act of the evening was doubly significant as Rowland had been Mathis's friend and chief supporter since she had joined his Metro Pictures company in 1917, and Campbell was the site where her dearest protégé, Rudolph Valentino, had been laid for public viewing less than a year earlier. Now, his remains were in her family crypt in Hollywood, and hers would soon be next to his. Both are still there.

Mathis's departure ended a story that might be logically started in Leadville, Colorado, in 1879 when Philip Hughes, her biological father, moved there from Moberly, Missouri where he had partnered with her future stepfather, William D. Mathis, in various business ventures.[10] Philip first lived with Richard and Alice Ledyard and partnered with their son Adelbert in various mining operations.[11] In tandem with this enterprise, Philip initiated the practice and promotion of the "Hughes System" for the cure of alcoholism in 1881 and married the Ledyard's daughter Alice. On August 10, Alice died somewhat mysteriously. The coroner concluded that the cause was "the effects of an overdose of morphine and chloral, taken by herself through a mistake, and thereby producing probably an embolism and paralysis of the heart."[12] These details would resound throughout the remainder of Philip's brief existence. Meanwhile, that same year, William Mathis moved to Minneapolis and two years later entered into a new drug store partnership with his brother-in-law, Samuel Friedlander.[13]

On April 1, 1883, the *Leadville Daily Herald* noted that Virginia (Jennie) Wilcox was a guest at a card party along with three male cousins.[14] She may have known Philip Hughes from when both lived in Illinois. But she must have spent a good amount of time in Leadville because she and Philip married on February 11, 1885.[15] He was twenty-five years old; she was eighteen. The Hughes's first daughter, whom they named Alice, was born in February 1886 and died about a month later, on March 17.[16] On June 30, 1887, June Beulah Hughes was born.

Over the next five years, Philip became extremely successful with his "cure" for alcoholism, but his activities guaranteed that his daughter's first decade would be filled with turmoil. In November 1887, one of his patients killed himself by slitting his throat while drunk.[17] The next few years were upsetting for the small Hughes family. On July 21, 1891, a six-man jury in Leadville pronounced Philip insane. The next day's *Denver Rocky Mountain News* stated, "He will be sent to Pueblo tomorrow [July 23]. Dr. Hughes has long been identified with the best interest of Leadville, and his dire afflic-tion is regretted by a large circle of acquaintances."[18]

Later in 1891, he arrived in Minneapolis with Jennie and June to reunite with William and establish the Hughes Institute for teaching and provid-ing Philip's marvelous cure.[19] At first, the institute enjoyed great success. In February and March 1892, the *Minneapolis Tribune* published personal testimonials, and the institute claimed a record of 800 successful treatments by year's end.[20] These glowing affirmations covered up the fact that in April 1892, one of his patients had died from acute meningitis caused by alcohol-ism. Shortly afterward, another died again by slitting his throat.[21] Then, on December 28, 1893, the *Tribune* reported that "the 'Hughes system' as it is called, included the hypodermic injection of morphine or other anodynes, and that many patients who go to this institute to be cured of the liquor habit become victims of one far more to be dreaded and harder to be cured, before they leave."[22] Reading this, one can hardly be surprised that Alice Ledyard Hughes's death had been shrouded in mystery due to the possibil-ity that she may have been one of Philip's early "patients" on whom he was testing his "cure."

On December 31, 1893, the *Tribune* reported that the county attor-ney and State Board of Examiners were ready to start hearings on whether Hughes could be charged with practicing without a license. William Mathis came to his partner's defense and said they had no thought of closing and no fear of an honest investigation.[23] But Philip's fortunes quickly declined and he returned to Leadville two months later to open a new Hughes Institute.[24] On October 30, 1894, Philip and Jennie separated. Philip was ordered to appear in a Salt Lake City court in February 1896 for divorce proceedings and custody of June, who was almost nine.[25] In April, Jennie was granted her divorce on the grounds of Philip's habitual drunkenness. William's son George served as her witness.[26]

On May 16, 1896, William and Jennie married in Salt Lake City, where they established the Eagle Pharmacy at which George Mathis worked as a clerk.[27] On May 31, Philip was returning home to Leadville from Park County, Colorado, when he stopped for the night at the London Mine boarding house. He went to bed early and was found dead there the next morning.[28]

Mathis never seems to have written or talked about these first years of her life and whether she was troubled by them, but she seems to have known something about Philip. Her description of her father as a physician and druggist in her Goldwyn biography draws more on his background than on William's. In the space for "Famous relatives," the studio reporter wrote that Mathis "comes from nine generations of doctors, lawyers and college professors. Her great-uncle is dean of one of the oldest colleges in England."[29] This statement appears to be total fiction, with the only possible connection to reality in the fact that Philip came from Wales.

While Jennie's first marriage was troubled, her relationship with William is not clear. When Mathis began her stage career in San Francisco at age fourteen, Jennie was there and then stayed with her on the road for much of the next fourteen years while William remained in Salt Lake City running his drug store.[30] One questionable account states that Jennie first took June to San Francisco for health reasons in 1896.[31] That would have been immediately after her marriage to William, which would certainly raise the possibility that theirs was a match of convenience, not love. Either is possible as Jennie knew him for as long as she had Philip, and William may have helped her through some very difficult years. With three children from his first marriage, Laura, Sam, and George, William was probably glad to receive help in parenting as well. Yet, Jennie and June were not around very much. Most often, the two were on the road with various theatrical companies until 1914.

Considering the heart condition that ultimately killed her, it seems that June did have significant health problems as a child, apparently respiratory and/or cardiac, that were never totally cured. On June 14, 1899, *The Salt Lake Tribune* mentioned that Jennie and June were returning to California to make Oakland their permanent home due to June's health. They had returned from there just a few weeks earlier but decided to go back after June suffered a relapse.[32] One brief article from later in her career claims

Mathis once overheard a doctor telling Jennie that she would not survive another day. But, because June disliked the doctor, she said, "I determined to live to discredit him. . . . I healed myself by my childish spiteful decision to live—and fool the doctor!"[33]

Jennie did take her to San Francisco supposedly for her health, and 1899 was probably the first time.[34] But why take a sickly child to a big city and initiate her into the strenuous life of professional theater? The first motivation most likely came from the child herself. Supposedly, June first caught the acting bug after seeing Sarah Bernhardt when she was three years old. She kept imitating "the divine Sarah" for days afterward.[35] Silent film producer/writer/director/actress Nell Shipman had a similar impetus to performance when she was six. After going to see a pantomime of *Dick Whittington* in London, little Nell came home and launched into a solo performance of the entire show. Writing of herself later, Shipman "knew what she wanted; her mind was made up; her course charted. She was going to be An Actress!"[36]

For other future film successes like Margery Wilson, Lillian Gish, and Mary Pickford, as well as untold thousands of other young women, the experience was the same. With no other media available at the time, a stage performance was the most exciting accessible attraction and the most likely to attract girls looking for a future outside the home. As Hilary Hallett states, professions like teaching and nursing demanded an education, barred marriage, and paid very poorly. "The stage," however, "offered the best chance for both self-support and social mobility for women with the fewest resources—women who otherwise would likely have worked from sunup to sundown in filthy factories, stood six and [a] half days at a department store counter selling products they could not afford, or served at the beck and call of a mistress nearly every hour of each day. Only as performers and writers did women earn the same or greater, wages as men for equal work."[37] For young girls starting this journey, the other important factor was support from their parents. Sometimes, as with Pickford, that was not a question as their work had to help support the family.[38] For Shipman, though only thirteen, her parents allowed her to head off with a touring company after receiving a simple promise that she would be well cared for.[39]

For Mathis, Jennie was a constant supporter who hoped her daughter could find more freedom than she had experienced. As a young woman, she was not content to stay home but left Illinois for adventures in Colorado. As a mother, she accompanied her only child to countless social

engagements for performances. Jennie may have had performance aspirations in her youth, and she performed with June at least once at a private
party in her hometown of Sterling, Illinois in 1901.[40] A popular 1890s educational movement to liven up school curricula by getting children more
active may also have influenced William and Jennie's thinking about June.
This philosophy was class-based as "discourses regarding aesthetic tastes
and dramatic instincts distinguished literate parents of the rising middle
class who sought to cultivate their children's aesthetic, moral, and literary
educations through dramatic literature and theatrical entertainments in
both private and public venues."[41] Another small incident reveals Jennie's
complicity with such thinking. In an age when many considered educating
girls to be a waste of time, Jennie told a minister who objected to the nine-
year-old June reading Balzac that "knowing the things of life will never hurt
her."[42] June later repeated this idea in scripts and interviews over and over.

This educational philosophy would have bolstered Jennie's decision to
take her little girl to San Francisco in 1899 to help her expand her horizons and bring credit to the family. It would continue what the two had
been doing for the previous two years. From 1896 to 1899, the *Salt Lake
Herald* regularly recorded children's performances at Democratic teas and
other events, usually giving June special notice. The report for an event on
October 7, 1898, mentioned, "Miss June Mathis captured the audience with
a recitation entitled 'Battle of Santiago, with Sampson Eleven Miles Away,'
for an encore she gave, 'Good Bye, God Bless You.'"[43] That Thanksgiving
Day, Mathis and another girl, pupils of Miss Louise Boyden, performed a
scene from *Ingomar* at the penitentiary as part of a show by the entire class.[44]
For a performance a few months later, the reviewer noted, "The entire pro-
gramme was fine and the recitation by little June Mathis deserves special
mention. The little lady shows a remarkable presence of mind and memory,
accompanied by a graceful carriage and splendid elocution. She recited 'Tit
for Tat' in true Irish brogue and for an encore 'Hol' Dem Philippines' in the
negro dialect. Both were well rendered and vigorously applauded."[45]

Another account of Mathis's early performances appears to be more
hyperbole than truth: "At 7 she was astonishing Salt Lake audiences by
her recitations and remarkably clever interpretations of characters from
standard plays. At 10 she had memorized 'Ingomar,' and was giving scenes
between the bandit and Parthenia, his Grecian love. She knew 'As You Like
It' from beginning to end, and could give entertaining bits from nearly all
of Shakespeare's plays long before she had entered her teens."[46] Mathis did

perform scenes from Maria Lovell's *Ingomar: The Barbarian* at ten, but she was still living in Minneapolis at seven. The earliest record of Mathis on stage states that she was the Maid of Honor in a children's play titled *The Marriage of Mr. Tom Thumb and Miss Minnie Warren* at Salt Lake's Unity Temple on April 4, 1897. An article published years later claimed that Mathis actually performed five of the parts herself that night because several other children had the mumps.[47] That would have been an ironic debut considering that ill health was to be a major factor in shaping Mathis's life.

Ann Douglas argues that in the nineteenth century, "the Victorian matriarch successfully attacked the Calvinist patriarchy, only to be hunted down in the twentieth century by the forces of masculinization bound together in that backlash we know as modernism."[48] Modernity, of course, had not waited until 1920 to begin. With the growth of industrialism and the consumer culture, work routines, lifestyles, and gender roles had already begun shifting in the late nineteenth century. Masculine culture was on the rise, as Douglas states, but it also established new requirements and provided new opportunities for women. Film scholar Ben Singer writes, "Modernity granted women a new freedom of social circulation—or rather, it might be more accurate to say that modernity required it. Female mobility was necessary for the sake of modern capitalism. As cheap labor in unskilled, semiskilled, and clerical occupations, women contributed greatly to the expansion of factory-based mass production and bureaucratic rationalization. As shoppers (and, again, as low-paid 'shopgirls' in department stores and other commercial concerns), women fueled the consumer economy on which capitalism depended."[49] Theatrical careers had long been an option for women and were growing as well along with industrialization and increased middle-class leisure time. Better rail travel and rising urbanization created more theaters all over the country and, thus, more touring companies. Very soon, the nascent film industry would provide women with even more opportunities that they would rush to fill.

In their move west in 1899, in what became June's first step toward a position in the film industry, Jennie was clearly as concerned with her child's career as with her health. San Francisco might have been chosen because Salt Lake City's Maude Adams, soon to achieve fame as Broadway's first Peter Pan, had begun her career there. Some unverifiable articles report that June received coaching and encouragement from Adams. While their connection was probably more incidental or even nonexistent, the famous local actress may still have provided inspiration.[50] The fact that in 1900

Jennie and June would live at 523 Eddy Street, just a few blocks from the office, at 6 Eddy Street, of theatrical agent Archie Levy, who would push June's career ahead, strongly suggests their thinking.[51]

The association with Levy in San Francisco could not have been entirely accidental. On July 11, 1901, he wrote to congratulate William "on the very great cleverness" of his daughter. Levy booked her with the Orpheum theater circuit and promised to put her "on the top of the ladder."[52] He had Mathis study with a "Professor Cooper, an instructor in dramatic art." Most likely, either Levy or Cooper developed the simple sketch she was to perform on every stop of her initial tour: "A school girl returns home from school after playing truant. Her mother is in the next room, and, as the child believes, receiving no answer to her calls, very much put out over her conduct. In order to calm the imminent storm, the girl recites for her mother, rendering several styles of elocution. Then she dances. Unable still to get an answer to her calls, the girl is terrified by the belief that her mother is dead. Finally the mother appears and clasps her daughter to her arms."[53] As this press report then explains, the piece, though crude in structure, allowed Mathis to have the stage for half an hour and display a wide range of movements and emotions. It provided her with a great test and a great forum. This was the piece Jennie later helped her perform in Sterling, Illinois. As an encore, Mathis would imitate some of the most popular stage performers of the day: Richard Mansfield, Henry Irving, May Irwin, and Maude Adams among them.

Levy wanted firm control of Mathis's career, offering a five-year contract. William and Jennie opted for a thirty-five-week agreement instead, one that committed June to an arduous travel schedule. She debuted in San Jose on Saturday, July 20, and was scheduled to then perform in several California cities including four-week engagements in San Francisco and Los Angeles. Then, she would head east, "playing Kansas City, Omaha, New Orleans, Chicago, and New York City. From the metropolis, the girl will play back to San Francisco over the northern route, taking in all the important cities."[54] While in Chicago, however, Mathis received a telegram asking her to play Baby in *Whose Baby Are You?* in Saginaw, Michigan. She went on the first night with no rehearsal. In January 1903, Mathis's half sister Laura joined the company, which added the play *My Friend from India* to its repertoire.[55] But Laura did not pursue a theatrical career. Reviews throughout Mathis's stage career consistently emphasized the excellence of her physical movements and facial expressions. She knew the importance of communicating through her body and possessed the talent to do so. Of her performance in *Whose Baby Are You?* one reviewer commented, "She [Mathis] is excellent in her specialty where she becomes the dancing girl of the hypnotist and quite charming where she concocts a whole costume, and a fairly good one, out of the draperies of the room. . . . A most appreciative silence was her reward in the dressing scene and when she finished it by replacing her cap with a lamp shade she was warmly applauded."[56]

Through these initial years of her career, Mathis's enthusiasm, dexterity, and expressiveness helped her get into roles and deliver lines right from the start. Her concern was not simply with memorization but also with feeling the emotions of a piece. On stage, the freedom she had always been granted to move and express herself enabled her to take advantage of her opportunities.

In July 1903, Mathis joined the cast of *The Vinegar Buyer* with Ezra Kendall. Among her many positive reviews was one in the *Elmira* (NY) *Advertiser*. In her role, it stated, June "at no time overdoes it and gives the country girl role about as true to life a characterization as possible."[57] Mathis next joined William T. Hodge in *Eighteen Miles from Home* and followed that with a very successful run as the lead in *The Girl Patsy* (1907), "which made her popular everywhere she appeared."[58] A review of *Brewster's Millions* later that year went far beyond standard commentary in its praise: "Miss June Mathis, as Peggy Grey, the staunch little friend of the millionaire, is an actress far above the average. She not only recites her lines well, but knows how and when to give expression to her emotions." To illustrate, the reviewer cites a scene in which Peggy learns that Brewster has not been manipulating her as she had feared: "Miss Mathis said nothing, but the expression that came to her face revealed feelings of gratitude that words could not."[59] For her performance in 1909's *Going Some*, the *Brooklyn Daily Eagle* reported, "all of the feminine portion of the cast join in the general enthusiasm and love-making with Miss June Mathis just one kiss in the lead. She plays Helen Blake, a Smith College girl. . . . She is charming as a dainty but plucky collegiate."[60]

Offstage, Mathis asserted herself and gained a small following by bringing attention to her physical characteristics. In 1907, one writer noted that she insisted on "having a sun parlor or its equivalent, and every morning at 9 o'clock an expert hairdresser must be in attendance to take care of her hair, which, I am assured, reaches to her heels, and which is almost a burden to her."[61] Publicity photos show that Mathis's hair was that long. Her existent studio portraits from that time usually show her in modest, sporty attire, perhaps twirling a parasol, and always beaming a bright smile. But she could take her persona over a broad range. One shot has her in drag, looking like a working-class tough, while another has her in a hazy goddess-like profile for a cigar box cover she once graced.[62] Still another depicted her as both characters at a table, with her hair, costuming, and expression distinctly different in each.[63]

Mathis's physical skills and attention to detail, as noted by reviews of her acting, eventually provided a basis for her writing. She understood the body in the way Charles Burnetts defines it, "as a vital mediator to thought, the privileged boundary or 'screen' between self and world."[64] Her use of gestures and facial expressions to wordlessly communicate with audiences fit with the development "from at least the 1840s forward," of more restrained and naturalistic acting. For actors to progress from the traditional histrionic movements of melodrama to more subtle performances would require a deeper understanding of characters. Mathis was inspired by this acting style and was able to learn it from one of the best practitioners of the times. Her childhood idol, Minnie Maddern Fiske, and James K. Hackett, with whom she spent a season in 1903 or '04, "brought what was recognized as a casual, quiet realism to their roles."[65] Mathis revealed the physical basis of her understanding of character not only through her acting but also in her study of pedestrian movements to develop her writing and her concern for motivating gestures and expressions in her scripts.

Mathis's success naturally affected her connections to home and family. Although she never considered a strictly domestic existence, Mathis always felt deep ties to her parents and siblings. Spending her first seven years with an alcoholic father may have influenced her desire for a loving homelife, and Jennie's marriage to William brought her stability, security, and companionship. For the rest of her life, she always expressed affection for her stepsiblings and stepfather. He acted like one of her biggest fans and filled one wall in his drug store with clippings about June.[66] It was a meaningful show of affection as her constant travel kept the family separated most of the time. A 1919 news item revealed that because William had suffered a stroke, he would now live in Hollywood "where the entire family will be united for the first time since Miss June Mathis started her stage career."[67]

By 1900, Jennie had spent a good amount of time living on her own even while married. It may even have been her preference, and there is no doubt that she gave taking care of June a high priority. June would certainly benefit from Jennie's assistance. Life in theatrical touring companies was not easy with poor accommodations, crowded low-quality transportation, and poor food. Mathis stuck it out for fourteen years. As she told the *Salt Lake Tribune* in 1926, "If there are any tank towns I didn't make when I was touring in dramatic productions, they have been built since I quit the road."[68] Money was also scarce, and June and Jennie had to work together to survive. At one point, they "found themselves with just barely enough coffee for breakfast and fifteen cents between them and starvation. They dressed in their very smartest best and went around the corner to the grocery and ordered sufficient food for two days. She told the man to deliver them to her apartment and if they were not home to leave them and she would pay for them the next day. Fortunately, the next day Mathis secured an engagement in an Al Woods production, and all was well."[69] A report of Jennie's presence at the office of vaudeville producers Cohan and Harris, when June was given a contract offer, further attests that she was always near.[70]

Touring life provided a physical education beyond those of books and classrooms during Mathis's most impressionable years. While most likely hoping for her first romantic encounters, she lived amid a number of callous veteran performers, some of whom would have probably been only too glad to introduce her to new experiences. As she later told the press, "I certainly saw life. Traveling across the United States in a car with the other members of the cast I got to know them mighty well." Mathis related an incident in which her drunk leading man attacked her while she prepared to go on. She responded by sinking her teeth into his shoulder, drawing blood. "A few minutes later I had to go on the stage for a love scene with him," she continued. "I could still see the blood trickling down his shoulder as I ran into his arms crying in my best ingenue manner, 'I don't know why I love you so, but oh, I love you so.'"[71] Life on the road provided many opportunities to build toughness and endurance.

Throughout her stage career, Mathis and her mother would sometimes be away from home for more than a year. June would frequently write stepfather William about her plans as she and Jennie toured the country. Besides the family contact, the letters also provided self-promotion for upcoming appearances and William would then pass along the information to the press. The Salt Lake City papers would usually print an article giving their source as "a letter received . . . by [June's] father" and mention June's "many Salt Lake friends," a true promotional statement. With a little advance notice, Mathis was able to fill theaters in Salt Lake City and elsewhere. In a late-November 1908 appearance in *Brewster's Millions* at the University of Missouri (William's alma mater), students bought every ticket and rose for a long ovation when she came on stage wearing the school colors. They "cheered the actress until their throats grew hoarse. It was several minutes before the play was able to proceed."[72]

By 1909, Mathis's stage career had included nine years of performances in a large number of cities and shows with constant movement between jobs—getting called from Chicago to Saginaw to begin *Whose Baby Are You?* and from New York to Boston to take the lead in *The Girl Patsy*.[73] The pressure may have led Mathis to consider a career change. At each stop, actors had to pay for their own accommodations, which Mathis finally tried to do something about in 1909 when she proposed a plan to build a series of hotels in major cities for the primary benefit of stage performers. An article in the *St. Louis Post-Dispatch* claimed that if the plan succeeded, Mathis "would leave the stage to take control of the hotel company."[74] After calling a meeting about the project in St. Louis, Mathis gained support from the Shubert organization and many successful actors including vaudeville star Eddie Foy. The plan certainly would have benefits but only for "white members of the profession." This reference in the *Billboard* article is a reminder of the highly segregated nature of the theatrical world and nation that Mathis did not question, although she did push its boundaries. After the St. Louis meeting, Mathis declined to schedule another meeting in Cincinnati, her company's next tour stop, and the effort apparently died.[75]

Mathis's brief feint toward a business career indicates growing desires for stability and higher status expressed in her 1910 career moves. That year, Mathis stepped toward her dream of becoming "the recognized successor of Minnie Maddern Fiske in the dramatic world and to essay the emotional roles of that great actress," when she landed a part in Clyde Fitch's *The City*, a searing condemnation of America's business and political elite. But she was soon off to begin the longest association of her theatrical career when she began a five-year stint with acclaimed female impersonator Julian Eltinge in his show *The Fascinating Widow*.[76] Unfortunately, nothing seems to be known about the Mathis/Eltinge relationship other than that it was quite successful and did not end when she left his company. She later transformed their theater production into a script for Eltinge, *The Fascinating Widower*, which was slated for filming at the star's own studio with Anna Nilsson costarring. Eltinge planned to wear only male clothes, but public pressure for him to display feminine fashions forced Mathis to do some rewrites.[77] In 1919, she also wrote a sketch for Eltinge's stage review titled "His Night at the Club."[78] Although Eltinge fought all accusations of homosexuality, sometimes with his fists, some evidence suggests that he was gay. Anthony Slide writes, "At least one vaudeville performer . . . was quite positive that Eltinge was a homosexual."[79] Mark Berger has suggested both to Laurence Senelick and this author rumors that Eltinge had homosexual affairs. But, more importantly, Senelick indicates how Eltinge may have influenced Mathis's attitudes on gender: "Eltinge's gender intermediacy qualified him to serve as a middleman between traditional standards of curried comeliness and the newer ideal of 'masculinized' femininity."[80] Melodrama already encouraged a certain amount of gender crossing. But as a central figure in the era's discourse on gender, Eltinge could very likely have broadened Mathis's understanding of it.

In 1914, Mathis landed another dramatic role for her final theatrical performance when she played blackface in Ridgely Torrence's *Granny Maumee*. Although she took the role because she and her family needed the income, it was a work of the dramatic nature to which Mathis had always aspired. Torrence was white and his cast was too, but his play was considered representative of a "new Negro theater." His liberal credentials were quite impressive, including correspondence with W. E. B. Du Bois, Langston Hughes, and Allen Tate. Poets within his immediate circle also included Robert Frost, Edward Arlington Robinson, and William Butler Yeats.[81]

The title character is an old Black woman whose son was mistakenly decreed guilty of murdering a white woman and burned at the stake years before the action begins. When Granny rushed up to try to save him, her eyes were burned, and she went blind. She has held a deep hatred of all whites from that time on. When the curtain rises, her granddaughter Sophie (Mathis) has brought home her new baby. Granny learns that the child was fathered, forcibly, by the son of the man who murdered her son. This kind of plot development is typical of melodrama's "'nonclassical' dramaturgy often derided as contrived."[82] The climax comes through Torrence's use of his character's "emblematic," in this case racist, identity. Because she is Black, Torrence shows Granny using tribal rituals to temporarily regain her sight, build a fire, and induce the death of the child's father by burning a photograph of him. This action is then painted as a reversion to a backward heritage when, at the critical moment, her martyred son appears in the flames and reminds her of her Christian beliefs. Granny is moved to forgiveness and revenge is rejected.[83]

Carl Van Vechten, a premier American literary scholar and critic of the time, wrote on May 9, 1914, in *The Literary Digest* that "'Granny Maumee' is fresh and novel. It breaks new paths and breaks them beautifully."[84] Black intellectuals agreed that it represented something new, with James Weldon Johnson calling Torrence's "Negro" plays "the most important single event in the entire history of the Negro in the American theatre."[85] Torrence received praise for his details of "black life," including his use of "negro dialect." Van Vechten wrote, "The dialogue of the play is one of its freshest winds." Ironically, however, his additional comments fit the tradition of valuing blackface's erasure of Black identity: "Soon one forgets that negroes are speaking and one becomes imbued with the universal philosophy and spirit of the piece and the tremendous force with which the idea that mind and soul are stronger than matter is presented."[86] One of the play's great problems is that it ignores the idea that Black people should work for justice by presenting Granny Maumee with only the choices of revenge or forgiveness. Yet, the notion of spirit as more important than physical force was one that grew out of nineteenth-century traditions and was still prevalent at the time. Mathis would draw on this idea throughout her career.

A play that marks Black people as possessing primitive beliefs and unchristian hatred even while acknowledging their suffering of brutal murder and rape by racist whites would hardly seem progressive. Yet, in terms of theater history, *Granny Maumee* was a very early work to go beyond "coon" stereotypes and depictions of Black people as other than comic and lazy. In 1917, it was performed by Broadway's first all-Black cast. In a sense, its history thus paralleled the larger history of Black people in American theater. Blackface was popularized by white actors who claimed to have developed their impersonations by observing southern Black people. It became popular in the nineteenth century because, as Michael Rogin writes, it upheld melting-pot mythology: "Minstrelsy claimed to speak for both races through the blacking up of one [and] in the service of Americanizing immigrants, pretended to the absence of conflict between black and white."[87] It was racist, but it provided an initial step, no matter how perverted, for recognition of Black life on American stages. It was so successful that many Black performers started by playing in blackface. In so doing, they were imitating the whites who were imitating Black people and not making the characters more authentic.[88] In this context, *Granny Maumee* could be respected as a dramatic step forward. But it was still white performers acting out a white writer's impression of Black lives.

It seems likely that Mathis's successful performance in the play led her to believe that she understood Black characters and felt no need to learn more. The requirements of melodrama would have reinforced Mathis's satisfaction with her understanding of various racial, ethnic, and gender identities. Gledhill notes that current responses to melodrama involve "the assumption that its characters lack psychological depth or authenticity."[89] She identifies this reaction as a result of melodrama's "personalization of the social." This characteristic defines the form's "means of staging psychology, putting considerable demands on the actor."[90] The negative side to this method of depiction is that it defines characters in terms of broad psychological "types" depending on their race, ethnicity, or gender, and Mathis most likely believed that years of expressing herself on stage through movement and facial expressions gave her a basis for her writing career.[91] As she developed her writing, she focused on physical details, believing that these would provide all the necessary psychological information about a character. Thus, when she began including Black people in her scripts with *Camille* in 1921, she generally presented them as background characters. Only *A Trip to Paradise* (1921) and *The Day of Faith* (1923) include individual Black characters making brief appearances, and both are racist stereotypes. Although she respected spiritual diversity and showed progress toward ethnic inclusiveness, she never moved beyond this limited and deeply problematic attitude toward persons of color.

Mathis's roles in *The City* and *Granny Maumee*, never noted as part of her stage career, represent efforts to break from the musical comedies in which she regularly appeared, a desire that she carried over into the movies. In September 1916, *Motography* reported that "although she is blond, cheerful, and wholesome looking, [June Mathis] declares that the ambition of her life has been to play 'Carmen.'"[92] It seems likely that Jennie encouraged this direction. Her "passionate wish" was to see her daughter's work provide "drops of balm" to people in need.[93]

Mathis's years in theater established her path in life and provided other benefits as well. Vaudeville and touring stock company actors "were used to unconventional lifestyles. They lived on the edge, from town to town and theater to theater."[94] In Susan A. Glenn's estimation, "Actresses on the popular stage were a proto-feminist vanguard 'helping to define the modern social and sexual terrain.'"[95] While Jennie would always be present as anchor and protector, Mathis would also gain an outsider's perspective on mainstream life. She could recognize a broad range of attitudes and personalities. Over fourteen years, she would also become familiar with narrative structure, particularly of melodrama, character types, and gags. She would know what audiences liked and how to create variations on standard melodramatic elements. She would gain ideas of what to aim for when she wished to go beyond conventional elements. All this would add to her influences from a childhood overseen by an alcoholic and criminal father. Though Mathis never discussed its impact on her, her screenplays depicting fractured families with children who lack spiritual guidance might be a product of that experience. Through her travels, she would indulge her passion for reading and thereby expand her knowledge of characters and dramatic situations.

By June 1913, Mathis had begun turning away from acting. The *New York Telegraph* noted that she had "taken up playwriting and that she slips away and studies, in her spare moments, and just writes and writes. If Miss Mathis can write as well as she can act her play should be a grand success." A constant reader since the age of nine, she very likely desired a life of the mind. She may have preferred a creative occupation in which she could constantly offer new ideas that would play a crucial role in the final production. Always eager for self-promotion, writing would bring her direct individual attention. She started writing poems, stories, and sketches in her spare time.[96] One story about her motivation is that she used to write an occasional piece for local newspapers wherever the Eltinge company played and one editor encouraged her to write more.[97] Another is that she was entertaining the company with a story on a train, and a film director on board overheard. When she finished, he suggested she had a talent for storytelling and should give writing for the screen a shot.[98] Both episodes could be parts of the actual story. While in Los Angeles with Eltinge, "she met a number of moving picture people."[99] They evidently gave her a positive impression of the industry, which Mathis chose to enter as a writer rather than an actor.

After leaving Eltinge in January 1914, Mathis went back to New York and began working on her writing with a magazine editor friend. The time was right to become a screenwriter. The movie industry was growing fast and encouraging submissions of stories and screenplays. A huge number of "how-to" manuals were published, and numerous competitions run through studios, magazines, and newspapers offered cash prizes and career opportunities.[100] Whether or not she made use of any of these is unknown. Her first step was actually to perform in blackface for *The Fairy and the Waif* for the Gustave Frohman Amusement Company in January 1915.[101] The substantial cast list for the film does not include her name, but she claimed to find acting for the camera uninteresting.[102] It took up only a small part of the day, and she was far more interested in using her mind: "She began studying all phases of film making. . . . She occupied all her spare time on sets, studying lighting, direction, action of others, and eventually the cutting and editing of films. Then she, like most individuals, got the urge to write for the screen."[103] The phrase "like most individuals" is ambiguous, but the idea that Mathis spent most of her time learning filmmaking makes sense as she continued to work on sets and fill her scripts with suggestions for cinematography and editing throughout her career. It would not be surprising that she decided from the start that learning how films were constructed would enable her to envision the production as she wrote.

As Mathis's transition to writing proceeded, she felt a heavy burden of responsibility to her family. In the beginning, she said, "I wrote stories and sent them out. They came back. I was heart-sick at times and terribly discouraged. I saw my funds dwindling. I knew that my father was carrying the burden of the family without the help I had always been able to give him, and it began to look as tho [sic] I was trying to do the impossible."[104] Mathis's concern was not unusual. Film scholar Ben Singer writes that "government statistics on women wage earners in 1910 indicate that among female workers under the age of twenty-one . . . almost 80 percent handed over their entire paycheck to the head of the household, usually the father. Only one young woman in a hundred was free to keep all her earnings."[105] From its beginnings then, Mathis's career was never just about herself but also her family, something her parents would have known from the start. She was pursuing her passion, and they needed the income.

In January 1915, Salt Lake City got the news that June Mathis had "quit the 'legitimate' [theater] for the 'movies.'" One reason for the move was "better money," a primary goal for most women entering the movie business. Other reasons involved more intrinsic needs: it would "not mean so much moving from city to city." She was able to start doing "all of her work at home, reporting at the studios only once a week" to "have much more time for writing scenarios."[106] She would need that time if she were to succeed. Other women like screenwriters Bess Meredyth and Frances Marion, writer/director Lois Weber, and actress Mary Pickford started by acting in films and then writing when they realized they could earn more that way. Meredyth's experience as she "jumped between assignments for several studios, churning out one-reelers, serials, and action dramas" while still acting illustrates the amount of work involved.[107] Why Mathis, now twenty-seven, having been onstage most of her life, gambled by focusing completely on writing is not clear. But she was ready for a career change.

Like many young women in early Hollywood, Mathis did not think of herself as feminist in the sense that a second-wave 1970s feminist would: "These women came of age at a time when women's roles were rapidly changing, especially in terms of careers and the movement into public life."[108] They wanted better choices for their futures, and the numerous small companies that looked to capitalize on a massive public hunger for this new entertainment offered plenty of opportunities. Personnel were needed for a wide range of jobs in and around the studios in front of and behind the cameras. Greater versatility meant greater chances to work and gender restrictions were loosened. Holliday writes, "Many women were promoted simply because they were there and the job needed to be done."[109]

In 1914, trumpeter and bandleader Benjamin Albert (B. A.) Rolfe formed Rolfe Photoplays, signing well-known acting talents including Mabel Taliaferro and Irving Cummings and distributing through Alco Film Corporation.[110] Pittsburgh theater owners Richard Rowland and James B. Clarke, who controlled part of Alco, stepped in when the company faltered in 1915 to form Metro Pictures. Their management team included Rowland as president, Clarke as vice president, and Louis B. Mayer, later to be president of Metro-Goldwyn-Mayer, as secretary. Unknown to Mathis, her stars were lining up through these corporate moves since Edwin Carewe worked for Rolfe, which was distributed by Metro.[111] When Metro assimilated the smaller company in 1917, Mathis gained a closer relationship to Rowland, who became vitally important to the rest of her career.

To fill their need for scenarios, the studios often sponsored screenwriting competitions, which produced the phenomenon of "scenario fever."[112] Mathis churned out scenarios throughout 1914 only to receive them all back with rejection slips, and her hopes dimmed. Thousands, if not millions, entered the competitions. In 1916, one screenwriting handbook author told his readers that "the average scenario department receives 100 to 150 scripts daily" and "Famous Players reports 'some days we receive as high as three and four hundred scripts, and many times not one is found acceptable.'"[113]

But it may be that June Mathis did not actually face such odds. First, she had the advantage of working in New York, where many of the new studios were. Second, it seems likely that she had connections. Somehow, whether through a contest in which her work finished second or through a writer who offered to team up with her, one of Mathis's efforts reached Edwin Carewe. Both stories came out in the press, but Mathis related the second in the most detail. After two months working with the Gustave Frohman film company, she said, "A playwright came to my house . . . when the world looked darkest and went over my stuff."[114] He admired her work, asked her to do a script based on a play he had in mind, and offered to go fifty-fifty with her if it were purchased. He took her script to Carewe who rejected the story but liked how it was handled, asked to meet the writer, and Mathis's life in movies began in earnest.

Exactly why her work was able to rise above all others to earn her a position with Rolfe in November 1915 will most likely never be known. The known facts are that she had a script titled *A Terrible Silence* accepted by the World Film Company. Whether or not this script was the one that Carewe first saw is not clear. But she then wrote her first screenplay to be filmed, *The House of Tears*, which Carewe directed and Rolfe released in December 1915.[115] While nothing about Mathis's work with Carewe seems to exist (films, scripts, or stories of how they worked together), both of them later described very similar philosophies of film and filmmaking, which likely contributed to their success.

2

Success at Metro, 1915–1921

In the 1920s, the Great War and the bankruptcy of the aristocratic order, the impersonality of business and consumerism, and the developments of Freudian psychology and greater sexual freedom all contributed to new searches for identity. Modernist writers and artists no longer looked outward to definable patterns of behavior, history, and social constructs. Instead, as Chip Rhodes writes, for modernism, "the 'real' is now itself a product of a point of view; it is a subjectively experienced vision of social reality that subordinates this reality to its apprehension."[1]

While modernists looked inward, melodramatic writers like Mathis continued to define reality by what they saw and a spiritual realm that existed out beyond what is visible. For Peter Brooks, melodrama seeks "to go beyond the surface of the real to the truer, hidden reality, to open up the world of spirit."[2] Mathis's key to success as a writer was to anchor melodrama's broad emotionalism in details of settings, scenery, costumes, appearance, and most importantly, actors' expressions and gestures. These details provided actors with realistic environments to relate to and helped them reveal what their characters were feeling and thinking. They were gateways to the characters' souls and often pointed to a spiritual realm as part of the reality she created. This greater dimension was critical for them to recognize.

Mathis wished to use physical details to refer to a larger reality, one that, according to Rhodes, made "absolutist claims to comprehensive truth in the metaphysical realm."[3] Characters could be in touch with this spiritual realm through mystical communications from dreams, visions, or ghosts. They might possess a supernatural capability to perform magic rituals or transcend boundaries of entrapment. Some details, such as the characters known as "the Trinity" in *Her Great Price* (1916) or the church's stained-glass windows in *Blue Jeans* (1917), might simply represent the constant presence of the spiritual. Characters needed to be alert to these signs. Those who were (mostly women, but not always) could provide guidance to others to help them achieve success or inner peace. A lack of such guidance could lead to tragedy and grief, which is true, for example, in *Blood and Sand* where Valentino's Juan Gallardo has no spiritual figure to help him. Mathis's screenplays often suggest a fear that society might no longer recognize this spiritual element, a logical fear in an age of growing industrialism and consumerism.

By 1915, feature-length films, many of which were based on literature, were gaining prominence, and Mathis defined her desire to see better adaptations as a great motivator for becoming a screenwriter: "It made me writhe to see a pasteurized version of a great novel so twisted and changed that few readers would have recognized the work of the author. . . . I wanted so much to see in the pictures what I had read or what I had seen on the stage—that is, as near to it as possible." The word "pasteurized" is important here. Mathis was not concerned with merely attempting to replicate the contents of what she had read or seen. She wanted to capture the impact of the original. "Hence," she wrote, "I began to experiment," and she drew on the resources of writers available to her, living or dead, for guidance.[4] During her years on the road, Mathis "snatch[ed] [her] education" while on train journeys or backstage.[5] She read authors she believed could teach her "perspective": Poe, Dickens, Thackeray, Maupassant. These added to the steady dose of Balzac she had begun in childhood.[6]

In 1923, Mathis explained how she focused on noticing details during her training as a writer: "I would stand at the window and see just what I could observe in five minutes. I'd then take twenty minutes to find out what I had missed in the scene in front of me. Then I'd repeat it, gradually working it down to three and then two minutes and then one. It's a fine exercise. Now I can go into a room and see a dozen or more things which escape the average person."[7]

Careful attention to details of physical movements and facial expressions became as important to Mathis's writing as they had been to her acting. Explaining how she became a screenwriter, Mathis stated, "I had been given an early dramatic training, after which I had spent years on the stage, absorbing every detail possible of that which I knew was to be my life work. I was interested in pictures from the first, and I went to see them for the double purpose of enjoyment and study."[8] Attention to detail, Mathis stated, formed the basis for her development of characters: "My first scenario, 'The

House of Tears,' had a scene in which a woman waits for her unfaithful husband to come home. At great length I pictured in the script her every act, how she went to the clock and wound it casually, as if she were not counting every tick of the minute hand, and told just what she did during those hours. When Edwin Carewe, the director, read it, he said, 'You can't tell me that you aren't married! You have given yourself away. No one but a married woman who had waited for her husband to come home could tell what you have told.' I said to him, 'I am not married, but I have watched my married friends wait for their husbands to come home.' And that was the truth." She mentioned that she had also "watched on the street cars how women of certain classes dressed and held their hands and feet."[9]

As a narrative structure, melodrama enabled the transition of Mathis's physical skills and knowledge from stage to page. Burnetts explains that in eighteenth-century France, unlicensed theaters were not allowed to use dialogue: "The use of facial and bodily gesture [thus] became . . . essential skills for actors, who had to convey emotions without the aid of the spoken word, engendering a style of acting that would clearly find continuities in the notorious gesturality of the silent cinema. These found properties of melodrama, at its purest a non-literary form, predisposed it to a close affinity with the expression of intense human emotion."[10] Through her years on the stage, June Mathis absorbed this understanding of the body's importance in communicating emotions and other characteristics of identity or interactions. In turning to writing, Mathis started by transferring her own emphasis of movement to studying that of others: "I began to make a close study of the different types I would come in contact with, and to watch for little dramatic or amusing situations that would crop up here and there."[11]

Mathis emphasized the importance of placing the minute physical details on the screen that reviewers had found in her stage performances: "A look in a woman's face, the way a man says a sentence, an exchange of glances—these things seem trivial, but if you are able to feel the undercurrent which goes with them, then you have touched something which provides the dramatic impetus to your life and mine. And that is what the pictures try to portray—Life!" Burnetts's words of almost a century later echo this idea about the importance of details. To help an actor achieve depth, Mathis believed she had to provide motivation for their movements as well as a description of them: "A scene must either show moving thought or moving form, but the mind cannot remain stationary or the scene doesn't get over. I try to give the actors through the script of my scenarios a good idea of just what each scene is intended to convey. If they know the thought which prompts a character to make a certain move, then they are able to put that thought and feeling behind the mere moving of the body and the scene gets over."[12]

Burnetts explains that such details have importance in sentimental melodrama because of its insistence "on the possibility of an ethics grounded not in an analytical or intellectual apprehension of the world but in a sensitivity to everyday phenomena and things. It is this intimacy with the world, and its anticipation of film, that Stanley Cavell identifies specifically in the writings of the nineteenth-century American writers Ralph Waldo Emerson and Henry David Thoreau when he describes their privileging of the 'everyday, the near, the low, the familiar.'"[13] This perspective was "deemed ill-founded and incompatible with the realities of . . . modern life" by George Santayana and other American intellectuals of the early twentieth century who defined and marginalized it as feminine.[14] Yet, because of this marginal position, sentimental melodrama was able to critically view what the violent capitalist materialism of the modern era could do to individuals.

From December 1915 to March 1916, Mathis quickly gained respect from Carewe and authored three scripts for him. In the remainder of that year, she wrote four more scripts, three of them also directed by Carewe. Seven complete scripts in a year sounds like a lot, but she was only beginning. Her pace that year may actually have been a bit deliberate since she was completely new to the profession and moved directly into feature-length productions. These may have been not much more than an hour long, but there is no indication that Mathis ever worked on the one- or two-reel productions that had been the standard through 1914. In fact, Mathis had a reputation for writing excessively long scripts throughout her career, and she frequently did multiple drafts of each. There is also little indication of what scripts she may have assisted with or how many she may have worked on that were not filmed.[15]

Mathis had collaborators on these first seven scripts, at least in the sense that all of them were adaptations. But a writer also had to work with company executives, directors, storywriters, and maybe others as well, so deciding how much to credit the scenarist might seem impossible. Understanding something of the production process of those days can help. The work might start with a story of two or three pages from a writer under contract, or it might be adapted from a play or published literature. Of Mathis's first seven scripts, four were from stories by frequent contributors to film productions: two were from Shannon Fife, one from the team of Channing Pollock and Rennold Wolf, and one from Frank M. Dazey. Two were based on plays, and one from an actress/writer of very low output, Florence Auer. These people, such as Fife and Dazey, et al., generally handed over the original material to the scriptwriter and then had little to do with the production. After the screenwriter completed the script (the continuity), the work would continue under the film's director.[16] Therefore, for Mathis's work in 1915–1916, Carewe would have been her most likely collaborator rather than the storywriter. Reviews of Mathis's scenarios of stories by Fife, *God's Half Acre* and *The Sunbeam* (both with Carewe in 1916), offer strong suggestions that her contributions were dominant. The *Moving Picture World* review of *God's* noted that the main character's innocence "was evidently the intention of the scenario writer June Mathis."[17] Of *Sunbeam*, *Motion Picture News* noted, "It is the joint product of Shannon Fife and June Mathis, who provided the artist with 'God's Half Acre.' Mr. Fife wrote the original story of 'The Sunbeam' and Miss Mathis adapted it for the screen."[18]

Mabel Taliaferro, who starred in several of the Carewe/Mathis films, later testified that Mathis's contributions to these early films had great significance: "June wrote her first scenario for me," Taliaferro said inaccurately. "She was studying the art with the Metro company for which I was making pictures. The man who was writing the scenes for me was growing a little stale. It was suggested that June have a chance at the next one. The regular scenarist wrote one. June wrote one. They submitted them. There was no comparison between them. June left the man so far behind. That was 'The Snowbird [1916].'"[19]

Looking back on her beginnings in the trade from the height of her career in 1923, Mathis claimed to have asserted an effort to shape her films right from the start: "In the beginning I did not have an easy time. I found myself working perhaps with a director who had been in the business for some time, who had set ideas, which, of course, did not coincide with mine. He did not see eye to eye with me, and wanted my scenario changed, saying that my continuity was all right for a story but that it was not feasible for his production." Other directors Mathis worked with besides Carewe in her first full year, 1916, are hard to identify. Only George A. Lessey on *The Purple Lady* can be spotted in existing credits. Mathis admitted she had to be patient and diplomatic: "As some directors did not change their opinions, I had to change mine. But, gradually I began to get my own way so far as the story was concerned, and I think I can claim that directors found that adherence to a good, smooth scenario was easier for them than trying to do it some other way."[20] Although perhaps filled with a bit of hubris after getting lauded as "the most powerful woman in motion pictures" at the time, Mathis's statement does have some basis in reality. She wrote in 1923, "There is a vast difference in the scenario of today compared with the scenario of ten years ago.... The day of the trick screen writer is over."[21]

In the years before Mathis started writing, directors often worked without a script, making up a plot during the course of producing a one- or two-reel film. Edwin Carewe may have had that era in mind when he wrote in 1927, "In the old days, a director paid little attention to his scenarist, and less to the scenarist's script. Often a picture was made with total disregard of the manuscript, the director following out the plot sequence only, and injecting his own dramatic situations and 'business' as he went."[22] Mathis may have encountered directors who still adhered to this method when she started. Carewe seems likely to have shifted toward more reliance on a script by the time he met Mathis since he was impressed with the first example of her work that he saw and wanted to see more. In fact, a 1924 article reports that "the experienced head" who read her first continuity told her, "Miss Mathis, this is the very first piece of writing for the screen in which I have detected the ear marks of an individual style."[23]

Mathis's detailed description of a suspicious wife constantly checking her clock was what first appealed to Edwin Carewe in her work, and the two of them shared a philosophy of promoting realism in the movies. This agreement may be one reason why Mathis and Carewe had such a successful collaboration. In 1916, Carewe made his argument by comparing movies to other arts. He stated, "Take the case of Tristan in Wagner's great opera. On his death bed, Tristan sings for fully half an hour before he passes away. He is always in strong voice and fairly raises the roof in his dying gasp. In reality, there are few men who sing for thirty minutes on their death bed. But this is one of the blessed liberties and licenses of grand opera. I am glad that it is so, for I love the opera." In terms of realism, Carewe finds similar weaknesses in painting and sculpture, referring to them as more distant from reality than a motion picture. For this reason, he concludes, "Motion picture audiences are the most critical in the world.... The public demands realism, and realism needs extreme and almost painful details. I am glad this is so. It bears out the contention of many that the motion picture is the greatest art of man."[24]

Mathis echoed these ideas in 1923 at the height of her fame when she became responsible for the production of *Ben-Hur*, telling journalist Katherine Lipke, "You can usually find a bit of drama whenever you stir out if your mind is trained to grasp it. A look in a woman's face, the way a man says a sentence, an exchange of glances—these things seem trivial, but if you are able to feel the undercurrent which goes with them, then you have touched something which provides the dramatic impetus to your life and mine. And that is what the motion pictures try to portray—Life!" She further claimed, "Personally, my idea is to portray life in such a way that children can't understand it. If a mother is taking a child to a picture she wants to see something mature, and yet something which will not injure the child's mind. I plan each picture so that a thing is created in a subtle way and my subtitles always help out with this thought."[25]

Beyond their concerns for details, Mathis and Carewe also shared a preference for simplicity. "'After all is said and done, I think we invariably find that simplicity is the greatest art,' . . . Carewe said. 'By that I mean we must not attempt to venture above the things that we all know and the things we experience.'"[26] Seven years later, Mathis stated in an advice article for prospective screenwriters, "Were I to whisper a few words to all ambitious screen tellers of tales, those words would be, 'You can really know only that which you have lived.' When that is remembered, talent and the capacity for hard work being equal, success is more nearly certain of coming."[27]

Nevertheless, although screenwriting offered a great opportunity in the midteens, studios had no interest in paying well and success was not guaranteed. Mathis later commented that it was considered "just a step above a janitor," paying thirty-five dollars a week.[28] The reason for this low remuneration related to the number of scripts solicited from amateurs. Film historian Cari Beauchamp writes, "Many stories were mailed directly to the film companies and a ten- or twenty-five-dollar check was sent back with a receipt and a release form. Seldom was there a writer's credit on the screen."[29] This disregard for writers continued well into the twenties. Writer Frederica Sagor Maas reveals that at Metro-Goldwyn-Mayer (MGM) in 1924, in her cubbyhole office "the damp and cold got to you so that you could hardly hold a pen or pencil, much less type. This was the atmosphere provided for those knocking their creative brains out to provide suitable fodder for the movie gins." She admits, "A few writers were ensconced in better offices in the executive building. But these were the exceptions."[30]

Despite the low pay, Mathis possessed the dedication to her career that she needed to succeed. Her motivation may have come from the pressure of competition, a belief that she always had to prove herself, or a desire for control. Or perhaps, after pushing herself as an actress from at least the age of seven, hard work was simply her nature. From the start of her career transition, Mathis possessed focus and determination and she quickly became essential at the B. A. Rolfe company. When she showed up at an early meeting of the Screen Writers' Guild in 1916 and asserted that she would soon be a member, she was also indicating her intention to be a major force in the profession.[31]

The debate over whether the director or writer had more control over individual productions in the silent film era continues today, and the outcome varies according to a number of factors: the year of production, the studio, and the director and writer. In 1918, fledgling writer Louise Boyer cast a negative light on directors in a letter to a friend about Metro's production process. "Having been shaped into a 'screen story,'" she wrote, "[the narrative] goes to the continuity writer, who holds a confab with the director and gets his point of view, if he has one. He usually does, but you would rather he didn't."[32]

Silent film script scholar Ian W. MacDonald argues that relationships between writers and directors during this early production era were "flatter, less structured and with less well-defined roles" than they are now.[33] Carewe did not have a great deal of experience when he started working with Mathis. He directed one film in 1908, one in 1914, and five in 1915 before *The House of Tears*.

The Mathis script told a story of a mother-daughter relationship, which in the 1910s, as Ruth Mayer notes, explored themes of "sexual maturation and procreation, or the transition from girlhood to womanhood."[34] They tended to "revolve around fatal decisions made in the past that come to haunt the daughter in the diegetic present, locking mother and daughter into tight affective loops."[35] But *House of Tears* does not penalize women who make their own decisions. The film uses the popular mirroring effect of the times in which the lead actress, in this case Emily Stevens, plays both roles and suffers through the same experience as each one. For example, in 1917's *The Law of Compensation*, Norma Talmadge plays a woman seduced into leaving her husband and daughter by a deceitful family friend, a choice that leads to her death. As the daughter, Talmadge marries whom her father chooses but finds domestic life boring as did her mother. Even though her husband keeps her from leaving and she lives unhappily, the film presents this outcome as best for her.[36]

The House of Tears heightens the similarities of the mother and daughter's experiences. The film relates through a series of fantastic events a tale of a mother, Alice (Emily Stevens), who leaves her husband Robert (Henri Bergman) (who paid far more attention to the stock market than to her) and child for a lover Henry Thorne (Walter Hitchcock). After fifteen years, Henry shoots Alice and leaves her for dead. Robert dies, but Henry meets and begins seducing Alice's daughter Gail, not realizing her identity. Gail meets Alice, who survived the gunshot, when she hits her mother with her car, and the two decide to work together and destroy their mutual seducer. They succeed by driving Henry mad, causing him to drive off a bridge. The story has many coincidental similarities to Mathis's own: the mother's name is Alice, much of the action is set in a mining town where the unscrupulous Henry tries to make his fortune, and the mother and daughter ultimately are on their own together. It is most likely that these elements were all created by the story's author Frank Dazey, but Mathis's experience of working the theater circuit with Jennie as protector might have influenced her conclusion. An early student of Mathis's work wrote, "For this reason, Mathis chose to end her story on a positive note with mother and daughter clasped in each other's arms."[37] Whether or not Mathis drew on her own experience, *The House of Tears* exemplifies a significant variation of popular melodrama in that Alice's decision is not fatal and she works with her daughter to achieve happiness. The film was a popular success that drew a wonderfully memorable review from a woman leaving a showing in Chicago who was heard to say, "My that was good. I feel like I've been through a perfect orgy."[38]

The March 1916 release, *Her Great Price* (Mathis's third script), included strong autobiographical elements for Mathis also. The main character is a young woman writer, Agnes Lambert (Mabel Taliaferro). Like Mathis in 1915, Agnes is talented but poor, and her work keeps getting rejected. Facing despair one New Year's Eve, Agnes is about to drink poison when she is interrupted by the wealthy young Tom Leighton (Henry Mortimer). He convinces her to try for one more year by loaning her $30,000 while giving her a life insurance policy of $50,000 with himself as beneficiary. He tells her that if she has still not succeeded by the next New Year's, she can drink her poison and he will gain $20,000. The plot continues as might be expected. Agnes has another unsuccessful year and appears to have taken the poison. Her three good friends (known as the Trinity) find her slumped over her typewriter. But when they knock on her window, she appears to miraculously revive. Rising up, she tells them she has just finished revising a remarkable story of failed romance. It's the story the audience has just watched as if it were a dream Agnes was having. In contrast to the melodramas Mayer discusses in which women suffer due to their own "fatal decisions," Mathis shows Agnes succeeding with the help of the spiritually figurative Trinity, thereby introducing a theme that will resurface throughout her work.[39]

Both *House of Tears* and *Her Great Price* depict women who, like Mathis, begin the struggle to find themselves at an early age. Other stories Mathis received for adaptation in her first year of screenwriting were also based on this situation, suggesting its cultural prevalence. *The Upstart* (Carewe, 1916) is a comedy in which Marguerite Snow plays Beatrice Mitchell, a wife who, when frustrated with her husband's lack of attention, decides to elope with their chauffeur. In *The Sunbeam* (Carewe, 1916), Mabel Taliaferro plays Prue Mason who marries a very wealthy man whose father disowns him. When her husband dies, Prue must struggle to stay alive until her father-in-law finally has a change of heart. A heavily melodramatic line might state the deep feelings of Mathis and many other young women of the time: "All her life Prue has been a sunbeam to others, but no one has ever thought of her."[40] Like many others called upon to contribute to family support, Mathis accepted this role as her natural responsibility, but some of her characters, like Alice, Gail, Agnes, Beatrice, and Prue, express clear desires for respect and recognition.

These films, although sometimes possessing interesting similarities to Mathis's life, cannot be completely cited as her creations. Credit must be given to Carewe and the original storywriters as well. But Mathis's impressive level of production gives credence to the idea that she had the main artistic input for many of these productions. In 1917, Mathis received screenplay credit or cocredit on at least nineteen films. For 1918–1920, her total was fifty-one.

In her extremely busy 1917, Mathis worked with Carewe on three more films. *The Barricade*, a March release from a story by Hamilton Smith, again features Mabel Taliaferro, this time as a young woman who torments an innocent man whom she believes has ruined her father.[41] July's *The Trail of the Shadow* received decidedly mixed reviews. *Wid's* called it "an ordinary melodrama with very, very convenient situations" while *Motion Picture*

News deemed it "thoroughly interesting on the whole."[42] *The Voice of Conscience*, a November release, is interesting because it involved Carewe's collaboration with his brother Finis Fox, who was credited with the story and codirected (uncredited). Carewe later stated that Fox was his favorite writer to work with.[43] To add realism, Carewe filmed on a plantation and used "two hundred Georgia 'darkies' picking cotton in the cotton-fields. . . . The life of an old Southern plantation will be reproduced in the Metro picture, showing both work and play in the Negro cabins." Mathis is credited with the scenario, which includes a number of Black characters working on a Savannah plantation. The casual racism in the reference to Black Americans as almost a nonhuman part of the scenery with an acceptable segregated existence is astonishing now but was common for the times. *Conscience* was released just two years after the blatantly racist *Birth of a Nation* (D. W. Griffith, 1915) and at the same time as the Broadway debut of *Granny Maumee* with an all-Black cast. In this context, Carewe, Fox, and Mathis may have actually believed they were taking a step forward by even including a large group of Black people and giving three key roles to Black actors, not whites in blackface as was the general practice.[44]

Mathis seems to draw on *Granny Maumee* with a scene in which a "negress" (Pauline Dempsey) performs a voodoo ceremony to elicit a resolution to the story's tragic circumstances.[45] In another possible sign of Mathis's contribution, an intertitle refers to one Black character, Uncle Mose (Anthony Byrd), as "the most onluckiest nigger on the plantation."[46] Mathis was not averse to using that racial slur.

In June 1917, Rowland realized that Metro needed to be much larger to survive. He, therefore, reincorporated by selling stock within the company and purchased the production studios Rolfe, Columbia, Popular Plays and Players, and Yorke. He also ramped up production under a new system in which "one of Metro's directing staff [would] complete the direction of one Super-Feature and another will begin at once on the direction of the next production."[47] Mathis's torrid schedule that year, which included becoming chief writer at the newly expanded company, introduced her to several directors and actors who became important to her future both positively and negatively. These included Metro vice president Maxwell Karger and directors Charles Brabin and Tod Browning. Karger soon started directing and collaborated with Mathis on nine films during their years at Metro. Brabin collaborated with her on the December 1917 release *Red, White, and Blue Blood*, starring the very popular team of Francis X. Bushman and Beverly Bayne, who had also starred in *The Voice of Conscience*.

Mathis's most valuable connection in 1917 may have been with the unfortunate young director John H. Collins, who succumbed to influenza in October 1918 at age twenty-five.[48] Metro wanted to sign his popular actress wife, Viola Dana, in 1916, and she insisted they hire Collins as well. After his death, Collins was nearly forgotten until the Eastman House restored and showed four of his films in 1975 and scholars recognized him as a talent who deserved recovery.

Mathis collaborated with Collins on five productions over two years starting with his first film for Metro, *A Wife by Proxy* (January 1917). Kevin Brownlow, who has watched a copy of the film kept in the MGM vaults, relates that it is a "very smooth, beautifully made little picture—could be a [Maurice] Tourneur—very well acted—art director marvellous [*sic*]— nice, cynical story of badger game and involvement of enchanting Irish girl. Small scale but charming."[49]

In June, the two combined on *Lady Barnacle*, a comedy in which Dana plays an East Indian woman who sneaks on board a cruise to America by attaching herself to a young man from Boston. *Moving Picture World* highly praised the directing, acting, and "originality of handling that is refreshing," though it criticized the "too long drawn out finish."[50] The next month saw the release of *Aladdin's Other Lamp*, a light comedy filled with dream scenes.[51]

December saw the pinnacle of the Mathis/Collins productions with the release of *Blue Jeans*. Dana had been disappointed to lose the rights to *The Poor Little Rich Girl* to Mary Pickford but was consoled by Metro when they offered her this property.[52] The play *Blue Jeans*, which served as the film's basis, was solid melodrama as it introduced the trope repeated in many action serials of a man laid on a conveyor belt headed toward a circular saw. It, therefore, neatly fit Mathis's talents and also expressed what became an important theme throughout her work, the dangers of restrictive religious conventions for women.

Metro announced that Mathis did the adaptation of the play when it released its plans for the production.[53] Charles Taylor is listed as coscenarist, but it is impossible to know what his contributions were as the script does not exist. Mathis seems likely to have been the film's major writer as she was head of Metro's scenario department, *Blue Jeans* was a prominent property, and Rowland had great confidence in her. In addition, the film addresses major Mathis themes of the need to protect the weak and home-less, recognize true Christian virtues, and reject the hypocrisy of men.

The plot centers on an orphan named Junie (Dana) who finds refuge in the home of an old couple who later discovers that she is actually their grand-daughter. She marries a young lawyer, Perry Bascom (Robert Walker), and has a child. But Perry is in a political campaign against a greedy and deceit-ful opponent named Bob Boone (Clifford Bruce). Seizing an opportunity to defame Bascom, Boone claims Perry is already married. While Perry goes in search of the woman Boone has hidden away who claims to be his wife, Junie is condemned by the community for having a child out of wedlock. Her grandparents evict her from their home, and she goes to live in a cold, barren home with her baby. Perry returns with proof of his innocence and goes to find Boone at the sawmill he owns while Junie follows him. Boone's accomplice, Sue Eudaly (Sally Crute), finds Junie and locks her in the mill office. Boone then overcomes Perry, knocks him out, lays him on the con-veyor belt of the giant saw, and turns it on. After he and Sue run away, Junie breaks out of the office and rescues Perry, leading to the film's happy ending.

Blue Jeans has all the elements of conventional melodrama: a high degree of coincidence, persecution of innocent characters by powerful organized forces, and the eventual triumph of goodness over evil. As a hungry orphan in the opening scene, Junie is an object of sympathy. Coincidence enters when she finds a home with a kindly old couple who turn out to be her grand-parents. They make her a cause for even greater sympathy when they force her and her child out into the snow and cold. Goodness triumphs through her perseverance and last-minute rescue of Perry. Melodrama also requires realism to achieve emotional catharsis and hope for the marginalized people it champions. As Gledhill and Williams argue, "Melodrama is . . . not the opposite of realism but an ongoing engagement with it."[54] Its engagement in *Blue Jeans* comes through the emotional struggles of Junie and Perry against the realities of political and business corruption, a church that is quicker to condemn than provide hope, and the powerlessness of women.

Jack Lodge refers to the film as Collins's "masterpiece." The director was fortunate to be working with cinematographer John Arnold who would have a long and distinguished career that included the silent classics *The Big Parade* (King Vidor, 1925) and *The Wind* (Victor Sjöström, 1927). He eventually became president of the American Society of Cinematogra-phers and head of MGM's camera department. The film's uses of close-ups, camera angles, and comparisons of characters through dissolves to graphic matches and balanced compositions give the narrative a modern treatment that keeps viewers involved. William K. Everson writes, "Collins's unerring sense of place and people, the perfectly selected rural locations, and the absolutely 'right' faces was quite remarkable."[55]

Collins begins with a very unflattering shot of Viola Dana, looking from a low angle up toward her rear end hanging over the top railing of the fence she sits on. He then cuts to a close-up of her face, childish, yet strong. However, in her reworked opening, Mathis emphasizes Junie's rebellious nature by including a flashback in which she attempts to steal flowers for her mother's grave and is roughed up by a policeman. She runs away and is alone and hungry when she encounters Perry. Mathis transforms the play's tricycle into an archaic high wheeler that Perry is riding. His fall with it, witnessed by an unseen Junie, parallels the conclusion in which Junie appears from off-screen to knock Perry off the conveyor belt to save his life.

Collins does more with the opening through the prominence of the wood in the mise-en-scène. The imagery of the fence rails and trees foreshadows the crucial lumber mill setting at the conclusion. As Perry eats, crossing branches behind him provide a hiding place from which Junie reaches around and tries to steal food. This pattern is effectively repeated in the sawmill where Collins often shoots characters under support beams near the ceiling to enhance the impending danger.

The acting, especially Dana's, enhances the film's realism. Dana shows comedy as she tries to steal Perry's lunch, strength when she defends him, and pain when her grandparents evict her. When she goes to church to ask that her starving baby be baptized, her tenderness and courage make her performance a major element in the film's success.

The church scene directly confronts organized religion's failure to address human suffering. During the Gilded Age, wealth accumulation received clerical blessings. T. J. Jackson Lears writes, "Protestant pastors, catering to their affluent flocks, dismissed the complaints of the underpaid and jobless. [Episcopal Bishop Phillips] Brooks reassured his congregations that in America 'excessive poverty, actual suffering for the necessities of life, terrible as it is, is comparatively rare.'"[56] Even liberal Protestantism, "like other official doctrines of nineteenth-century America, came to terms with modernity by denying its darker side. The specter of class conflict, the pain of passions thwarted, the spiritual sterility of the positivist world view—all were overlooked on the highroad of progress."[57] *Blue Jeans* reveals the cost of this spiritual aridity to women.

Mathis's influence on the film seems most evident in the church scene as its significant use of stained-glass windows indicates her fondness for using works of art in her scripts. Junie is in her apartment holding her baby when she hears the church bells ring. She goes there and sits in the back as the minister christens four children. But when Junie walks forward, he refuses to anoint her child, saying, "You have dishonored the laws of morality and caused shock and panic among the faithful."[58] As Junie turns to leave, Collins shows the stained glass from her point of view that reads, "Suffer the little children to come unto me." Her grandparents are in the congregation. Jacob (Russell Simpson) was insistent about her eviction. But his wife Cindy (Margaret McWade) always believed in Junie's goodness.

As Junie walks away, Cindy stands up to comfort her. She turns to the minister as he prays and shouts the line for him, "And forgive us our trespasses." Turning to address the congregation, she says, "Let he who is without sin cast the first stone." This use of three sayings of Jesus to reveal the hypocrisy of the men who claim to preach his word is a standard Mathis element.

The struggle of Boone and Eudaly against Perry and Junie is one of individualism/materialism versus spirituality. This becomes a familiar conflict in several Mathis scripts in which men of hypocrisy and greed contrast with spiritual figures. These are usually women but could be a man such as Valentino's Amos Judd in *The Young Rajah*, who must fight the oppression of those who can only see the temporal world. Mathis was not alone in this view. As Lears puts it, already by the 1880s, "myriads of thoughtful Americans . . . had begun to question the very basis of industrial capitalist society: not merely the unjust distribution of wealth and power but the modern ethic of instrumental rationality that desanctified the outer world of nature and inner world of the self, reducing both to manipulable objects."[59] In *Blue Jeans*, Ben Boone is clearly able to use the modern ethic of reliance on "reason" and "a basic sense of decency" to manipulate the local Christian community and put Perry, Junie, and their child in danger. In contrast, Junie and Cindy understand reality to include both physical and spiritual dimensions and appeal to audiences both in and out of the film to see it with them. In the church scene, the congregation is shown to value conformity over true spirituality. Only Junie and Cindy recognize both the physical and spiritual dimensions of reality, as evident from Junie's point of view of the windows and Cindy's powerful use of Christ's words.

This conflict of materialism and spirituality suggests what film theorists, such as Paul Schrader and Henri Agel, define as a transcendental theme: "films that incite spiritual reflection but that do not tend to have religious subject matter."[60] Agel was "interested specifically in films that succeed in escaping the immanence [the constant presence] of inner life."[61] Escaping immanence means that the audience is raised to a level of contemplation that goes beyond the temporal events presented in the film; it suggests the presence of a spiritual realm for viewers to contemplate. This multidimensional reality appears when Junie looks at the stained glass and Cindy quotes Jesus. The film's resolution not only brings Ben Boone to justice but returns to a sense of values based in community rather than individualism. Audiences, especially today, might consider the narrative sentimental and simplistic. But it has a serious message that Mathis and Collins present in a transcendental style. William Everson writes, "*Blue Jeans* can still be taken quite seriously, and needs neither apologies nor weak suggestions that it be regarded as 'camp' or unintended lampoon."[62]

For Mathis, reality most often includes a spiritual realm with forces such as the four horsemen of the apocalypse or the ghost of Joan of Arc that can play critical roles in human affairs. The melodramatic form Mathis utilized is not the same as transcendental style, defined by Paul Schrader as one that "creates a sense of unease the viewer must resolve." Mathis sought to reassure viewers rather than leave them uneasy. Like D. W. Griffith famously stated, she wanted to teach people "how to see." Her details, like the church's stained-glass windows in *Blue Jeans* and the picture of Joan of Arc that comes to life in *The Legion of Death*, linked the visible world to the spiritual. Like many artists, as Schrader explains, Mathis "used 'realism' as a springboard for other interpretations of life, overlaying a seemingly realistic environment with fantasy, folk-myth, expressionism, and so forth. Carried to the extreme, this tendency to create an underminable reality results in the everyday. Most of these artificial 'realities' are designed with built-in loopholes which the film-maker can conveniently slip through later in the film."[63] For Mathis, women characters or males who possess what she called "the feminine quality" were the portals to the mystical realm. They channeled a transcendent force, an "external, nonideological reality" that is "beyond normal sense experience" and transcends the immanent.[64]

Powerful businessmen and their intellectual confederates never gave such ideas any consideration: "While the male world of laissez-faire capitalism excluded any ethical design from its culture, its cloistered intelligentsia

[was] framed . . . in terms of a privileged liberal elite, one removed, physically and logically, from the American dynamism of free enterprise."[65] But anti-capitalists also criticized sentimental perspectives as a "consoling reification of the status quo and 'social position' over a more tragic articulation of social conflict and its losses."[66] Mathis's beliefs did indeed have roots in childish superstition. In 1901, stepfather William gave her a mystical "snake ring" that supposedly had belonged to the King of Belgium and now brought luck to "little June." This could well be the same ring she wore as a writer and said always brought her ideas.[67]

As she grew, her belief that physical and spiritual realities are intertwined developed further. In 1917, Mathis wrote that ideas travel in electric currents that anyone might tap into. Therefore, writers who believe their ideas have been stolen may not have been working with original material anyhow.[68] Most famously, Mathis later attended séances with Valentino and actress Alla Nazimova and met with Sir Arthur Conan Doyle who had a powerful belief in spiritualism.[69] Doyle, creator of Sherlock Holmes, "lost his brother, his son Kingsley, two brothers-in-law, and many nephews" in World War I.[70] Spiritualism and Theosophy enjoyed strong popularity in the postwar era when millions like him sought consolation for deep losses. When he visited Hollywood in 1923, "in June Mathis, editorial director, with whom he had a lengthy conference, the novelist found a hearty sympathizer. . . . In other words, Miss Mathis is a firm and reverent believer in the fluent tenets of spiritualism."[71] In 1924, Mathis revealed her specific belief in response to her mother's death: "I have the consolation of theosophy . . . and know that death is nothing. Age is nothing. The lives we lived before live again in us."[72] Theosophy holds "that there is a deeper spiritual reality and that direct contact with that reality can be established through intuition, meditation, revelation, or some other state transcending normal human consciousness." In addition, "most theosophists also affirm an overarching, all-encompassing unity that subsumes all differentiation. . . . and that humans are sparks of the divine trapped in the material world who desire to return to their spiritual home."[73] Recognizing that Mathis believed this spark to be most prominent in women helps explain her work.

As women increasingly moved into the workforce, America's entry into the Great War gave them another opportunity to expand their lives. Most Americans at the time probably did not recognize that women faced the war not only with dread and heartbreak but also with a desire for involvement. During the Great War, "twenty-five thousand American women, most of them educated and middle-to-upper class, eager to find a useful alternative to marriage, went overseas as part of the war effort." These experiences expanded the horizons of countless American women. But literary scholar John Limon writes that if the war "raised hopes of political, professional, and sexual freedom for women, the post-war era was a retrenchment."[74]

For June Mathis and American movies as a whole, the Great War provided a means for adding new depth to melodrama. Characters could now struggle with questions of life and death, self-interest versus a greater concern, the struggle to maintain romance in the midst of chaos, and the ultimate meaning of it all. Spiritual ideals could be clearly contrasted with temporal desires. When the war ended, questions of what it was all about, what had been gained or lost, and how to continue could be addressed. Mathis's work would significantly explore each of these issues, especially the opposition between spirituality and violence. Through this conflict, Mathis attempted to define the moral basis for society. Did life have to be a constant struggle for economic security and dominance? Or could spiritual values (possessed mainly by women) provide guidance? Finally, what would be the costs if such guidance were not present?

Film industry historian Garth Jowett called the war "the ideal opportunity [for the film industry] to consolidate its role in American society."[75] Many in the movie industry actively supported the war effort, including Richard Rowland who served on a commission advising the government how to best use motion pictures to achieve victory.[76] He very likely encouraged the production of four propaganda films Mathis scripted: *Somewhere in America* (William C. Dowlan, 1917), *Draft 258* (William Christy Cabanne, November 1917), *To Hell with the Kaiser* (George Irving, June 1918), and *The Great Victory* (Charles Miller, January 1919). These superpatriotic tales were easy to praise by reviewers who knew the phrases to use. The films demonize Germans (especially the Kaiser), pacifists (always dupes of German agents), and striking workers (always incited by foreign subversives). Noting *Draft 258* "opens in 1914, with alien war lords gathered together for the consultation that disrupted Europe," and includes an exciting "charge of a troop of United States cavalry," a Pittsburgh reviewer deemed the film "a truthful 'history of our own times.'"[77] *To Hell* included a scene in which the Kaiser leads a raid on a Belgian convent and evilly selects a girl for his own pleasure. He tells his troops to do the same. *Variety* called it "a wonderfully effective propaganda picture . . . bound to arouse enthusiasm wherever shown."[78] In *The Great Victory*, the Kaiser orders that all unmarried women be given to soldiers to bear sons for the army.

However, these films do capitalize not only on the public's eager acceptance of propaganda but also on women's interests in being part of the action. They perpetuated the "sustained fantasy of female power" identified by Ben Singer in the popular serial-queen melodramas of the decade.[79] These heroines, Singer notes, "represented a commercial strategy to engage female spectators," an indication of the studios' understanding of women's interests.[80] In *Draft 258*, Mabel Taliaferro inspires her pacifist brother to become active in the war effort. He changes his attitude in time to recognize the presence of enemy spies and save his sister from German kidnappers. In *To Hell with the Kaiser*, Olive Tell contacts her American aviator boyfriend so his squad can capture the Bosch leader. *The Great Victory* explains the fate of Edith Cavell, the real-life British nurse who was executed by the Germans, as her punishment for helping an American woman escape their clutches.

But these shallow formulaic crowd-pleasers stand in stark contrast to Mathis's script for *The Legion of Death*, directed by Tod Browning and released by Metro in January 1918. Like most others in her profession, Mathis strongly supported the war effort. Besides her propaganda screenplays, she undertook as a personal project a campaign to collect old shirts to be repurposed as clothing for children in beleaguered countries.[81] In another admirable effort, Mathis helped get Metro films to Navy hospitals to entertain the wounded.[82] In *The Legion of Death*, based on the actual experiences of a Russian all-women brigade that fought in 1917, Mathis included several references to American patriotism. Two of her favorite themes besides patriotism, female leadership and spirituality, are also prominent. Gathering her material from articles published in many newspapers, Mathis "based her original story on the fact that since the time of Catherine the Great, women have been potent factors in Russian history."[83] The film is not available to be judged. But in her script, Mathis shows women deeply involved in the Great War on many levels, capable in battle, and ready to move on to broader social roles when the conflict ceased.

On January 23, 1918, Metro president Richard Rowland sent his friend Louise Boyer a copy of *The Legion of Death* script to study. Boyer would soon be coming to Metro to pursue her dream of learning screenwriting from Mathis. Rowland noted, "Of course this is altogether too long and has too many scenes for a five reel picture but was gotten out as a special, but it gives an idea of the amount of scenes and action necessary to keep the audiences interested continually." He added that he was also including the revised script, which "the California studios cut down from the one furnished by Miss Mathis. . . . You will note that the original had 500 scenes which they cut down to 400."[84]

Mathis's usual emphasis on details may have contributed to the excessive length, a common fact for several of her scripts. Although it includes romance, *The Legion of Death* is more of an action melodrama like the popular serials. As in *Blue Jeans*, the plot involves a woman who rises from a subordinate role to take charge in a crisis. Her heroine in *The Legion of Death*, Marya (based on the Legion's actual commander Maria Bochkareva), is an intellectual who becomes a physically strong military leader. The American patriotic prowar elements begin in the opening scene where Marya (Edith Storey) and her brother Paul (Fred Malatesta) are in Washington, DC, seeking support for their anti-Czarist struggle. As they watch a troop of American soldiers march by, Marya remarks, "If Russia had men like that to fight for her liberty, she would have no cause to fear."[85] When she returns to Russia, Marya tells a meeting of Revolutionaries, "America—the Mother of Democracy—will be the first to greet us when we win our fight for Freedom!"[86]

In Washington, Paul seems to be totally in charge, making all the decisions, communicating with their undercover contact, and fighting enemy spies while Marya prepares for bed. But, when they return to Russia, this situation is completely reversed. Russia does not seem to need men like the Americans as much as it needs women like Marya. When Russian leader Alexander Kerensky decides that rural villagers must be informed about a planned uprising, Marya steps up to take the job. Mathis blends in more American patriotism by showing her as a modern Paul Revere driving from farm to farm to tell people, "On the morrow, for Russia!"[87] Later, she is practically Kerensky's top assistant. Mathis again makes her a pro-American spokesperson when the premier introduces her at a rally as "Princess Marya who carries a message of Liberty from America." After her speech, Marya takes a Russian flag from a child in the crowd and puts it in a group of flags on the podium right next to the stars and stripes.[88]

But *The Legion of Death* had to go beyond showing women as patriotic supporters of the war effort. In the *New York World*, one of the Russian women soldiers told a reporter, "How did I feel on taking a human life? I had no sensation except to rid my country of an enemy. There was no sentimentality. We were trying to kill them and they were trying to kill us—that is all."[89] Mathis used this material in her screenplay and included a battle scene in which most of the Russian women are killed, wounded, or taken prisoner while fighting the Germans.[90] Mathis also gave a valid account of the Battalion's origins. A crowd calls a group of Russian soldiers cowards as they return from the front. One soldier yells, "Why fight? It isn't getting us anywhere. Besides—Germany will pay us if we quit." Marya speaks to the crowd from her veranda: "From the earliest History of Russia, women have been the dominant spirit for Good or Evil." There is an insert of a German heel grinding down an anthill after the next statement when Marya says, "Let us take the places of the men who are proving themselves cowardly traitors to Russia!"[91] This statement relates to the fact that Russian Premier Kerensky encouraged the Battalion's formation as part of an effort to humiliate reluctant men.

A scene in which Marya joins Kerensky on stage and presents her plea for women soldiers was also derived from an actual event. On May 21, 1917, Maria Bochkareva joined Kerensky at Petrograd's Marynsky Theater where she told the crowd, "Men and women-citizens! . . . Our mother is perishing. Our mother is Russia. I want to help save her. I want women whose hearts are pure crystal, whose souls are pure, whose impulses are lofty. With such women setting an example of self-sacrifice, you men will realize your duty in this grave hour."[92]

Bochkareva claimed peasant status, but stated that "[her] original group included women of prominent families, university graduates, peasants, . . . and servants."[93] Mathis indicates her character's authenticity by showing Marya pick up a volume of Tolstoy in an early scene, a detail that was cut for the final version.[94] During scenes of the February 1917 Revolution in Petrograd, Russia, Mathis accurately shows the feared Cossacks, enforcers of the Czar's privilege, going among the people and randomly killing children.[95] As historian G. J. Meyer states, this development was a sure sign that the Czar's rule was ending.[96]

Most significantly, Mathis suggests the "Legion of Death" received its name because each of its members carried a small vial of cyanide in case she were captured and faced "a fate worse than death" from the enemy. Opinions on the accuracy of this idea differ with Russian scholar Richard Stites stating only that "Death Battalions" received their name "to underline their savage determination to perish in defense of the country if necessary."[97] Mathis uses the more sensational explanation, which helped her incorporate the rape trope that had entered war films of the time in D. W. Griffith's 1915 *The Birth of a Nation*.[98] She may have actually believed the cyanide idea to be accurate, and she may have been correct. The *New York World* piece that seems to have been a major source for Mathis also printed this explanation.

To make Marya a spiritual figure, Mathis employed the popular Joan of Arc trope for American prowar films of the time that began with Cecil B. DeMille's *Joan the Woman* of 1915. In a key scene, Marya agonizes over what to do as more Russians flee the front lines and she feels the need to act. She opens a book to a picture of Joan of Arc, which materializes and transforms into Marya in a soldier's uniform. Mathis then provides an intertitle reading, "And thus another woman is inspired to rally a fear ridden army." Robin Blaetz explains that in DeMille's work, "the message of the film is that women and war do not mix. Women are welcome to sacrifice themselves for the crusade, but the deeds of war itself and the attendant glory are reserved for men alone."[99] Mathis clearly thought differently and put her "Joan" on the battlefield where she actually had been.

Blaetz also argues that "the chronicle of events that makes up Joan of Arc's life only signifies something in Western culture if it appears as a rebirth story."[100] In Mathis's script, Joan is clearly reborn through Marya and represents not merely an answer for Russia's problems but also for the world's. Marya, already a warrior, becomes a spiritual figure as well, transformed by Joan of Arc's spirit. In this, she resembles Alla Nazimova in Mathis's *The Red Lantern* (1919), where she is a spiritual figure who becomes a leader of the Boxer Rebellion in China. Together, they represent distinctive perspectives on gender and war that merit recovery. *The Legion of Death* uses what Blaetz defines as a romance structure: "The romance, like myth, is based on the ethical axis of good and evil, with the world, or experience, in need of deliverance. The heroic representative of light and virtue transcends the corruption and darkness of the world in order to redeem it."[101] Marya is that heroic figure who will cut through the darkness of the times.

Mathis presents Marya as a truly multitalented woman. She is a spy, organizer, orator, and soldier. One of Mathis's scenes crossed out in the final draft of the screenplay showed Marya receiving news that the evil Count Orloff (Charles Gerard) has turned traitor and is helping the Germans. Marya knows she must get word to Kerensky and get his orders. She spots a dispatch rider who refuses her order to give up his motorcycle and takes off. Marya shoots him and takes his cycle. He fires at her and hits her helmet but does not stop her. After succeeding in her mission, she returns to her troops, only to get shot off the motorcycle and captured. Her lifelong servant, a gigantic peasant named Dmitri (Pomeroy Cannon), comes to her aid but is also captured.

With this development (as with the Joan of Arc apparition), Mathis again shows an interrelationship of spiritual and physical elements through a setting that defines Dmitri as a modern-day Samson. In the Bible, when Samson is bound in his enemy's palace and believes his strength has gone, he prays for one last burst of energy in order to pull down the columns and destroy his people's oppressors. Mathis sets up this allusion in an early scene in which Marya refers to Dmitri as "a Giant, who does not realize his strength, but some day Russia will break the bonds of autocracy and stand unshackled before the altar of Liberty."[102]

But Tod Browning's script revisions almost completely obscured this biblical reference. Mathis wrote that following her capture, Marya is brought to Orloff whom (in melodramatic tradition) she has known for a long time. When he threatens to rape her, and her hands are tied, she buys time by telling him she has always desired him. She sees Dmitri tied to a post outside, awaiting execution. Orloff grants her permission to speak to him one last time. Marya cannot reach her vial of cyanide, so she asks Dmitri to strangle her. He reluctantly agrees to but cannot. He then unties her hands, but Orloff gets there before she can drink the poison. Orloff begins holding and kissing Marya, which angers Dmitri so that he uproots the post he is tied to, completing the Samson analogy. He falls on Orloff, who then angrily orders Marya to go to the firing squad in Dmitri's place. Mathis, recognizing how potentially ridiculous this scene could become, added to her script, "NOTE: I AM AFRAID THAT IF THE STAKE TO WHICH DMITRI IS BOUND, STRIKES THE GRAND DUKE ON THE HEAD, IT MIGHT MAKE A 'KEY STONE' EFFECT, AND CAUSE A LAUGH."[103]

The most important of Marya's many positive qualities is that she keeps her personal goals and duties ahead of her love interest, the American Rodney Wainwright (Philo McCullough). His encounters with Marya go back several years, and his squadron eventually rescues her from the firing squad. Mathis was clearly breaking from historical accuracy to get propaganda mileage out of this character, putting the Americans in Russia several months before they actually were. Marya's priorities are clear in a scene that was improved in the final version of the script. In the original, Mathis thoroughly suppressed any romance in a scene in which Kerensky personally orders Paul and Marya to the front. They simply go. Even in Browning's revised version, Marya's duty comes first. Rodney is there and proposes, but Marya says, "My work is not yet done. When Russia's freedom is assured. . . ."[104]

The revised ending, however, was not nearly as strong about Marya's own goals as Mathis's version had been. In the final version (either written by Browning or done so under his instructions), Orloff kills Dmitri and tries to rape Marya. She begins screaming, but Rodney and his American soldiers are at that moment chasing retreating Germans past the hut where Orloff is holding Marya. Rodney hears her screams and runs in. Orloff has given up on rape and is choking her instead. Rodney stops him in time. Browning then concluded with American soldiers and Russian women troops marching past the camera and a cut to an intertitle: "When the flare of the sun is in ashes / And the thunder of cannons cease. / These shall be living—when all earthly, passes. / LIBERTY—LOVE—AND—PEACE."[105]

Mathis's original avoided such empty proclamations and once again emphasized women's sacrifices and continued commitment. After Dmitri's struggles with Orloff, some Germans shoot him. But he lives long enough to tell Rodney where Marya is and facilitate her rescue from a firing squad. After Marya collapses into Rodney's arms, Mathis cuts to a later scene in which she is visiting wounded soldiers, some of whom are women. Marya tells Rodney, "TOMORROW I RETURN TO MY REGIMENT, AND IF I LIVE,—REMEMBER—I AM NOT A PRINCESS ANY LONGER. I'M JUST LIKE ANY AMERICAN GIRL." Rodney does not insist on their love coming first. Instead, he replies, "GEE, THE RUSSIAN REVOLUTION'S DONE A LOT FOR ME!" and gives her a mock salute.[106] Thus, in Mathis's version, Marya still puts her own commitments first and does not reject any possible future roles. Mathis does not finish with a shot of an embrace or a promise of eternal peace. Instead, she stays focused on Marya and a suggestion of new roles for women in the future.

Nevertheless, Count Orloff's attempted rape of Marya continued a disturbing anti-feminist trend of the World War I films. In *The Little American* (DeMille, 1917), *Draft 258*, *To Hell with the Kaiser*, and *The Legion of Death*, German captors of American women constantly have rape in mind. As Gaylyn Studlar documents in *This Mad Masquerade: Stardom and Masculinity in the Jazz Age*, concerns about masculinity were already prominent in America in the late teens.[107] War, with its omnipresent threat of destruction, is the ultimate demasculinizing force. Movies with women on the battlefield, therefore, conveniently fit propaganda needs in two ways. First, emphasizing threats to women obscured the dangers to men. Instead, men reassert their heroic persona by rescuing the woman from her would-be rapist. Second, the films could capitalize on the popularity of active women in adventure serials while still suggesting that females do not belong on battlefields. As Singer wrote of the female adventure serials, these films included "contradictory extremes of female prowess and distress, empowerment and imperilment."[108] Women's contributions to the war effort could be briefly recognized and then quickly forgotten afterward. But their fade from history was not due to a lack of effort from June Mathis and other women filmmakers of the era.

In many ways, Mathis's *The Legion of Death* was far from the realities of World War I. But it was close to the realities of women's identities and outlooks at the time. Until 2015's *Battalion* (Dmitriy Meskhiev), it was the only fictional work to depict the Battalion of Death, which it does through accurate historic facts and events. It is a reminder that women actually fought and died on the front lines during the war. Most important, it shows a woman as a leader, rising up and taking an active role that is intended as an example for men. Dorothy Goldman states that during the teens, "the impact of contemporary cultural mores—that the public sphere was reserved for men while women could exert influence in the private sphere of the home—should not be underestimated."[109] Mathis's script for *The Legion of Death* is a reminder to look beyond this formula and recognize the true complexity of women at the time.

3

Metro's Women Writers, 1917–1921

To achieve success, Mathis used a tremendous work ethic and high ambitions to profit from her cultural experiences and personal connections. She fought and struggled to get what she wanted, but she was not alone. She was part of a contingent of women born in the 1880s and '90s who entered the workforce in large numbers. The film industry offered talented women great opportunities not simply to find work but to take a relatively equal share in production with their male colleagues.[1] By January 1917, Metro's chief scenario writer Harry Hoyt had left his position to begin an independent scenario company. Later that year, Mathis moved into Hoyt's old position. One of her colleagues was Katharine Kavanaugh, an experienced actress and playwright who remained an associate and sometime cowriter with Mathis through 1927. Another was Louise Boyer, wife of Pittsburgh architect Ernest Boyer and an old friend of Richard Rowland who came to New York to begin writing screenplays.[2] Boyer wrote Ernest that she was thrilled when Mathis remembered that a mutual friend, a musician named John Clare, had said Boyer "was so well grounded in the Classics!" She gushed in her letter, "O hug me, Ernest, hug me!"[3]

In another letter, Boyer wrote, "The place we work is a cubby hole over the studio—the stage, they call it. You go up a steep flight of stairs and come to a very small room, three desks littered up."[4] Whether Mathis spent much time there is open to question, but her collaborations with Carewe, Collins, and others show that she got to know her colleagues very well. Boyer reveals her opinion of Mathis's personality in some very specific comments: "Give a human being a sufficient amount of rope and they either hang or climb. June climbs. And hangs at the same time." Her comments sound like a logical description of someone who had worked her way up through years with traveling theater companies while hoping for the chance to create great drama: "She has . . . the faculty for cheapening every fine and subtle thing that comes to her notice. She is bourgois [*sic*] to the finger tips. Her laughter is course [*sic*], her vanity is cheap, her point of view is rotten. But on top of that she manages to be a very decent sort of animal."[5]

Of Mathis's talents, Boyer writes, "She is a splendid comedian and mimic, an able actress, and she knows the business of making a working continuity as well as any one in the game today." Later, she wrote that Mathis "knows the picture making business from the synopsis writing to the cutting of the film."[6] This private comment lends credence to Mathis's account of her 1915 production stint with Frohman during which she claimed to have spent most of her time studying the work behind the camera. On February 19, 1918, Boyer's letter to her husband confirms Mathis's constant efforts: "Went to dinner with Miss Mathis yesterday. She is a very clever woman + she knows her game technically, but she lacks finesse. She is studying playwriting now. She is a fiend for work. Working sometimes till two and three in the morning and keeping three stories going at a time!"[7]

Recognizing that "June Mathis is high cockalorum at Metro. Chief Scenario writer," Boyer was willing to take Vice President Maxwell Karger's advice about learning from her, but only to a certain extent. Karger recommended that she be "June Mathis' poodle dog for awhile—follow her everywhere—listen to her talk to the directors—get her method—for he thinks she's great. I told him I'd gladly be June's pup if June would let me. He seemed to think she would—said June was a darling. He thought I could learn alot [*sic*] about the game by typing Mathis' stuff—But while I don't mind being a dog, I draw the line on being a stenographer."[8] Boyer did not mind this arrangement at first, but it seemed to have limited benefits. She wrote to her husband about one evening with Rowland, his wife, and June Mathis: "Miss Mathis has several of my stories, [and] that dinner [the] Rowlands gave June and me was for the express purpose of discussing those same stories and their possibilities, but June didn't mention them. I didn't think she would. She did what she usually does, talked about herself. Which I enjoyed far more than I would any discussion of me."[9]

Later, though, Mathis's gruff personality started to wear on Boyer and Kavanaugh. Boyer wrote to her husband, "Miss [Katharine] Kavanaugh is finer in perception than June Mathis is—Miss Mathis is a shade flamboyant."[10] She later tells Ernest she has written a story, "Breath of Spring," and given it to Mathis to read. Kavanaugh advised her "to get it from Miss M. immediately and put it on the market. Said she wished she had written it herself. We had a heart to heart about the fair June, too—We agree on

June. We think she's a little boot licking four flusher."[11] Two years later, on April 23, 1920, Boyer presents a different (or supplementary) impression of Mathis as she fondly reminisces to Kavanaugh about her days at Metro: "Old 61st Street on the job again, the racket, the yells of 'camer-r-r-ah' with the temperamental Boss registering dynamics all over the place, and the festive June being gracious, but not compromisingly so—and two whole 'well-known playwrights' (whoever they are) to boot (literally, to boot, if Mr. Karger hasn't changed his opinion of authors)."[12] Then, in January 1923, Boyer apparently asked Mathis for a recommendation to help her get into a scenario writing course. Mathis wrote to her in a personal letter, "The only thing I had to say was that I knew your marvelous reading capacity and also that you had written many interesting things. I shall always remember our association at Metro very pleasantly and also the friendship that drew us together, for long before I knew you I felt on intimate terms from just hearing about you."[13]

Born in 1874, Katharine Kavanaugh is another woman of great talent, ambition, and fortitude largely forgotten by film history with a biography much like June Mathis's. She was multitalented, publishing some songs in 1898.[14] Kavanaugh's parents died when she was in late adolescence, motivating her to learn the business of testimony transcripts and open her own office. At that point, she began writing and starring in her own plays at Elks and Rotary clubs, churches, and schools around her home city of Baltimore. After about a decade of writing and starring in her own plays, Kavanaugh married longtime colleague and theater company manager Oliver C. Ziegfeld in 1910. But she quickly went back on the road with vaudeville star Valerie Bergere, writing and performing in skits with her for the next six years.[15] In 1916, she sent a screenplay, *The Wheel of the Law*, to Metro. While performing in Philadelphia, she went over to New York to find out their response. Metro purchased the work and starred Emily Stevens in the film. It was the start of a film career that lasted until 1940.[16]

On December 9, 1916, *Motion Picture News* briefly announced that Metro had signed "three writers of prominence": Kavanaugh, Charles A. Logue, and J. F. Poland.[17] At the end of 1917, Kavanaugh won second place in a *Photoplay* screenwriting contest with a script titled *Betty Takes a Hand*, which Metro filmed in 1918 with Olive Thomas in the lead role.[18] As head of Metro's story department, she wrote several stories in 1918 adapted by Mathis, starting with a western, *The Winding Trail*, directed by John Collins and released in January. In May and June of that year, Kavanaugh wrote the stories for *Social Quicksands* and *The House of Gold* and collaborated with Mathis on the scenarios for those along with ones for *The Winning of Beatrice, A Successful Adventure,* and *The Silent Woman. House of Gold* deserves recognition for the review in *Variety* that read, "If you are at all nervous or sensitive don't go to see 'The House of Gold' in the evening or you will be likely to suffer from nightmare[s]. It is a frightful concoction of murder, bacchanalian revels, the incarceration of an innocent man in an insane asylum, delirium tremens, a court room trial for murder, etc."[19] Although their work was not usually so extreme, this example shows that Mathis and Kavanaugh did not shy away from shocking material. Kavanaugh also wrote stories titled "For Revenue Only" and "The Scheme" with scripts by Mathis.[20]

Kavanaugh was a kindred spirit with Mathis and Boyer through her love of literature. In 1908, she told the *Baltimore Sun* that she reads "two thirds of the time" and that her tastes are "almost universal." Her favorite poet was Kipling, especially "The Rubaiyat," and to a desert island she would take *Anna Karenina*, which she had read three times. She spoke of her writing in a manner that may very well have been true for many screenplay and drama authors of the time: "People say that all of my plays are melodramatic. Well, I don't think that that charge is altogether true, but consider the houses in which I have played and the audiences I have had to write to. I have played in middle-price houses and to church audiences. You always have to have a loud shot or two. Under such conditions I have adapted my plays to my people."[21] This statement comparing her literary knowledge with her popular work indicates something important about the careers of June Mathis and many other writers. Their work drew on "great" literature, popular melodrama, and personal experience and aimed at popular audiences. And they were conscious of each element and purpose.

On February 19, 1918, Boyer wrote, "Miss Kavanaugh is a very able woman, and she is being used for hack work. . . . [She] is tired [of] being nothing but a buffer between the agents for stories and Karger, who has no idea how difficult stories are to get. . . . She would develop very well as a continuity writer if she only had the chance."[22] Boyer wasn't the only one to think so. Kavanaugh then wrote the screenplay for *The Divorcee* (released in January 1919) for Ethel Barrymore, who did not care for Mathis. She then returned to her native Baltimore to strike out on her own as producer, writer, and director of her own company and open a school for "stage and photoplay arts."[23] She made a three-reeler, *Love's Crossroads,* using local performers and settings. It opened in November 1919 at Baltimore's Albaugh's Theater, where Kavanaugh had spent much of her career, sharing the bill with a "playlet," *The Liar*, for which she was again writer and lead actress.[24] But a few years later, after Mathis had joined Goldwyn, Kavanaugh followed to become head of its story department.[25] While there, she assisted on Mathis's screenplay for *The Day of Faith* (1923). In 1924, Kavanaugh said later, "When June went to First National, I joined her and we worked together for several years."[26] Two years later, Mathis trusted Kavanaugh with writing the screenplay of *The Far Cry*, directed by Mathis's husband, Silvano Balboni.

Evidence of Katharine Kavanaugh's talent is available on the Internet Archive, which contains twenty-four of her plays. Her work generally attacks social restrictions on young women with much good humor, but she uses heavy melodrama as well.[27] Like so many creative women in the silent film industry, she worked under rough conditions and was well liked. She worked with June Mathis a great deal in various capacities. After her death, First National demanded proof of Mathis's work on a final scenario she owed them. In letters about the issue, Kavanaugh is referred to as Mathis's secretary and personal assistant and submitted a Mathis story titled "Her Boy Friend" as evidence of progress toward fulfilling the contract.[28]

Richard Rowland was the dominant force leading Metro to high prominence in the industry by 1917. But as Louise Boyer's comments imply, it was Metro cofounder and vice president Maxwell Karger's voice that drove the company's workers every day. Carolyn Lowrey describes Karger as "a creative and imaginative executive. An indefatigable worker, his day's activity frequently covers eighteen hours. His intense enthusiasm for motion pictures and his infinite faith in their splendid future, arouse an inspiration which welds him to his task."[29] On January 26, 1918, Louise Boyer wrote her husband Ernest that Karger was dead tired and wanted to break her in as a dependable writer. Later, she added, "I found out that we work all day Saturday, in fact we work a little longer on Saturday than we do any other day, because Karger wants to take so many scripts home with him to read over Sunday."[30] Two days later, in another letter to Ernest, she noted, "Karger is a very able man but he has [not] got confidence enough in some one else to train them to do his work for him, so he wastes a lot of time doing things that some one else could do just as well, and then hasn't time to attend to the things that no one else can do. He is wearing himself out."[31]

Karger's extraordinary efforts also limited the opportunities for Metro's talented women and thus hurt the company. Boyer wrote Ernest that she suggested to Dick Rowland that Karger spend at least one hour a week helping to improve morale and cultivate the talent of the women writers on his staff. The women would then use their ideas to help the company "instead of hanging on to them for their own profit from some other source." Rowland liked the idea but said he had to make Karger think it was his (Karger's) idea or it would not get done. He had repeatedly asked Karger to formally organize the scenario department only to be told it was not possible. Karger would not take the time, to which Boyer had the sarcastic response, "Poor Devil! He hasn't got the time to take."[32]

Karger's great enthusiasm and energy were often displayed through his strong temper and vulgar vocabulary. Boyer wrote Ernest that she had "heard him cursing everything and everybody down on the stage. You don't need to fear for my tender ears by the time I'm through with this place." She concluded that their friend Elmer "may have a bigger and choicer vocabulary than Karger, but Karger makes up by repetition what he lacks in variety. I'm thinking of asking Dick [Rowland] to give Elmer a job as Karger's coach—it may help him to relieve his feelings."[33] Karger's exuberance belied a lack of organizational skills that could have better served the young company. Writer Channing Pollock—who contributed stories to Metro in 1916 and 1917, including two scripted by Mathis, *The Dawn of Love* and *His Father's Son*—describes Karger as very confused and confusing in his memoir, *Harvest of My Years*. Pollock relates how Karger asked him to create a script so they could get more use from the set they had built for *Romeo and Juliet* (1916). Pollock did so but later received a call from Karger, who said the script was no good because they could not afford to build the set it would require. Pollock had to remind him that the script had been written specifically to make use of the set they already had.[34]

The costs to Metro of Karger's tendency to overwork himself rather than focus on utilizing studio personnel wisely is evident in one more private example. On July 21, 1918, one of Boyer's former Metro colleagues wrote to tell her why he was now at Fox: "Mr. Rowland's snippiness to me, and Mr. Karger's lack of organization and his indifference, and my low salary, etc., etc. made up the sum total of my discontent. . . . I was wearing myself out for people who didn't care."[35] Boyer had a much better relationship with Rowland but would soon leave Metro as well. The wife of accomplished architect Ernest Boyer, Louise would eventually find her true talents in drawing. Today, her work in that medium and the more highly regarded pieces by her daughter, Helen King Boyer, are present in several major galleries.

Mathis's work at Metro during the late teens was filled with dozens more screenplays prior to her large career-boosting success with *The Four Horsemen of the Apocalypse*. The productions provide critical depictions of gender, race, and spirituality that would be major themes in her work. They also provide examples of her work with male directors and producers during her rise to prominence in the industry. Most importantly, they include Mathis's collaboration with one of the major theatrical and film figures of the era, Alla Nazimova, which lasted into the early twenties.

4

The Nazimova Films, 1917–1921

Mathis's Metro years were the happiest of her career. In summer 1918, Rowland settled her into what *Motion Picture News* called a "cool little office overlooking Central Park through which a breeze is always blowing. The soft greens of the walls, the grey of the wicker furniture, and the green grey cretonnes, make it a veritable oasis these hot days."[1] Mathis became a booster for the studio, teaching her pet parrot to say "Metro." *Camera!* magazine joked that she was next going to teach it to say "Screen Classics" and then "fewer, bigger, and better pictures."[2] She even became "the good luck joss of the Metro baseball team."[3] The work never ended, but that was not necessarily due to company orders. In 1919, *Motion Picture News* wrote that she insists on staying busy, but at the moment is writing only two scenarios at once.[4] Still, even the heavy workload could be mixed with fun. At one point, she resorted to buying a hat over the phone, a noteworthy event for the press.[5]

Mathis's destiny was set at a very young age, and it seems she may only have found happiness in a creative career. Although there were rough points and she sometimes claimed that the work was too much, Mathis never expressed any regrets about her choices. As she moved further into her career, she continually intensified her efforts. Rewards like a stylish office, her own staff, greater influence, and eventually her own production unit and the highest salary of any woman in Hollywood kept coming.

Mathis often idealized her reasons for becoming a writer. The apparent promise of steady income and greater domestic stability had been important. But in the press, she usually emphasized her desire to improve the movies. In one advice article she stated, "I first became a scenario writer for the reason that I was not satisfied at the time with the pictures then being shown."[6] To achieve her goals, Mathis's diligent effort to use details, to understand narrative structure, and to know all aspects of filmmaking helped her succeed. Her use of verse for intertitles in her first screenplay illustrated her willingness to take chances to infuse her work with artistry, and her partnerships at Metro with seasoned artists like Carewe, Collins, Kavanaugh, and Karger helped her focus on serious themes.

Her most notable work in this period would be her collaborations with Alla Nazimova, a major star with great control over her projects. Nazimova is credited with revolutionizing American stage acting with her performances of Ibsen in 1906. She maintained her prominence through 1915 when she decided to begin making films. At Metro, she chose her own projects and often wrote, directed, and edited. For Mathis, with her love of serious drama, the prospect of working with Nazimova must have been exciting. Between 1918 and 1921, Mathis and Nazimova made six films together in which they exploited Orientalism, a style popular for its "exotic and mysterious" qualities. Orientalist characteristics are notable for denigrating all Asian, Arab, and African people, and other people of color, and justifying their exploitation by whites. Yet, in *Eye for Eye* (1918) and *The Red Lantern* (1919), Mathis and Nazimova condemn the brutality of Western white males and promote female spirituality. In *Out of the Fog* (1919) and *Camille* (1921), they further argue against the dangerous control of older men over young women. The extant screenplays available for these works exhibit strong statements on race, gender, and materialism, making them critical for understanding Mathis's purpose because the completed films were generally temporized by Nazimova and others.

While at Metro, Mathis created many of the kinds of films she preferred, films that would "touch the heartstrings." She admitted, "Comedy is necessary" but believed "it doesn't make the lasting impression that is made by the soul-searching story—the story that gets under the skin of all of us and shows that mortals are weak, groping atoms in a cosmic wilderness and that . . . their brief span of existence is crowded with infinitely more sorrow than happiness."[7] Most viewers actually do not wish to hear that they are weak individuals whose lives are filled with sorrow, but these were the stories Mathis wanted to tell.

Mathis expressed her preference for drama throughout her life in minor ways: her statement that she wanted to reach the top ranks of dramatic actors, her desire to play Carmen, her constant reading of canonical authors, and her work in *The City* (1910) and *Granny Maumee* (1914). Whether she wished to address the themes focused on in this chapter or whether these were titles selected by Rowland, Nazimova, Collins, or others to which she was assigned is a fair question. But the answer may not make much difference because evidence of Mathis's work and ideas are discernible throughout her life and career regardless of any project's origins.

As an actress, Mathis developed the persona of the "winsome" young woman evident in the cheerful images beaming out from each of her promotional photographs. She displays an energetic personality that characterizes her years of high productivity at Metro. In 1950, Adela Rogers St. Johns suggested that this cheerful energy suffused all her work: "When June swept through the studio onto sets, into offices and dressing rooms, appearing as by magic wherever there was a crisis, her fierce authority lit in others some of her own divine fire."[8]

These references and images played well in the popular press and overshadowed Mathis's occasional statements about her preference for serious drama. But they cannot discount her bleak assessment of humans. Mathis had grown up in a fractured family and was constantly on the road with her mother, absorbing lessons from world literature and earthy colleagues, and fighting for better conditions for actors. She worked hard for every achievement and sometimes must have felt like a single atom in an expansive wilderness. World War I and the influenza epidemic that each claimed millions of lives could have only exacerbated this feeling.

Her preference for producing topical dramas that addressed serious issues inadvertently received strong assistance from Metro's policies. From 1915 to 1917, Metro had phenomenal success. Rowland made millions by hiring talented actors, directors, writers, and technicians and pushing profits back into new productions. Among his signings were the popular duo of Francis X. Bushman and Beverly Bayne who mainly starred in mysteries and detective films at Metro from 1916 to 1921, some of which were based on stories and screenplays by Mathis and Kavanaugh. Director John Collins and actress Viola Dana, as discussed previously, were other important signings.

These four would do much to establish Metro's reputation for high-quality productions: "Rowland wanted exhibitors to identify Metro's logo with superior scripts and high production values (i.e., spectacular scenes, elaborate sets, and professional photography and editing). Furthermore, he wanted exhibitors to be assured that when they booked a Metro product, particularly a feature, it would contain one or more bona fide stars."[9] His most important signing, however, was Alla Nazimova, considered by some to be the greatest actress of her day. Referred to by Louise Boyer as "deyvilish tricky to work with," Nazimova was a Jewish Russian immigrant who had revolutionized dramatic performance styles with her stagings of Ibsen starting in 1906.[10] Alan Dale of the *New York American* wrote, "She did more than Duse ever did. Her fame will be a household word."[11] As a musician, dancer, and actress who had trained in Moscow, she brought an artistry and passion to her acting that American audiences and critics had not seen. She toured with a repertory of Ibsen's *Hedda Gabler, A Doll's House,* and *The Master Builder.* The young Eugene O'Neill, who saw her ten times during the tour, later said her performances gave him his "first conception of a modern theater."[12]

In 1915, Nazimova entered filmmaking with an adaptation of a playlet she had been touring with, an antiwar work titled *War Brides.* She stated that her admiration of director Herbert Brenon's *A Daughter of the Gods* (1915) gave her the confidence to start working before the camera. But not everyone was thrilled with her screen debut. *Moving Picture World*'s Edward Weitzel felt "that Nazimova had not fully adapted to the medium: she 'gave too freely of her inward fire,' and he advised her to study Gertrude Berkeley's superb performance as the mother." Brenon, however, remarked that Nazimova's acting was beyond impressive: "men who have been with me a long time, all through the work of producing *A Daughter of the Gods,* have forgotten the Cooper-Hewitts, the camera and all the accessories, and have had to turn away and dry their eyes."[13]

In 1917, Nazimova returned to the Broadway stage in *'Ception Shoals,* a play about a sixteen-year-old girl restricted from all knowledge of sex by her Puritan father. Karger saw her in it and urged Rowland to sign her. Rowland announced that she had returned to the screen for good when he signed her to a five-year contract at $13,000 a week with approval rights for her scripts, directors, and leading men. Her first film for the studio was *Revelation* (George Baker, 1918), based on the play *The Rosebush of a Thousand Years.* Set during the early months of World War I, the story features her as a cabaret singer, Joline, who touches a rosebush at a convent that immediately blooms. It's declared a miracle and another follows. She therefore ends her singing career to become a war nurse. During the film's premiere in February 1918, "when the lights went up at intermission halfway through the movie, the dazzled audience at the [New York] Lyric Theatre spotted Nazimova sitting in a box and 'greeted her with shouts and handclapping.' The same thing happened at the end, and 'not until she had left the theatre did the people stop their applause.'"[14]

Meanwhile, Richard Rowland was fighting to maintain independent control of Metro. Screenwriter and personal friend Louise Boyer called him "a real business genius. He has some common sense." Rowland had started with $30,000 in capital in 1915, was worth $6 million in 1918, and refused "to loose [*sic*] control of the company or imperil it by borrowing."[15] Metro's films had been making money, but that had been immediately used for funding more productions. As a result, the company had few alliances with theater chains or investments in its own theaters, which left it without the strong distribution enjoyed by other studios. Rowland tried to compensate by instituting policies designed to give Metro films more appeal for exhibitors. He dropped block booking so that theater owners would only need to book the Metro films they wanted. He announced Metro would make fewer and better films, and, with Nazimova and Dana under contract, he decided to withdraw from bidding for other top stars. Metro films would emphasize quality narratives, talented directors, and strong performances over big-name performers.[16]

Within this context, Mathis could feel confident about her opportunities to produce the dramatic "meaningful" films that she valued most because these were exactly what Rowland was calling for, and her approaching period of collaboration with Nazimova would provide a needed stimulus.

Hollywood's major woman filmmakers tended not to produce work that argued for equal inclusion in the male-dominated social structure. It is not surprising, therefore, that Western women would adopt the personas of even more greatly marginalized and oppressed women, "the Oriental," as a means of asserting their own importance and condemning masculine oppression. As Edward Said has famously shown, "Orientalism" was a construction of the Western view of "the Orient" through the distanced observations of prominent male writers whose experiences of Middle Eastern and Asian lands came mainly through artifacts, museums, and other texts produced in the same way.[17] Matthew Bernstein adds that it instilled in Western culture "a distinctive means of representing race, nationality and Otherness."[18] As Gaylyn Studlar has explored, the vogue for Orientalism coincided with the development of cinema: "Even though early cinema learned to borrow from almost every mode of popular entertainment and trend in art appearing during its time, Orientalism was a particularly powerful attraction, especially in the United States. . . . Across high and low culture, in many venues, including consumer advertising, dance, the decorative arts, fashion, movie palace architecture, literature, theater, and vaudeville, the Orient was figured through narrative tropes and visual conventions based on a tradition that had been thoroughly codified by Victorian culture."[19]

These racist concepts included the idea that "Oriental women" were mysterious, both sexually and spiritually, which meant that men could not control them. Studlar argues, "the orientalized female was a subject whose exhibitionism was not just passive but was associated with dance's construction of self-assertive, highly charged identities that temporarily broke down the binary roles through which not only femininity but ethnicity and race were conceived."[20] Similarly, Mari Yoshihara argues, "It was not incidental that [numerous] Orientalist performances by white women took place at the same time that many white women were becoming New Women of the twentieth century, who challenged Victorian gender norms and the ideology of the separate spheres by participating in the women's suffrage movement . . . , expressing themselves in arts and letters, [and behaving in many other nonconformist ways]."[21] Orientalism was an ideal concept for movies because it designated "a place where personal identity is liminal, where identities are lost, transmuted, recovered."[22] For Nazimova, already considered exotic and mysterious, as well as for Mathis and director Albert Capellani, the concept was perfect for exploitation.

Studlar relates that the history of Orientalism on stage originated in Sarah Bernhardt's performances of *Cleopatra* in the 1880s.[23] In silent film, the persona was first taken up most famously by Theda Bara (née Theodosia Goodman) whose studio-created name was said to be an anagram of Arab Death. Her stardom, says Studlar, "stood at the intersection of transformative femininity, sexual anarchy, and Orientalism."[24] In 1915, Bara had a smash hit in *A Fool There Was*, a story of a woman "vamping" a happy family man and destroying his life. She followed that with more films in which she played wicked seductresses and Orientalized characters such as *Carmen* (1915) and *Cleopatra* (1917). In the midst of this mania for Orientalism and exotic women, Nazimova accepted *Toys of Fate* (1917) as her second Metro production and her first Orientalized movie role. Gavin Lambert defines the plot as a "lurid sexual melodrama" that "allowed Nazimova to run the gamut between dual roles. Fade in on a wild, passionate gypsy who deserts her tribe when she falls in love with a wealthy Englishman . . . and commits suicide after he abandons her. Fade out, and fade in again, twenty years later, on the gypsy's wild, passionate daughter intent on revenge." Mathis and Metro were capitalizing not only on Orientalism but also on successful elements from *The House of Tears* with its story of revenge against an abusive man and the female lead playing both mother and daughter. Nazimova became as popular as Pickford and Norma Talmadge and "Metro's most important asset."[25]

Yet, critics would often fault Nazimova for exerting too much control over her films. Writing in *Moving Picture World*, Weitzel noted, "The necessity for making 'Toys of Fate' a seven-part feature has forced June Mathis, the author, to stretch her story to the limit. This Screen Classic, produced by Metro, successfully answers its purpose of providing Nazimova with her full share of forceful acting."[26] Nazimova's understandable desire for self-promotion trumped Mathis's work in *Toys, Eye for Eye*, later in *Camille*, and possibly in their other collaborations as well, often considerably subordinating Mathis's themes. Yet, the two apparently had a strong friendship. Though comments about each other do not seem to exist, they worked together for at least five years through six completed films and one uncompleted project.

Mathis was a guest at some of Nazimova's famous parties at her home, the "Garden of Alla." Their relationship might be understood by the fact that Nazimova could be extremely critical of directors. For example, after completing her third successful film with Capellani in 1919, *The Red Lantern*, she dismissed him because she was tired of his personality. Interestingly, Mathis and Capellani seem to have worked well together. Besides the Nazimova films, they also collaborated on *Daybreak, The House of Mirth* (both 1918), and the scenario for *The Parisian Tigress* (1919) for director Herbert Blaché. Their productivity may be due to their sharing the same philosophy. Scholar Kristin Thompson states, "In all his films, Capellani clearly gave precise movements and business to each actor present, no matter how insignificant, and their faces, stances, and gestures, often fairly broad, make up for the almost entire lack of cut-ins."[27]

For *Camille* (1921) and *Salome* (1923), Nazimova's directors (Ray Smallwood and Charles Bryant) were merely nominal as she actually directed herself (uncredited). She never expressed criticism of Mathis, perhaps because they did not have to work together closely every day. Nazimova heavily revised the script for *Camille*, but Mathis seems to have recognized at this point in her career that such alterations were part of the system. Later, after her bitter experiences with *Ben-Hur* and with producer John McCormick at First National, she would show more resistance to the studios' pressures.

But at Metro in the teens, Mathis had the great good fortune of working with the excellent actors, directors, and cameramen hired by Rowland
whose talents, perspectives, and artistry meshed well with hers. In addition, Metro's financial shifts, whether up or down, were excellently timed
to give her opportunities and freedom when she needed them. Finally, she
also benefited from the popular fascination with Orientalism. Not only did
the style move her narratives to new countries, as in *Toys of Fate*, but it
also enabled her to depict spiritual females in greater depth. In *Eye for Eye*
and *The Red Lantern*, although both "Orientalist" productions, Nazimova's characters possess notable abilities for rebirth and renewal, overcoming male oppression, and transcending cultural and physical boundaries.
Studlar hints at the spiritual element in these films when she states that
"women's fascination with the Orient should be viewed not just in terms of
the appeal of luxurious consumables but as part of a search for intensified
experience. That desire has been associated with modern culture's search
for personal meaning."[28] She adds that the "aesthetic topography [of the
East] held the promise of a different feminine identity—preposterous and
improbable—but also destructive of the claims of the prevailing ideology."[29]
That element has power as each film ends with intrusive white males forced
to confront their own guilt and responsibilities in a final encounter with
Nazimova's character (even if she has died).

In 1918, Nazimova selected Henry Kistemaekers's play *L'Occident* for
production, requested that Mathis write it, and changed the title to *Eye for
Eye* because she felt it indicated the narrative content better.[30] Mathis, in
turn, suggested Capellani direct it because of his reputation for understanding actresses and success in his films with the star Clara Kimball Young.
With Capellani's history of achievement in France including a highly
acclaimed version of *Les Misérables* (1912), she also felt his name would
lend the film prestige.[31] Kistemaekers's play was extremely critical of French
military actions in Palestine. The main character, Hacina, loses her family to cannon fire launched from the French battleship commanded by the
officer she later falls in love with. Her father and three brothers were killed
by bombs, her sister had her leg and head blown off, and her mother survived but went insane. A friend from her home tells her that the violence
occurred when one tribe attacked another and a third attacked the "Christians" (the French). The Christians retaliated by assaulting all the "Arabs"
with no concern about exactly who had attacked them.

The drama's lead male character is a French officer, Cadiere, who has come to Toulon (the setting) to rescue his friend Arnoud from opium addiction. Like several other French officers, Arnoud is sick of the military because he thinks politicians interfere too much. Cadiere feels the same, but he does not see any alternatives. He believes French men are all part of a chain constructed by culture, customs, and feelings that must be passed on. He feels that Arab men are freer because they are more individualistic but nevertheless thinks that Arnoud must stay in the French tradition.[32]

In 1918, this depiction of America's allies in the Great War would not be allowed on screens. *War Brides* had been withdrawn from circulation, then redistributed with new titles identifying the violent soldiers as German.[33] Larry Wayne Ward writes that the government used "pressure" to get antiwar films withdrawn and force changes in negative depictions of US allies. In response to filmmaker Robert Goldstein's *The Spirit of '76*, which depicted British brutality during the Revolutionary War, "the courts convicted the film's director under the Espionage Act, sentenced him to a ten year prison term, and confiscated the film."[34] It seems astounding, therefore, that Metro would approve the production of *L'Occident*. That they did indicates Nazimova's tremendous stature and the studio's trust in Mathis to transform it into something acceptable to the censors. She did so by expanding brief references in the play into narrative events that moved the action from Palestine to Morocco and eventually to Paris, opening it up from the restricted settings of the stage. She emphasized the sexual and spiritual powers of Nazimova's character, now named Hassouna. She also made Cadiere (Charles Bryant) more worthy of sympathy, and the completed version was altered to even make him innocent of killing Hassouna's family. However, Mathis's greatest alteration was to make Hassouna the lead character instead of Cadiere. A *Photoplay* review indicates the narrative apparently underwent still further revisions, stating that "the tale concerns Hassouna's struggle with her growing love for [Cadiere] and the Arab duty to kill one who had subjugated her tribe—and caused the death of her family."[35] Mathis's script, written in June 1918 and owned by artist Georgina Starr, includes no such struggle, which indicates possible revisions.

Reviews suggest the completed film (not known to exist) emphasized revenge, but Mathis's extant script emphasizes Hassouna's persistence and spirituality. These qualities replace the Orientalist conceit of the "exotic Arab woman" as irresistible to Western white males present in *L'Occident*. Kistemaekers has Cadiere tell Hassouna she appeals to him because of her magic (a typical Orientalist element). He gives into it too often and cannot recognize himself when he does. She replies that, if she had him, she would not hurt him, and they begin to kiss passionately and violently.[36] Mathis keeps Hassouna's passion but drops the intellect and love of reading that she possesses in the play. Instead, Mathis gives her a spiritual nature that places her beyond the understanding or control of men.

Other events referred to only briefly in the first act of *L'Occident* provided Mathis with cues for building her narrative structure and creating new scenes. In the play, Cadiere relates how Hacina had been sold to a tribe in Africa at age twelve and later became a carnival dancer in Montmartre. The carnival manager tried to return her to Africa, but she found temporary shelter in a convent. She suddenly disappeared one morning and lived on the road a few years before Cadiere found her in a Montmartre club.[37] These references left narrative gaps in which Mathis created scenes of birth imagery to show how Hassouna's spirit could not be contained.

In Mathis's opening scene of *Eye for Eye*, her description of Hassouna emerging from the dark interior of her tent suggests a baby leaving the womb.[38] Shortly thereafter, her father throws her into an empty grave after discovering she helped their captive Legionnaire (Cadiere) escape. He promises to return to execute her in the morning. But Hassouna escapes this womb-like environment when men from a rival tribe discover her, lift her out, and sell her to a circus in Tangiers.[39] Later, Cadiere takes her from there (thus conflating the Montmartre club with the circus), but she then escapes the convent he sends her to by climbing a tree to go over its wall.[40] Like her father and the circus owner, Cadiere is unable to restrict and define Hassouna. Her frequent rebirths (most of which are escapes from places where men have tried to confine her) reveal her constant movement toward freedom and self-definition, a pattern Nazimova and Mathis had played out in their own lives as well.

Eye for Eye maintains what Ella Shohat defines as the feminizing of the land in American Orientalist films. In *L'Occident*, Cadiere is in love with Hacina at the start of the play. They live together, and he says he thinks of her as an island that he needs to explore.[41] Mathis uses this idea when she defines the country through her description of Hassouna in her opening scene: "the passion and mystery of the desert are in her smile, as she leans her body sensuously against the tent."[42] She thus takes this male Orientalist perspective as the definition of the gaze upon the female. Mathis's placement of Hassouna inside the tent and strong identification of her with a sensuous yet destructive land (a description also of the stereotypical vamp), defines her as "mirroring the mystery of the Orient itself, [which] requires a process of Western unveiling for comprehension." Furthermore, Shohat explains that this process "comes to allegorize the Western masculinist power of possession, that she, as a metaphor for her land, becomes available for Western penetration and knowledge."[43] However, in *Eye for Eye*, the Western male has no knowledge of the country and his attempted penetration of the land fails from the start.

Shortly after introducing Hassouna, Mathis presents her father and his men dragging Cadiere, bloody and beaten, into their desert camp. They push him into a tent and tie him to a post to await execution the next morning. Hassouna, therefore, as the protagonist, is the one to take action and penetrate this enclosure to cut him free and enable his escape.[44] Cadiere, in other words, has become the treasure hidden in the Arab lands that must be liberated, and it is the Arab woman who must follow her instincts to do it. Hassouna can also be seen as that treasure, one discovered by Cadiere. But their final reunion ultimately results much more from her actions than from his.

She is with him in Paris at the conclusion entirely because of her own indomitable spirit. Her escapes from the grave and the convent might suggest God's continued presence with her in response to her prayer in the opening scene, even while "leaning sensuously" against the tent.

The content of that Islamic prayer is not presented, but Mathis makes it central for Hassouna. Her presence in Paris at the end has been motivated by her refusal to exchange Islam for Christianity.[45] At the convent, Mathis writes, as she observes the nuns in prayer, "Slowly the chapel begins to dissolve—leaving Hassouna standing in foreground—the chapel dissolves to a Moorish mosque—the Two [sic] Korans in the back, each side of the praying Priests—a fountain playing—the arabs [sic] coming in with their shoes off, and kneeling on their prayer rugs."[46] She then decides to leave the convent. As she does, "she registers the fact that the burdensome air of the Christian church is not for the free daughter of Mohammed."[47]

When she reaches Cadiere, he is reading a farewell note from his wife, whom Mathis has strongly associated with Western culture by naming her Helene.[48] Helene's idea of freedom is to have as much fun and as many possessions as she can, which her husband seems uninterested in providing. By contrast, Mathis defines Hassouna as a pagan and associates her with animals, particularly dogs, throughout the script. The final scene easily suggests a puppy waiting for affection from its master. Hassouna even uses this term for him twice in the final intertitles: "FORGIVE ME, MASTER, BUT I COULDN'T OBEY THY WISH. LET HASSOUNA STAY WITH THEE, MASTER."[49] *Photoplay* ended its glowing review with an acknowledgment of this bow to racist and nationalist conventions: "The psychology of the thing is at fault in Hassouna's final acceptance of Western civilization . . . but then. . . ."[50] Yet, Hassouna displays not just loyalty, but also, as stated when she left the convent, freedom. Her presence asserts a challenge to Cadiere (and Western white males) to accept his (their) responsibility. Despite his attempt to distance himself, he has rescued her and she won't let him walk away. Optimistically, the film ends with the lieutenant accepting her: "Hassouna looks at him—he doesn't answer—but looks at her, stroking her hair—she moves closer to him—he bends forward—puts his hand on both her shoulders—and draws her to him. FADE OUT. THE END."[51] Her submissiveness is somewhat paradoxical because she has used her own physical and spiritual strength to obtain this goal. Mathis's script shows Hassouna there to find comfort despite the weakness, decadence, and lack of understanding from Westerners.

Eye for Eye's success with both the public and the critics caused Metro to quickly follow it with productions of *Out of the Fog* and *The Red Lantern*. The production schedule was so packed that in October 1918, the filming of *Fog*, editing of *Eye*, and writing of *Lantern* were occurring simultaneously.[52] Though *Out of the Fog* came first, *The Red Lantern* seems more appropriate to discuss here because of its Orientalism. Set in China during the Boxer Rebellion of 1899–1901, Metro invested huge amounts not only in Nazimova's salary of $13,000 a week but also in thousands of extras, glamorous gowns, and marvelous sets. Christine Leteux writes, "Henri Menessier [yet another talented Metro artist . . .] recreated a sumptuous Peking with its temples, open markets, missions, and crowded streets. He reproduced Peking's famous 'Dragon Room,' where the emperor's throne stood . . . [and] made watercolor sketches of all the interiors, which were later built. He also created a garden for the mission." Finally, sculptor Victor Andre created a massive Goddess of Peace statue, measuring twenty-two feet high by six feet wide, copied from a rare antique of Capellani's.[53]

The film was the first production at Metro's new West Coast studio, and they hyped it with a (huge for the time) $250,000 publicity campaign, including the filming of a night scene that thousands of spectators were able to view.[54] These expenditures were rewarded with great box office success.

In *The Red Lantern*, Nazimova, in another dual role, plays a Chinese-British woman named Mahlee and her white American half sister, Blanche Sackville. Her character possesses several trademarks for female characters in melodrama: spiritual, innocent, and abused. But she is not passive as she seeks acceptance in either the Western society or the Chinese. Her battle for recognition and justice parallels Junie's in *Blue Jeans*. More importantly, Mathis deviates from the conventional Orientalist narrative in that none of the Western men in the film—her father, an American missionary, or the missionary's son—come to Mahlee's aid. Their presence does not provide any solutions for the Chinese they are supposedly there to help.

Nevertheless, Mathis's script maintains blatant stereotypes and fulfills audience expectations for depictions of Western superiority. It seems obvious the production was not interested in cultural accuracy, but rather in popular attitudes toward Asians. The film, in fact, was based on the novel of the same name published by Edith Wherry, who had lived in China with her missionary parents. But Wherry had little interaction with the Chinese as her private journal, written in 1891 when she was fifteen, reveals.[55] Mathis also drew on the two-volume history of the Boxer Rebellion by Arthur H. Smith, *China in Convulsion* (1901). In it, Smith comments, "The fact that Christians refuse to conform to the customs of the country is, to the literati especially, a heinous, an unpardonable, offense. It is a saying of great antiquity in China that upon entering a village one should learn what is customary, and upon entering a country ascertain what is forbidden—with a view, that is, to conforming to the custom, and eschewing what is for any reason taboo. But here is a set of teachers, alien to China, who deliberately narcotize the Chinese themselves, so that they presently become obstinate nonconformists."[56] In this statement, Smith identifies the distance and prejudice of the Europeans toward the Chinese that Mathis emphasizes as the source of great suffering in her film. In *The Red Lantern*, Nazimova's Mahlee falls in love with Andrew Templeton, the missionary's son. But when both the Templetons and her British father refuse to accept her, she fully commits herself to the Boxers.

Mathis establishes spiritual themes very early. Madame Ling (Margaret McWade), Mahlee's grandmother, suffers a terminal illness in the coffin shop built by her late husband. But for her, death is not the final destination as an intertitle defines this setting as a womb-like environment for her. She will proceed through "a dark passage" (suggestive of a birth canal) to "Nirvana."[57] Once again, Mathis associates women with Theosophy's all-encompassing spiritual unity. Madame Ling possesses significant negative qualities. Her beliefs are highly superstitious and self-serving as is evident when she tries to force Mahlee to cut off her own feet. Madame Ling's goal is to reach nirvana, which she believes she may not enter unless she can achieve remittance for not binding Mahlee's feet as a child.

Both script and film present enough caricatured depictions and derogatory remarks about the Chinese to fulfill all the qualities of a truly ugly Orientalist production. Mathis's script opens with a title defining the setting as "THE SHOP OF THE COFFIN-MAKER'S WIDOW, WHERE FATE STALKS IN SICKLY GUISE." A title immediately following reads, "WITH TRUE ORIENTAL OPTIMISM, THE ANCIENT CHINESE CRONE FACES THE DARK JOURNEY UP THE RIVER OF SOULS TO THE CHINESE PARADISE—NIRVANA."[58] Thus, Mathis introduces Chinese beliefs as strangely, and perhaps even sickly, other. Yet, she includes a countermotif that criticizes Western beliefs and presents her broad approach to spirituality. The suggestion that Madame Ling's soul will ascend to nirvana rather than Christian heaven is only one of several ways in which Mathis undercuts Western assertions of Christianity's superiority. She also shows that the Chinese understand the spiritual world far differently than Westerners, and yet accurately. Madame Ling says she knows she will die when she spots an owl for the third time, and she is soon proven correct.[59]

The next scene is set on a nearby street. Mahlee approaches a vegetable stand where there are flowers on the counter. Mathis instructs that she "stands where the blossoms frame her face, to make the same comparison that was made in the book, when it compared Mahlee to the Chinese flowers."[60] In the film, Nazimova actually pauses at a tree to smell its small round blossoms, a very effective choice as it contrasts Mahlee's association with beauty and feminine circularity to the phallic imagery of men's swords. While Capellani very likely chose the shot, Maxwell Karger was also much involved in the production. Mathis refers to him throughout the script as with a note for this scene: "Mr. Karger says: Be sure that a great many atmospheric close-ups are taken of all these scenes."[61] Mahlee then endures cruel mocking about her large feet from a number of men. But an ancient holy man who is passing by prophesies that Mahlee will achieve great importance but, after that, darkness and the trip to nirvana.[62] The film's revision of this title to omit the word "nirvana" has a more negative message, as it ends with the reference to "darkness." It lacks the acceptance of spiritual diversity in Mathis's original text.

The holy man's prophecies also function as a forceful narrative device, possessing a strong similarity to Shakespeare's witches in *Macbeth*. Both passages come immediately after the works' prologues and, while Mathis's script is not comparable to Shakespeare's play in terms of quality, she deserves credit for including a similarly functioning character, whether by accident or on purpose. Like the witches' prophecy, the holy man's comes true. But also, like Macbeth, Mahlee reads far more into it than she needs to. When Macbeth is told he will be king, he is not told that he will need to murder Duncan to do so. He does not have to do anything, but he takes drastic action that ultimately undermines his goals. Mahlee also does not need to fear the prophecy. She is not given a timeline but is merely told that she will eventually die like everyone else. Moreover (at least in the script), she will be rewarded in eternity. Yet, afterward, she lives with a sense of foreboding that haunts her till her death.

What is most interesting is that this prophecy is revealed to Mahlee, the greatest outcast in the plot, from a priestly figure for a religion that the film at times defines as inferior. Yet, the conventions of popular narrative film encourage viewers to take such pronouncements to the major character seriously. Thus, Western viewers face a conflict between their sympathy for Mahlee, a Chinese woman, and intertitles that reaffirm beliefs in the superiority of Christianity. The film is exceptional for its lack of a significant Western male protagonist with important goals. None are major characters and none can be trusted.

Mathis then includes the first of two important womb imagery scenes, each one tainted with death. In these, European male penetration has caused desecration of the womb. The first (the only one in the extant film) is a flashback to Mahlee's birth. Madame Ling reveals to Mahlee, "A FOREIGN MANDARIN DEVIL LOVED MY DAUGHTER—YOUR MOTHER—AND PAID ME A HANDSOME PRICE FOR HER. SHE GAVE HER LIFE FOR YOURS." The setting is "A CHINESE ROOM, CONSIDERABLY RICHER THAN THE COFFIN SHOP, AS THOUGH THE FOREIGN MANDARIN HAD BEEN WEALTHY AND HAD FITTED UP A PLACE TO LIVE IN COMFORT WITH HIS CHINESE WIFE."[63] The exotic furnishings, along with the money paid for the "wife," suggest a brothel in which Mahlee's mother has been the prostitute. Mahlee's grandmother, Madame Ling, holds her while her mother lies dying on a cot. Her father, Sir Philip Sackville (Frank Currier), tosses down some money as his apparent total contribution to the care of his child. He departs with what Mathis's script calls a "regretful glance."[64]

Mathis here suggests, as another aspect of Orientalism, that for Westerners at the time, their real fear was sexual. Her depiction of Sir Philip illustrates Nick Browne's point: "The racial unconscious of American popular culture in this period is predicated on a specific prohibition: No white woman can have sanctioned sexual relations with a non-white man. The male prerogative in this system is expressed in the asymmetrical fact that a white man can under certain circumstances (for example, when residing in a foreign, non-white country) have relations with non-white women."[65] Neither *Eye for Eye* nor *The Red Lantern* revokes these privileges, as is evident when Sir Philip gives Mahlee's grandmother strict orders never to have her feet cut. But both films emphasize the privileges' costs to Eastern women and the debts that white males accrue.

Shortly afterward, Mathis includes another flashback. This one explains the origins of the hatred Boxer Rebellion leader Sam Wang (Noah Beery) holds toward all Europeans and their Christian religion. In another dark tent, young Sam watches as his European father stabs his Chinese mother to death and then leaves.[66] Together, the scenes emphasize two forms of European male penetration, one sexual and one malicious. In each case, procreation has been perverted and leads immediately to death. The tent, representing a womb, becomes a tomb that only the adult white male escapes.

With these scenes, *The Red Lantern* initiates the Orientalist pattern of a feminized land invaded by white men who most often rescue an oppressed woman and provide social uplift. But the white men in *The Red Lantern* are not heroes. Their penetration does not bring coherent insight but oppression, rebellion, and death. The children born from their possession of Chinese women, Mahlee and Sam Wang, eventually lead a bloody rebellion partly due to their rejections from their white fathers. Rather than enlightenment, the white males attempt to repress the truth through violence and money.

Not for the first time, Mathis found her script changed during production, omitting the scene of the murder of Sam's mother. Instead, a flashback to his social exclusion in America during his three years of study there is included. Just who was responsible for this revision is unknown. While Sam mentions that his European father was just as evil as Mahlee's, the omission of Mathis's murder scene makes his motivation for revolution seem petty.

Even worse, he later tries to rape Mahlee and then provides the poison that will kill her. These changes minimize the film's depictions of Western oppression. The American missionary couple, the Templetons (Winter Hall and Amy Van Ness), might be criticized for their desire to indoctrinate the Chinese in white Christian beliefs while maintaining a comfortable distance from them. Their Ark of the Covenant Mission is set off apart from the city rather than in the midst of the people, suggesting that fear and concern for their own safety trumps their desire to truly help. The Mission has elegant interior design with Chinese columns, dark paneling, a full organ, and a beautiful garden. The Templetons fully support an American education for Sam, believing he wants to practice medicine. But their failure to recognize Western oppression leads to his assault against their mission.

After Mahlee fails to sever her own feet, Andrew finds her passed out on the coffin shop floor and takes her to the Mission to help her recover. While she lives there, Mahlee helps with the Templetons' outreach, falls in love with Andrew, and nurses him to health after he is beaten by a Boxer gang. Mahlee's presence gives the Templetons a great opportunity to promote integration and prevent a great deal of hardship and bloodshed. But they fail to transcend their racist beliefs. Mrs. Templeton tells Mahlee that she can never be Andrew's wife "BECAUSE YOU ARE OF ANOTHER RACE—A RACE THAT NEEDS YOUR HELP TO LEAD THEM AND TO SHOW THEM THE WAY."[67] Mrs. Templeton never explains why Mahlee could not perform these duties as Andrew's wife, and so her racism drives Mahlee away and enables Sam to enlist her support for the rebellion.

The existing film of *The Red Lantern* suggests that Nazimova's choice of this project is part of the trend for white female artists of the time to identify with "Orientals" to assert their own importance and condemn masculine oppression. As Mahlee, Nazimova uses clichéd Asian characteristics of mincing steps, humble bowing, and inquisitive head tilting. Yet, she is a strong character, holding her head high, indulging in the fragrance of flowers, playing the organ at the Mission, reading, and teaching English. She fights the insults of the Chinese who mock her and stands up to Mrs. Templeton and her father who reject her for racist reasons. Her height and broad shoulders allow her to tower over all the other women in the film and emphasize her strength even as she is constantly vulnerable. Most significantly, her major goal is to find her identity and a community to accept her. But prejudice and hatred deny her wishes and lead to tragedy for both her and the country.

Mathis contrasts men's temporal and women's spiritual natures through her two main characters. Sam pursues his goals by lying about his purpose for going to America. He tells the Boxers that it is part of his plan to drive all Westerners from China. Mahlee employs powers of transcendence. Her mercurial, spiritual nature enables her to easily transition back and forth between the European and Asian cultures, from Mathis's strange depictions of Buddhism and Chinese mysticism to Christianity and back, from leading the rebellion to trying to protect the Mission occupants from it, and from alternately loving and hating both Sam and Andrew. Her final transcendence is represented by her death and her prophesied trip to nirvana.[68] Mathis constructs this reading of the conclusion by her association of Mahlee with spirituality throughout the film. For example, in her work at the Mission, Mahlee is a far more effective evangelist than either Andrew or his parents. In one scene, she fixes her hair to look like the Virgin Mary in a picture she has. When she goes over to the Boxers, she impersonates their spiritual leader, "The Goddess of the Red Lantern." Sam even defines her in spiritual terms when he claims she will become "The Jean D' Arc of China."[69] Through all these transitions, Mahlee shows her ability to succeed within either culture, to embody the highest feminine spiritual figures of either, and to potentially unify them through her ability to teach, comfort, and heal.

Mahlee and Sam are victims of the binary view of ethnicity and culture strictly maintained by each side because they are offspring of blendings of the two. They give the lie to Kipling's "Oh, East is East and West is West / And never the twain shall meet," used twice in the film. But their tragedy is that Kipling's dictum is based not on culture, politics, or religion as much as on skin color. The flashback to Sam's experience in America shows one example. Mahlee first experiences this prejudice with Mrs. Templeton's rebuke. She suffers much more from her rejection by Andrew. As Mahlee nurses him back to health, Andrew's attachment to her grows. He is about to express his affection when he "catches one of her hands, starts to raise it to his lips, when the rays of the moonlight sift through the boughs of the trees and he sees her yellow hand. The thought of the difference in race crosses his mind—he realizes the gulf between them—drops her hand quickly and turns away."[70]

The crucial question here is whether Mathis and Nazimova held the same racist attitudes. Despite the film's criticism of white behavior and atrocity, the answer is probably that they did. In her script, Mathis draws on "the traditions of realist and sentimental literature and legitimate theater which, best embodied by the countless theatrical representations of *Uncle Tom's Cabin* . . . staged complex forms of identification that conveyed 'racial sympathy' and a 'melodramatic crossracial recognition of virtue.'"[71] Her use of these conventions did not need to be motivated by antiracist beliefs. Thus, her racial slurs in this script and others suggest her agreement with Nazimova who wrote that one negative aspect of making *The Red Lantern* was her need to be around "the hundreds of Chinese & Mexicans and Indians (the latter two were camouflaged as Chinamen) . . . for neither of them had ever been [in] the vicinity of a bathtub or the ocean, and to be constantly in their midst did not encourage my desire to know more of the Far East!"[72] In other words, Orientalism fetishized high culture objects isolated from actual societies. It had no concern for the lives of the masses. Yet, Mathis's use of melodrama and focus on details push her *Red Lantern* script beyond her limited views. Her work gets underneath the decorative spectacles of both the missionaries and the Chinese to suggest that what is unseen— hidden desires, rape and murder, and a spiritual ability for transcendence— is more powerful than what is visible: pathetic missionary efforts, violent rebellion, foreign intervention.

Besides transcending spiritual boundaries, Mahlee also has the power to constantly shift her identity and to pass through physical barriers. These mercurial powers suggest an identity less grounded in the temporal world and more potentially unifying than those of men. While fierce fighting goes on in Pekin, Mahlee heads to the Mission in a final desperate attempt to gain recognition from her father, Sir Philip Sackville. Mathis's extant script contains two versions of this scene, and each presents one of her most damning portraits of a paternal figure. Sir Philip goes to extremes to repress his guilt over his exploitation and abuse of Mahlee and her mother. He is willing to sacrifice his daughter so that he can deny any connection to the Chinese. As she heads to the Mission during the rebellion, Mahlee transcends gender boundaries by disguising herself as a young male coolie to sneak through the barricades and bridge the division between the two sides by slipping through a crevice in the Mission wall.[73]

The film contains a blend of the two versions in Mathis's script. In her male disguise, Mahlee breaks from behind the attacking Chinese to approach the Mission. She does not enter through a crevice but by calling that she has an important message for Sir Philip, an element from the second version. She is allowed inside and confronts Sir Philip with "Don't you recognize me? I am Mahlee, the Eurasian—the grandchild of Madame Ling." Sir Philip looks at her softly and bows his head with a slight sense of shame as Mahlee leans toward him with arms open and a hopeful expression. Sir Philip then gazes off toward Blanche as she holds a baby and Andrew stands next to her. Mahlee also looks at them with a smile of appreciation. Then, turning back to him, she states, "I want my father to acknowledge me."[74] Sir Philip raises into a tall forceful posture and shakes his head no while saying something for which there is no intertitle. These two shots suggest that his response is most likely based on the idea that he will not risk letting Blanche know about Mahlee, which gives him a final excuse to reject her. Not only does he wish to stay away from any taint of miscegenation, he does not want to make Blanche cope with that shame. She is the favored daughter, and his assertion of this idea most likely found favor with audiences of the time.

Kneeling in the posture of a beggar, Mahlee replies, "You do not have the right to disown me."[75] When her father still refuses to accept her, she says, "You have severed the last tie which bound me to the white race. I am back to serve the Yellow cause, and I shall know peace nor rest as long as a single foreigner remains in China."[76] Mahlee turns away angrily, pushes past Andrew, and leaves through the gate.

In the second version of the scene, Mahlee is commissioned by the Empress of China to go to the Mission and ask for favorable terms of surrender. But upon arrival, she tells Sir Philip that her only intention was to talk to him. Both versions include a line that presents Mahlee sympathetically but does not appear in the film. Both also privilege whiteness and may signify Mathis's racism as well. But they may be excusable in that Mahlee's need for acceptance would cause her to claim her father's identity. But when she fails, she immediately accepts herself as Chinese. In version one, she tells her father, "I am not yellow—my heart is white—give me a chance to live."[77] The suggestion that Mahlee is not just pleading for her identity but for her life is significant and makes Sir Philip more cruel for his refusal. The second version is only slightly less desperate as she says, "I AM NOT YELLOW—MY HEART IS EUROPEAN—I AM SO LONELY."[78] Here, Philip's refusal will not deny her life, only companionship. But Mahlee's statement is a powerful expression of the multiethnic individual's life, and Philip is still abandoning her. He Europeanized her with his refusal to let her feet be cut, but he will not help her find refuge from her isolation.

Also significant in the second version is that Blanche approaches Mahlee to ask forgiveness for an earlier offense in a scene also missing from the extant film. She begins to ask Mahlee to stay, but Mahlee sees Sir Philip's cold stare and refuses the offer. Mahlee notices Blanche's affection for Andrew and puts their hands together in a gesture equivalent to her look at them in the film. As she leaves, Blanche again starts to ask her not to. But Sir Philip again stops her and then makes a statement of guilt: "GOD FORGIVE ME—SHE IS YOUR SISTER." None of this material appears in the film, and its existence shows an effort to make the script less racist and misogynistic. Mathis completes the scene with Andrew asserting segregation's inevitability. Blanche first realizes her sisterhood "with horror and then an expression of eager joy, as she starts to call after Mahlee to bring her back—but it is too late. Mahlee's figure has disappeared through the barricade, and Andrew puts his hand on her [Blanche's] arm in sympathy but with the realization that it is best."[79]

In the end, Mahlee is the tragic victim, an object of sympathy due to her father's rejection. As the Boxers are defeated and Sam has been killed, Mahlee has nowhere to go; she drinks poison and dies on the empress's throne. Her father, stepsister Blanche, and Andrew arrive too late to save her. Mahlee has learned the truth of Kipling's statement too late. Mathis maintains conventions of Orientalism in that the Western white males only suffer emotionally at most while the "Oriental" woman is punished simply for who she is. But despite Mathis's complicity and agreement with these racist elements, her conclusion emphasizes the murderous racism of Western whites and their ineffectual responses to their sins while Nazimova is the object of viewers' admiration and sympathy.

The major irony in *Eye for Eye* and *The Red Lantern* is that even though Hassouna and Mahlee have greater moral character and endurance than the men, they are either submissive or dead in the conclusion. Jane Gaines refers to such endings as signifying "contradictory positions that *were* unresolvable in life and that therefore stubbornly remained so in these narratives."[80] Each conclusion suggests tragedy and sympathy for the marginalized woman crushed by the masculine hierarchy. They place blame on white Western patriarchy, though the implications are not emphatic. The conclusion of *The Red Lantern* backs away from a strong condemnation of white males. As Mahlee sits dead on the imperial throne, her father, stepsister, and Andrew, having driven her to her fate, feel remorse but will face no punishment. As Gaines states, "Following the novel, [Mathis and Capellani] end the problem of her doubleness without resolving it. Mahlee commits suicide in the end, an event made strange by the excessiveness of its staging."[81] The scene is arranged like a tableau of the crucifixion with the young man kneeling beside her on the right and father and daughter embracing on the left and turning their heads like Mary and the disciple who comforts her. Mahlee receives sympathy and even appears as a Christ figure. If read as such, we are left with the subtle question (perhaps too subtle), for whose sins has she died?

As mentioned, Nazimova forced Capellani out of Metro immediately upon completion of *The Red Lantern* even though they had made three very successful films together. She apparently could not tolerate a skillful director who demanded respect. She explained to her sister Nina, "On account of my pictures being such a success he maintains that it is due to him and therefore he ought to be treated like Griffith. . . . Also, he wanted an increase of salary (750 a week instead of 500) and many other things that were impossible."[82] The actress obviously did not consider her own $13,000-a-week salary impossible.

Prior to *The Red Lantern*, Mathis, Nazimova, and Capellani made one other film, *Out of the Fog*, the loss of which is particularly regrettable. Art director Menessier remarked, "I can say without being unduly excessive that it was the best picture Capellani ever made."[83] *Film Daily* advised exhibitors, "In some roles there is no finer screen actress than Nazimova, and with each picture her hold is becoming stronger with regular fans, also with theatergoers who are interested in truly artistic impersonations. The picture is so far out of the ordinary in its possession of artistic qualities that I would make a special appeal to the most critical element in your community [to have it play a local theater]."[84]

In this work, Nazimova addressed the crucial issue of women's rights to birth control information by taking her production of the original play, 'Ception Shoals, to Broadway in January 1917. Many others addressed the topic in actions, writings, plays, and films as well and faced strong opposition. In 1916, activist Margaret Sanger was jailed for publishing information on the topic that was judged obscene. She then produced and starred in a film, *Birth Control*, that the courts would not allow to be shown.[85] Lois Weber also engaged the issue with *The Hand That Rocks the Cradle* (1917), which suffered at the box office when she was unable to show it in New York City.[86] The topic became so prominent that *New York Tribune* columnist Heywood Broun declared 'Ception Shoals playwright H. Austin Adams had done well to put his heroine in a lighthouse because "Where else, indeed, could anyone escape the clamor of sex education these days?"[87] But

Nazimova, who had suffered physical abuse and resorted to prostitution in Russia, probably welcomed the chance to support women's rights to control of their bodies.[88] When she signed with Metro, she enlisted Mathis into creating the film adaptation of the play. Mathis's comment in scene 136½ of the script indicates Nazimova was involved in the writing as well: "<u>Insert Poem</u>: Will have to get the words from Madame Nazimova."

Nazimova's character in *Out of the Fog* is Eve Coffin, whose uncle Job Coffin (Henry Harman) keeps her on the isolated island of 'Ception Shoals where he works at the lighthouse. His oppressive religious notions have already caused great suffering, and his confinement of Eve promises more. After Eve's mother, Faith (Nazimova in another double role), gives birth "out of wedlock," he brings them to the island to keep them away from the evils of the world. But Faith responds to this threatened imprisonment by leaping to her death. The characters' biblically derived first names define their identities. Job suffers greatly, but he does not keep his faith. Instead, he tries to block out reality, and his last name blatantly associates him with death. Eve's name is also doubly symbolic. Like the original Eve, she is innocent, but her last name is portentous. With Faith gone, Job keeps Eve away from all knowledge of life she needs and desires. When Eve asks about feelings she does not understand, Job gives her a four-letter solution: "P-R-A-Y." Eve's response cuts through his desire to keep her ignorant and under his control: "You can bend my body with your strength, but you can't bend my soul and that wants—LIFE—LIFE!"[89]

This is melodramatic writing, not realistic human dialogue. It adopts a strident moral tone in response to upper-class efforts to impose restrictions on the poor and working classes as it adheres to a gospel of material progress over one of compassion. For example, at a National Board of Review discussion following their private screening to evaluate the film, Mrs. G. L. Mulliner, lawyer, and president of the Camp Fire Girls, condemned *Out of the Fog*'s "dangerous realism of primitive passions," which she found "contrary to the effort of education to uplift and civilize." She further denounced the "negative value of holding up to decent minded people the sordid incidents of the lower classes," which she associated with "dangerous Bolshevik propaganda."[90] Mulliner responded not to the needs of the oppressed but to the fact that she had to view their behavior in the realism of this melodramatic film.

Mathis's script follows the pattern she began with *The House of Tears*. She places responsibility for disruption and tragedy on the efforts of men to control women and shows that this control will eventually hurt both genders as Faith and Job both die. Eve, too, is left vulnerable and only realizes what her first romantic encounter could have led to after the fact. In scene 45, Mathis asks for a "close up of Eve" as she watches a woman give birth: "Her face lights up with a strange excitement. At last here is a chance to learn what she has endeavored vainly to find out all her life. She hysterically says—'You mean—[she is going to be] a—mother!'" Then in scene 82, another close-up shows "the terrible realization that the little kiss and embrace which she had received from the stranger might have resulted disastrously had not the man controlled himself, [and] lends a wild expression of terror to her face." Through extrapolation, viewers might also realize that women who are kept from knowledge of sexuality will not be able to contribute to society. The idea that one small kiss could lead to an unwanted child might sound overly cautious. But how could a young woman kept in extreme isolation be expected to function out in the world? She might well be terrorized by possibilities, and her potential will never be recognized.

In theatrical touring companies, Mathis learned about sexual exploitation and knew that young women were better protected by knowledge than ignorance. Her statement on censorship to the *Los Angeles Times* in 1923 provides a forceful response to Mrs. Mulliner: "In the good old books by Mrs. Southworth and all the rest, if a sin was committed, the dire and awful results were pictured vividly. They were enough to make a girl travel wisely all the rest of her life. But here in the pictures, if we picture the same idea, the dire and awful results are immediately cut out by the censor, leaving merely the scene with the girl in the ermine coat and the diamond pendant." Mathis recognized the dangers of failing to depict what could happen to women kept ignorant of possible exploitation: "The censors claim that the sad ending is unfit for the young maid, but what effect does the sight of the girl in her ermine coat have? To a part of the girls who view it, with no moral tacked on, it would just mean, 'I'll get me an ermine coat of my own!'"[91] Thus, while *Out of the Fog* might now sound excessively melodramatic, it represented a new honesty about sexuality, which Mathis felt was needed.

Eve's statement that Job might bend her body but not her soul suggests the gender essentialism that exists throughout Mathis's oeuvre, the association of men with physical existence and women with spiritual. Like their biblical namesakes, Job is associated with physical suffering while Eve is associated with the origins of life, the abundance of Eden, and the desire to learn. There is effective irony in the fact that while the biblical Eve is said to have introduced death and suffering to the world through her effort to gain knowledge (for which Solomon is later exalted), Eve Coffin would be likely to die if she failed to do so. Job Coffin follows the traditional message of "humanity's fall" from the story of Eve and the apple: that is, limiting woman's knowledge prevents suffering. But the story of Eve in *Out of the Fog* could lead viewers to reconsider that meaning, a possibility aided by the heavy symbolism of the names.

Mathis did not create this idea since she was adapting the play by Adams that had been another Broadway triumph for Nazimova. Yet Mathis, Nazimova, and Capellani can be credited (along with Metro's managers) for keeping this powerful message at a time when censorship pressures on the industry were growing. In the Board of Review's discussions, a member in agreement with Mrs. Mulliner stated, "The scene in 'Out of the Fog' with the satyr was one of the most revolting exhibitions—if not the most that it has been my misfortune to witness."[92]

Yet, this production reinforces Mathis's claim throughout her career that she aimed to lift the artistry and integrity of motion pictures by addressing vital concerns. Review Board comments support this idea. Board member Arthur Clark, for example, despite criticizing some characterizations, concluded, "The average motion picture has sunk to the level of the dime novel. . . . Unless motion picture production is refreshed with plays such as 'Out of the Fog' . . . I venture to predict that an industry now ranked as one of the foremost will fall of its own unintelligent, monotonous dead weight to a very much lesser place." G. R. Lomer, assistant editor of *The Chronicles of America* at Yale University Press, stated, "There was very little to suggest that the story was only acted; i. e. it produced to the highest degree the illusion of reality owing to the good methods of Mme. Nazimova. The story had artistic 'momentum'—i. e. there was enough in it to carry it along and you never felt that it dragged." George Smith, a Board of Education member (city unstated), felt, "Some of the most beautiful effects are obtained in 'Out of the Fog,' e.g., the vision of the drowned mother, the face in the light."[93] Ultimately, *Out of the Fog* "was selected by the National Board of Review of Motion Pictures as the representative American production to be shown at a demonstration of European and American Artistry in Photoplay Production" in March 1920.[94]

"Six of [Nazimova's] Metro films had the advantage of being written or cowritten by June Mathis, whose flair for drama was always sure and everything she wrote bore the mark of innate good taste," writes DeWitt Bodeen.[95] His praise is certainly hyperbolic, especially in relation to *The Brat*, a *Pygmalion*-styled work adapted by Mathis from Nazimova's treatment of an original play by Oscar Morosco.[96] It was Nazimova's first screen comedy, and while it earned a modest profit it marked the start of a downward slide in her film career. She followed it in 1920 with *Stronger than Death, The Heart of a Child, Madame Peacock,* and *Billions. Stronger than Death,* for which Nazimova was both writer and star when Mathis was unavailable, was a box office success.[97] The next three, however, received as much ridicule as praise. But even though Nazimova was able to choose her projects and exert her control over writing, directing, and editing, she later blamed anonymous others for her decline: "I went into the pictures and nothing would do but I must be a little hoyden, a harum-scarum, naïve child. . . . How I hated all that 'Heart of a Child' sort of thing, kicking my heels and standing on tip-toe to kiss the strong hero-man!"[98]

In *Out of the Fog*, she successfully played a sixteen-year-old while she was thirty-seven. But when she attempted to do the same in *The Brat, The Heart of a Child,* and *Billions,* all nominally directed by Ray Smallwood, but actually by Nazimova herself, her work fell flat. Gavin Lambert reaches a reasonable conclusion that these films failed "perhaps because her public didn't really approve of Nazimova venturing into Mary Pickford territory."[99] *Fog* achieved critical success in its own time, and her 1923 *Salome*, in which she played a fourteen-year-old at the age of forty-two has received both praise and ridicule for its artistry from then until now. But Nazimova's attempts at comic childishness were artistic miscalculations.

As Nazimova struggled to reconfigure her cinematic identity following Capellani's departure, she found a new collaborator in Natacha Rambova, a dancer and designer who worked with her on both *Camille* and *Salome*. Each film featured Rambova's exotic designs of jet-black and pearl white contrasts, prominent circles and swirls, erotic costuming and makeup, and further surreal elements inspired by the work of the 1890s "decadent" artist Aubrey Beardsley.[100]

Camille was not Nazimova's first choice for her final Metro production. But when Karger vetoed the plans she and Mathis had for an adaptation of Pierre Louÿs's scandalous play *Aphrodite, Camille* became an acceptable replacement. In the meantime, Mathis had initiated the next step in her career with her production of *The Four Horsemen of the Apocalypse* that included her daring choice of the little-known Rudolph Valentino for the lead. Following *The Four Horsemen*'s successful New York premiere, Mathis believed her "discovery" had a great future and promoted him for the role of Armand Duval in *Camille*, a move that would help connect their fortunes. Nazimova would later claim that she had discovered Valentino, as would Rex Ingram.[101] But there is no doubt that June Mathis secured Valentino's fame, for which he was eternally grateful.

The extant script for *Camille* reveals that Nazimova was solidly in control as she has crossed out of much of Mathis's original version. In her screenplay, Mathis opened and closed with Armand Duvalier (Valentino) speaking to the author of the novel *Manon Liscout*, a romance of the French Revolution, that he and Marguerite (Camille/"the Lady of the Camellias") romanticized about during their relationship. Their story thus appears as a flashback that begins with Armand outside a jewelry store watching Count Andre de Varville (Arthur Hoyt), Marguerite's latest paramour, buy her something very expensive.[102] In the novel, she is buying jewelry alone, presumably with the Count's money. Both versions reveal that Armand has worshipped Marguerite from afar for a long time. He is like a puppy following her around and hoping for affection.

Nazimova was probably wise in cutting the framing material that shifted focus from her character to Valentino's. After all, as the star she had a right to demand the most attention, and she made a logical choice. The opening scene in which she meets Valentino on a grand staircase and the closing in which she dies provide greater spectacle than Mathis's material would have. To quote Gavin Lambert, "Nazimova makes her first entrance at the head of a stairway leading down to the lobby of a theatre. Extraordinarily slim, huge curly black wig above a deathly-pale face with bee-stung lips, she wears a gown with a camellia pattern and a black fur train that opens out like a fan."[103] Gaston Reux (Rex Cherryman) introduces his friend Armand to her as a law student, but Marguerite (Nazimova) mocks him by saying, "He should study love instead." She and her friends laugh and walk away and leave Armand embarrassed. But he will get his lessons in love from her in the rest of the film.

In the next scene, Mathis planned to further the association of Armand with dogs. While Marguerite hosts a dinner party provided by the Count in her apartment, Gaston and Armand try to get her attention from the window of a neighboring apartment because they want to be invited. Gaston scratches at the window and barks to let Marguerite know he is there.[104] Mathis's associations of Valentino with animals began in *Four Horsemen* and would continue in *The Conquering Power* and *Blood and Sand*. Mainly present near the start of the films, these animals suggest the nature of his characters at the start: weak, pampered, or brutish. Their absence toward the conclusions provides a measure of how much his character has grown. But Nazimova cut the begging scene, and Ingram would axe the scenes of Valentino with a poodle in *The Conquering Power* as well. All that remains of this motif in *Camille* occurs when Armand realizes Marguerite is sick and literally killing herself by continuing to throw herself at wealthy men. He tells her, "I wish I were a relative—your servant—a dog—that I might care for you, nurse you—cure you."[105] Mathis lifted this typically melodramatic line from Dumas's theatrical version of *Camille*. Most commentators have suggested that Valentino's scenes, including his presence at Marguerite's deathbed, were removed because Nazimova didn't want to give him more attention at a time when his career was heading up while hers was in decline. The destruction of Mathis's work as a result also deserves recognition.

Unlike her other films scripted by Mathis, Nazimova is not a moral or spiritual guide for the male lead in *Camille*. But Marguerite is strong in coping with heartbreak, knowledgeable in the ways of the world, and she tries to provide the guidance Armand needs. From the beginning, she tells him that their love cannot succeed saying, "You know who—what I am. Go home—forget that we have ever met." Still, he persists and their love grows until Armand's father forces her to reject his son. After that, Marguerite must show courage, as she alone knows the truth that she cannot share with Armand. To discourage him, she returns to Count de Varville and pretends to be carefree. But, in actuality, she allows her health to deteriorate and dies the victim of social conformity. From this perspective, Nazimova was justified in concluding the film by emphasizing her character, a strong woman destroyed by hypocrisy.

Mathis's original conclusion for *Camille* would have presented her concern about the lack of proper guidance for young men after the war. Armand's father had secretly met with Marguerite to tell her to stay away from his son because she would ruin his future. Marguerite reluctantly agrees and publicly spurns Armand though it causes the heartbreak that kills her. In her conclusion, Mathis returns to the conversation between Armand and the novelist as a framing device for the plot. She cuts from a close-up of the deceased Marguerite to a "FOREGROUND DISSOLVE TO THE AUTHOR'S STUDY. The author and Armand facing each other, and

Armand finishing telling the story as in scene 6. Armand looking at the author—with a sad appealing expression—and without a word, the author rises—hands him the book, looking into his face with pity. He puts his hand on the young man's shoulder, and there is a silent sympathy expressed by the author—Armand thanking him in silence. FADE OUT."[106]

The scene 6 to which Mathis refers is missing from the existing copy of her script; in making her changes, Nazimova most likely discarded it. In her ending, Nazimova cuts from a long shot of Marguerite's friends kneeling around her bed to a close-up of church bells. With her death, Marguerite has obviously suffered the most of any character. The refusal to allow her to love is cause for mourning. By contrast, Mathis's script shows two powerless men mourning lost ideals. The author does no more than offer sympathy. Armand's emptiness due to lack of spiritual guidance would have been an apt image for the postwar era.

Mathis's script for *Camille* was not intended to be her final collaboration with Nazimova. In 1921 or '22, Charles Bryant issued a press release that Mathis had signed to write the screenplays for Nazimova's *Salome* and *A Doll's House*.[107] It is doubtful, however, that Mathis contributed anything to these projects as she was very busy at Famous Players-Lasky Studio and Goldwyn in 1922. Thus, she ended her extremely productive and rarely examined associations with Metro and Alla Nazimova. But in Metro's *Camille* and *The Four Horsemen of the Apocalypse*, her even more memorable association with Rudolph Valentino had begun. Like her work with Nazimova, her films with Valentino would have great relevance for the times but not in the manner in which most people think of the star. As Nazimova did not fit the mold of either the wicked vamp or the melodramatic heroine in her Mathis films, neither would Valentino resemble the dashing Sheik he would become famous for in his.

Mathis in young man's wardrobe during her acting days.

Promotional photo from Mathis's stage career, circa 1910.

LA FLOR DE
TAMPA-CUBA

HABANA

Mathis's picture on a cigar box, her prize for winning a 1912 beauty contest. The government later distributed 260,000 of these to US soldiers during World War I.

Premier female impersonator Julian Eltinge. Mathis performed with him from 1910 to 1914. Courtesy of Bruce Calvert.

Director Edwin Carewe, first Native American director. He gave Mathis her first big break in 1915. Courtesy of the Edwin Carewe Legacy Archive (edwincarewe.com).

METRO
PICTURES CORPORATION
presents
MABEL
TALIAFERRO
in
HER GREAT PRICE
A Metro wonderplay
in Five Acts by
June Mathis from
the romance by
Florence Auer
Directed by Edwin Carewe
Produced by
ROLFE PHOTOPLAYS, Inc.

Released
on the
Metro Program
March 20th

Publicity for *Her Great Price*, 1916. Courtesy of the Edwin Carewe Legacy Archive (edwincarewe.com).

Viola Dana, star of Mathis's *Blue Jeans* (1917) and *The Willow Tree* (1920). Photo from the Library of Congress.

Metro action star Edith Storey, lead in Mathis's *The Legion of Death* (1918). Courtesy of Bruce Calvert.

Publicity photo from 1920 or 1921.

Mathis gazes happily at Rex Ingram in a photo of *The Four Horsemen of the Apocalypse* cast and crew, 1921. Valentino is seated just behind her right shoulder with Nigel de Brulier and Alice Terry to his immediate right. Courtesy of Donna Hill.

Notre Dame football coach Knute Rockne and his famous four horsemen backfield visit Mathis, 1921.

Valentino, Mathis, and Fred Niblo clowning on the set of *Blood and Sand*, 1922. Courtesy of Donna Hill.

Valentino in costume for *The Young Rajah*, 1922.

Mathis, Valentino, Phil Rosen, and Wanda Hawley during the filming of *The Young Rajah*, 1922. Courtesy of Donna Hill.

Valentino's text reads, "To my dear and clever June, the only one I owe my success and place in life. Ever grateful, Rudy. Dec. 14, 1922."

Mathis at her writing desk, circa 1923.

Mathis annotating a book in her office.

Mathis with her car: year, make, and model unknown.

Mathis with Arthur Conan Doyle, who stopped by the Goldwyn lot to talk with her during his lecture tour on spiritualism, 1923. Courtesy of Kevin Brownlow.

Mathis and an unknown Goldwyn employee by a tally board for the public's choice for *Ben-Hur*. Courtesy of Kevin Brownlow.

Top box office performer Colleen Moore, star of four Mathis productions, 1925–1926. Courtesy of Bruce Calvert.

Mathis next to Colleen Moore in the center of a group of cast and crew members of *Sally*, 1925. The Yale football team was visiting. Moore's double is third from the left. Silvano Balboni is on the far right in back.

Corinne Griffith, star of
Mathis's *Classified* (1925).
Courtesy of Bruce Calvert.

Mathis with husband, cameraman/director Silvano Balboni. They collaborated on
The Far Cry (1926) and *The Masked Woman* (1927).

Mathis with her pet birds, circa 1926. Her parrots were named Metro and Mayer.

Poster for Mathis's final World War I epic, *The Greater Glory*, 1926.

Mathis and Balboni playing Puff Billiards, a game craze of 1926–1927. Courtesy of Kevin Brownlow.

First National personnel pose for mock publicity shot showing that they've started filming *The Masked Woman* on time. From left to right: Mathis, General Executive Manager M. C. Levee, General Production Manager John McCormick, actress Ruth Roland, Balboni, actor Holbrook Blinn. Courtesy of Kevin Brownlow.

Mathis and Balboni examine footage from *The Masked Woman*, the first picture made at First National's Burbank Studios. Courtesy of Kevin Brownlow.

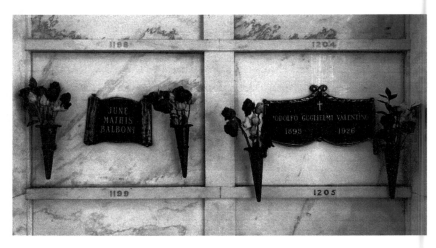

The start of Mathis's hand-written will written on the night before her abdominal surgery, March 16, 1926. Author's personal copy from County of Los Angeles Estate Case No. 90235, June Balboni. (Mathis writes, "Fifth Ave. Hospital. March 16th. Be it known that this is my last will and testament [*sic*] and supercedes [*sic*] all other written word in regard to the distribution of my property both real and personal. "I hereby bequeath all property both real and personal to my beloved husband Silvano Balboni and to my beloved grand-mother Emily Hawkes, said property bequeathed is to be hers—my grandmother during her life—and then is to revert in turn to my dearly beloved husband.")

The final resting place for Mathis and Valentino in the Mathis family crypt, Hollywood Forever Cemetery.

5

The Valentino Films, 1921

In his *History of the American Film Industry*, Benjamin Hampton writes that when Richard Rowland handed June Mathis responsibility for producing *The Four Horsemen of the Apocalypse*, she "developed immediately into a competent executive and organized a staff that worked enthusiastically with her and the director to plan the details of camera work before photography began." As a result of her technical knowledge and ability to completely envision the film before shooting started, Hampton concluded, "Miss Mathis' carefully and skillfully planned 'Four Horsemen' came through the studio with a reasonable total cost and proved enormously popular. Because of Rowland's confidence in the girl's [*sic*] ability, Metro reaped a profit of several millions on this one picture."[1]

Despite Mathis's efforts, however, those millions would not be enough to save Metro as an independent studio during the film industry's convulsions of the late teens and early twenties. In 1917, Wall Street began to notice that motion pictures were gaining stability and becoming a promising investment, and Rowland soon began negotiating Metro's sale to theater magnate Marcus Loew, who needed productions to fill his houses. By January 1920, Metro was part of Loew's Enterprises and thus began the movement toward the creation of Metro-Goldwyn-Mayer (MGM).[2] But first, perhaps through the persuasiveness of June Mathis, Rowland purchased the rights to Vicente Blasco Ibáñez's highly successful World War I novel, *The Four Horsemen of the Apocalypse*.[3]

The Four Horsemen was one of five Mathis screenplays in which Valentino either starred or had a leading role in 1921–1922. *Camille* (already discussed) and *The Conquering Power* (both 1921) and *Blood and Sand* and *The Young Rajah* (both 1922) were the others. In her Valentino screenplays, Mathis confronted the emptiness of the masculine values that had contributed to a crippling war and a generation of lost youth. She made the destructive influences of patriarchy and violence the primary concerns of these scripts. What Mathis hoped to achieve in her effort to redefine masculinity can only be recognized by studying these written works because much of the crucial material never appeared on-screen. Thus, although the unproduced aspects of the work did not have a cultural impact, the scripts reveal that women in the silent film industry had significant criticisms of patriarchy that have not been recognized. Mathis's Valentino scripts are especially valuable because they suggest an alternative definition of masculinity that deserved consideration in the post–World War I era and still do.

When Rowland assigned Mathis to produce *The Four Horsemen*, he told her, "You've got to make good on this for me. Everyone in the world thinks I'm crazy."[4] "Everyone" might have had good reason to question Rowland's sanity. While the war provided good material for "plots, settings, and bits of business" to use in films of any genre, the number of features specifically focused on the war sank to a low of about nine in 1921.[5] Devoting a million dollars to a new epic on the conflict, especially from a studio with few resources, was notably daring.

The gamble was grounded in Rowland's efforts to cope with Metro's financial struggles and his eventual need to sell out to Marcus Loew. Loew immediately put $2 million into Metro to construct a new state-of-the-art studio on the West Coast and begin construction of what was planned to be the largest studio on the East Coast on Staten Island.[6] In 1920, Mathis moved to California to take occupation of a new suite of offices and a large personal staff. Her first project there would be *The Four Horsemen of the Apocalypse*.[7] With a new state-of-the-art facility, new offices and staff, and immense freedom to write, cast, and hire the crew, she could now use her experience, artistry, and ideas to create the work she envisioned and establish herself as a major figure in the industry. She told the press that "to have only one production on my mind at a time and remain with it from start to finish had never been my privilege."[8] Mathis reached her goals with such efficiency that the production's history seems completely untroubled and with such artistry that the film became one of those rare achievements: an adaptation as greatly enthralling as its highly beloved source.

Crucial to her success was her ability to work well with her collaborators, the most important being twenty-seven-year-old director Rex Ingram, whom she selected to make *The Four Horsemen*.[9] Many women screenwriters and directors of the teens gained their opportunities through partnerships with male collaborators: Anita Loos with John Emerson, Lois Weber with Phillips Smalley, Julia Crawford Ivers with William Desmond Taylor, Ida May Park with Joseph De Grasse. Mathis had several multifilm partners through the teens: Edwin Carewe, John Collins, Albert Capellani, and Henry Otto. Her partnership with Ingram began on *Shore Acres* (for which she is uncredited) and *Hearts Are Trumps*. They may have envisioned further collaborations as well as they followed *The Four Horsemen* with *The Conquering Power* and started on *Turn to the Right*, although that script was finished by Mary O'Hara.[10]

Mathis's work with Ingram was further blessed by the skills of cameraman John Seitz. Ingram and Seitz met during the production of *Shore Acres*. Ingram, a Harvard-trained painter and sculptor, was frustrated with the high contrasts in the film's images. Seitz got what Ingram wanted by decreasing the development time of the negatives.[11] That same softening of contrasts, a moody darkness to capture the atmosphere of the Argentinian cantina and the misty gray of the battlefield scenes, gave *The Four Horsemen* a dampened look suitable to a somber topic. Viewers were not distracted from the brutality of war and the complexity of their feelings about it. Instead, they were able to review their subjective feelings without any false reassurance from an artificial resolution. Mathis's instincts about the screenplay, to base the ending on the one in the novel, proved correct and established a model for all subsequent World War I films.

Beyond planning, writing, and choosing Ingram, Mathis's most momentous decision on the film was her selection of Valentino for the lead. When asked later about who "discovered" him, Valentino responded, "June Mathis . . . for it was her genius, not only for production but for the management of men and women, that was responsible for the wonderful success 'The Four Horsemen' made. She is, I think, the most brilliant woman it has ever been my privilege to know, and it was she who did any 'discovering' that was done about me."[12] Others, mostly Ingram, would try to take credit. In his unpublished memoirs, Ingram claims he told Mathis, "We'll have to get a professional dancer, . . . and I know the guy. But I can't remember his name. It's something like Gugliano. He is South American or Italian."[13]

Their relationship began before they ever met. The accepted story is that Mathis saw him from a distance and then watched his performance in *Eyes of Youth* (Albert Parker, 1919) in which Valentino plays a low-life "cabaret parasite."[14] He only appears in a third of the film, and his character is nothing like Julio Desnoyers, his character in *The Four Horsemen of the Apocalypse*. But Mathis appreciated his looks and his physical grace and felt he was right for the role. She sought him out, and Valentino did not get the message. But he thought he might be able to dance the tango in the film, so he went to Maxwell Karger and was surprised to discover that they had been looking for him. In Mathis's office, he met her for the first time and "liked her right away. She was so friendly and so human." After a few words with colleagues, Mathis turned and asked him if he would like to play the lead in *The Four Horsemen*.[15]

Mathis's selection of Valentino came in the wake of a cultural move-ment in America to aestheticize ghettos, the poor, and immigrant minori-ties, begun in the 1890s by photographers such as Jacob A. Riis and Alfred Stiglitz and writers such as Theodore Dreiser and Henry James.[16] Their work softened the threatening elements of these places and people. In the movies, Anglo-American actor George Beban's "feature-length cinematic impersonations of charming but ill-fated Italian immigrants catapulted him to stardom" in films such as *The Italian* (Reginald Barker, 1915) and *The Pawn of Fate* (Maurice Tourneur, 1916). For movie audiences, "If Beban, as a much-celebrated character actor, was successful in creating emotional solidarity for his racialized, yet utterly desexualized, immigrant charac-ters, Valentino and the star machine around him succeeded in attaching his star persona and his celebrated performances to the romantic and sen-sual stereotype of the Latin lover."[17] In *The Four Horsemen,* his affair with Marguerite Laurier (Alice Terry) and his striking good looks add to his sensuality. These elements helped Mathis overcome the low-life persona formerly associated with Valentino's ethnicity and launch him into star-dom. White women could now fantasize about his sexual prowess with-out having to completely renounce racist attitudes. His on-screen presence as a thoughtful, troubled, and gallant lover to the white Alice Terry made him acceptable. But, while Julio had great sex appeal, Valentino would not become known as "the great lover" until after he made *The Sheik* later that year. Mathis's Valentino was much different because the characters she cre-ated for him had goals beyond sexual triumph. As this chapter will argue, studying Mathis's work allows us to see her Valentino characters as part of a redefinition of masculinity in response to World War I. They had to learn humility as well as daring or be left to face loneliness or death.

Choosing Valentino may have been influenced by Rowland's policy of not bidding on big-name stars, though Marcus Loew, who was already pay-ing for Metro's largest budget ever, may have been willing to support any choice Mathis made. Metro needed a big return on its investment, so a safe choice would have been to put big names in the leads. Rowland's first idea of who should play Julio was Metro star Carlyle Blackwell.[18] But Mathis was certain that it was time to bring passion and lust into the open and deal with them honestly. As her colleague Erich von Stroheim stated, "[Audiences] had become weary of . . . doll-like heroines and their hairless, flat-chested heroes who were as lily-white as the heroines." Emily Leider adds, "Women were ready to respond to a leading man whose face suggested undercurrents of cruelty and whose every gesture promised a new kind of dangerous sensuality."[19]

With this choice, Mathis also demonstrated a sense of the times that other film producers seem to have lacked. In the early 1920s, American cinema was attempting to negotiate massive changes that followed the end of the war: women gained the vote, Prohibition started, and xenophobia surged. The economy also suffered a short but very serious depression.[20] Ironically, the war's devastation prompted a cultural response in the United States that promoted men's need to risk life and limb to prove their masculinity. Utopian male fantasies of the time were prominently represented by the rugged physical adventure films of Douglas Fairbanks. In the teens, Fairbanks's films celebrated what Studlar defines as "boy culture" as a means for building masculinity. His characters begin as pampered youth from the East Coast who somehow transform into aggressive, athletic men once they encounter America's western wilderness. In the twenties, he shifted to adaptations of adventure stories such as *The Mark of Zorro* (1920) and *The Three Musketeers* (1921). In none of these is Fairbanks's character attached to any family or practical concerns.[21] By contrast, Mathis's Valentino scripts continually illustrate the frustrations of "wounded" young men attempting to achieve maturity in the midst of family pressures who require alternatives to violence and adventure as a basis for identity. In sum, they reflect Mathis's greater interest in realism rather than fantasy. As a result, the films did not become as wildly popular among men and boys. Instead, men felt threatened by Valentino who "called into question the very idea of a stable sexual identity."[22]

Mathis and Valentino films, like Fairbanks's, are staged in Europe but in the contemporary world and facing the future, whether with dread (*Blood and Sand*), hopefulness (*The Conquering Power*), or uncertainty (*The Four Horsemen, Camille*). Valentino's characters try to define their masculinity in the midst of social turmoil and families that hamper and restrict them, but that they still love. His characters learn that if there is any hope at all for the future, they will not find it in the patriarchal ideals of the past. But reconstruction by the female offers a chance of "becoming": not a resolution but a new path to follow. Mathis's Valentino scripts redefine masculinity in the wake of World War I according to a socially useful, sexually open, antimaterialist, nonviolent model. In these films, Mathis focuses on Valentino's characters as lost young men seeking to reach maturity without a father figure to guide them. Instead, they must hope for a woman's spiritual guidance. Without such aid, as in *Camille* and *Blood and Sand*, Valentino's character is left frustrated or dead. The importance of these films is thus in their offering an alternative path for a generation of young men whose fathers were killed or traumatized in the war. They do so through motifs of male immaturity, sexuality, spirituality, and the continual failure of patriarchy.

Mathis's explanation of her method of adaptation enhances the thesis that she considered each Valentino character in terms of his immaturity, need for guidance, and spirituality. First, she explains, "I have held fast to one fixed rule all during my writing career, and that is, that the theme of a story is ALL IMPORTANT. No combination of circumstances has ever been able to make me deviate from that rule."[23] Her next step would be to "find as many people as possible who have read the story or the play and ascertain from them the most striking features of the work" because their ideas often differed from hers. She then noted each critical dramatic point and how many people found it to be so, concluding, "I find that I want at least seven-tenths of opinions to be in favor of certain situations before I set them down as the dramatic points of the scenario. Then I start constructing the story or sketching in the high lights, which are gradually filled in, of course, to make the sequences logical."[24] How much and how often she actually followed this process is difficult to say. She wrote so many scripts that she would not have had enough time to do so consistently, and her adaptations always show a reenvisioning of the original work and the inclusion of thematic motifs that could not have emerged from collaboration. Still, when director Al Santell years later accused Mathis of just listening to others and stealing their ideas, he may have been observing her in this practice of opinion gathering.[25]

For *The Four Horsemen*, her process was somewhat different, and her main collaborator was the novel's author. En route to Los Angeles with her mother, Mathis stopped in Chicago to meet Ibáñez about the production. She told the press, "I had, of course, discussed the production with Richard Rowland, president of Metro, in New York, and I told Senor Ibanez that

I had read the book carefully and outlined the book mentally, but that I wanted to talk them over with Mr. Karger before proceeding further with the scenario."[26] Ibáñez told Mathis he was impressed with her screenplays for *Out of the Fog* and *To Hell with the Kaiser*, and the two worked together on *The Four Horsemen* scenario in California.[27]

Karger's advice may not have been too valuable. One idea he gave Ingram was to "cut out the war stuff, or just make it allegorical. . . . Build up the South American stuff." When Ingram rejected that idea, Karger offered another. The four horsemen presented in the Book of Revelations are associated with famine, war, pestilence, and death. Karger suggested literalizing them: "The Four Horsemen: The Kaiser, The Emperor of Austria, The Sultan of Turkey and The King of Bulgaria. How's that?"[28] This idea sounds like a continuation of the early propaganda film tropes where the Kaiser would be caricatured as "The Beast of Berlin." Mathis understood that the film instead had to address issues of what had been gained in the war, what had been lost, and what it was all about. She looked to maintain the mythical horsemen as powerful apocalyptic forces rather than mere human villains.

With *The Four Horsemen*, a major production from a minor studio coming at a time when distant impersonal Wall Street forces were gaining control of the industry, Mathis and Ingram worked together quite smoothly. A perfect example of their collaboration is in the scene that introduces Valentino's Julio in a small dank Argentinian cantina where he gives his famous tango performance. Seitz says that Ingram did not revise scripts, but the director took credit for adding a personal touch to this scene. Mathis's extant script only states that the scene will include the tango and "General little touches to be found on the set."[29] Ingram used that cue to insert action drawn from an early film of his at Universal, *The Pulse of Life* (1917). That sequence "showed an adventurous youth going into a Bowery dive and taking the dancer after he had first floored her partner. Bones and marrow, I transposed this action to South America." Julio's initial appearance is in a close-up, suddenly blocking out everyone else in the grimy saloon with his striking good looks. Seitz lights Valentino "so softly that his features seem rounded and youthful and almost feminine, before teasing the viewer with cigarette smoke that drifts across the set, temporarily obscuring them."[30] Julio then approaches the lone couple on the dance floor, smirking in disdain at the man's dancing. He pushes the man away, even using his whip as intimidation. When Julio takes over the dance floor, his tango is slower, more calculated, and smoother than that of the man he has just chased away. His dips are incorporated into his movement, not separate displays, and complete the sensuality of the dance.

Some tensions might have existed between Mathis and Ingram as Mathis was on the set every day to guide Valentino through his performance. Valentino told interviewers, "When I would rehearse I could tell by June's face whether she was pleased with the way I was doing the scene, and if she was not she would call me over to her, very quietly, and say, 'I wouldn't do it quite like that, Rudy, I think it would go better like this.' I'd watch her all the time and if there was a frown between her eyes I'd change my tactics." As a former actor with knowledge of performance skills, Mathis firmly believed in the importance of great acting to create a great film. She felt it was extremely important for actors to understand their characters. As Valentino noted, "In between scenes we would talk about Julio, and June would tell me what she thought he would do in such and such a circumstance, how he would reason, what kind of a man she thought he was."[31]

Mathis's selection and guidance of Valentino complemented her script, which asserted ideas about masculinity that were present in her earlier work and now spoke in response to capitalism and militarism. The immediate postwar years, as Gaylyn Studlar has argued, were "an era marked by fears of national and masculine enfeeblement" in which "there was a veritable obsession with the attainment of masculinity." Valentino became a "star" at this time, "culturally poised between a traditional order of masculinity and a utopian feminine ideal, between an enticing sensual excess ascribed to the Old World and the functional ideal of the New."[32] The "utopian feminine ideal" was one in which men would promote peace and understanding and not just become the fodder for all-out war, paper pushers at office desks, or production workers on assembly lines that the New World of industrial capitalism was trying to make them. Mathis's Valentino scripts promote this feminine ideal.

In these scripts, Mathis continued to use a melodramatic structure in which incredible coincidences, conflicts of good and evil, and a transcendent spirituality were crucial elements. At the same time, she also began to infuse more carnal sexuality. Overall, she now used these elements to present a needed path for masculinity in the transition from the prewar world to the present. Within the context of the war's desecration of masculinity, Mathis condemned the idea of male identity based on violence and greed. Importantly, she created female characters who possess the courage and values needed to reconstruct masculinity in a positive fashion.

An analysis of masculinity from more recent films can aid in understanding the confusion Valentino's character faces in his. In "Turning the Male Inside Out," Phil Powrie, Bruce Babbington, and Ann Davies state that there was "a difference in the damaged man [of the 1990s] in comparison with earlier periods of film. The damaged man is more often than not damaged . . . from the start of the film in which he appears."[33] Yet, the same was true for Valentino's character in each of the Mathis screenplays. Each begins with Valentino's loss of a dear male friend, grandfather, or father, and sometimes his fortune as well. This depiction seems particularly appropriate for the post–World War I era, in which thousands of veterans faced traumas. Historian Stephen O'Shea writes that "some 67 million men" fought in the war. "One in every six of these men was killed. Of the remainder, approximately half were wounded."[34] Casting Valentino, so strongly identified as an "other," in this role certainly benefited Mathis in displacing American male wounds from the war onto Europeans. But this suffering man (though not weak or effeminate) was capable of finding strength through female influences. As Pat Kirkham notes, in Frank Borzage's films of the 1920s, "The ideal man is one who is partly de-masculinized in order to be partly feminized: who is *deconstructed* to be *reconstructed*. . . . Wounding makes men more accessible to women's imagination."[35] Mathis consistently uses this pattern.

Valentino's characters, such as Julio Desnoyers and Juan Gallardo (in *Blood and Sand*), do not conquer the world with laughter and enthusiasm as did Fairbanks's. They struggle and die, sometimes without finding an answer, and need help from women not simply to survive or to become "good." They need the chance to redefine themselves by leaving violence and greed in the past. Powrie, Babbington, and Davies note that "men are not somehow 'better' because they seem more like women, particularly not, one might argue, when 'being like a woman' involves passivity, masochism, disempowerment. Such reductiveness merely reinforces the binary oppositions upon which patriarchy and capitalism thrive." But films can often present "*moments of becoming*, the interstitial moments which undermine fixed ontologies, as cinema attempts to come to terms with change."[36]

As novels, both *The Four Horsemen of the Apocalypse* and *Blood and Sand* begin in medias res. In the former, Julio is awaiting a secret rendezvous with Marguerite in Paris, having just returned from a trip to Argentina. In the latter, Juan is at a favorite hotel, awaiting his next fight. But Mathis tells each story in chronological order, thus emphasizing Valentino's characters' struggle for maturity. Her scripts show that his character's suffering "is not just a climax, a moment of spectacular display, as might be the case . . . for the shoot-out of the western, the war film, or the action movie." These men are "damaged *from the start*."[37] As a creator of melodramas in the immediate postwar years, Mathis worked to define a specific vision of reality in which the physical and spiritual realms intertwine. The spiritual is always present, working through the physical to control events, both upholding and confounding social order. The spiritual is a higher realm but also part of everyday reality. Both transcendent and immanent, it is comprehensible and yet mysterious. Characters' personal problems involve tragedies of unseen circumstances and forbidden desires that audiences can easily understand, not obscure psychological issues. The work focuses on external realities as audiences watch the main characters search for answers to their problems, answers from the spiritual realm that viewers might learn to seek as well.

This was different from the work of modernists, epitomized by Hemingway, who would attempt to strip their prose to the starkest possible degrees. Their work represented their protagonists' struggles to comprehend and express their troubled minds and environments. They focused inward, disturbed by problems they could never fully grasp. But Mathis's work, while considering the same circumstances of broken lives that concerned the modernists, continued in the traditional melodramatic form.

Spirituality is the great equalizer, a source of power that oppressors cannot understand, one that can reveal social injustice. In Mathis's work, a spiritually transcendental realm often suffuses temporal reality but remains heavily emotional and sentimental. Characters who discover this spirituality have the best chance to achieve inner peace and fulfillment.

It is therefore crucial to recognize that in both the novel and film of *The Four Horsemen*, Julio's lover, Marguerite Laurier, is his guide toward honor and heroism. In a pattern that Ibáñez would repeat in *Blood and Sand*, Julio is not well served by the men in his life. He grows up in Argentina, the favored grandson of a wealthy landowner. This grandfather teaches him to spend his time dancing in taverns, wasting his money, and using women. As seen in the previous chapter's discussion of *Camille*, Mathis sometimes creates parallels and connections between Valentino's character and animals to ridicule traditional masculinity and mock wealth and privilege. In *The Four Horsemen*, as Julio wastes away his young life on his grandfather's estate, Mathis includes scenes of a monkey fighting with a parrot, an expression of his desire for elegance that is not part of his nature. He believes his grandfather Madariaga's false promise that he will inherit the old man's entire estate. But the monkey represents his jealousy and anxiety over what he does not possess. Later, the monkey follows Julio into battle and is destroyed by the shell that also kills his master, an event that defines the action as one of thoughtless foolishness as much as it is of bravery.[38]

The Four Horsemen blends melodrama and politics through its background story of Julio's birth to French and Spanish parents in Argentina. His mother's sister marries a German, and both families live on Madariaga's estate until he dies. Julio is profoundly discouraged to learn that the old man has divided his wealth between both families. Julio's father then moves his family to his native France while his uncle takes his family to Germany just before the outbreak of the Great War. Julio and his German cousins end up on opposite sides. The Germans are presented as stereotypical militarists while the French Julio and his father Marcelo are devoted to pleasure and materialism. Marcelo wastes the family fortune on antiques, which he keeps at a large country manor purchased just for that reason. Meanwhile, he hypocritically denies Julio money for his bohemian lifestyle as he continues to behave as he did in Argentina. But Marcelo is partly responsible for this situation because he never provided guidance for his son. As one Mathis intertitle states, "What chance had Julio Desnoyers to be other than a youthful libertine?"[39]

With the action moved to Paris, Mathis brings Julio's discreet activities more into the open. At his art studio, Julio paints three women posed in togas, one with a breast fully exposed. This scene appears innocent, but his behavior soon begins to have consequences. Madariaga fathered children across his estate with no fear of retribution.[40] But when Julio dances with Marguerite at a stylish ballroom, they draw disapproving comments. A short while later, Marcelo and Marguerite's husband catch the adulterous couple together at his studio.

Later, with the Germans approaching his estate and antiques, Marcelo leaves his home and family and heads toward the fighting merely to try to protect his possessions. At his castle, a squad of occupying German soldiers get drunk and parade in drag, shocking Marcelo and his house staff (and probably many viewers). Mathis was especially proud of this scene and recognized that a segment of the audience would have a knowledgeable reading of it. She told the *Los Angeles Times* that to most people the scene represented "nothing more than a masquerade party," but "to those who had lived and read and understood life, that scene stood out as one of the most terrific things in the picture."[41] Mathis never exhibited any inclinations other than heterosexuality, but she certainly gained knowledge of gay society through her lengthy stage career, her long association with Julian Eltinge, and her years with Nazimova. With the postwar culture of open cars, hip flasks, and jazz, her desire to include an updated "realism" in her work is unsurprising. Especially since in the 1920s, as William J. Mann writes, "gay Hollywood could only have been more visible if the pages of the fan magazines had been printed in lavender. Not to the average moviegoer, of course—but to more sophisticated readers."[42] Mathis's comment seems particularly bold and perhaps represents her confidence at this time—at the height of her success—about infusing more sexual honesty into the movies. The presence of a possibly lesbian couple at the ballroom where Julio and Marguerite tango is another aspect of this realism.

Simply by casting Valentino, whose swarthy complexion suggested a forbidden sexuality, Mathis already moved toward a fresh honesty toward sex. But here Mathis had him portray a troubled young man searching for identity in a world where sexual diversity is a factor in the collapse of traditional order. That fact raises a troublesome point in that the presence of men in drag and lesbians, while recognizing diversity, also makes them part of the confusing new world Julio must leave behind to redeem himself. Mathis's adaptation captured postwar desires to make sense of the past while moving into the future. One of the film's contemporary reviewers probably stated it best: "The patriotism that swept the world in 1914 and 1915 has been turned into cynicism by bungling peace delegates, by exposures of money wasted on aircraft equipment and armament and by squabbling politicians. But the nerves of the public are still sensitive to the emotionalism of a period that becomes more momentous as it looms farther into the background of the calendar."[43] Whether decadent enemy soldiers in drag or lesbians in "tango parlors" were to be accepted as part of the restored order is questionable since Julio must escape that environment to fulfill his destiny.

By casting Valentino as Julio, Mathis was selecting an appropriately ambiguous figure: an unknown to play a major lead, and an Italian to play an Argentinian who would fight for the French. As in the novel, Marguerite becomes Julio's guide; Mathis's subtle contrast between Julio's merely physical interest in his female models and his reverence toward Marguerite reveals his growth. Importantly, Mathis reveals that Marguerite's influence over Julio grows from her possession of a spiritual nature. Ibáñez includes a scene in the novel in which Julio makes a short trip home after being wounded. While he and his father are walking down the street, they spy Marguerite attending her husband who's been blinded in the war. Julio suppresses his feelings and ignores her, but his father observes her gazing at him longingly. It is their final encounter, and Julio believes that Marguerite never saw him.[44] In the film, Mathis uses an earlier scene from the book to show their final meeting in which Julio visits Marguerite as she comforts her husband in a sanatorium. Mathis places the scene outdoors in a setting fittingly labeled a "SACRED GROTTO."[45] In her nurse's uniform, Marguerite appears angelic; Julio stands behind her reverently lifting and kissing her veil. At this point, Julio is still a civilian who hopes that Marguerite will want to forget about the war and continue their affair. As a noncitizen, he has no obligation to fight. But after he sees Marguerite don a uniform, become a nurse, and devote herself to her wounded husband, Julio also puts on a uniform, becomes a soldier, and devotes himself to the French cause.

Having witnessed German atrocities and debauchery, Marcelo has returned to his family when Julio comes to tell them he has joined the army. In a fit of madness, Julio's father tells him that he must kill every German he finds and have no concern that one of them may be his cousin. With Marcelo obsessed with the idea of mass killing, Julio backs away in shock as his father collapses. By contrast, Marguerite's sanctity in the sanatorium scene establishes the basis for Julio's spirit to return to her at the end of the film. After Julio's death, Mathis has Marguerite consider leaving her wounded husband. She writes a note and starts to go when the spirit of the newly deceased Julio appears. Marguerite does not see him but only feels his presence, which emphasizes his spirituality. He slowly shakes his head and Marguerite turns and stays. In this way, Julio's spirit reminds Marguerite that the most important lesson he has learned from her is compassion.[46]

Ibáñez sets the closing scene of the novel at a massive graveyard as the Desnoyers family searches for Julio's final resting place. After they find it, Marcelo realizes that the furies unleashed by the war will not be restrained by its end: "All the rest was a dream. The four horsemen were the reality."[47]

Metro was worried that the downbeat ending would hurt the box office, so they had Mathis write a happy ending for *The Four Horsemen* and Ingram filmed it. In this ending, Julio survives, Marguerite's husband dies, and the two of them return to Argentina to get married. However, Metro discarded the alternative ending and went with the original of Julio's spirit returning to Marguerite. It was a choice much to Mathis's liking. At the end of the happy alternative she added a typed note: "I hope to goodness this ending will not be used. J. M."[48] Like the novel, the film finishes in a massive graveyard with small white crosses stretching as far as the eye can see. Julio's family searches for his resting place. The novel ends with Julio's sister embracing her wounded husband and Ibáñez comparing the sight of her to that of a Grecian vase. Mathis starts her description of the final scene with "I do not exactly know how to write detail of this until we know what graveyard scenes we can get from the News Weekly but this is the scene of [the] book with the exception that I bring the stranger to the battlefield."[49] The Stranger is a Russian mystic, Tchernoff, who lives upstairs from Julio's art studio. The two meet as Tchernoff has a vision of the four horsemen of the apocalypse thundering across the sky on the night that war is declared. In the graveyard scene at the end, Marcelo Desnoyers asks if the Stranger knew his son, and Tchernoff becomes a blatant Christ figure. Spreading his arms, he answers, "I knew them all." Then, looking straight into the camera, he speaks the final title: "Only when love replaces hatred in men's hearts will the terror of the four horsemen end."

Mathis did not include the outstretched hands or the same words for the final statement in her script. Instead, the Stranger, "raising his eyes to Heaven he looks—grasps Desnoyers' arm and points off. There we see the title from one of the chapters of the book about —The Apocalyptic beast has received his deathwound[.] But the Beast will not die . . . the Four Horsemen will go on through the minds and souls until mankind turns to right living. We show the apparition of the Four Horsemen fleeing before the Angel of Peace. AND THEN FADE OUT ON LONG SHOT OF BAT-TLEFIELD."[50] This description contains important Mathis elements not as forcefully present in the completed film. She had wanted "all the sky . . . blood red" in this scene to emphasize the war's cost and the responsibility for change rather than a sense of resolution.[51] The existing finish, while effective, does not leave viewers as shaken as Mathis's would have.

Mathis's other two Valentino scripts of 1921 were adaptations of *Camille*, by Alexandre Dumas fils, and *Eugenie Grandet*, by Honore de Bal-zac. These works attack greed more than violence and have strong simi-larities. In *Camille*, Valentino plays an immature young man who falls in love with a very worldly woman. His father forces an end to the romance, his lover dies, and he is left alone. As discussed in chapter 3, *Camille*'s title character is a classic passive melodramatic female who is nevertheless the strongest character in the story. Although forced to reject Armand Duval, she never abandons her love for him and takes it with her to the grave. She is forced to suffer, but she values true love more than anyone else.

Balzac's eponymous Eugenie Grandet is similarly passive but strong. She is raised in complete ignorance of the outside world and dedicated to her abusive and greedy father. From this isolation, she learns to value love and loyalty rather than the capitalist exploitation that dominates the rest of society. Eugenie never lets herself become financially indebted to any man, twice refusing money from her father. She also refuses a lawyer who offers to help her gain her father's hidden wealth. But she is not simply ignorant or innocent. After inheriting her father's fortune, Eugenie keeps living in the family's decrepit old house so that she can help the poor with her wealth. Balzac writes, "For her money was neither power nor consolation; her existence lay only in love, religion, and faith in the future. Love explained to her the meaning of eternity."[52] This love does not cost her her independence. When she needs to marry, she does so only on the condition that she will not consummate the union. Thus, she maintains control of her body and sanctity while her greedy, ambitious husband (similar to all the selfish men in the novel) dies in an accident.

In Mathis's adaptation, *The Conquering Power*, Valentino's Charles Grandet is an immature young man at the beginning. His father abandons him by killing himself and Charles soon falls in love, but Eugenie, unlike Camille, has been loved and protected by her father. But just like Camille to Armand and Marguerite to Julio, she will be crucial to helping Valentino's character reach maturity. She and Charles develop a deep love that enables their togetherness at the end.

The Conquering Power again teamed Mathis with Ingram and Valentino, but relations between them had deteriorated. John Seitz reports that Mathis felt that she deserved the most credit for *The Four Horsemen*'s success since she had cast Valentino and that Ingram had been credited too much. Seitz also states that Ingram did not do much rewriting of scripts as far as he knew.[53] Yet, Mathis attempted to greatly expand the role of Valentino's Charles Grandet from the novel, but Ingram cut most of that material. The director seemed to feel that he was competing with Valentino and resented the great attention his star was receiving. He suggested that Valentino no longer took direction well and resented getting corrected during filming.[54] Valentino's irritation with Ingram had started during *Four Horsemen*. He told cameraman Robert Florey that Ingram "seemed to think more about his compositions and his lighting effects than about my performance, and that sometimes annoyed me."[55] He complained that Ingram had not allowed him to do what he wanted on *The Four Horsemen*, and the same was true for *The Conquering Power*. Valentino, who took great care to assemble his costumes, received flack about them from Ingram and resented that his days of practice with manipulating a monocle received little use.[56] He can only be seen twice briefly and skillfully popping it from his eye into his vest pocket. But what may have upset him most was his horrible treatment by Metro who had paid him a paltry $350 a week for *Four Horsemen*. He begged Ingram for a $100 raise but was granted only $50.[57]

Mathis seems most likely to have supported Valentino rather than Ingram in this dispute. Commentators on her *Conquering Power* usually make this point but give no further consideration to the material Ingram cut from her script or its purpose. They leave the impression that Mathis merely attempted to give Valentino more screen time. But examining her adaptation, especially in relation to Valentino's character, helps us understand that her work had a purpose. The parallels with *The Four Horsemen* script on issues of masculinity, young men who need guidance, materialism, and women's spirituality are significant. Viewing the script from this perspective suggests that this material was meant to add and continue important ideas. One of Mathis's additions to the narrative was to open with a scene in which Valentino, as in *The Four Horsemen*, is immersed in revelry and unknowingly suffering because he has been taught to rely on wealth and materialism rather than character.

The film and the script open with Charles celebrating his twenty-seventh birthday in his father's Paris mansion with wealthy friends, and Mathis's version contains blatantly sexual references that did not make it into the film. It continues the honest revealing of her ideas about gender and sexuality begun in *Four Horsemen*. Mathis states that the setting is to be decorated as an Arabian tent with a "Negro" jazz band dressed in Egyptian costumes and playing exotic instruments in the background. The women are to wear Oriental veils and the men Bedouin costumes. Charles indicates that it is time for the guests to receive their gifts, which are on little boats in the center of the dining table that the guests pull toward themselves.[58]

The prop for this scene is an unusual round table with troughs of water running from the center toward each place setting. Mathis envisioned using this setting to mock several of the guests. For scene 8, she states that while pulling the boats, "Some of the women lean far forward. If delicately worked we might get a little suggestion of one of the men leaning forward as a lady." Of the women, Mathis wanted cuts to show physical similarities between each one and the boat she pulled: yacht, speedboat, tugboat, and battleship.[59] But Ingram ignored all these opportunities for the close-ups.

Mathis uses this situation to also humiliate the wealthy, pampered Charles in a scene that Ingram may have considered too suggestive. She writes that as Charles offers to help his lover Annette put on the jeweled garter he bought for her,

> we cut,
> 23 FOREGROUND SHOT OF NEGRO JAZZ BAND
> Man with trombone in front—he draws out the trombone to its full length.
> 24 FLASH BACK TO FULL SCENE
> Charles just raising up as though he had kissed her knee—the man finishing drawing out trombone and general shout of merriment from the guests. The negro orchestra now starts to play.[60]

Mathis's suggestion that Charles could have been kissing something besides her knee and that it obviously affected him is not lost on anyone present, and she includes a blatant racist stereotype to make sure the point is clear: "the [N]egro orchestra looks on—their eyes almost bulging from their eye-sockets at this unusual occurrence."[61] Ingram makes the garter a bracelet and does not use Black musicians. But he does include four Black men wearing only waistcloths and turbans who carry a tabletop with a dancing girl on it. They are part of the furniture.

Mathis intended more for the opening party scene. As it concludes, the guests were to get up and dance around the tables, and she writes that "here we can get in that little bit of business with the Arab cape that we spoke about."[62] Whether this note was meant for Ingram, Valentino, or both is not clear. But the purpose would seem to have been to exploit Valentino's dancing, a sensible commercial move that Ingram was apparently having none of.

In more scenes absent from the film, Mathis includes a poodle as a mocking symbol of Valentino's Charles, a useless socialite. She feminizes him when she describes his room as "a very elaborate affair that but for the dark colors might be the bedroom of a young woman." As he prepares to visit his uncle, where he will meet and fall in love with his cousin Eugenie (Alice Terry), Mathis describes a "very smart French poodle . . . on an elaborate cushion on a chair near Charles and he is feeding it with dainties—and making the servants wait while he does so."[63] For his drive, both Charles and the poodle wear a motor cap and goggles.[64] Charles's immersion in pleasure and association with animals makes him similar to Armand Duval and Julio Desnoyers.

While the party goes on, Charles's father, Victor (Eric Mayne) returns home and learns that he has lost his fortune. He calls Charles out of his party to wish him a happy birthday and ask him to visit his (Victor's) brother to try to breach their twenty-five-year estrangement. Charles shows no knowledge of his father's business or circumstances when he asks whether Victor's trip was successful. But he shows deep affection when he gets a chair for his father, hugs him, and agrees to leave for his uncle's the next day. When he leaves, Victor sends a letter to his brother with Charles to say that he has killed himself. Charles now moves in with his uncle, who controls most of the property in the rural community where he lives. He is a miser who causes his family suffering and betrays Charles just as Armand's father betrays him.

Fortunately, but unsurprisingly as this is a melodramatic romance, Victor's brother has a beautiful daughter, Eugenie, just a few years younger than Charles. But there is a slight reversal from Marguerite's relationship with Julio as Eugenie is more active in her influence on Charles.

Mathis uses a number of parallels between the opening scene and the first scene at Charles's uncle's house to establish that both have been equally deprived by fathers who are too worldly-minded. On the day Charles arrives, Eugenie is also celebrating her birthday. Like Charles, she also loves her father, referred to only as Pere Grandet (Ralph Lewis). Her birthday party also centers around materialism though the scene contrasts greatly with Charles's party. Although he is extremely wealthy and owns a castle, Pere Grandet keeps his family in a dilapidated cottage, and the party guests are just families with young men who hope to marry Eugenie. Her father calls Eugenie to him to bestow his conventional gift upon her, a gold coin, which he greedily fondles before handing it over. Eugenie receives it gratefully and lovingly. Although Pere Grandet is as restrictive as Victor was indulgent, he teaches the same lesson that wealth is what matters.

Shortly after Charles's arrival, Pere Grandet shows him Victor's letter revealing his suicide. They are by a garden bench with Eugenie leaning out from behind a tree a short distance away to eavesdrop. Charles reads the letter, is overcome by grief, and sits. His uncle tells him, "My boy, now you understand you are penniless." Charles responds with exasperation, "What is that to me when my father is dead?" When Pere Grandet leaves, Eugenie comes out to comfort Charles as he sits crying.

Eugenie quickly becomes an angelic figure for Charles just as Marguerite is for Julio in *The Four Horsemen*. Mathis includes several references to ensure that viewers see Eugenie this way. As she looks in on Charles while he is asleep in a chair an intertitle states, "Woman has this in common with the angels—all suffering creatures are under her protection." Eugenie reads his goodbye letter to Annette on the table in front of him in which he writes that Eugenie "has a face like an angel." As the letter also tells her that Charles is broke, she tries to give him her coins while he is sleeping. When he wakes and tries to stop her, she tells him, "Until to-day, I did not realize the value of money. It is only to bring happiness to those you—you hold dear." A short while later, they are walking in the garden and spy a nest holding three eggs. Charles says, "Our Lady watches over them while the mother bird is away." The next shot reveals a Madonna statue in a small cabinet on the tree behind them. Eugenie, as the actual lady watching over the nest, has just been spiritually elevated.

Valentino's performance is excellent. In the opening scene as the pampered fop at his own party, he is convincingly anxious and a bit naive as he gives Annette the bracelet. In his face and posture, slightly leaning forward, he personifies the young man trying to believe that his beloved actually loves him though he knows it is not true. As he falls in love with Eugenie, he does so as one simultaneously gaining romance and maturity, a complex combination of emotions. He cannot help appearing mawkish with some of the material as Mathis reverts to her tendency to employ poesy rather than believable dialogue in her intertitle. Charles gives Eugenie a gold toilet case to hold until he can repay the money she has given him. When Eugenie tucks the key to it inside her dress he tells her, "My heart shall always be there with it."

Ultimately, Valentino believed his performance could have been even more impressive if the director had not dismissed both his contributions and Mathis's for petty reasons: "I went to Ingram, at which he confessed too, to his antagonistic cutting out of several of my best scenes in 'The Conquering Power.'"[65] Valentino may have been referring to the scenes of the party and with the poodle. More likely, he had in mind a scene that Mathis kept from the novel of Charles going to see Annette one last time before traveling to the West Indies to manage the legacy left to him by his mother. It is a long sequence of many scenes in which Annette pretends to show sympathy to Charles while Alphonse, who has always been her real lover, acts annoyed. Annette sees Charles off and promises to wait for him, then invites Alphonse back into her home. They smile at Charles's innocence.[66]

The scene of Charles in the West Indies, one in which Mathis included more racist caricature as a "comic touch," was also revised from the script. It was to begin with a scene of "some of the natives . . . fooling with a large oorangutang—grouped round a stack of cocoanuts."[67] It was to finish with the insulting image of Black workers as ignorant and lazy: "IF A LARGE ENOUGH MONKEY CAN BE GOTTEN MIGHT HAVE HIM FLING A COCOANUT TOWARD A SLEEPING NATIVE. WAKING HIM UP."[68] The completed scene shows Charles at a desk in a hut with several Black men visibly at work in the background. But one sitting on the floor who is to keep the fan going over his white boss's head gets a close-up as he falls asleep. Charles picks up something and angrily throws it at him. The extant script suggests that far more material may have been cut from earlier drafts as well, as these West Indies scenes are numbered in the 500s while later ones are in the 300s. Valentino, therefore, may have been referring to far more than what is now discernible.

As in *The Four Horsemen*, *The Conquering Power* presents another woman helping a man become a better person. Mathis's Eugenie Grandet is not as strong as Balzac's. In the novel, Charles becomes a cruel, exploitative capitalist and Eugenie must endure an unwanted marriage. In Mathis's version, Charles returns to her just after she announces that she will marry one of the men who has pursued her for over twenty years. The film ends with Charles and Eugenie romantically together in the garden. But to read Mathis's adaptation as merely providing a commercially desirable happy ending is to not fully consider Eugenie's character. As in the novel, she still must defy her father, suffer through several years of separation from Charles, and get locked in her room for several months when her father realizes she has given Charles her gold pieces. He threatens her as he "grasps some heavy object as though to strike her" and then attacks her dignity: "What else did he steal from you besides the gold?"[69] In response, "Eugenie looks at her father in horror as she realizes what he means."[70] Her painful endurance is less noticeable because much of her suffering takes place off-screen and is quickly covered by an elliptical cut. Furthermore, Eugenie gains much of her strength by discovering that Charles has been writing to her from the West Indies, whereas in the novel he completely neglects her after he leaves. Mathis has Eugenie find Charles's letters in her father's desk and confront him. He yells, "How dare you meddle in my desk?" But she stands up to him and replies, "How dare you keep us apart—how dare you cheat Charles of his inheritance and me—of my happiness?"[71]

The scene shows Eugenie's self-determination, though present-day audiences might find it sexist, especially when Mathis includes intertitles like "Woman's is the passive part—the web of life interwoven with love, sorrow and hope" and "While the man busies himself with the present and looks to the future for consolation."[72] But these assertions define women's happiness in relation to emotions as opposed to money, the concern of men, which does not provide reassurance. Women may be passive, but they are also associated with "life." They appreciate and comprehend its daily beauties and sorrows while money and materialism separate men from emotions and from the present. They can only hope to find consolation for their alienated existence in the future. Despite the regressive nature of these concepts of gender, they explain why Mathis believed women have a distinct voice that the movies need.

Ingram seems to have changed a lot from the film Mathis and Valentino had envisioned, but Mathis's script indicates how she was guiding her protégé. When Charles arrives at his uncle's cottage, Mathis describes the shot seen in the film of everyone inside looking at this strange guest standing in the doorway with his dandyish suit and monocle.[73] For Charles's return, she offers a "Note—I do not know exactly how you are going to make your garden location, so you will have to use your judgment as to entrances and exits."[74] These comments reveal Mathis's desire to understand sets and focus on details so she could thoroughly envision the film.

For the conclusion, however, Mathis only provided a sliver of what ends up on the screen. Early on, an old villager that Pere Grandet cheated tells him that his gold will kill him some day.[75] When Grandet later gets locked in his secret vault, Mathis writes, "Figures of all Grandet has known appear to him and then the walls start closing in. Has pulled cabinet full of gold over on himself, crushing him as the peasant said."[76] Ingram filled in this brief description of spirit figures typical of Mathis with material inspired by his memory of a childhood nightmare. After his mother died, Ingram was with his family at their big house in Galway. In his nightmare, he passed the family vault where his aunt and uncle were buried and a house where a miser had lived. His uncle had told Rex that the man used to rock a cradle. As he looked through a window, Ingram could hear "a sound like the slow tock-tock of a grandfather clock, only there was a creak to it, and occasionally the clink of something that hit the floor. And I knew it was the miser rocking the cradle full of gold coins. . . . And as he rocked it the layer of coins on the top of the cradle began to undulate and two gold hands, that looked more like the claws of bats than hands, pushed up through the gold and seized the miser by the throat."[77] In the film, Ingram translated his nightmare into a scene showing the spirits of people Grandet cheated in the past tormenting him to death. Grandet looks on fearfully as gold coins pour from the mouth of one of the ghosts.

After Charles goes to the West Indies, he remains separated from Eugenie for many years because Pere Grandet writes him that she is married. When he finally returns, he finds Eugenie in the garden and learns that was a lie. Eugenie is not as strong of an influence on Charles as Marguerite is on Julio. The influence between them is not only in one direction, but she is a necessary guide for him following the failures of both his father and his uncle. First in the garden and then in his room, she actively approaches and comforts him, gives him money, and says that she has learned from him. The brief final scene allows Valentino an impressive conclusion to his performance. Wearing a neat mustache and goatee, a unique haircut with the sides clipped short, and a suit fit to Charles's age and status, Valentino adopts a new posture and expression that is simultaneously composed and weary. Whether Ingram or Mathis were coaching him this time, Valentino clearly has adopted Mathis's idea that he can use a knowledge of his character to make his performance effective.

The Conquering Power did only moderately well at the box office.[78] Critics were impressed and gave overwhelming credit for the film to Ingram, which makes sense since he had successfully diminished much of Mathis's and Valentino's work.[79] Ingram guaranteed that he would no longer need to cope with Valentino by convincing Richard Rowland that the success of *Four Horsemen* was a one-shot event. Whether Rowland tried to keep Mathis at Metro after 1921 is unknown. But 1922 saw another major transition in her life and career when she signed with Famous Players-Lasky. With Valentino already under contract, Jesse Lasky attracted Mathis by promising that she would be able to continue creating scripts for him.[80]

6

The Valentino Films, 1922

"After a period of unprecedented growth, Famous Players-Lasky was facing an economic crunch and had set out to eliminate or crop all expenditures they considered excessive," writes Emily Leider. Part of their cost-reduction strategy was to sign Rudolph Valentino for $400 a week, which represented a considerable savings after letting go of James Kirkwood, who had been earning $1,750 weekly. Besides, Kirkwood lacked the complexion needed for the lead in Famous Players' planned production of *The Sheik*.[1] Released in October 1921, *The Sheik* was Valentino's fifth film of the year. In 1922, the star would reunite with his good friend June Mathis to make *Blood and Sand* and *The Young Rajah*.

In the 1908 novel, *Blood and Sand*, Blasco Ibáñez condemns the growing popularity of violence and war. He attacks bullfighting as a vicious capitalistic enterprise that sacrifices both men and beasts to the whims of the crowd and exemplifies a love of brutality that exists everywhere. As in *The Four Horsemen*, nothing is solved. After Juan Gallardo's last fight, the ring is merely cleaned for the next event. There is no end in sight to the violence.

Ibáñez's real concern in his novels is not bullfighting or war, but the shaping of masculinity. In each work, a young man follows his desires for passion, love, and fame into a violent world that ultimately destroys him. Both Julio and Juan believe they must either achieve greatness or die trying, and all the men around them fail to help them find any alternative. Julio, at least, finds purpose and a pathway toward a spiritual identity through his guidance from Tchernoff and Marguerite. Juan, by contrast, never finds influences strong enough to lead him away from (or through) dangers determined for him by the patriarchal process of masculinization.

As Mathis began adapting *Blood and Sand*, she may have envisioned an evolution of Valentino's persona from the self-centered immature youngster who must find female guidance in the first four scripts to the spiritually

109

defined yet confused young man of *The Young Rajah*. She thought of his characters as essential to her goals for these films and wanted audiences to consider them carefully. Who Valentino portrayed and his characters' need for growth were more important to her than the actor's good looks and physical appeal. Mathis may have come up with this plan for the development of Valentino's characters over several films sometime before leaving Metro. Certainly, Mathis's Valentino characters were totally different from the intoxicating Sheik for which he gained his greatest fame.

In her adaptation, Mathis's construction of Ibáñez's bullfighter Juan Gallardo fits within the postwar context of a young generation lacking male guidance. Juan's father, a cobbler, is present at the start of the film but soon dies of some unstated cause. His only comment is about his disappointment in his son for not fulfilling his apprenticeship in the family shop. Juan is much more influenced by the glamour of the bull ring and the men who surround him, all of whom value fame, violence, and wealth over family, fidelity, or spirituality. This situation leads to Juan's early and lonely death. As psychologist Roger Horrocks suggests, "male fascination with damage and with death are 'the result of masculinization itself, the process of becoming a man under patriarchy, which is deeply damaging.'"[2] Horrocks's thesis, published in 1995, helps to thematically connect Mathis's Valentino screenplays in 1921 and 1922 because they explicitly accuse the masculine patriarchal order of leading to the horror and bloodshed the world had just endured. This message is especially clear in the Ibáñez adaptations and directly evident in *Blood and Sand*.

These elements suggest that Gaylyn Studlar's conclusion that these Valentino films foreground "a transformation of masculinity," one "that tempers the hero's hard masculinity in the beginning" might be expanded. True enough, in the first part of each film, Valentino's character is a wild young man in search of pleasure through drinking, dancing, or bullfighting, all of which fulfill sexual desires. He treats women as objects, tossing them about on the dance floor as in *The Four Horsemen* and *Blood and Sand* or watching them dance erotically in *The Conquering Power*. These opening displays of debauchery would help hook the white female spectator, the New Woman, whose desire for sexual freedom represented by the exotic (dark-skinned) Other was culturally repressed. As Studlar explains, the female viewer could enjoy the tango "as a 'safe display' of dangerously eroticized heterosexual relations because she can rely on the conventionalized patriarchal dynamics of dance to displace responsibility for her own arousal onto the powerful male dancer."[3] After safely escaping into this erotic world, the viewer would be reassured through Valentino's loss and loneliness that he did have a tender side, and she would also be reassured that through her "maternal instincts," she could guide this poor boy into maturity and that her love would be returned.

The fact that Mathis wrote both screenplays suggests that these similarities are not accidental. In addition to continuity with her ideas in the screenplays already discussed, Mathis's close relationship with Valentino from their first meeting suggests that her constructions of his characters may have been related to her own repressed desires and mothering instincts in addition to cultural influences and box office considerations. Mathis shows that beyond their becoming safer figures of affection, a more important signification is their need for spiritual guidance.

The film's first title, printed over a drawing of a gladiator killing a lion in an arena, states, "The wide world over, cruelty is disguised as sport to gratify man's lust for excitement. From the early ages, humanity has congregated to watch combating forces of man and beast." In the second title, the arena remains the same, but a bullfighter has replaced the gladiator, and the title card reads, "To the Spaniard, the love of the bull-fight is inborn. A heritage of barbarism—its heroes embody the bravery of the knights of old." An early intertitle refers to Juan as "playing at bullfighting," and he pictures himself as a heroic knight. But the bullring is no place for play as he should learn when his friend is gored to death in a small rural ring. Juan cries over his friend's body when he dies. But when he returns home soon afterward, he has forgotten or repressed his grief. He acts like a child as he sits with his arms around his mother and promises her riches while she sews his pant leg. In this scene, Studlar notes "Juan's boyish interaction with his mother, whom he unashamedly kisses and caresses on a number of occasions. The emotional and physical closeness of mother and son demonstrated in *Four Horsemen* is duplicated to great effect."[4] Yet, she continues to treat him like a child through the rest of the film, and appropriately so. Juan's affection does not blind her to his problems and weaknesses.

Juan believes that bullfighting provides him with an opportunity to achieve masculinity. His posture as he prepares for the kill during an early triumph in the ring signifies his feeling of phallic power, one enhanced by the sword he draws out. He stands rigidly straight, raising the sword above his head and lunging toward the bull. But despite appearances, he has not reached a mature and self-confident manhood.

Studlar asserts what most who have written about Valentino recognize in one way or another: that his popularity came from his blending of compassionate and macho attitudes.[5] But consideration of Mathis's narratives within the contexts of her oeuvre opens these films to additionally possible feminist readings. When he returns home after his first success in the bullring, Juan spots Carmen (Lila Lee), his childhood sweetheart, at the back of a crowd that surrounds him. She has just returned from several years in a convent, and she tosses him a flower. Shortly afterward, Juan leaves a tavern where he is carousing with fans and his entourage to serenade Carmen under her window. In their study of masculinity in 1990s cinema, Powrie et al. note, "The damaged male forces male and female viewers to reconstruct a theoretical space which precedes patriarchal law."[6] The scene shows Carmen's potential for providing Juan with such a space, one that still attracts him due to his innocence. But as a traditional melodramatic love interest, Carmen is both unassertive and asexual and she fails to provide the guidance he needs. Studlar concludes that *Blood and Sand* reassured female viewers that "the patriarchal system is really benign as [it] fulfill[s] her deeper need to symbolically recover, through heterosexuality, a mother's love that promises that the heroine will have all her needs passively satisfied."[7] But that does not happen, and Carmen's passivity is largely to blame. She is the love of his life, and without her near Juan is vulnerable to the destructiveness of traditional patriarchy.

Don Joselito (Charles Belcher), a mystic like Tchernoff in *The Four Horsemen*, might have helped Juan understand reality as the Russian had for Julio. In contrast to those who find violence and killing glamorous, Don Joselito sees a record of man's barbarism in history. In his dim study, he keeps ancient torture instruments on which the ghostly suffering figures of their victims appear. He also keeps a giant ledger filled with notes about crucial issues, and he follows Juan's life with interest. But he does not offer practical help; he can only define the way things are. He jots down thoughts such as "Passion is a game invented by the devil that only two can play" and then stares off into the distance as if he has just expressed something profound. At the wedding party scene, he puts his arms around Juan and Carmen and tells Juan to remember that the crowd's admiration can be as fickle as a woman's. Juan listens thoughtfully and then turns to embrace Carmen. In her script, Mathis directed that Juan "looks toward her with the realization of possession. Yet at the same time there is a great timidity— he is humble before her innocence." This statement illustrates the hardness and softening trajectory Studlar outlines. But his attraction to her from the moment they reunite shows he is looking for something more. Unless Carmen can show him a spiritual path to maturity, neither his possessiveness nor his timidity will help him achieve it.

But on their wedding night, after all the guests have left, Carmen looks fearful when Juan turns to her. He gently leads her upstairs as the camera pulls back behind the closed outer gates of the house. We are barred from seeing what will happen. But perhaps their lovemaking is not to be. His happiest moment in the movie is when he plays at bullfighting with his two little nephews. The scene hearkens back to the first intertitle about him in relation to the sport. He still has the same attitude he had from the beginning. As Carmen watches them, a title states, "Her husband's love of children was a constant reproach." This statement has many possible interpretations. One is that Carmen was unable to have children, which is suggested in the novel, or that Juan is sterile. Another is that their marriage has never been consummated. A final possible reading of the title is that Juan is happier with the two boys than with her; they could be replacements for the two young friends he lost at the opening of the film, which shows them happily walking down an open country road, arms entwined, seeking adventure in rural bullrings.

Mathis emphasizes that Juan's lack of sexual maturity is his most critical shortcoming, and his desire to gain it is his fatal flaw. Due to that desire, he is susceptible to the sultry Dona Sol (Nita Naldi) and unable to resist her temptations. While Juan feels possessive toward Carmen, Dona Sol has the same attitude toward him. Unlike him, she also acts on it because she sees him as an object while Carmen sees him as the sensitive boy he no longer is. Carmen first makes contact with Juan by tossing him a flower; Dona Sol tosses him her serpent ring in the same manner. The phallic power of the serpent is what Juan wants, and Carmen does not offer this. Carmen is associated with soft, feminine flower imagery throughout the film. Twice, she walks through the house with a bunch of flowers. But Dona Sol is able to associate the flower with sexuality; she finally seduces Juan when she plucks a flower from a bouquet surrounding a small bronze statue of a naked woman, actually another phallic image. Following this gesture, Juan responds forcefully in his longing for sexual maturity.

Miriam Hansen recognizes that traditional melodramatic vamps such as Dona Sol are defined by their appropriations of the gaze, which makes them evil.[8] Such women spot Valentino first and lure him toward destruction when he returns their gaze. Dona Sol emphasizes her possession of the gaze when she tells her friends that she finds Juan "a very interesting study—just like a big, fine animal." Again, Mathis has associated Valentino's character with an animal in Dona Sol's objectification of him. Her conception of him in terms of brute sexuality expresses her belief that she can manipulate him for her own purposes. Juan is powerless against her because, cognitively, he is only a boy with no idea of how to respond to overt sexuality.

Dona Sol, a stereotypical vamp, is an obvious representation of sexual deviance. She always dresses in black, and when Juan first visits her, she is lying back on a plush couch in an exotic "Arab" room. Her servants are dressed in short "Arab" garb, and one of them sits by her head, serenading her. She offers Juan and his manager, Don Jose (an ineffectual male adviser who has pulled him away from his home), something to smoke, possibly opium. In fact, in the script, Mathis had Dona Sol assert of her "cigarettes," "I import them from China—they carry the message of the poppy!"[9] Her association with a serpent motivates Juan to call her a "serpent from Hell," a line that has been ridiculed but fits Juan's immaturity. Don Joselito, another poor guide for Juan, obviously refers to her when he writes in his ledger, "Woman was created for the happiness of man, but instead, she destroyed the tranquility of the world." Mathis enhanced this character from the novel, but his declarations give Juan no direction.

By contrast, Dona Sol lures Juan toward the masculinity he longs for, an aggressive nature that thrilled women when Valentino demonstrated it to Agnes Ayers in *The Sheik*. During one of their encounters, she expresses her desire for him to grow up when she tells him, "One day you will beat me with those hands." But every time they are together, he continues to act like the boy he is rather than the man she wants. Niblo's direction of Valentino, in this regard, seems excellent. Throughout the movie, Valentino continually slouches, hangs his head, and shuffles his feet. Rather than exemplifying the great lover, his performance captures Mathis's notion of Juan's immaturity. Rather than struggling valiantly to overcome his material, as Jeanine Basinger asserts, Valentino is giving the portrayal the film needs.[10]

The mystic's advice about the fickleness of the crowd might have warned Juan about the path he is on, but he already knows the dangers. He recognizes from his first amateur fight that death in the arena could come at any time. His friend was gored to death. But he represses this fear. We know because every time he is reminded of the danger, as when the bandit Plumitas (Walter Long) mentions it to him, he freezes like when he is with Dona Sol, and he has the same boyish expressions. Subliminally, he realizes that the path he has chosen toward manhood is also a path toward death. By only experiencing patriarchal guidance, Juan will not discover the reconstruction of his masculinity through women's influence that he requires—the alternative Mathis promotes.

Near the end of the film, Juan, humiliated by Dona Sol and abandoned by his family due to his infidelity, has spent a year in dissipation. He sits in a café with just two companions and two anonymous customers who pay no attention to him. The scene contrasts with two earlier ones in which the cafés were crowded and Juan was the admired center of attention. He reads a letter from Carmen asking him to give up the arena, but his assistants counsel against it. One says that he cannot give up his pigtail before he is thirty; the other says that quitting would sink him into poverty. Earlier, Plumitas had told him that the only way men like them could earn money would be by killing and risking their lives. Juan does not want to become like his father, the cobbler, or the beggars outside his home on his wedding night. So he goes along with these older men whom he respects, even though he will lose everything in his next fight. He staggers away from the table, forgets about Carmen, and sneaks off for a final rendezvous with Dona Sol.

Carmen's passivity is ineffectual and mainly refers to her suppression of reality. She knows about Juan's affair with Dona Sol, yet she refuses to confront him or help him in any way except through prayer, and that is not enough. She goes to Rinconada, the family cottage, and discovers Juan and Dona Sol there only because Juan's brother-in-law Antonio (Leo White) states that the two of them are there so loudly that she cannot help hearing. When she is finally alone there with Juan, she says nothing but only turns her back and moves away from him. He gives up trying to get a response from her and gets his hat and cape to leave, mentioning that the season's last fight will be the next day and that anything can happen. He asks her to at least say goodbye, but she still refuses. At the end, she goes to the arena in Madrid. But instead of trying to stop him, she prays again. After he has been gored and lies dying, she kneels by him and looks down. He asks forgiveness, says she is the only one he has ever loved, and finally takes off the serpent ring and drops it on the floor. This action is not simply a rejection of Dona Sol; it also represents his failure to reach maturity. Furthermore, it could suggest a rejection of fame and physical conquest as a path to maturity. Carmen's loving look at him is one more of pity than of unity. He was lost to her long before through the path to maturity he chose.

But it was the only one available to him, which defines the film's main issue. Mathis copies *The Four Horsemen*'s ending by once again giving the final line to the mystic character to condemn humanity's love of violence. Don Joselito gazes at the crowd in the arena and claims, "Out there is the real beast. The one with ten thousand heads."[11] From Mathis's perspective, patriarchy in *Blood and Sand* does not seem as benign as it is broken and destructive.

Recent scholarship has criticized *Blood and Sand* by claiming that the story gets "too religious and moralistic" without examining what these morals are or their basis. Jeanine Basinger writes that the film "has to undercut the handsome hero to make its point. Valentino does his best . . . [;] however, the role weakens his energy and robs him of his trademark: he's at his best when he plays the aggressor."[12] But Valentino felt he did his best work in the Mathis films. He enjoyed playing Julio Desnoyers and Juan Gallardo because in these characters "there was the opportunity to show . . . a complete life from early youth to death." By contrast, he "felt little in common with the Sheik." Professional viewers such as Charlie Chaplin and French director René Clair also preferred his work as Juan for its "fine repression [and] sudden tenderness." Clair proclaimed that in Gallardo, Valentino created "a character 'at once noble, vulgar, sensual and full of pride. . . . His ennui, desire and rage . . . are the expressions of a great actor.'"[13] Perhaps Valentino believed Mathis was trying to do more in her work to speak to great contemporary issues and did his best to help.

Valentino offered this argument after the movie's release when he claimed that Mathis's work in editing the film would have made his performance even better had Niblo kept it. He told an interviewer, "The [narrative] thread was negligible through his [Niblo's] scenes. Miss M[athis] knew that it couldn't continue and she edited the film herself to perfection, took charge of the biggest possible chunk of the storyline and cut N[iblo]'s unnecessary dramatic effects. This was a harsh blow to N[iblo]'s self-esteem and he took a tough position by making one of the most important scenes exclusively his. Despite Miss M[athis]'s wishes." While she and Valentino wished to further develop his character, Niblo and Famous Players President Jesse Lasky wanted a faster pace and more action. Valentino explained that Niblo's stubbornness "only served to convince Lasky—who said, in parenthesis, that he did not grasp at all how film could be art—that the scene was unnecessary, it dragged and was going on totally too long. It ran about 7 minutes!! Well, that was quite my best scene, concerning matters of life and death and besides it was quite necessary for the motivation."[14]

Mathis's final screenplay for Valentino to be filmed, *The Young Rajah*, brought closure to the redefining of masculinity she began in the previous scripts. Not surprisingly, the narrative is again heavily melodramatic. Valentino plays Amos Judd, native of India whose royal father sends him to his uncle Joshua (Charles Ogle) in the United States as a boy when an insurrection puts his family in danger. Amos grows up there in secret, shielded from turmoil he escaped but also from knowledge of his true identity. This causes problems when he starts having visions of the future that inevitably come true. His uncle finally reveals that Amos has inherited this gift from a prince who bestowed it on his family in the distant past. The men who have it are marked by a thumbprint on their foreheads. This is told in flashback near the start of the film so the audience can see Amos's arrival at his uncle's house. He apparently does not remember that he came from India even though he appears to be between eight and twelve years old and gives his guardians a snappy salute when they leave.

The story then jumps to his life at Harvard where he is a star of the rowing team and very popular. He falls in love with Molly Cabot (Wanda Hawley) when she and her father show up at a "reincarnation party" where everyone comes as someone from the past. In another conventionally melodramatic turn, the Cabots immediately decide to spend their summer in Amos's hometown and his relationship to Molly becomes serious. But Molly agrees to marry Horace Bennett (Robert Ober) because she says she "could never marry someone who is not one of her people." But right after she accepts his proposal, Horace encounters Amos and repeats a false accusation that Amos murdered Horace's old friend. Amos forces Horace to recant, but Horace hits him in the head with a rock, almost killing him. Molly then leaves Horace for Amos. Meanwhile, the insurrectionist from Amos's home in India has learned of his existence. He sends men to kill Amos, but they fail and Amos becomes convinced to go back to India and save his birthplace. He ends up as a restored prince with a new American wife.

Viewed in relation to Mathis's previous work, especially her other Valentino films, her enthusiasm for making *The Young Rajah* is easy to understand. Once again, Valentino is a young man seeking his identity and guidance. His father is absent and his substitute father disappears early in the film. A strong spiritual element ultimately produces a resolution, and there is even a mystic figure as there was in *The Four Horsemen* and *Blood and Sand*, Narada (Josef Swickard, Marcelo Desnoyers in *The Four Horsemen*). This time the mystic is also involved in the plot. He foresees that Amos is in danger and leads a rescue team to save him. The focus on Hinduism parallels the emphases on Islam in *Eye for Eye* and Buddhism in *The Red Lantern*. These elements are partly more Orientalist exploitation, but in *Rajah*, they also present a message of respect for religious diversity. Amos's room is filled with sacred artifacts including open copies of the Koran, the Torah, and the Bible. When Molly asks him which one he believes, he tells her, "There are many roads—all lead to God." Shortly afterward, Molly reads a short verse she finds in Amos's room: "Men should be judged, not by the tint of their skin, . . . But by the quality of thought they think." This strong antiracist statement is quite unique for Hollywood at that time but has always been overlooked in discussions of the film.

Mathis might also have seen *The Young Rajah* as an expression of theosophy, as "most theosophical speculation reveals a fascination with supernatural or other extraordinary occurrences and with the achievement of higher psychic and spiritual powers. Theosophists maintain that knowledge of the divine wisdom gives access to the mysteries of nature and humankind's inner essence."[15] All of the theosophical elements of a universal spiritual realm that humans can access are present in *The Young Rajah*, making Mathis's choice of the project and desire to direct understandable.[16]

Since *The Young Rajah* includes many elements that Mathis had used successfully in the past, its critical failure raises questions as to what went wrong. *The Film Daily* found it hard to accept a character who could foretell the future.[17] The *Exhibitor's Herald* stated that "as a story . . . it hardly holds water." The *Herald* also stated that "Jesse Lasky and June Mathis . . . cannot be criticized for having seized upon a story so palpably meant for Valentino's personality."[18] That opinion seems valid, yet Alan Arnold writes that "Rodolpho [*sic*] did not like the subject and instinctively knew that it wasn't suited for him."[19] Both statements could be true. Mathis, as explained, had good reasons for thinking this film would be great for Valentino. Valentino, however, may have been looking for something different or just too frustrated for any work at all. He had just spent time in jail on a bigamy charge. Some politically motivated prosecutors deemed his marriage to Rambova followed his divorce of his first wife, Jean Acker, too closely. Mathis helped bail him out when Famous Players-Lasky completely abandoned him.[20]

Valentino was depressed by an enforced separation from Rambova. He was deeply upset with Lasky for skimping on the production of *Blood and Sand* and underpaying him, and he did not care much for the role.

In recent writing about the film, Emily Leider calls it a "dud" and draws on *Variety*'s comment that while Valentino's best work comes "spiked with 'a dash of paprika.' . . . this one resembled a milk shake."[21] In the actor's favor, the reviewer added, "'Rodolfo [*sic*] really does his very best with a perfectly idiotic role.'"[22] Jeanine Basinger also reports that "*The Young Rajah* . . . was poorly received by reviewers" and quotes the same *Variety* review.[23] Other reviewers noted that the film was aiming for something different. Mary Kelly, in *Moving Picture World*, writes that it "makes an appeal that is slightly new. . . . Instead of relying on an intensely physical theme, . . . the picture resorts to mysticism as the strongest appeal."[24] The *Film Daily* notes that Valentino "has little real acting to do."[25]

A possible explanation for the film's failure may be that the studio had no interest in doing anything positive for Valentino. Perhaps Lasky was convinced, as Rowland had been, that Valentino was little more than a short-term phenomenon who should be quickly exploited and discarded. The studio did nothing to help him get out of prison. He complained that he sometimes had to work all night with "cheap sets, cheap casts, cheap everything." His worry over how Rambova was being treated left him so miserable that scenes had to be cut due to his bad appearance.[26] But Famous Players-Lasky was more interested in controlling Valentino than supporting him, and the film's failure strengthened their hand. Its poor outcome "was a blow to his prestige and a setback in his fight for independent choice. . . . The outcome of this was that Famous Players-Lasky insisted upon absolute right to decide what films Valentino made in the future." When Rambova encouraged him not to give in to their demands, the studio was able to keep him off the screen for the next two years.[27]

Mathis's role in all this is unknown, but there must have been something she could have done to help achieve a compromise between the actor and the studio. She may have had a strong belief in the property, but she might also have become too arrogant to look for an alternative that could have pleased both sides. Her star was still rising, and by the end of the year, she would be editorial director at Goldwyn Studios. She had much less to lose than Valentino with his poor contract that gave Lasky the right to suspend him and the hint of scandal due to the bigamy charge. Following the Roscoe "Fatty" Arbuckle murder case of the previous year, it's not too surprising that studios would distance themselves from him. In addition, Valentino's swarthy southern Italian appearance and his challenge to popular notions of masculinity, largely shaped by Mathis, had created an undercurrent of spite for him throughout the culture. Nevertheless, Mathis stood by him, and Valentino told journalist Adela Rogers St. Johns, "I am not discouraged because my dear friend June Mathis has promised me that we will create art together."[28] That art may have come through Mathis's production of *Ben-Hur*, for which she wanted Valentino for the lead.

Mathis might have hurt *The Young Rajah* by choosing or agreeing to Philip Rosen as director, "an experienced cameraman but an undistinguished director," when she was not allowed to take the position.[29] She may have been following Nazimova's practice of choosing weak directors or hoping to replicate her own experience choosing the little-known Ingram for *The Four Horsemen*. Some critics found Rosen's work to be the best part of the film. *The Film Daily* wrote that the film's situations "cannot provide serious entertainment despite the efforts of Director Philip Rosen to make them do so."[30] *Exhibitor's Herald* believed, "In spite of Director Rosen's good work the story fails to be more than a fairy tale."[31] But the reconstructed version of *Rajah* now available shows many opportunities for action, close-ups, and fast-paced editing that Rosen may not have taken advantage of: a crew race, a fight among the college students, an ancient battle, an imperial court rebellion, an attempted assassination, and a final overthrow of the unlawful ruler. The one good action scene in the existing footage shows Valentino spinning quickly and grabbing Ober in a one-handed choke hold that pins him to a tree. It's a powerful and deft move. By contrast, the climactic overthrow merely shows Valentino slowly leading a group of horsemen into the ruler's city unopposed. Similarly, the reincarnation party scene does not show Valentino dancing. He only gazes at Wanda Hawley from a distance and then sits and talks to her. The film's biggest flaw, however, may not be with the studio, Rosen, or Valentino but with the fact that in making Valentino the spiritual force, Mathis left the female lead with no importance. This was a significant deviance from her usual work.

Despite its many flaws, however, *The Young Rajah* is important because it includes June Mathis's creation of her ideal male: one who is strong, handsome, and athletic, but also intellectual and spiritual. Amos Judd crosses boundaries of ethnicity and ideology for movie heroes at a time when immigration barriers were used for racist goals, African American veterans were neglected and oppressed, and nonwhites in general suffered from segregation and white violence. The film, in fact, condemns prejudice against interracial romance and encourages women to admire men with positive qualities regardless of their lineage. Valentino's Amos Judd is not simply a fatherless boy who suffers and requires rescue by a strong and caring woman. Instead, he triumphs through the strength of his own spirituality. He represents a fulfillment of Mathis's redefined masculinity for a postwar, post–sacred age.

June Mathis sought to promote Valentino as neither hero nor tragic victim. Indeed, her scripts show that she was a skillful adapter who structured her work around an alternative definition of masculinity through Rudolph Valentino's characters. Her scripts for Valentino reveal her own ideas and do not reflect the same goals as the scripts written for him by others. Recognizing this fact not only provides her with long-overdue credit but also provides new legitimacy for studying even unproduced and obscure screenplays that may reveal new ideas and rich possibilities that have been unfortunately ignored by the dominant culture.

Overall, Mathis could be said to have written nine screenplays for Valentino. There were the five completed films discussed in the previous chapter and this one, plus four that have been only lightly acknowledged. The first was *The Spanish Cavalier* (1923), a work that had to be rewritten as *The Spanish Dancer* for Pola Negri when Valentino proved unavailable.[32] Mathis wanted Valentino to play Ben-Hur but he still was not available.[33] It would have made an excellent sixth Mathis/Valentino production as the main character is once again a young man set adrift in the world in search of a father figure and spiritual guidance. Another possible Mathis/Valentino work may have been *Cobra* (Joseph Henabery, 1925) for the actor's independent Ritz-Carlton Pictures. Anthony Coldeway is credited for the scenario, but actress Colleen Moore claimed that Mathis actually wrote it.[34] Perhaps Coldeway, who had revised Mathis's script for Valentino's uncompleted *The Hooded Falcon* in 1924, was called in to rewrite this one as well.[35] After Valentino's death, Mathis even offered to write a script for his brother Alberto to give him a start in pictures.[36]

With *The Four Horsemen*, Mathis and Valentino boosted each other's careers. She lifted him from obscurity, and his performance secured her reputation as a talent spotter. Journalists quizzed her on her casting decisions, and fan magazines ran articles such as "Aspiring Valentinos Seek Aid of June Mathis."[37] When Valentino and Rambova rejected Mathis's script for *The Hooded Falcon*, the two close friends kept away from each other for a year. Otherwise, for the rest of their brief lives, they remained devoted companions. Mathis and her mother were guests for spaghetti dinners prepared by Valentino at his home. She accompanied Valentino to the premieres of *The Young Rajah* and *The Son of the Sheik*; when he faced serious physical problems while filming *The Son of the Sheik*, she visited the set and "begged him to take a long rest."[38]

Valentino was practically a part of the Mathis family. He loved Jennie Mathis and would take flowers to her crypt following her death.[39] He called June Mathis "'little mother' and described himself as her adopted son." Nita Naldi, costar of *Blood and Sand*, commented, "[Mathis] mothered Rudy, and my dear, she worshipped him and he worshipped her."[40] After a visit from Mathis and her husband Silvano Balboni on the set of *The Son of the Sheik*, Valentino said, "We three shall be together as long as I live."[41] Tragically, that would not be much longer. After his death at age thirty-one on August 23, 1926, Mathis commented, "My heart is too full of sorrow at this moment to speak coherently. My grief is deep."[42] She then granted permission for his body to be laid in her family crypt. Less than a year later, hers would be placed next to it in what became a permanent arrangement. In their collaborations, they may have achieved much more than they realized.

7

Crucial Films and Transitions, 1920–1923

Despite the great popular and critical responses to *The Four Horsemen*, mainstream discourse over masculinity veered in the totally opposite direction of what Mathis promoted in the film. Disregarding the war's horrors and over fifty thousand American deaths in barely one year of battle, national concerns still focused on the fear that men were too heavily influenced by women and lacked the vigor they needed to keep the country strong. Rather than follow a female-defined spiritual path, the preferred solution was to cut loose from all former restrictions and decorum. Ann Douglas states that following the Great War, America "was a Cinderella magically clothed in the most stunning dress at the ball, a ball to which Cinderella had not even been invited; immense gains with no visible price tag seemed to be the American destiny."[1] As her statement implies, Americans were generally not interested in contemplating the costs of violence and war, and they certainly were not eager to blend spirituality into their popular culture. Instead, "modern America, led by New York, was free to promote, not an egalitarian society, but something like an egalitarian popular and mass culture aggressively appropriating forms and ideas across race, class, and gender lines. This culture billed itself as irreverent if not irreligious, the first such in American annals, alert to questions of honesty but hostile to all moralizing."[2]

Douglas describes a culture that is not buying what June Mathis was selling. By 1924, Douglas Fairbanks is being "touted as 'the most popular man in the world.'"[3] Valentino's popularity skyrockets as well. But it comes from his title role in *The Sheik*, created in 1921 by director George Melford and screenwriter Monte Katterjohn, rather than his portrayals of Julio Desnoyers or Juan Gallardo. *The Sheik* has greater similarity to Fairbanks's adventure films of the decade: grand action-fantasies with few ties to reality.

Lea Jacobs explains that in the twenties "sentimentality began to be judged to be inappropriate for masculine action stories," an opinion that extended to romantic dramas as well.[4] While *The Sheik* achieved huge success, inspiring numerous cheap imitations, some critics found it too tame. *Variety* mockingly referred to the scene in which Valentino's Ahmed decides to release his captive English Lady Diana: "So painful is the decision, so heroic the renunciation, a great light breaks on him. He loves her. Not only loves her, but loves her truly, nobly, as great souls love. Ooh, la, la!"[5] *Blood and Sand* received this attack as well; the *New York Times* found it "flat and insipid," remarking that it "takes great pains to reassure timidly and tyrannically conventional folk as to its constant moral purpose. It is loaded with platitudinous subtitles, and among its characters is a tedious old fool who comes forward every now and then to utter some trite aphorism or stale word of warning. All this is extremely annoying to the person who simply wants a good story."[6] Jacobs explains these criticisms as part of a trend toward more modern film techniques in various genres. In comedy, "filmmakers such as Chaplin and Lubitsch pushed [new] principles in the direction of increasingly reduced depictions of story events and an increasingly understated dramaturgy . . . part of a coming trend, an efficient and streamlined approach to directing."[7] Similarly, war films moved toward "a departure from more traditional, sentimental, representations."[8] Critics wondered about the long-term prospects for these trends, but "there was nevertheless a sense that these films represented an advance in filmmaking technique."[9]

Jacobs argues that the work of Chaplin, Lubitsch, Vidor, and Sternberg represents an important departure from sentimentality and movement toward modern techniques. The progression was toward greater ambiguity of both characters and narrative, natural dialogue, explicit violence and sexuality, and the rejection of ideas about morality and guidance. These were male-infused characteristics of a new male-dominated cinema. One of the key genres marking the transition was the gangster film of which Gilbert Seldes writes, "They brought a sense of actuality and a rude male vigor to an art given to prettiness and sentimentality, they shifted emphasis from women to men and created stars who were neither clothes models nor movie actors, but players in a new medium."[10] These films demanded male characters of a much different nature than Mathis created for Valentino.

Complementary to the concern with masculinity were issues of immigration and race. Studlar writes, "The notion of race suicide was an obsession during the 1910s and 1920s." Heading these fears was the fact that most newcomers were no longer from white European regions. Studlar continues, "The immigration debate began to take on the tone of a racial argument as politicians, influenced by nativists, turned their concerns toward southern and eastern Europe. The assimilation of these new immigrants was regarded as a threat rather than a solution: it would lead to a mongrelization of the Nordic/Anglo-Saxon 'race' in the United States."[11]

Mathis, as noted in earlier chapters, shared many of the racist attitudes of her day, and sometimes made them evident in her work. In *Five Thousand an Hour* (Ralph W. Ince, 1918), for example, Johnny I. Gamble (Hale Hamilton) faces financial ruin by betting his last $100 on a horse that finishes second. But the winner is disqualified on a penalty, and so Johnny earns his first $5,000. As he celebrates, Mathis creates a joke when Johnny kisses the horse and its jockey but then steps back to shake hands with its Black trainer. The "joke" is that kissing the Black man would be more repulsive than kissing the horse. In writing about European films in 1925, Mathis casually uses the phrase "the nigger in the woodpile" to define what she sees as the films' weaknesses.[12] The racist stereotypes she uses in *The Red Lantern* show a similar attitude toward Asians. As Michelle Su-Mei Liu writes, "That a virulent strain of anti-Asian sentiment underlay the vogue for orientalism in American arts must not be forgotten."[13] Anti-Semitism is present as well. In *Hearts Are Trumps* (Rex Ingram, 1920), a greedy Jewish character named Israel Fell (Brinsley Shaw) meets a gruesome fate when he is killed in a landslide at the conclusion. Besides placing the dark-complected Valentino in lead roles, Mathis's scripts for him did not address the immigration question. Only one of his characters in the five Mathis films, Amos Judd, spends any time in the United States and even he does not face questions about assimilation. He faces antagonism from a jealous rival who accuses him of bribery and murder, and his love interest shies away from him due to either religious or "racial" issues. But his rival reveals his own hypocrisy and Amos eventually marries and settles with his wife in India.

Another issue of major importance throughout the silent era and therefore a source of great box office potential was that of labor struggles. On occasion, as with D. W. Griffith's scenes of militiamen shooting down strikers in *The Mother and the Law* (1914) and *Intolerance* (1916), depictions of labor strife could be surprisingly critical of owners' tactics. But these depictions were also shaped by popular trends. With anti-union hysteria sweeping the country, Griffith's reissue of *The Mother and the Law* in 1917 included a new intertitle during the massacre: "The militiamen having used blank cartridges, the workmen now fear only the company guards."[14] Film-makers were generally unwilling to take sides on an issue if it could mean losing a large portion of their audience.

Mathis, however, through her use of melodrama, a genre that, as Christine Gledhill writes, "sides with the underdog," and her long experience, was prepared to address these issues. Her training had included years of hard work on the stage, learning all aspects of filmmaking, gaining credits on seventy-seven films from December 1915 to December 1920, making contributions to many others, and taking efforts to become a playwright. She was well settled into a practice of relying on hard work and pushing ahead with her ideas. Of *The Four Horsemen* Kevin Brownlow writes, "It was astonishing for such a big picture to go into production with no star names . . . and without a star director. It was an act of faith by June Mathis."[15]

However, the cult of hypermasculinity represented by Fairbanks and the corresponding "decline of sentiment" as defined by Lea Jacobs were not the only trends of the postwar era.[16] As Gaylyn Studlar notes, femi-ninity in the 1920s cannot be easily divided between "true womanhood" and "the New Woman." Victorian womanhood was always "dynamically fluctuating, formed and re-formed by competing discourses, both progres-sive and traditional."[17] Already in the late nineteenth century, "matinee girls" were flocking to theaters to idolize favorite actors such as the British import Harry Montague.[18] As the movies grew, film producers understood that responding to women's tastes was in their financial interests. Studlar notes that "there is no doubt that female fans, especially middle-class fans, were a coveted audience. They were believed to go frequently, to control the film-going habits of their family, and have the money to spend on tie-ins and industry-related items, including fan magazines."[19] Part of their influ-ence is evident in "the era's ideal of masculinity [which] did not exclude gentleness or gentlemanliness, or even an admission of the need for a little touch of the feminine in a well-balanced man. At the same time, there was demonstrable fear of the masculine antiself personified by the adolescent sissy or boyishly immature mollycoddle."[20]

Mathis's work with Valentino therefore accomplished several import-ant advancements at once. It raised an actor from a negatively stereotyped ethnicity into a starring role in a major production. It "softened" his image, as Studlar argues. But the main factor was not in the character's relationship to his mother, but in his construction as a young man seeking his identity in a violent and unstable world. Valentino's characters thus avoided the mollycoddle label. Their strength came not from athletic feats like Fairbanks's but from inner searching.

Mathis's model of masculinity built on women's guidance and spirituality was quite distinct from the popular Fairbanks model and her association with Valentino was the most important factor in her career. Her work on *The Four Horsemen of the Apocalypse* was a crucial challenge at a major transitional point for both her career and the motion picture industry. Marcus Loew's buyout of Metro provided the support Mathis needed to make the film as she wished and move her to a position of great influence. The film's remarkable success enabled Mathis to move on to Famous Players-Lasky to make *Blood and Sand* and *The Young Rajah* in 1922 and then to a position of great influence at Goldwyn.

But these were not the only films in which her talent and ideas would find expression in this period. On May 8, 1920, *Motion Picture News* reported that in the previous four months, Mathis had completed continuities for *Hearts Are Trumps, The Right of Way, The Saphead* (Buster Keaton's first feature film), and *Parlor, Bedroom, and Bath*. Each of these was an adaptation. The *News* added, "Miss Mathis is an exceptionally quick worker, and although she frequently rewrites her scripts entirely has been known to complete one in two weeks."[21] A year later, columnist Nora B. Giebler stated that "her self-imposed duties are not ended when the continuity is completed. She hovers around the stages and sets and confers with the directors daily, and she follows the film into the cutting and editorial rooms and writes the titles."[22]

Simply mentioning these other films, however, only credits Mathis with speed and intensity, but ignores her imprint on them through her artistry and ideas. Whether she is recognized as an artist or not, these issues are the most important to address because they indicate the degree of her influence on American film. In her remaining two and a half years at Metro and her later positions at Famous Players-Lasky, Goldwyn, and First National, she would influence countless other films. Therefore, while her specific contributions may not always be identifiable, Mathis's presence throughout American cinema of the 1920s is undeniably large. To start the new decade, Mathis continued long-term collaborations with directors Henry Otto and Maxwell Karger on films that addressed issues of race, class, and materialism. Of the three to be examined here, each is of a vastly different style from the others. *The Willow Tree* (Otto, 1920) is a mystical Orientalist production that again involves an American male/Asian female relationship with spiritual elements and an antiwar message. *A Trip to Paradise* and *The Idle Rich* (both Karger, 1921) focused on working-class Americans struggling to survive in a shabby superficial culture. The former, the first film treatment of the play *Liliom*, eventually adapted as the musical *Carousel*, has a strong spiritual theme, while the latter presents Mathis's strongest depiction of the United States as a multicultural society.[23] In 1923, Mathis emphasized spirituality and a cooperative social system as a response to economic hardship in *The Day of Faith*, one of her two "pet projects" along with *In the Palace of the King*.[24] Throughout the year, while she served as Goldwyn's editorial director and shouldered responsibility for writing and producing *Ben-Hur*, she simultaneously researched and wrote a screenplay for *The Spanish Dancer*, a film meant to be a major transitional work for Pola Negri, reviewed scripts and preproduction plans, and assisted Erich von Stroheim in the development of his massive production of *Greed*.

Studlar's recognition of the continuing trend of feminine sentiment shows that Mathis's troubles in the twenties were not because she was somehow out of touch with modern "masculine" styles. Instead, her participation in a male-dominated studio system that would never accept her as an equal in its top ranks worked against the recognition of her achievements. Ironically, as she gained greater influence, she also faced greater resistance to her ideas from male colleagues. Powerful new studios like Metro-Goldwyn-Mayer, controlled by white men with connections to big money sources, excluded women from the top ranks. This problem was part of a larger social characteristic. Elaine Showalter declares, "The difference between the modern woman [of the 1920s], and the suffragist or feminist of the nineteenth century, was her insistence on the right to self-fulfillment in both public life and in relationships with men."[25] But, she continues, "no amount of personal and individual growth and change on women's part could succeed without a corresponding adjustment in social structure and sex roles generally."[26]

The male controllers of the film industry certainly never contemplated making any such adjustments. Cari Beauchamp writes of women silent film writers, "They were products of their time, priding themselves on their femininity, and they were so inculcated in the system that they had learned to be superb office politicians. . . . But of course they never were totally accepted."[27] The women in the business had little choice but to accept its established gender roles if they wished to remain part of it. They might have high ideals of their own, but they embraced a system that would never grant them equality. Gaines argues that Mathis's assessment of the US film industry in the postwar era was "an expression of the capitalist optimism of market supremacy, that brashness tempered with a secret ingredient slipped in undetected, noisy cheer at odds with a quietly genuine 'something.' Neither can one miss in Mathis the obtuseness of an American capitalist optimism that cannot see beyond its nose to the worlds into which it exported emotional merchandise."[28] "Obtuseness" is correct. Despite the ideals expressed in her work, Mathis understood that studio heads were mainly concerned with profits, bigger markets, and economy in production, and she did not question these goals. But then, Mathis had seen work in the entertainment industry as a way of earning money and a means of self-expression from age eleven. She never separated the two, and it is likely that other early women filmmakers did not do so either.

As financial powerhouses like Marcus Loew and William Fox took control of the industry, they empowered their own associates, often people never before involved with movies, with new responsibilities. These men (always men) could cause havoc with traditional practices at the studios, which meant that women filmmakers might quickly lose the respect they had built over many years. One of these new authority figures, playwright and novelist Bayard Veiller, informally known as Baydie, had come to Metro's West Coast studio as assistant to general manager Joseph W. Engel.[29] One day, Rex Ingram found Mathis crying in a hallway and asked what was wrong. "Baydie," she said, "Baydie just ran The Right of Way. He locked me out of the projection room. I wrote the scenario. I'm not going to stay here another day. . . . After all I've done for Metro . . . To be treated this way. . . . I'm not going to write another line for Metro if they expect me to take orders from a little thing like that! I won't! I won't! I won't. . . . Supervisor! He knows nothing about pictures. Nothing!"[30] Mathis's secretary chimed in, "It's an outrage, that little insignificant person! And Miss Mathis has been here since the company started. Locking her out of the projection room—the idea! She'll never submit to him!"[31]

Fortunately, Ingram was able to smooth things over. He later wrote in his unpublished memoirs, "June Mathis and I were having quite a problem with the scenario of the Drury Lane show [*Shore Acres*], for the play was nothing more than an agglomeration of scenes—spectacular enough on the Drury Lane stage, but nothing out of the way for Hollywood." Marcus Loew helped Ingram become friends with Veiller, and Ingram gave him that script to read, "a gesture that soothed his ruffled feelings." What ruffled them is not clear. Perhaps he had been reprimanded for being too forceful. Ingram continues, "He made some suggestions, and when he learned they had been included in my working script, said some complimentary things to June. That afternoon she told me she had discovered that Baydie had—in a rather ruthless way—sex appeal."[32]

Corporate changes did not only affect women. Filmmakers with careers established in the teens like Ingram, Marshall Neilan, Maurice Tourneur, and Erich von Stroheim, writes Thomas Schatz, who encountered the new "centralized production and division of labor under the emerging studio system, . . . found themselves at odds with the very industry they had helped create. None could adjust to the steady fragmentation and the increasing constraints of studio filmmaking."[33] These directors also considered themselves producers of their films. But so did filmmakers such as Nazimova, Weber, and Mathis who had worked just as hard to establish the industry and would also suffer major setbacks because the new system could not tolerate their independent natures.

One reason Mathis did not criticize the system was that she did not define the industry solely in financial terms. She believed women were part of a business that was a force of moral superiority in the world. In fact, she asserted shortly before her death that for the film moguls, profits were secondary to the production of artistic works: "For it is a great industry, with many high-minded men at the head of it. They have frequently been criticized as being commercial and money-mad; but this is not true. Many of them have a desire to do fine things, and sometimes produce a number of strictly 'commercial' pictures in order to afford the losses from one great artistic venture that will be for the betterment of the industry."[34]

In her 1923 article "Harmony in Picture-Making," Mathis argues, "Biological creation takes two elements: male and female. . . . It is a significant fact that most of the best-known and most successful scenario writers are women. The greatest directors are men, and the harmonious endeavors of a man and a woman have resulted in the best pictures." She adds that the "greatest artists, surgeons, authors and musicians have the feminine quality in their nature, and the successful scenarist also has this enviable quality, or reflects it from a home in which the feminine influence is strongly felt in the person of wife or mother."[35] For Mathis, men of great achievement had integrated feminine qualities into their nature; without them, the greatest works of arts and sciences that humanity requires would not exist.

Marcus Loew's impact on Metro's financial security in 1920 must have helped solidify Mathis's idealism because his importance in helping her achieve her artistic goals at this time cannot be underestimated. He asserted his hands-off approach to production, saying, "Metro is a separate organization, and will remain so to a great extent. The gentlemen who handle its affairs agree with us absolutely, and have been working along these lines before we had anything to do with Metro. They will continue to remain in charge."[36] While Bayard Veiller's presence shows that Loew was not going to let the old production system continue, Mathis received great support and little interference from him with her Metro projects of 1920–1922. That she succeeded in repeatedly asserting her ideals throughout her work as her career progressed is unquestionable. She defined some profoundly progressive ideas in her scripts even though she was strongly conservative both socially and politically and never criticized American expansionism or racism.

Mathis's interactions with and depictions of marginalized Others are complex. Her recital of "'Hol' Dem Philippines' in the negro dialect" as a ten-year-old reveals notions about race and imperialism that she never outgrew. In a racist, segregated industry and society, the inability to learn about others as individuals is not surprising. As a result, Mathis constantly refers to ethnic minorities in her scripts as "types," a practice that suggests a clear social distance from them. This perspective would be the most likely at a time when, as Sumiko Higashi writes, for whites in America "immigrants like Italians and Jews—not to mention 'new women' active in the public sphere—required an identity firmly anchored in a subject-object dichotomy that commodified the 'Other.'"[37]

Higashi further asserts that "to introduce a fluid spectrum of colors in a pluralistic culture as opposed to a strict bifurcation of races into white and non-white categories, was threatening to the status quo."[38] Mathis, like the rest of white American filmmakers, did not create pictures of a racially integrated society. She recognizes the growing Black influence on popular culture with the jazz bands she includes in *Camille*, *The Conquering Power*, and *A Trip to Paradise*, and her *Ben-Hur* script also emphasizes inclusiveness. Yet, she never depicts or even refers to Black people as an integral part of society even when she had the chance to as in the script for *The Idle Rich*. It is commendable that Mathis expanded the number of ethnic groups from those included in the short story "Junk" that the film was based on. It is also admirable that this entertaining comedy, created in collaboration with director Maxwell Karger, includes a strong critique of materialism and commercialism. That criticism, whether intentional or not, still tolerates or even endorses American capitalism's racism. Nevertheless, as Ann Cvetkovich writes, critics and scholars who condemned popular melodrama and erased women writers and directors from cultural history promoted "the disparagement of cultural forms that appealed to marginalized groups, such as the working-class or women. The subtext of dismissals of the sensation novel as bad art is the fear that it encourages those who enjoy it to rebel against social restrictions."[39] Cvetkovich does not argue that affective works are inherently liberatory. She points out that if "sensationalism or the expression of affect challenges or transforms structures of power, it is only because it can also maintain or enforce those structures. By the same token, mass culture can be subversive, but it can also be conservative. Or it can be both simultaneously, producing, in other words, multiple and unpredictable effects."[40]

The importance of sexual, racial, and ethnic Others in Mathis's career, whether as characters she played on stage, professional colleagues, or characters in her screenplays, especially during the teens, is striking. Her final stage work in a dramatic role was in blackface in a play that acknowledged the reality of lynching. One of Mathis's extant poems is an ode to Lincoln, which is a slight indication of sympathy for the oppressed, and her film career would never have started without the help of Edwin Carewe, the first American Indian director.[41] As a proponent of "realism," Mathis would not always present a world devoid of racial and ethnic Others. Instead, as with her films with Nazimova and Valentino, they were often her main characters. In others such as *Ben-Hur* and *The Idle Rich*, she worked to include as many marginalized groups as possible. They may not have been presented as equal to whites, but they were present and necessary, a baseline standard for inclusiveness that Hollywood rarely exceeded for the next several decades.

Racist attitudes, therefore, do not completely define Mathis's relationships or writing, and she became increasingly progressive in her criticisms of masculinity, commercialism, and war and her openness to various faiths, cultures, and racial identities. Her work suggests that spirituality and female leadership can overcome the oppression, exploitation, and violence of Western white males. Most importantly, she refrains from didacticism and prefers to encourage viewers to find their own answers. In her emphasis on details, her lengthy scripts, and her frequent references to artworks as models for the mise-en-scène, Mathis suggests that viewers need to pay careful attention. She understood that a film's meaning is not imposed on viewers but created in their interactions with the text. In a First National press release from late 1924, Mathis said, "The public, individually, is a self-conscious actor. It is only in the mass, in its reflexes, that it reaches perfection in histrionics, and it is the scenario writer's part to stimulate this subconscious reaction."[42]

The Willow Tree, released in January 1920, with significant self-reflective elements, provides an important case study for arguing that Mathis wanted viewers to take responsibility for finding their own answers. The reflexivity also suggests that film and art can provide a peaceful alternative reality. It is difficult to define the differences between the film adaptation and the original Broadway play of 1917 that it was taken from because neither the dramatic text nor the screenplay is available. But the film reveals that Mathis, Otto, and cameraman John Arnold rethought the stage play in cinematic terms. The play began with a "lacquered screen [that] when folded towards the wings reveals a Japanese garden with a pagoda occupying the center of the stage."[43] Similarly, when the film begins, two Japanese women open cabinet doors following an intertitle that states, "Let us peep behind the Sacred Peak of Nippon—in the shadow of which nestles the tiny village of Ito."[44] The title appears on a Japanese print of mountains and trees, so when the doors open, viewers are doing exactly what it requests.

The camera tracks in to the first shots of the film narrative on a screen within the cabinet: a film within a film. *Variety* refers to the film as "a beauty picture for the benefit of the artistic, not a rousing story calculated to set the hearts of the masses on fire."[45] Mathis's love of art is evident, and Otto and Arnold produce some beautiful well-lit and well-framed compositions. The filmmakers, in fact, seem to have had the idea of having the production resemble a Japanese print. Indeed, two of Mathis's intertitles serve this purpose. One that introduces O-riu (Viola Dana), reentering the narrative after running away from her arranged marriage, simply reads, "A bit of driftwood in the sea of moonlight." It is printed against a minimalist image of a mountain, thin clouds, and trees. A later title reads, "The still and peaceful beauty of Nippon night." The film then cuts to a shot of O-riu and her British admirer Dick Hamilton (Pell Trenton) walking in his garden, which appears as a beautiful setting, especially with the gentle moonlight effect of this shot.

With *The Willow Tree*, Mathis returned to the mysterious "Oriental" woman she had created in earlier films with Nazimova and maintained some of the negative stereotypes of interracial relationships. O-riu fits the childlike, dependent, and vulnerable nature of the "good Oriental" woman.[46] In her first appearance, she plays with children in her father's garden. She is modern only in the sense of resisting her father's efforts to marry her to a wealthy man so that her brother can attend college in New York. She wants to be like the American girls her brother tells her about, but her father says, "My son I give to modern Japan—but my daughter belongs to Old Japan and must obey its customs." He then raises a stick to beat her, but O-riu bows and pledges to obey.

O-riu resembles a wooden statue of a mythic princess carved by her father. The princess in the legend emerged from a willow tree to comfort a warrior who had fled Japan to seek peace. When companions find him later and beg him to return to fight for his country, he refuses. The princess then takes his sword and stabs the tree, which ends her life, so the warrior goes back. Back in the present-day story, O-riu's father refuses to sell the statue, prizing it above his daughter. But when O-riu runs off and makes him believe she has drowned, he sells the statue to Dick to get the college money for his son.

The narrative has some obvious problems of racism and sexism. It justifies the white Westerner's love as one that breaks the evil of Eastern patriarchy while also obscuring colonial history. As Gina Marchetti writes, in this context, "[Western] bourgeois, patriarchal power legitimizes itself through the religion of love."[47] Dick and O-riu are made for each other as both wish only to find someone with whom they can escape from the worlds they were born into. O-riu sees Dick first as he admires the statue; she wishes to be the figure so he would admire her. Dick's goal is possession, first of the statue and then of O-riu, and the love narrative, the fact that she desires possession by him, makes his goal acceptable. When he finally buys the treasure and brings it home, she is hiding in his house. Yet, *The Willow Tree* also possesses significant differences with the tradition of films depicting Eastern/Western relationships. While most up until 1920 presented tragic romances, as in *The Red Lantern*, *The Willow Tree* does not. Instead, Mathis and Otto seem more concerned with depicting a mythical world, a blending of fantasy and reality, one self-reflexively defined as cinematic, which can provide refuge from the actual world of violence and materialism. The film invites viewers to seek a peaceful refuge as do the main characters and suggests that the movie's blend of reality and fantasy is a place to find it.

In addition to the self-reflexive title cards that blend with the scenery, the narrative includes numerous mirroring devices between the fantasy and "real" stories within the diegesis. The characters and events in the legend and the present are exact duplicates. A mirror even becomes a key prop that bridges fantasy and reality within the film. On the first morning that he has the statue, Dick is preparing to shave when he remembers O-riu's father telling him a legend of a carver who put a mirror in a statue's bosom and brought it to life. As he thinks about this, O-riu emerges from hiding and takes the statue's place. Dick decides to put his mirror on her bosom and starts to shave. He is completely fooled at first when she impersonates it, an illogical event that suggests he cannot tell the difference between wood and skin. While he begins, Mathis and Otto insert a racist reference to Asian weakness and superstition as O-riu yawns and causes a servant to run in fright. Then, as O-riu reveals herself, both she and Dick have what they want and are ready to spend their lives away from the world.

A second mirroring segment within the overall mirroring structure occurs when Otto, Arnold, and the film's editor create a beautiful shot/reverse shot of Dana as the mythical princess who came to life looking in through a barn window at her warrior admirer sleeping across a pile of bundled reeds. In the reverse shot through the window, she is framed in the shadows of willow branches with her face first half and then completely dark. She walks back out to the willow tree from which she emerged in another beautifully framed composition. The narrative as a mirror of social reality completes this motif. Near the conclusion of this sequence, the war theme appears in parallel to the mythic tale as Dick returns to England to serve. As he leaves, O-riu comes out and stands in the light to watch him go and a storm begins to surround her, a metaphor for the war encompassing the world. As darkness closes in around O-riu, she stands gazing upward to the left, backlighting beautifully outlining her torso and profile.

Dick believes O-riu dies in that storm that also destroys the willow in his garden. A final title states, "Four years—Then peace returns to bless a weary war-torn world." Dick returns unharmed to his Japanese home and discovers that O-riu is still alive. In an effective parallel to the film's opening, the final scene begins as a servant opens the door to Dick's old house to reveal O-riu collecting flowers in the garden. In contrast to earlier shots throughout the film, the door is now clearly within the diegetic world, which suggests a transformation from fantasy to reality, but one that retains peaceful, mystical elements. As an analogy to the recent historical past, the characters have passed through the storm and returned to the garden. It now becomes important to put conflict aside and focus on beauty, which is exactly what Dick does throughout the film. At the end, he and O-riu walk out onto his porch, silhouetted against the garden in the light, but, as in *Eye for Eye*, there is no final embrace or kiss. His relationship to O-riu is never physical. He has her on a pedestal to admire her like the sculpture she resembles. She is not a modern active woman. But the idea of admiration rather than possession maintained in the conclusion is appropriate to the film's messages and mood. To renounce conflict and seek beauty is exactly what the film wants viewers to do.

Some critics were biased toward "a rousing story calculated to set the hearts of the masses on fire" and unwilling to consider the merits of a film that did otherwise or to accept Viola Dana in a role that was a distinct departure from her previous work, which hurt its box office in small towns.[48] Responses from theater owners in *Exhibitors Herald* were largely negative. The manager of the Leroy Theater in Lampasas, Texas called it "Not as good as *Please Get Married* [Dana's previous film]. Star well liked here."[49] The owner of the Kenton, Ohio opera house thought "This picture must have been made for Chinese fans as it certainly is no good for Americans."[50] *Variety* thought the story too slight.[51] But many recognized the film as aiming more at artistry than narrative impact. *Wid's Daily* called it a "decided novelty with wonderfully beautiful settings and wholly artistic atmosphere."[52] Writing for *Motion Picture News*, J. S. Dickerson noted, "It strikes us as being well out of the ordinary and therefore worthy of attention for that reason if no other."[53] The *Exhibitors Herald* reviewer wrote, "A thing of beauty, both as to appearance and import, it gives audiences jaded with mathematical realism and mechanically perfect emotion a relief that should be welcome."[54] Given the contexts of its production within the supportive situation at Metro and Mathis's oeuvre, *The Willow Tree* is worth consideration as a distinct artistic response to the horrors of the Great War. Although it might be criticized as an escapist philosophy, the pursuit of peace rather than a competitive or militaristic life makes sense, though it is difficult to present as entertainment.

Even more difficult is to pose spirituality as a response to labor problems. Mathis tries to do so in *A Trip to Paradise*. Because two sets of values, labor and capital, were involved and moviemakers did not want to alienate the adherents of either, films on the issue tended not to make strong statements.[55] Kay Sloan writes that the movies "acted as a diplomat, negotiating between owners and workers and inevitably resolving the conflict in a fashion that did not require the massive changes demanded by radical labor activists. The melodrama offered reassurance to average men and women who feared both the insecurities of everyday life and the sweeping changes suggested by Socialists."[56]

Mathis had first addressed working-class struggles for material needs in *The Man Who* (Karger, 1921). Like *A Trip to Paradise* would a few months later, it offered a reassuring resolution but also critically addressed social hypocrisy and capitalist exploitation. The original short story for *The Man Who* in the *Saturday Evening Post* is classified as a comedy. But the narrative of this film, now considered lost, sounds more dramatic. Bert Lytell plays Bedford Mills, a wounded veteran who falls in love with the aristocratic Helen Jessup (Lucy Cotton) at a party her father gives for returning soldiers. But Helen spurns him when she learns he is only a bank clerk. Bedford then decides to protest the high price of shoes by refusing to wear any, but he is harassed by the public and eventually arrested. Mary Turner (Virginia Valli), an artist, comes to his aid and marches with him despite the fact that her father is director of "the shoe trust." Public support then goes to the veteran rather than the manufacturers and Bedford wins his battle and the girl.

With *A Trip to Paradise*, Mathis returned to labor issues and depicted a woman as redeemer and guide for yet another broken and confused male. Its source, *Liliom*, is a drama written by Hungarian playwright Ferenc Molnár in 1909 and first produced in his home country. Molnár's "masterpiece" is surrealistic, blending states of life and death, wakefulness and dreaming. Although it was not a hit initially ten years later, Benjamin F. Glazer tracked down interpretations of texts written in various Hungarian dialects, and the play became successful on Broadway. Commenting on its success in his "Introduction" to the published edition of the play, Glazer notes, "Perhaps the wide circulation of the play in printed form had made its beauty and significance clearer. Perhaps the tragedy of the war had made Molnar's public more sensitive to spiritual values."[57]

In her adaptation, Mathis makes major changes in Molnár's play, perhaps the greatest being that in the play she renames main character, Liliom, Curly Flynn (Bert Lytell) who also remains unchanged and gives him an essential goodness that others eventually recognize. Ultimately saved by the prayers of his wife Nora (Virginia Valli), Curly is allowed to continue his life on Earth and rejoin her at the end. Mathis again indicates the importance of women's influences, especially of a spiritual nature, in establishing hope for a peaceful future.

Mathis's script's opening scene humorously depicts the cheap artificiality of modern culture. As a lady frantically searches for her dog near a hot dog stand, worried that her pooch might now be meat, a customer looks at his hot dog suspiciously.[58] One wonders if this incident was inspired by Upton Sinclair's *The Jungle* and if Mathis was counting on audiences to make that connection. In any case, the joke suggests an undercurrent of threatening qualities in modern life. But then Mathis includes a racist reference in her script likely to erase the humor of her initial joke for modern readers. Curly Flynn is a skilled carnival barker, luring customers into a ride called A Trip to Paradise. His success has made him highly conceited as is evident in his late arrival to work in a rickshaw pulled by "a huge Negro." When Curly gets out, Mathis writes, "he flips the nigger a coin."[59]

Following this unpleasant note, Mathis continues the opening scene with further emphasis on the deficient value of popular culture. In one of the many references to classic art in her screenplays, she emphasizes that the set should look cheap and crude and writes, "Each side is a cheap idea of duplicating the effect gained in Paradise lost—and Purgatory by Dore."[60] Early on, Curly attracts customers by inviting them on a "ten-cent trip to Paradise."[61] What they actually purchase is a shoddy imitation that provides temporary escape but not much more. Throughout the script, as her emphasis on the oppressive conditions for the working class continues, these opening comments could suggest their acceptance of very small rewards in return, even in the "happy ending."

One of the major sources of class oppression brought by modernity was the institution of the time clock. Working-class people increasingly lost control of their labor to the needs of mass production and consumerism and thus gained a greater consciousness of time. Anti-modernists protested the dehumanizing nature of this change, and Mathis emphasizes that effect throughout the first third of her screenplay. At the start, Curly's boss is worried about his tardiness but says nothing because he brings in a lot of business right away. But Nora's boss at the diner where she works threatens to fire her if she does not return from her break on time.

Through this detail, Mathis constructs Nora as a young woman who wants to break traditional restrictions. She is not a passive, long-suffering melodramatic heroine. Besides her boss, the aunt she lives with, Madame Smiley (Victory Bateman) has also given her a time constraint—she must be home by midnight or get locked out. Ignoring these pressures, Nora consciously rejects the entrapments of home and work one night after she has finished her shift at the diner. She and her friend Mary (Eva Gordon) stop by the Trip to Paradise ride, and Curly is very attracted to her. The safe, long-suffering path for Nora would have been to go home and wait for Curly to come to her. But at this point, she is mainly interested in immediate gratification. Curly's pitch to carnival goers in the opening scene suggests the ride's romantic possibilities: "Filled with thrills, filled with bliss— / In the darkness, steal a kiss— / That's Paradise!" A young couple about to enter a rival attraction "look at each other . . . giggle and . . . hurry across the street followed by three or four others."[62] After Nora and Mary take the ride, Curly gives them another for free and then gets in with them for a third trip. While in a tunnel, "Curly's arm steals round Nora, and when the lights come up again—he removes it quickly and apologetically while Nora registers the fact that he has impressed her and that he was not displeasing."[63] Mary then warns her not to stay with Curly and forgo work because "It ain't so easy to get a job these days."[64] But Nora is determined to set her own destiny.

During their night together, Curly and Nora first take a walk on the beach. Mathis introduces a policeman who comes by "as though scanning the beach for spooning couples after hours."[65] Though it is not blatant, the implication is that Curly and Nora are not chaste as Nora's pregnancy soon proves.[66]

In her adaptation, Mathis softens Curly the same as she did for Julio Desnoyers and Juan Gallardo. But the significance of this transformation again goes beyond just making him acceptable to feminine sensibilities. Like Mathis's Valentino characters, Curly needs guidance to help him cope with economic pressures. Throughout the screenplay, he faces a choice between the unfeeling, carnal, masculine path of worldly treasure or the spiritual path of love and compassion. Curly's other important acquaintances like the Widow Boland (Eunice Vin Moore), his boss at the amusement park, Madame Smiley, who becomes his second boss, and his friend Jim Meek (Brinsley Shaw), with whom he attempts a robbery, are mean, aggressive characters who put their faith in money and try to influence him to do the same. But Nora's more powerful influence on his better, softer nature has been present from their first meeting. When the Widow Boland jealously threatens Nora, Curly leaves his job. That night, he tells Nora, "I never knew there were such feelings in the world until" and then writes in the sand "YOU."[67]

The extant *Paradise* script reveals that Mathis worked very hard and with great precision on this project. It is clearly not the first draft as Mathis notes several scenes she has cut: 140–142, 200, 211–216, and 230–231. She also frequently provides specific instructions for shooting to define the mise-en-scène and to make the editing easier. For example, she includes the following directions during the film's wedding scene:

CLOSEUP
FADE IN DOUBLE EXPOSURE NOTES OF WEDDING
MARCH—
TAKE WITH AND WITHOUT NOTES
To cover footage for continuity.
Clerk whistling and conducting Wedding March.[68]

At other times, Mathis more specifically defines the mise-en-scène, sometimes with an indication to consult her for her exact ideas. Nora's aunt, Madame Smiley, runs a photography studio. As she is taking a picture, Mathis states that her subject should be "a very wizened faced old man, with a silk hat. A distinct type (whom I have in mind)."[69]

Curly and Nora quitting their jobs are particularly rash acts because during times of high unemployment, workers are especially powerless. This was a significant issue for audiences in 1921 left unacknowledged by the negative characters of the Widow and Madame Smiley. Madame Smiley established her studio in a poor location far from the other amusement park attractions but blames Curly for her failure. Eventually, he tries to find something that pays better but he's told at the employment office, "There's a hundred men to one job these days."[70]

The *Paradise* script suggests that Mathis's knowledge and confidence had grown during 1921, and that rather than exhausting her, the intensive work on *Camille* and *The Four Horsemen* earlier that year had actually energized her. For example, in scene 159, as Curly returns from his fruitless job hunt, Mathis appears to suggest the use of a graphic match when she indicates that Curly should show his frustration while still outside and that they should "HOLD THIS FOR CUT INTO PHOTOGRAPH GALLERY AND CARRY HIM ALONG INTO GALLERY." Scene 161 then begins with the "INTERIOR [OF THE] PHOTOGRAPH GALLERY." In other words, the instruction appears to suggest a cut from Curly standing just outside the gallery to a matching shot from the inside to show that he has entered rather than showing him walking in. This is much more detail than necessary, and most likely unmatched in any of her earlier scripts. It would be sufficient to describe scene 160 as outside and 161 as inside and allow Karger to decide whether it would be done in one or two shots.

These indications of intensive effort, along with the heavily revised narrative and themes of spirituality presented through the female lead strongly suggest that Mathis took up *A Trip to Paradise* as a project for personal expression. Mathis shows what happens to honest people under brutal economic conditions: they starve and lose their homes. As Curly grows frustrated in his job search, his friend Jim Meek suggests a plan for a robbery. Curly resists at first, but when Madame Smiley receives an eviction notice and blames him, Curly agrees to the scheme. Their plan goes terribly wrong, but in reworking Molnár's surrealism as melodrama Mathis is able to insert an uplifting spiritual conclusion. She changes the original work by enhancing the connections between the living and the souls of their loved ones in the next world. In *Liliom*, Molnár's main character kills himself and then willingly forfeits his chance to return to his earthly existence at the end because he knows he will continue to be cruel to his wife.[71] By contrast, in *Paradise*, Curly is wounded when the owner of the house he and Jim Meek are robbing surprises them with a gun. Jim holds a little girl in front of himself while attempting to shoot her father. Curly jumps in the way to prevent the murder. As he then lies near death while in surgery, Nora prays for him.

While Glazer is credited with the adaptation and may have worked on some revisions with her, Mathis's hand is clearly evident in references that only she could have provided. The scene in which Curly has been shot and his soul ascends to paradise while his body hovers between life and death is a great example. She calls for a

LONG SHOT
As Curly walks toward great doors and if we can get a foreground shot so that doors can be in foreground and can open in a rift of clouds such as we have in [May] Allison picture taken up at Big Bear, and see Curly enter with the Heavenly Policemen, it would be a marvelous effect.[72]

This specific reference to an earlier Metro production is something Mathis would know, but not Glazer as this was his first film work.

Mathis's conclusion emphasizes her point that by moving beyond violence, men can reach maturity through women's help. Curly has a dream of the future as his life and soul hang in the balance. In the dream, Nora tells their daughter Rose, "Your father was like a great boy."[73] In Curly's return to Earth, he does not slap his daughter as Molnár had Liliom do.[74] Instead, Curly tries to show his daughter love by squeezing her hand. But he does it too hard and hurts her. The Heavenly police encourage him to reveal who he is. But Curly humbly states he would rather die than disgrace his wife and daughter.[75] With this act, Curly has completely committed himself to learning the compassionate feminine characteristics modeled for him by Nora. In this new masculine identity, he has secured his chance for happiness as the Heavenly Judge hears Nora's prayers and grants him permission to live.

Mathis's ending completes her transformation of Molnár's narrative into a conventional melodrama as she defines paradise in earthly terms and reassures her audience that "There is justice in God's court."[76] Unfortunately, this conclusion is a shallow response to the problems Mathis raises in the script as Curly escapes punishment for his big mistake via the transition from a tale of economic struggle to one of personal drama and romance. The closing scene has a reformed Curly, his equally repentant boss, and his wife and daughter reunited at the carnival and happily setting off for a ride together. While he has matured a little, Curly appears as another example of the popular Fairbanksian boyish man at the end, not the enlightened male Mathis preferred, and the ride is still just a cheap amusement. The ending offers audiences reassurance, but little has changed.

With her next film *The Idle Rich*, Mathis again worked with Maxwell Karger, Bert Lytell, and Virginia Valli and addressed issues of commercialism, materialism, classism, and ethnic diversity through a very entertaining comedy. The extant script is a valuable resource for understanding Mathis's collaborative work with Maxwell Karger who supervised the production of many Mathis films as Metro's director general from 1917 to 1921 and directed six in 1921–1922.[77] Mathis's scripts frequently include parenthetical notes stating "Mr. Karger wants . . ." to include his concerns with images or costs in a specific scene. In *The Idle Rich*, Karger has frequent questions and large revisions that focus on sharpening the narrative and the comedy and reducing costs. Though his suggestions caused a lot of work as evidenced by the incredibly jumbled order of the scenes, Mathis was used to heavy rewritings and seems to have been comfortable working with Karger.

At least in this film, their collaboration produced an impressive result for which reviews were universally positive.[78]

Mathis opens her script with a short sequence of an immigrant named Sam Weatherbee trading with the Spanish, a white miner, and American Indians, all of whom she refers to as "distinct types."[79] Nevertheless, this degree of ethnic diversity is notable, going beyond what was mentioned in the short story and making a point that all of these groups were part of this story of American success. In her biography of William Fox, Vanda Krefft notes the minimal efforts of the silent film industry to promote racial equality. In *The Idle Rich*, Mathis does little more than mention diverse ethnicities. But this was more than most films did in "an era that emphasized homogenization over cultural diversity" and is therefore recognizable as a conscious effort on Mathis's part.[80]

An elliptical cut of several years introduces Sam's grandson, young Sam (Lytell), who first appears as the lazy inheritor of the fortune his grandfather acquired through his bartering business. Another ethnic group is represented by his Japanese valet. Young Sam lives in a mansion built by his grandfather and wastes his inheritance on extravagant parties for his friends. In the opening, he is hosting a party with a pioneer theme to celebrate the anniversary of his grandfather's arrival in San Francisco. An intertitle states that young Sam "knew not and cared less for the value of a dollar."[81] Mathis includes some action in which youngsters enter on ponies with dark kerchiefs over their faces to look like highwaymen. They stop the waltz and give everyone half tokens; to find a dance partner, partiers must find a match for their half. Sam and his fiancée, Mattie Walling (Valli), each get half a heart.

The scene appears fairly clear, but Karger writes, "Don't understand." His confusion may have come from where Mathis mistakenly types that Sam has received a full token when she meant his rival Dillingham Coolidge (John Davidson). Still, that mistake is easy to spot. Karger then adds a more relevant comment: "Isn't this episode too corny?" Across the top of the page, he adds a specific question relating to budget concerns, "How will these [party] favors be made?"[82] Mathis then includes a scene of a fiddler jumping around while playing a Virginia Reel and enough of the dance to show the hilarity of it. Karger logically asks, "Hasn't this been done too often?"[83] Comic incidents do not seem to have been Mathis's strong suit and she much preferred to work with drama to get at what she believed to be the important issues of life.

Before his party ends, Sam learns how superficial his wealth is. He receives a telegram that his broker has killed himself after losing the Weatherbee fortune through several bad investments. Sam will soon be out on his own along with his dog, making his situation an exact replica of Charles Grandet's at the start of *The Conquering Power*. In a later sequence, workers remove all of his possessions while Sam is having coffee. In a light touch, he stands and a worker takes his chair away. The man then returns as Sam finishes his coffee to take the cup.

After he loses the family fortune, an intertitle reads: "With a pocket full of pawn tickets and one suit to his back, Sam found Chinatown the best place to avoid his friends."[84] With help from people with a variety of ethnic identities and a providential legacy from an unknown aunt, Sam's regeneration begins. He goes to his aunt's estate, meets an elderly pair of Irish caretakers, the O'Reillys (Joseph Harrington and Victory Bateman), and finds an attic full of junk. He makes his first trade when Mr. O'Reilly tells him their Portuguese neighbor has a load of beans he wants to trade for a load of bricks Sam has. Sam tells Mr. O'Reilly, "For the love of Mike, swap him! You can eat beans, but bricks don't digest worth a cent!"

Mathis and Karger's acknowledgment of so many groups as part of the nation's foundation is admirable and effective. Their presence reinforces the film's major theme that every individual deserves respect. Sam states this idea when it occurs to him that just like the unwanted items in which he has found value, there are too many people who become discarded but still have value too.[85] Yet, this picture is still conventional for the times because the members of all these groups are defined as servants (the Irish and Japanese), insignificant others (the Chinese), or customers from whom the Anglo Weatherbees can make their fortune.[86]

Very soon, Mathis has a chance to bring some spirit communication into the narrative as Mattie sits in a nearby house annoyed at a vision of Sam. Meanwhile, Sam is antagonized by images of Mattie's eyes appearing all around him, a representation through double exposure of what is in his mind as he tries to read a newspaper. To break his haunting by Mattie, Sam stands up and throws down his newspaper, which providentially lands with the classifieds section facing him, revealing many requests for barter. In double exposure, his grandfather looks benevolently over his shoulder. Mathis describes Sam putting his head back until it almost touches old Sam. An intertitle informs us, "The spirit of Samuel Weatherbee I had taken possession of young Sam, and every piece of junk had a meaning all its own."[87]

He immediately starts his bartering business like his grandfather had by trading with a Jewish tailor and his son.[88]

Dillingham Coolidge represents a suitable melodramatic bad guy as the greedy, malicious nemesis of the innocent underdog Sam. Whether or not "Junk's" author purposefully selected the character's name as a reference to the well-known figure soon to be president is impossible to learn. But the fact that this Coolidge ("Dill") is a shallow, deceitful capitalist who will stop at nothing to get what he wants, including Mattie, in both the story and film, might have been intended as a commentary on his real-life namesake and the financial system he represented. Not only does Dill try to take Mattie, but he also tries to thwart Sam's business.

Sam's grandfather's first trade was for a bolt of checked cloth that he used to make a pair of trousers that people recognized as a trademark for his business.[89] At the start of the film, Sam's home is presented through an intertitle that reads, "Upon the heights overlooking the Golden Gate stood the Weatherbee mansion—a monument to perseverance—and checked trousers."[90] Sam's first trade outdoes his grandfather by having the Jewish tailor he trades with make him an entire checked suit. Later, the large trade center he builds downtown has checked floors, checked borders around the walls, and service people who wear checked overalls; Sam's secretary also wears a checked skirt. This element, however, allows Mathis and Karger to criticize classism as Sam's gaudy establishment embarrasses the other business people of the area, including Dillingham.

Showing their prejudice, some of the other business owners complain about Sam to Dill's wealthy father. One calls his clients a health hazard. But Sam, like Mathis, achieved his success by working directly with these "Others," people often marginalized and excluded in American film and society. In the film's philosophy, these people simply need to find the right place to be useful. But the film's most culturally critical line comes from Sam's complaint about the self-humiliation required for commercial success: "I've sacrificed my pride—worn these freak clothes, labeled myself the 'Junk King.'"

He recognizes the hollowness of his image, partly because his goal is not the money or power but to win the woman he loves. Sam justifies himself in the end, a point at which Karger's suggestions seem most questionable. In scenes 247–265, Karger cuts the sequence in which Sam asserts the value and honor of his business to Dill and talks of people being discarded as well. Karger doesn't see the need for all this though it is important for the film's message. Fortunately, the material stayed in.

The Idle Rich exemplifies how melodrama could focus on politics or social systems such as capitalism, socialism, or communism. But its message of hope for unity and peace had to appeal to a broad audience and therefore avoid the suggestion of practical proposals that might prove divisive. As a result, spiritual forces such as the ghost of Samuel Weatherbee I, which could negate the worst consequences of capitalism and modernity, could be a logical choice. As a comedy, *The Idle Rich* could address social issues and stay in tune with audience tastes. Following the suffering and chaos of the Great War, people wanted to cut loose and have fun. Order, regimentation, militarism, and social hierarchies had produced years of death and gloom. The public might make a nod toward serious considerations of peace. But mainly, it seemed to want new cars, new fashions, easy profits, and fun.[91] In contrast, serious melodrama and spirituality looked past the physical world to a larger realm of existence.

Mathis and Karger followed up on *The Idle Rich* with a similar tale of business and love titled *Kisses* (1922). In this film, Alice Lake plays a young woman just out of college with a great candy recipe and friends to help her market her product. When her father dies leaving her with large debts, her fiancé leaves her. But her business success brings her a new love and financial relief. Reviewers generally praised the film's balance of comedy and drama with Mary Kelly writing in *Moving Picture World*, "The love affair is not precipitated but is kept subordinate for the sake of getting a more novel dramatic effect." She adds that pictures of this type "offer a refreshing change to anyone satiated with purely sentimental entertainment."[92]

For her final Metro production, Mathis again teamed up with Karger and Lake for *Hate*, a crime drama. In the story, "Babe Lenox [Lake] receives the attentions of two gamblers who are deadly enemies. One of the men kills himself and circumstantial evidence convicts the other. The girl fights for his life and after saving him by finding a note left by the gambler before he died, turns about and marries the prosecuting attorney."[93] Reviewers offered significantly high praise for Mathis's work with Kelly writing, "It offers a relief from the obviously moral picture with its sharp delineations of the good man and the bad man. Each one of the girl's suitors is a human composite of weakness and strength, and the shifting of sympathies is one of the several proofs of the film's realism."[94] While the *Film Daily* reviewer found the plot too complicated, those from *Variety* and *Motion Picture News* specifically praised Mathis.[95] Mary Kelly opined, "The conventional plot twists have been avoided and the result is

146

the ingenious development of a quadrangular love affair with just enough uncertainty to make it fascinating."[96]

In July 1922, Mathis left Famous Players-Lasky when Goldwyn gained the rights to *Ben-Hur* and signed her to produce it and write the screenplay. Goldwyn's new president Joe Godsol believed in her ability to take this major project and achieve the same success as she had with *The Four Horsemen*.[97] Unfortunately, Mathis's *Ben-Hur* production would drag on for two years and finally be disbanded although several reports stated that she had a draft of the script completed by December 1922.[98] Part of the reason for the delay was that Godsol added to Mathis's responsibilities by promoting her to editorial director by the end of the year. As a result, almost nothing was accomplished on Goldwyn's epic production through all of 1923 as Mathis approved other projects, wrote scripts and articles, did research, hired directors, and contributed to various other works in a variety of ways. Three of those films were Victor Sjöström's *Name the Man*, Herbert Brenon's *The Spanish Dancer*, and Tod Browning's *The Day of Faith*.

Mathis's move to bring acclaimed director Victor Sjöström to Goldwyn from Sweden indicates her awareness of international cinema and desire to work with filmmakers interested in artistic achievement. She defined him as "a man whom a London critic has called the greatest director in the world. . . . And in intellectual capacity and all around culture he will compare favorably with the leaders of any other art in the world."[99] Sjöström did not return the compliment. In a letter to his wife in March 1923, he wrote, "Remember what rubbish 'Blood and Sand' was. Miss Mathis over here wrote the script. Nisse [a close friend or colleague] has frequently talked about it and seems so proud of it. Oh, well—every once in a while I marvel to myself at his strange ideas."[100]

Sjöström provided more evidence of Mathis's full involvement in productions and attention to detail when he wrote home to his wife about the search for a suitable hairstyle for the female lead in *Name the Man*, his first American film: "Miss Mathis suggested braids twisted over her forehead, and I think it would be a good idea; we're going to try it anyway."[101] But in terms of budget management, Sjöström found the Goldwyn people quite lax: "Now they are going to find a man to write the script. They're going to look for someone whom they regard as the very best. Can you imagine, I heard them ([Goldwyn vice president Abraham] Lehr and Miss Mathis) talking about it and discussing what this man would ask for, and Miss Mathis said that she was quite sure he would want $4,000—more than

15,000 kronor in other words. 'Well then, that's what he's going to get,' Lehr answered. That's no small pittance, let me tell you."[102]

This expenditure was apparently worthwhile as *Name the Man* was both a critical and commercial success, but Mathis's production decisions indicate why Goldwyn experienced serious financial problems under her guidance. The film went 25 percent over budget with Sjöström shooting much more footage than he needed. Mathis was not bothered by this; she said they could just cut later, which she did, reducing the film's twelve acts to eight.[103]

Mathis's intense efforts often produced successful results when pursued in collaboration with the men around her. Director Herbert Brenon's production notes on *The Spanish Dancer* exemplify what Mathis may have defined as an ideal director/writer collaboration. Originally intended for Valentino, the production demanded extra work when it had to be rewritten for Pola Negri due to Valentino's contract dispute with Famous Players-Lasky.[104] Mathis's emphasis on detail, which she considered essential to artistic creation, is evident in the director's responses to her work. Brenon comments on one of Mathis's suggestions for cinematography: "I think I should shoot from the mansion toward the balustrade, as Miss Mathis suggests."[105] On the narrative, Brenon writes, "Miss Mathis makes the Spanish king of the play King Philip IV. All other adaptations agree in making him King Charles II. I strongly advise following Miss Mathis. Philip is a more vital and interesting personality than Charles—his court is more interesting—and the costumes of his period more attractive."[106]

Brenon directly credits Mathis with a number of other revisions including the following: "The death cart and Lazarillo's request for the body is from the Mathis continuity—it's all taken for granted in the play and no explanation offered as to why nobody disposed of the 'corpse' or evinced surprise when there was no 'corpse' to dispose of."[107] Brenon further comments, "Why should the King risk everything by coming to a private house (with a fete in progress, in all but the Mathis version!) when in a very few hours he is to have the lady all to himself at the hunting lodge?"[108] *The Spanish Dancer* was a potentially important transition film for its star, European import Negri, as she attempted to build a following by softening her vamp image. Mathis hit the target with her construction of the character as a "recuperation of the vamp, where Negri's character is neither a vision of purity nor a caricature of feminine evil: 'Here, rather than destroying her lover, she rehabilitates him.'"[109] This summary defines the same relationship of male and female leads in many of Mathis's most important works, which might suggest that her task was not too burdensome. Yet, for Mathis to take time to insert this amount of accurate detail into the script during this busy, high-pressure point in her career seems remarkable. Most critics deemed the effort superior to Mary Pickford's *Rosita* (Ernst Lubitsch), adapted from the same source and released simultaneously.[110] But it was not enough to fulfill Negri's goals as her "gypsy" character and vamp persona may have held her too tightly. Agata Frymus quotes Edward Said's relevant comment, "The very possibility of development, transformation, human movement— in the deepest sense of the world—is denied the Orient and the Oriental."[111]

In *The Day of Faith* (1923), which Katharine Kavanaugh coscripted, the main character exemplifies the classic melodramatic heroine who reforms others through spiritual goodness. Mathis's belief in the production may have been hers alone. Commenting on its sappy philosophy of "My Neighbor is Perfect," Goldwyn staff reader Margorie Eggleston commented, "For my part, I hesitate to believe that there is a public which would be seriously impressed with so uninteresting, undramatic, untrue a phrase."[112] Her skepticism is understandable, but some curious circumstances surrounding the production may explain Mathis's motivations. As the studio made plans to film *Ben-Hur* in Italy, it first produced a remake adaptation of Hall Caine's novel *The Eternal City*, originally filmed in 1915. The 1900 novel and original film both promoted Christian socialism. But Goldwyn revised its 1923 remake to include Mussolini as a heroic figure, much to Caine's displeasure.[113] At the same time, Victor Sjöström agreed to film Caine's *The Master of Man: The Story of a Sin* as *Name the Man*. As Goldwyn's editorial director, Mathis would have been involved in these decisions, and it is not impossible that she would have pushed Caine's novel to Sjöström as an appeasement to the author. In addition, the novel focuses on a woman carrying the child of a powerful judge and pressured to name him. Her *Ben-Hur* script would give prominence to the character Iras missing from all other adaptations of the work, and *Day of Faith* features a female leader of a broad humanitarian movement.

Although Tod Browning was struggling with alcohol, Goldwyn signed him to a very generous contract in February 1923. A week later, he presented Mathis with an original story he wanted to develop, which she found "very excellent." But she counseled he would be wiser to choose a well-known work to begin with and he agreed. She pushed a 1910 novel by Charles Tenney Jackson called *The Day of Souls* for which Goldwyn owned the rights. Browning said he liked it but that he would consider it for the future. For the present, he wanted something that promised a larger commercial success. After rejecting several other possibilities, he ended up with directorial duties for a different story of redemption with a similar title, *The Day of Faith.*[114]

In retrospect, Margorie Eggleston's feelings about the project may have been the most accurate. Audiences found scant validity in the story of Jane Maynard (Eleanor Boardman in her first starring role), who adopts the slogan "My Neighbor is Perfect" as the basis for the work of her Bland Hendricks Foundation, named after her inspiration, the man who first promoted it. Hendricks believed forgiveness would always work better than arrest and punishment, and Jane produces a successful movement based on that idea.

Among those who come to Jane's Foundation are lawbreakers who are forgiven and change their ways, a lame girl who has left her abusive father and miraculously regains her ability to walk, and cynical reporter Tom Barnett (Raymond Griffith) who intends to ridicule the organization but becomes a major promoter. Barnett's boss, newspaper magnate Michael Anstell (Tyrone Power) is furious at first but then sees a chance to use Jane's work for his own profit. Working as an unscrupulous and deceptive partner, Anstell builds enough resources to create the community of Anstellville. At a massive inaugural rally, his secretary reveals that Anstell only intends to use the Hendricks name to cheat people. The celebration quickly turns ugly as the crowd viciously attacks and kills Anstell's son. Holding his son's body, Anstell looks up to see a picture of Christ and the inscription "What does it profit a man to gain the whole world."[115] The script then quickly concludes with Anstell saying goodbye to Jane and Tom who have just won a declaration from Congress that every state should declare a Day of Faith. A title proclaims, "The idea can't be commercialized. The world will accept it when it's ready."[116]

Reviews of *The Day of Faith* were largely negative. Managers at the Ashland, Ohio, Palace Theater complained, "Booked it three days, ran it two days. Broke all records for poor business and we got all the business the picture deserved." The Russellville, Kentucky, Dixie Theater manager pronounced it "Absolutely rotten. Nothing to it. Lay off if you have it booked. Let them keep it in the exchange."[117] A summary of newspaper opinions in *Motion Picture News* included a series of glowing statements applauding the film as a "forceful compelling drama."[118] However, George T. Pardy found that the picture "lacks conviction . . . sincerity of purpose . . . and freedom from slushy sentiment."[119]

Writing in *Motion Picture News*, Laurence Reid seems to place most of the blame on the writing when he notes that the "melodramatic touches are so arbitrary—that reality is never suggested."[120] He praises Browning for keeping it interesting and guiding his cast well. In 1972, however, Boardman related, "I was brand new, scared and found Mr. Browning unattractive."[121] Browning worked hard at times as he got the film's budget increased and produced versions of twelve, nine, and ten reels that August. But he accepted some responsibility for the outcome, later admitting, "I wouldn't listen to reason. I was as stubborn as a mule—I wouldn't budge or make concessions, even when I knew inside that I was wrong. I quarreled constantly with the various and assorted swivel-chair bosses, and finally blew up and stalked out."[122] Whether these disagreements occurred during the filming, the editing, or both is unclear.

Whatever the production's flaws, Mathis now had to get focused on making *Ben-Hur*.

8

June Mathis's *Ben-Hur,* 1922–1924

Lea Jacobs, Gaylyn Studlar, and Ann Douglas all define American culture in the 1920s as dominated by a masculine ethos that demanded greater efficiency, productivity, and accountability. It was a time in which both the informal studio operations of the teens and the popularity of sentiment were rapidly falling. But matriarchal/feminine perspectives were still present, women were still fighting for and occupying executive positions, and June Mathis was still using melodrama to criticize war, violence, and greed, and elevate art and spirituality.

A summary of Mathis's professional life in 1922–1923 reveals that it was an incredibly busy period of transition. In 1922, she received credit on six feature films from two different studios, Metro and Famous Players-Lasky, and began work at a third, Goldwyn. Her assignment there would be to write the screenplay for one of the most highly anticipated productions of the era, *Ben-Hur*. Mathis began work on the script in July and was expected to finish by December, which she may have done.[1] But then she was offered and accepted the position of editor general at Goldwyn.[2] It seems that she could not say no to a challenge. As a result, 1923 was filled with hiring directors, approving and overseeing various productions, and writing three more scripts: *The Spanish Dancer, The Day of Faith,* and *In the Palace of the King*. She accomplished almost nothing on *Ben-Hur* during the entire year.

Meanwhile, the public became well aware of Mathis through her increased presence in the press. Goldwyn hyped her position by taking out a million-dollar life insurance policy on her and dubbing her "the million-dollar girl."[3] *Motion Picture Classic* published a spread of photos of her home, and *Photoplay* called her "probably the most powerful woman in the motion picture industry today."[4] The 1923 *Blue Book of the Screen* emphasized Mathis as "the only woman studio manager extant. She is in sole charge of Goldwyn production, with a corps of nine notable directors in action making special film productions."[5] The *Los Angeles Times* published a large article focused on her career and opinions.[6] She even had a cameo appearance in Rupert Hughes's comedy set in the film studios, *Souls for Sale*.[7]

But the publicity machine paid little attention to the personal upheavals she experienced simultaneously with these large career changes. No one can know the depths of her concerns about Valentino as she helped bail him out of jail and watched his career stagnate as Jesse Lasky forced him off the screen.[8] Her involvement in the dispute between Valentino and Ingram during *The Conquering Power*, which ended her creative partnership with the director, had potential emotional effects as well. Most important, though, was the death of her mother in New York on September 6, 1922.[9] She was followed in death by Mathis's stepfather in September 1923.[10] Mathis makes a brief comment about Virginia's death when questioned for a January 1924 article, and she mentions missing her stepfather in a 1926 article.[11] But to know the impact of these losses or of other disturbing events from her early childhood is sadly impossible. Mathis certainly knew of her biological father, the alcoholic con man Philip Hughes. Her 1922 Goldwyn biographical form refers to her father as descending from a long line of British scholars, which may be more of a reference to Philip, who emigrated from Wales as a child, than to stepfather William Mathis.[12] Whether Mathis knew about a sister, Alice, born in 1885 who died a year later and its impact on her is unknown. A 1923 picture of her in which she looks far older than her thirty-six years may provide some indication of the costs exacted by the combined stresses of grief and work. But we can only speculate that perhaps this series of personal losses and a life spent more on the road than at home may have influenced her desire to create great dramatic statements.

The film industry was also in a tumultuous period, especially for small companies and independent producers now being swallowed up by corporations. Thomas Schatz mentions that directors like Ingram, Stroheim, Maurice Tourneur, and Marshall Neilan who also wrote, produced, and edited their films were in serious conflict with the new centralized production system: "None could adjust to the steady fragmentation and the increasing constraints of studio filmmaking, and by . . . the late 1920s, . . . each of their careers was effectively finished."[13] Schatz does not mention women filmmakers such as Weber, Nazimova, and Mathis as similar artists who were also endangered by this trend. That responsibility fell to Karen Ward Mahar who writes eighteen years later, "Although Weber said in 1917 that she was not an 'idealist,' adding that all filmmakers were in business to make money, her methods sacrificed efficiency for art. 'Efficiency?' Weber exclaimed in 1918. 'Oh, how I hate that word!'" Weber preferred shooting scenes in sequence to assist actors' character development "long after other directors took all the shots requiring a particular background at once to save money."[14] In 1924, Mathis similarly explained, "I have my own ideas on how a picture should be filmed. Expense and arguments to the contrary notwithstanding. I believe our present habit of filming pictures in haphazard fashion without regard to continuity is very injurious to the spirit of a picture. How can an actor portray the little subtleties of a character if just because a company happens to be on location he has to play youth one morning and old age the next?"[15]

Mathis's move to Goldwyn in 1922 meant that her career would include working for both companies that soon merged into Metro-Goldwyn as each one lost its independence. Goldwyn's new owner, Joe Godsol, and president, Abe Lehr, were in desperate need of help when they signed Mathis to write the script for *Ben-Hur* on July 15. Production had slowed to a trickle with only seven films going before the cameras that year. Despite Goldwyn's shaky financial condition, Mathis had good reasons to sign with them. First of all, there was money. Benjamin Hampton writes, "Attracted by Miss Mathis' splendid success [with *The Four Horsemen*, Godsol] offered her a large salary to take full charge of his studio's professional department, and she accepted."[16] Second, Goldwyn had fine production facilities, and finally, she hoped to work with Valentino again on *Ben-Hur*. They had discussed making *Ben-Hur* together during the filming of *The Four Horsemen*, and she later tried to negotiate his release from Famous Players-Lasky to make his appearance possible.[17] Mathis's research assistant, Abe Mass, had further thoughts about the casting. He noted at the end of eighteen pages of research, "What a wonderful pair to have playing as the two friends— Valentino as Ben-Hur, and Ben-Ami as Messala, the Roman. The acting would prove a knockout. Ben-Ami being a Jew and naturally having the habit of gesticulating in his speech, would make a marvelous Roman."[18]

As conditions deteriorated, Godsol and Lehr turned increasingly to Mathis for help and made her greatest goals look obtainable. On September 8, 1922, Abe Erlanger, possessor of production rights for *Ben-Hur*, announced that Mathis had signed to write the scenario, collaborate on the production, and edit the film.[19] A November 18 report stated that Mathis was traveling from New York to Los Angeles where she would complete work on the screenplay in collaboration with Goldwyn executives.[20] But then Godsol, hoping to protect the millions he had invested into the studio, decided to put Mathis in charge of all production decisions by naming her editorial director in December 1922.[21] The press, as noted, followed with a chorus of praise. In August 1923, Frederick Van Vranken wrote in *Motion Picture Magazine*, "The part June Mathis alone has played in the evolution of the cinema is sufficient reason to give women a high and permanent rank in picture production. She is the Editorial Director of Goldwyn Pictures and the first woman ever to hold so responsible a post, which carries with it the responsibility for the outlay of millions of dollars yearly."[22] Mathis made some strong moves by bringing in skilled directors like Marshall Neilan, King Vidor, Tod Browning, and Victor Sjöström, and best-selling novelist Elinor Glyn as well.[23] In 1923, Goldwyn's production rose to fifteen films. But neither June Mathis nor any other individual was likely to have the skills needed to help the studio survive. In particular, Mathis's missteps on *Ben-Hur* show that her ignorance of the film industry's new organization and efficiency methods left her unable to meet the studio's needs at this critical time. Her attempt to control the project as she had *The Four Horsemen* would fail because her practices were out of step with the changes in Hollywood.

As Hampton writes, producing a single blockbuster is very different from managing a full schedule of productions: "It is one matter to organize a small staff, a single unit, to produce one picture in four to six months, but it is quite another to direct the operations of a large studio."[24] In addition, "Women filmmakers were incompatible with [the] newly emerging image of an efficient, big-business Hollywood, particularly in the eyes of New York capital; Wall Streeters would trust their dollars only to other men."[25] Mathis may have been particularly ill-suited for her high position at this time because her interests were with reaching her artistic goals, not with solving the company's financial problems. Godsol and Lehr deserve credit for promoting a woman at a time when most other companies were cutting them. But Mathis's privileging of art over commerce was totally at odds with Hollywood's profit orientation. As Hampton argues, Mathis sabotaged her own efforts: "When Miss Mathis assumed the duties of her Goldwyn position she organized a committee to pass on production, and made the mistake of including in it authors of smart stage plays, a professional dramatic critic, and a few writers whose principal work had been confined to essays and articles for intellectual magazines. These sophisticates strenuously and sarcastically condemned as 'melodrama' and 'hokum' all suggestions of widely popular themes and treatments, and Miss Mathis permitted herself to be convinced that movie audiences were ready to assimilate a higher class or ration."[26]

Most likely, Mathis appointed members with views that she knew supported her own. Hampton continues, "The studio steadily swung away from the showman ingredients of screen construction, and most of its offerings became smart, modernistic themes selected to win the approval of the intelligentsia. Many of the pictures produced under Miss Mathis' administration were technically excellent, but too many of them were almost totally lacking in entertainment value for large audiences. The costs were very high, and the burden of losses became so great that the corporation succumbed and its properties passed into a merger of several companies."[27]

Goldwyn's moves created a huge increase in Mathis's workload, to which she responded by making her situation more difficult. Rather than reviewing all productions to find cost savings and contacting financiers to find the best path forward, Mathis immediately used her influence to have Lehr hire director Erich von Stroheim, thereby committing the studio to a second massive production impossible to complete: *Greed*.[28] Stroheim was a talented and eccentric writer/director whose obsession with realism and details far outdistanced Mathis's, which may be why she admired him. While at Universal, he made the highly acclaimed *Blind Husbands* (1919) and *Foolish Wives* (1922), neither without controversy over his methods and expenses, before Irving Thalberg fired him from the filming of *Merry-Go-Round*, which was finished by director Rupert Julien. Stroheim then needed a place to make his massive adaptation of novelist Frank Norris's *McTeague*, which was eventually re-titled *Greed*. Mathis gave him a new home at Goldwyn with no restrictions on his contract.[29]

Mathis claimed to have a special affinity for Stroheim's project, and he considered her a kindred spirit. He is pictured with his arm around her in the 1923 *Blue Book of the Screen*.[30] Mathis noted that as a girl, she had "lived on the very street in the heart of the very district in which Norris laid his novel." In February 1924, she told the press, "It gives me a great deal of pleasure that McTeague is coming to the screen just as Frank Norris wrote it."[31] Historian Lewis Jacobs writes of *Greed*'s production in the same manner as Brownlow does about *The Four Horsemen*, marking it as another example of Mathis's daring and dedication to what she considered meaningful: "It is singular that any studio should have allowed this ex-Austrian [Stroheim] to direct such a highly realistic dramatization of American working-class life, a dramatization certainly out of tune with the times. *Greed* was, at any rate, the last of the films about the working man in that period: the culmination of the tradition that had borne [Edwin S.] Porter and [D. W.] Griffith."[32] Stroheim's intention to capture the gritty realism of working-class life and his pronounced intention to film the entire novel as written probably further attracted Mathis. She added to her comments, "You may hear that [the film's characters] have been exaggerated, that they are not true to life, but I can tell you they are real, vital human beings described by Norris as they actually were, as he knew them and as I knew them."[33]

Stroheim's experience with this acknowledged masterpiece involved creating an original version of forty-two or forty-five reels, approximately nine hours, which was eventually reduced to a two-hour version of ten reels.[34] Over the years, film historians have written various accounts of Mathis's role in this massive cut most of which have damaged her reputation. Jacobs was the first to claim that Mathis cut the film from forty-two reels to ten, even though he refers to her as "the most esteemed scenarist in Hollywood."[35] In 1960, Bosley Crowther wrote that Abe Lehr "despairingly gave [Stroheim's complete film] to June Mathis . . . to cut. She trimmed about a third" of it.[36] Roger Manvell states that Stroheim gave his forty-two reels to Ingram and Mathis who cut it from ten hours of screen time to four.[37] Then in 1972, Georges Sadoul sullied Mathis's reputation when he wrote of the final editing, "Irving Thalberg . . . stepped in, took the final cut of *Greed* out of Stroheim's hands, and turned it over to the pork butcher, June Mathis, to chop into pieces."[38] A decade later, Richard Koszarski argues that as Stroheim's contract required a film of twelve reels, Mathis created a thirteen-reel version by January 21, 1924.[39] More recently, Ruth Barton states that Ingram gave a twenty-six- to twenty-eight-reel version to editor Grant Whytock in March 1924 who divided the film in two and cut unnecessary parts.[40] For the final release version, Metro-Goldwyn-Mayer (MGM), now in control of the property, handed the film to Joseph Farnham, whom Stroheim said "had nothing on his mind but a hat."[41]

Mathis's exact role in cutting the large bulk of material from *Greed* will never be known. But evidence of skillfully suggested cuts she made for part of the film at a time when her life could not have been busier does exist. On February 10, 1924, the New York *Morning Telegraph* reported, "June Mathis is the essence of the motion picture business. She fairly lives and breathes motion pictures, and if ever a woman had her hand on the pulse of the film industry, it is this indefatigable worker. . . . In addition to her preparation of the script of 'Ben-Hur' she has been hovering like a guardian angel over Von Stroheim's production of 'Greed.'"[42] On January 29, eight days before leaving for Europe, Mathis telegrammed a seven-page memo defining further cuts for *Greed* that suggest the guardian angel metaphor was fairly accurate and reveal her skill for excising unnecessary material.[43] These suggestions were for brief cuts from most of the reels and some shifting of material from one reel to another to cover gaps. Some of these were of little consequence except to quicken the pace. For example, in reel 7, she cuts shots of a cat's head and an iris down to its eyes. In reel 8, she cut shots of Trina, the female lead, crying and saying, "Oh, Mac—we're ruined!" Cuts of thirteen scenes (in a silent film script, a scene might refer to just one shot or several) in reel 9 heighten the tension between Mac and Trina. But the cuts could also have thematic significance. Her cut in reel 6 of Trina looking happy as gold coins pour through her hands not only condenses the material but gives more emphasis to the hands, an important motif in *Greed*, as what hands do and what they reach for tells a lot about people. In a previous dinner scene, characters are reminded about cleanliness and civility when they reach across the table for food. Here, Trina's small hands cannot hold many coins, but she enjoys playing with them anyway. Eventually, she loses a finger and can hold even less. Mac ultimately dies from having his hands cuffed to another character in the desert.[44]

Eight days after submitting these cuts, Mathis left for Rome, and editing on *Greed* halted until after Goldwyn was absorbed by Metro-Goldwyn. Their executives, Louis B. Mayer and Irving Thalberg, gave the twenty-four-reel version to either Joseph Farnham or Arthur Ripley, who produced the ten-reel version. Some inept final titles like the infamous "Let's go over and sit on the sewer" lent a ludicrous tone to the production.[45] For the released version, "Farnham received screen credit for editing, and Mathis shared writing credit with von Stroheim, a contractual billing." Koszarski adds, "If June Mathis had stayed on the project, the results might have been better."[46]

But editing *Greed* was only one task Mathis had to complete before sailing for Europe on February 6; she still had to pull the production of *Ben-Hur* together. The novel by General Lew Wallace, published in 1880, was a huge bestseller. Mark Vieira writes, "By the end of the century, only the Bible was selling more copies." As a stage play, "the property's success again exceeded expectations, running consistently into the 1920s."[47] To obtain the rights to *Ben-Hur* from theater entrepreneur Abraham Erlanger, Goldwyn granted him the right of final approval on "the cast, the scenario and all the various details of the production," which may have contributed to the production's massive delays.⁴⁸ Erlanger had to review and approve Mathis's every decision and revision before she could move on. Furthermore, although Mathis was not supposed to be finished with the script until the end of the year, grumblings about the project at Goldwyn began much sooner. In June 1922, writer Paul Bern began a regular correspondence with casting director R. B. McIntyre about people interested in working on *Ben-Hur*. On November 3, he mentioned someone named Macey Harlam, noting, "He might be a good name to remember when we make the production, which ought to be sometime within the next ten or twelve years."⁴⁹ With important studio personnel like Bern already complaining about the slow pace of production, Mathis's promotion to editor general in December 1922 does not seem to have been wise. Godsol was obviously hoping for a repeat of *The Four Horsemen*'s success.

But despite the pressure, very little progress on *Ben-Hur* occurred throughout 1923, a mystery that raises serious questions about Mathis's management capabilities and those of the Goldwyn organization in general. While their attention turned to productions like *In the Palace of the King* and *The Day of Faith*, critical decisions about issues such as location, costumes, wigs, the cast, and the director of *Ben-Hur* were delayed. On July 1, 1922, *Motion Picture News* reported, "The picture will be but partly made at the Culver City studios of the Goldwyn Corporation; steps are already under way for an expedition to Palastine [*sic*] itself, where most of the action takes place, to film the exteriors. Entire temporary cities will be built there in order to reproduce the civic and architectural features of Palastine [*sic*] in the time of Christ. An army of experts will be employed for that purpose. Parts of the picture will be made in Italy."⁵⁰ Kevin Brownlow asserts that it was Mathis who insisted that the film be shot in Italy.⁵¹ But maybe she began to have doubts because on January 20, 1923, screenwriting colleague Carey Wilson (who eventually cowrote the script for the MGM production with Bess Meredyth) sent Mathis a memo about a possible location "thirty-seven miles from San Diego, [in the] town of Redondo, Mexico, from which may be secured a vista of country and hills [which is] practically an exact replica of the Holy Land and Mount of Olives."⁵² Wilson also let her know where she could get further information and photos of the location. Nevertheless, on October 13, *Motion Picture World* reported, "Nothing, not even the interior shots, will be made in American studios. Models of the settings have been made and these will be taken abroad to be constructed on a vast scale in Italy, Egypt and the Holy City."[53] The article also states that set construction and principal photography were expected to take about a year.

On February 1, 1923, producer/distributor George Kleine stopped to see Erlanger at his office in New York to discuss *Ben-Hur*. Erlanger tried to claim that the production was going well and give himself credit: "Mr. Erlanger indicated a great deal of self-confidence in passing judgment upon film production; stated that Miss Mathis had worked out a Ben Hur scenario at his desk and under his direction which was stronger than either the play or the book."[54] In the existing script, Erlanger's influence is only occasionally evident as when Mathis notes, "This should be a man who is to be made up like the picture of Joseph [in the scene of Jesus's birth] in Mr. Erlanger's book."[55] In another scene, she writes, "Mr. Erlanger would like to have the sound of the real trumpet in this scene."[56] (Mathis's script is for a gala presentation that would include an orchestra and choir.)

Kleine's memo shows he was not buying Erlanger's story: "It was probably a matter of tactics on his part that [Erlanger] did not refer to Ben Hur until toward the end of our interview." Kleine's notes suggest Erlanger did not actually feel confident about the status of the project at all, and his use of his time to visit Erlanger and type his memo indicates that people with financial interests in the project were feeling nervous. In another paragraph, Kleine focuses on the costs such as one single set priced at $60,000 and the overall production estimated to run between $700,000 and $1,400,000. Erlanger may have been trying to boost Kleine's confidence when "some one telephoned him, and he stated that it would be worth $100,000.00 if Miss Mathis came East, presumably in connection with the script."[57] Most likely, Erlanger's apparent willingness to suddenly add such a huge amount to the budget only added to Kleine's concerns.

On October 23, 1923, Mathis named Charles Brabin as director because she said she had long admired him "and considered his directorial method perfect." She claimed that she "had selected Rex Ingram to direct the 'Four Horsemen' because he had worked under Brabin."[58] Brabin did have his admirers, especially for his film *Driven*, an independent production of 1923.[59] *Moving Picture World* noted some attributes of questionable relevance: "He has been a student of Bible history for many years, knows Europe and the continent perfectly, and is an accomplished linguist." More defensible was the idea that "Mathis and Brabin were working shoulder to shoulder in the old Metro days and Miss Mathis knows what Mr. Brabin can do."[60]

This statement carries some validity as Mathis later noted her planning for the production made considerations for Brabin's preferences. Mathis clearly constructed part of her script with Brabin in mind because it contains her considerations of how to work with him and the need to move fast on revisions when the time came. Furthermore, she was cleverly attempting to use the arrangement with Erlanger and the need to pick up the work pace to gain leverage with the director. She noted, "This picture is heavily scene numbered, but I have played safe with numbers and scenes, knowing Mr. Brabin's dislike to taking close-ups, and feeling that once the script is okayed by Mr. Erlanger, he will agree to take close-ups without discussion which would take up time, and of course time is the most important item I can name."[61] This would be useful knowledge and smart tactics, but the true nature of the Mathis/Brabin relationship is questionable. While they may have conversed about various projects during their days together at Metro, their only previously completed films were *Red, White and Blue Blood* (1917), a Bushman and Bayne mystery, and *His Bonded Wife* (1918), a film whose bizarre plot sounds like a comedy until the description of the wife shooting her husband near the end. Ultimately, when they finally got to Italy, Brabin was in charge of his set and uninterested in any contributions from Mathis.

But the major topic in the press about *Ben-Hur* throughout 1923 was who would play the lead. A poll in April placed Valentino as the top choice among fans.[62] Judah Ben-Hur would have been remarkably similar to the characters Mathis created for him in the other five films they did together, and the work contained a similar theme. Fatherless from the start, Ben-Hur (like Julio Desnoyers et al.) also spends the narrative seeking a father figure and trying to get home. His ultimate guidance comes through the light of Christ, not the wealthy merchants who assist him or the Romans who train him. But with Valentino out of the running, the search for the lead dragged on. Among those considered were "John Bowers, Bob Fraser, Antonio Moreno, Ben Lyon, Edmund Lowe, Ramon Novarro, Bill Desmond, [and] Allan Forrest."[63] In May, *Photoplay*'s Herbert Howe quipped that they had discovered who would play Ben-Hur. It was child star Jackie Coogan, and the film would probably win best picture for 1940.[64]

Mathis finally awarded the part to George Walsh, brother of director Raoul, in December. Harry Carr of *Motion Picture Magazine* expressed strong doubts about the selection: "Walsh has been on the screen for years and his screen career, to be frank about it, has not been much of a success."[65] But he had made a successful comeback six months earlier in Hugo Ballin's

Vanity Fair (1923), which influenced Mathis to sign him to Goldwyn and Mary Pickford to cast him as her costar in *Rosita*. In the same issue of *Motion Picture Magazine*, journalist Tamar Lane boasted that she had been "the first to suggest Walsh as the logical Ben-Hur" because he "answer[ed] the demands of the role better than any other player on the screen today."[66] *Motion Picture Classic*, however, emphasized the doubts about his ability. It greeted the news with a couple of pictures of Walsh in costume and a brief caption stating, "What magic Miss Mathis used we do not know, but they finally decided to let George do it. Perhaps these poses helped their decision. He looks like Ben-Hur anyway."[67] Other press items suggested that romance was involved in the casting as Walsh and Mathis were secretly engaged.[68]

Mathis explained her reasons, which are consistent with how she always spoke of actors in relation to themes. She told *Screenland*'s Eunice Marshall, "Because of his eyes mostly. They have the so-rare quality of spirituality. Did you see Rosita in the dungeon scene, where Walsh took the sacrament? Did you see the spiritual look in his eyes—the light of one who dreams and dreams and sees visions? That was the spirit I wanted for Ben. Too, he has an 'old world' face."[69] Mathis had a logical reason for basing her decisions on actors' eyes: "Whenever I view a possible choice for a role, I first notice the eyes. There I find what I call the soul. You may alter everything except your eyes, in these days when tucks are taken in necks, chins blunted or sharpened and noses remodeled at will. Hair may be dyed, eyebrows plucked and teeth replaced, but the soul that looks out of the eyes is the real 'you.'"[70] But she also considered the body: "Ben-Hur had a beautiful body; he gloried in it." She related this to the story's theme, which she defined as "the spirit of revenge conquered at last by the message of the Christ; a man of enormous strength and virility, motivated for years by the lust for revenge for a terrible wrong, softened at the last by a spiritual love."[71] The spiritual overcoming the physical was Mathis's constant theme. Nevertheless, Marshall was unconvinced and finished her piece by writing, "It all sounds great. But, oh, June Mathis! We wish you hadn't let George do it!"[72]

As preparations dragged on into 1924, other issues behind the scenes were also causing problems. On January 5, 7, and 9, Mathis, Goldwyn vice president Abraham Lehr, and casting director McIntyre sent memos to each other regarding wigs.[73] On January 9, 1924, a telegram from Lehr to Mathis indicates that negotiations with the Wallace family during the previous year may have also caused delay. Lehr refers to a memo from Godsol that offered "Congratulations [on the] Outcome [of] Wallace Matters to Date" and said that the studio should "Consider Delays [a] Blessing In Disguise [as] Preliminary Preparations Research Will Effect Economics And Excellent Production."[74]

Much of the casting was also yet to be completed in early 1924. On January 23, McIntyre sent a memo to Lehr stating,

> Miss Mathis does not want Marc McDermott
> Miss Mathis is interested in the man who played "Nelson" in "Lord and Lady Hamilton" and the somnambulist in "The Cabinet of Dr. Caligari." As far as Miss Mathis is concerned, she is willing to wait until after she gets abroad and considers this other man before we make a decision [for the part of Simonides].[75]

Mathis's recognition of the remarkable Conrad Veidt in *Caligari* speaks well of her ability to recognize talent. But she ultimately decided on Nigel de Brulier to play Simonides, whom McIntyre considered "an erratic damn fool."[76]

Yet, despite her heavy workload on *Greed* and *Ben-Hur*, immediately after departure for Europe, Mathis paid due deference to Goldwyn's men in charge with a telegram to Lehr: "Many Thanks Shall Do All In My Power To Make You Proud Of Me."[77]

Once in Europe, Mathis indulged in her lifelong affection for museums and wrote to her sister Laura Mary that in Paris she had gone "to Napoleon's tomb which is in a church, and to the Louvre and Trocadero Museums. Saw the outside of Notre Dame, but it was dark and I could not get in." Mathis was impressed, and perhaps thrilled, by the history she related. She had climbed to the top of her profession and was now experiencing a world she could have only dreamed about through reading. Past and present were opening to her as she explored Italy: "I forgot to tell you," she wrote Laura Mary, "about the trip to Anzio. Left Rome by the Appian Way, and then connected with the seaport town—all roads built by Caesar himself. We are going to do the Galley sequence down there, and it is a beautiful seaport on an arm of the Mediterranean; ancient wharfs built by Caesar, and the foundations of Nero's Summer palace, wave-washed at the present time; but one can pick up bits of marble here and there that had once been in the palace."[78] These places and their history meant something to Mathis. She shows a dedication to getting the names and details correct and seeing just "bits of marble here and there" could inspire her imagination of grandiose events.

Mathis's report on the trip to Anzio shows something of the American company's attitude toward Italians, whom they seemed to regard as quaint and unsophisticated. She wrote,

> The citizens tendered us some sort of ceremony, at Anzio, where we are to do the galley scenes. The city was presented with one hundred and fifty dollars—I never saw such a fuss made over that sum of money before. Colonel Braden (technical director), Mr. Brabin, Mr. Edington, the business manager, Mr. Boyle the cinematographer and myself partook of the repast they gave us.
>
> There were 25 Italian officials connected with the city and shipyards. They stood around and made speeches, to the accompaniment of the popping of champagne corks and the booming of vermouth and cordial bottles. Although it was seven o'clock in the evening they served us nothing but cake, pastries— and champagne.[79]

At this point, Mathis might still have been expecting, or just hoping, to achieve her vision for *Ben-Hur*. Discussions of the silent *Ben-Hur* production by Brownlow, Scott Eyman, and Andre Soares have focused on all the delays, disputes, and disasters of the Mathis/Brabin effort and Irving Thalberg's/Metro-Goldwyn's rescue of the project.[80] Practically no attention has been given to Mathis's script except to comment on its length, 1,722 scenes. Just as Victor Sjöström had scoffed at *Blood and Sand*, King Vidor, an early contender to direct *Ben-Hur*, dismissed the script he saw, which he said reminded him of the simple version (apparently the 1907 one-reeler) he had seen as a child.[81] Fred Niblo, who took over as director for MGM, was slightly more generous, calling it "a beautiful continuity of the terribly long story of Ben Hur as Lew Wallace wrote it. Nothing added and nothing left out. Just an impossibly long story and twice as long a continuity as it should be."[82]

But Mathis had a history of creating overly long scripts and was used to having directors alter or delete some of her work. Her attitude toward her *Ben-Hur* script was no different. In her "Cutting Notes on Ben-Hur" memo of January 26, she outlined plans to cut 177 scenes and explained that she had written far more scenes than necessary for the purpose of efficiency:

"All these same closeups and numbers will help us to eliminate footage later on, as they are written for cutting and not for directorial drama; for after all this picture is entirely cut in my own head now, and with a picture of this character, one must stop long walks and slowness of movement, or else we will have a very slow moving thing. This can only be eliminated in photographing many scenes, so that action can be broken up in cutting. And when all is said and done, even though the tempo of the scene action may be slow, the picture will move and not be draggy."[83] On January 30, 1924, a telegram from studio executive Edward Bowes promised a cut of at least 300 scenes.[84] Both messages show concern with saving time during the filming and the running of the film. Mathis also looked to save time during editing: "There are . . . many closeups which may not be used in the final cutting, and, of course, many of them will be taken all in one, without extra camera set-ups. This will take film but not extra time, and will form a sort of insurance." Mathis also refers to the problem of Erlanger's rights: "I did not attempt to cut on this until I had seen Mr. Erlanger as he had okayed the other continuity version, and I did not wish to have the Goldwyn people run into legal complications until I have seen him and discussed it, with the logical explanations, of which I think I can convince him."[85] Erlanger, it seems, certainly might have contributed to the delays due to exercising his contract rights.

Mathis's foresight in building considerations for filming, editing, and working with Erlanger into her script displays her professionalism. More importantly, the content of her work gives evidence of her devotion to artistry through her uses of imagery, narrative parallels, and characters to present her major theme of spiritual love overcoming the desire for revenge. Her inspiration may have come partially from her mother who, as one journalist stated, had the "passionate wish . . . that her daughter should be a force in bringing the drops of balm that 'Ben-Hur' has always been to other aching hearts."[86]

Since Mathis begins her script as the novel did, with the Magi as they become inspired to seek the Christ child, Niblo's impression of her script as overly faithful to the source is understandable. He might also be justified with his claim that Mathis's scenario was double the length that it should be. In commercial terms, a film of much more than two hours is a large gamble. Yet, the extremely successful 1959 version of *Ben-Hur* was three and a half hours long, and Mathis viewed her work similar to the way Stroheim approached his production of *Greed*. She had always emphasized her desire to capture the full spirit of a novel as Stroheim did with *Greed*. But while Stroheim's struggle became a major case history for film studies, Mathis's effort received scant recognition.

With *Ben-Hur*, Mathis was working in familiar melodramatic territory. To David Mayer, Judah Ben-Hur is a typical melodramatic character, a mere shell to be manipulated according to the omniscient narrator's will in order to illustrate his message.[87] The work's genre features include its spectacular plot with characters who, though often missing and presumed dead, or having no knowledge of their past connections, and despite being separated by hundreds of miles at a time of poor transportation, keep meeting each other at exactly the right times in order to resolve their conflicts or achieve their goals. This world is one in which order exists; characters simply need to acclimate themselves to it.

Mathis opens her script by setting the stage for the film's premiere as she refers to a "specially designed curtain . . . disclosing a dark stage." Then, in a device that might typically be associated with the avant-garde, Mathis introduces her major motif through the projector's beam, God-like and spiritual, enlightening the screen.[88] This detail firmly establishes the need for the audience and all humankind to lift their heads to receive a new light. Characters' continual gaze toward the heavens signifies an awakened people anticipating a light to lift their oppression.[89] This motif begins when the projector's beam hits the screen and continues through scenes of angels and stars that appear to the wise men who will seek Jesus at his birth. Mathis begins by showing the Old Testament prophet Isaiah on a mountaintop. Archangel Michael appears to him in a ray of light that slowly shines down from heaven. Then the angels Jophiel and Raphael show the wise men Balthazar and Melchior stars that first appear in the water below them and then rise into the sky. The angel Uriel, holding a book, appears to the wise man Caspar, and the book dissolves into a star. In each case, the angels and stars either literally or figuratively awaken men and lift their eyes to the heavens.[90]

Mathis associates light from above and below with Christ at the stable in Bethlehem. She first describes a great rock that conceals the place with light coming from below. The light from the star grows bright and comes to meet it, which creates a rainbow to be shown through double exposure over the setting. Appropriately, the following title quotes the Old Testament book of Isaiah: "The people that walk in darkness have seen a great light. They that dwell in the land of the Shadow of Death; upon them hath the light shined."[91]

Mathis's idea of light as providing guidance for troubled humanity was not original to her adaptation. In 1890, after years of resistance, Lew Wallace finally allowed a stage adaptation of *Ben-Hur* with the proviso that Jesus was not to be depicted by an actor but by a beam of light.[92] Wallace, a former Union General and lawyer, wrote *Ben-Hur* while serving as governor of the territory of New Mexico. While the novel presents a classically modeled male-centered tale focused on the wealthy and powerful, women, servants, and people of all races and faiths play positive and important roles. These messages were relevant for a postwar United States struggling with the temptations of rampant capitalism and imperialism and the challenges of incorporating cultural diversity. Wallace defines Christianity as a religion with a primary message of love and acceptance set in contrast with Roman values of militarism and oppression. He wrote with the belief that these messages were needed in post–Civil War America.[93] As previously noted, Mathis's work, like much of American silent film, sometimes expresses racist attitudes. Nevertheless, her works from the early twenties, like *Ben-Hur*, often exhibit these themes of tolerance and inclusion.

In her screenplays, Mathis consistently emphasizes diversity in terms of both faith and ethnicity. *The Four Horsemen of the Apocalypse*, *A Trip to Paradise*, and *Hearts Are Trumps* (all 1921); *Blood and Sand* and *The Young Rajah* (both 1922); and *The Day of Faith* (1923) use iconography from and references to Christianity, Hinduism, mythology, and mysticism to present themes of spiritual guidance. She had a similar vision of *Ben-Hur*, saying, "It is the most widely read novel in the world, having its appeal for Christian and Jew alike."[94] Thus, Mathis has each of the wise men leave their old traditions in search of a new and unifying answer, an apt idea for the post–World War I era. Balthazar is introduced speaking to his Egyptian countrymen about monotheism. Feeling rejected, he walks to an ancient shrine created by the Pharaohs; a light that appears in the water surrounding the shrine forms into a star.[95] Melchior is introduced in front of an ancient rock-hewn shrine built to the Hindu God Brahma, and Caspar is found asleep in front of a Greek temple after a pan down from Olympus.[96]

As the angels call to the wise men, Mathis begins to establish her theme of tolerance and diversity with references to the Magi's nationalities similar to the way she references a wide range of ethnicities at the start of *The Idle Rich*. The angels who call the Magi name their homelands of Athens, Egypt, and India as Mathis wants it clear that they come "from the far quarters of the earth [to] see the Redeemer, and witness that he hath come!"[97]

On her approach to the adaptation, Mathis said, "Faithfulness to General Wallace's story was a requisite and I have been faithful to it in preparing the continuity; . . . those who see the completed film will find that the story has not been distorted in any particular in turning it into a motion picture."[98] For Mathis, this statement was largely true, yet she makes several purposeful changes. She introduces the Hurs' servant and custodian of their fortune, Simonides, at the Hur household at the beginning so that the audience gets to know him although Judah does not. Introducing Simonides early establishes his close relationship with the family. Similarly, Thord, the gladiator instructor, is introduced while training Judah during his years in the tribune Arrius's household in Rome. Wallace does not introduce him until his description of the athletic competition just before the chariot race and after Judah left Rome. Mathis also has Judah learn about the chariot race and his enemy Messala's participation in it from a poster he sees during his first visit with Simonides at his home in Athens. Wallace has him making all these decisions about participation in the race in a moment of inspiration just after saving the wise man Balthazar and his daughter Iras from Messala's chariot in the Grove of Daphne. Overall, these changes combine material from two scenes into one, help audiences identify characters, and make Judah Ben-Hur a much more human and believable character, better able to use his intelligence rather than giving in to impulse.

Faithfulness to the novel also gives Mathis another opportunity to present homosexual desire on-screen as she had done in *The Four Horsemen*. It occurs in a scene revised from the novel as the Romans are indulging in wild debauchery on the night before the chariot race. Wallace's passage reads, "from the floor where he had fallen, a youth was brought forward, so effeminately beautiful he might have passed for the drinking-god himself— only the crown would have dropped from his head and the thyrsus from his hand." Ben-Hur's childhood friend, now his enemy, Messala pays homage to the boy as a representative of Bacchus, and Wallace finishes the chapter with "There was a shout that set the floor to shaking and the grim Atlantes to dancing, and the orgies began."[99] Mathis transcribes this in her script as,

> Just at this point a huge dark-skinned slave, bronzed all over to
> reflect the light and to make him a thing of beauty, enters, bearing
> upon his back a white boy, who has been painted silver. He is
> nude but for a jeweled clout, and wearing a weird headdress,
> with cymbals in his hands; he is carried to the table clanging the

cymbals. The slave places him upon the table where he starts to dance. This relieves the tenseness of the situation. The Romans sink back upon their couches, and start to sip their wine, and look toward the dancer with interest. Messala still sits, a trifle serious; and after a moment disperses the thought and proceeds to join in the revelry.[100]

Mathis's more specific description of male nudity and homoerotic desires suggests that she is once again consciously communicating with those in the audience "who had truly lived" as she had with the Germans-in-drag scene in *The Four Horsemen*.

In the chariot race, the major spectacle of *Ben-Hur*, Mathis continues to emphasize ethnic and religious diversity and unity. Shots of the crowd show Arabs and Jews separately but united in their support for Ben-Hur and hatred of Rome. As Messala cheats by using his whip on Ben-Hur's horses late in the race, their owner, Sheik Ilderim, cries from the stands, "May Allah strike thee as thou hast my desert beauties!"[101] Shortly thereafter, his prayer is answered as Messala experiences a crippling accident. At the same time, as Ben-Hur realizes his impending victory, "a gleam of triumph comes into his eyes. God has answered his prayer. His score is settled with his enemy."[102] Thus, it would seem, the deities of two faiths have cooperated in producing this outcome. Characteristically, Mathis then blends in a reference to mythic determinism in a title following the race: "The weaver sits weaving, and as the shuttle flies the cloth increases; the figure grows, and the dreams develop! Of such is the fabric of life."[103]

Beyond her depictions of ethnic and religious diversity, Mathis also intended to present sexuality and women with honesty and complexity. The MGM production would include both men and women as objects of visual pleasure. In a galley scene, a naked man is chained to a wall, his back to the camera, but fully visible from head to knees. The most logical explanation of this would be that he is a galley slave receiving punishment. Illogically, though, he appears to be in great physical condition. Maybe he had just arrived and had not learned how to behave yet. Female nudity appears with several bare-breasted women leading a parade through Rome celebrating Ben-Hur's athletic triumphs, a spectacle increased by filming the scene in color.

Mathis's more thoughtful handling of sexuality combined with a notable blending with spirituality is evident in the character of Iras. This character's plea for Judah to show mercy to the crippled Messala is a deeply Christian moment, in a feminist sense, not included in any version of *Ben-Hur*. As a writer steeped in melodrama, adapting an epic novel that audiences loved for its stereotypical characters, Mathis might have been expected to simply condense the book, throw in some favorite moments from the stage play, and celebrate the heroic main character. Yet, she did none of these. Instead, her version emphasizes spiritual guidance over masculine heroism. Mathis presents these ideas through the major motif of light as both the light of Christ and of the cinema, the theme of spiritual and ethnic inclusiveness, and the spiritual message that once again comes via a woman. Mathis, however, does not have the sweetly innocent Esther, Ben-Hur's fiancée, nor Tirzah, his sister, Amrah, the treasured family servant, or his beloved mother convey this message. It comes instead from the unrepentantly wicked Iras, a great contrast to the long-suffering heroines of her earlier films played by Alla Nazimova, Viola Dana, and Eleanor Boardman. In melodrama, as stated, reality includes a spiritual realm, both morally and ethically stable, that the main character needs to recognize and grow into. But here, Mathis gives the film's most enlightened statement to the woman who remains unredeemed.

David Mayer asks why a character in a standard role, Iras, "so central to the functioning of melodrama, . . . one of the more interesting of all nineteenth-century adventuresses be marginalized or excised in stage and film adaptations of the novel?" His conclusion is that perhaps "her sexualized subversiveness has been considered inappropriate to a narrative that also contains Jesus."[104] In both the novel and the stage play, Iras is the daughter of the wise man Balthazar who first worshipped the Christ child, but she does not accept his idea of Jesus as the promised savior. She is solely interested in personal gain, constantly shifting allegiance between Ben-Hur and Messala to obtain the best situation for herself. Wallace makes her a major character but eventually finishes her off according to the simplistic morality of standard melodrama. He suggests that Iras, weary of caring for the broken and impoverished Messala after the chariot race and incapable of seeking redemption (though the righteous Esther promises she and Ben-Hur will forgive, befriend, and care for her), finally murders him and then drowns herself.[105] At the conclusion of William Young's play, Ben-Hur still hates Iras for her betrayal and refuses to forgive her or his childhood friend. Most readers and viewers of 1880–1920 would have been likely to cheer these outcomes as just punishments for the evil.

Film versions, as David Mayer notes, have done even less with the character: "Fred Niblo's 1925 *Ben-Hur* allowed Iras the merest walk-on part, whilst [William] Wyler's 1959 adaptation eliminated her altogether."[106] Niblo's Iras is simply evil, a vamp who tries to help Messala destroy Ben-Hur and then disappears. She is not the daughter of Balthazar, and she has no motivation. For filmmakers, it seems, Iras added too much complexity to an already-loaded plot. Mayer concludes, "With the women's healing [ridding Ben-Hur's mother and sister of leprosy] and Judah's conversion still to be dramatized, both directors found it far easier to kill off Messala and to elide the episodes in which Judah [Ben-Hur] is lured to the Palace of Ildernee and confronts Iras."[107]

Mathis's Iras is more human, more complex, and therefore more sympathetic. More modern woman than melodramatic vamp, she shows "great love for Messala" although he is crippled and penniless. In a key scene, she ironically presents a more Christian attitude than the main character. Coming to Ben-Hur, Iras begs on Messala's behalf: "He did thee wrong—but deeply did he deplore it! Forgive the past—restore his fortune—save him from poverty!"[108] She thus challenges Ben-Hur to fulfill Christ's commandment to love our enemies. But Judah responds with only contempt and refusal, which may have pleased audiences but is far from Christlike.

Mathis's conclusion makes no mention of the main character. Instead, the spiritual light remains the source of hope for all, a theme that blends elements of Victorian attitudes with modern assertions of greater honesty about sex and straightforward depictions of the dilemmas faced by modern women. Paradoxically, this radical change from any other version may have been motivated by a desire for fidelity to the source. No adaptation of *Ben-Hur* gives any consideration to Wallace's final chapters in which Judah becomes a leader in the fledgling religion inspired by Jesus. But Mathis's reading, consistent with the themes of so many of her scripts, may have been that Wallace's message was not in the triumph of Ben-Hur, but in the promise of Christianity. Taking Wallace's subtitle of *A Tale of the Christ* as a major theme, June Mathis, more than any other adapter, emphasizes the radical nature of the light of Christ and challenges viewers to recognize it. Her work possesses what T. J. Jackson Lears refers to as "the paradoxically antimodern impulse animating many forms of modernist thought."[109] At the same time that modernization was standardizing work and regulating daily routines, "a widespread yearning for regeneration—for rebirth that was variously spiritual, moral, and physical—penetrated public life, inspiring movements and policies that formed the foundation for American society in the twentieth century."[110] The plea for forgiveness, for finding love in our souls, even for our enemies, was also a major postwar theme that Mathis presents in many works.

This theme looks to the future, arguing the need for spiritual alternatives to war. In emphasizing the light of Christ over the triumph of the male hero, Mathis's ending not only contrasts with MGM's but also promotes the values under attack from patriarchal society. For the men of the times who set the standards for American public opinion and behavior, "home" could be achieved through hard work. Victorian and Christian ideology defined men's places as heads of household and controllers of the public spheres of business, labor, and politics. They were to provide "a crucial centripetal force against the centrifugal energies of markets and monies." Within the industrial/consumer society, the ideal man was to be "so hardworking . . . that he produced his own success, his own social identity" and became a "paragon of autonomy" and "the apotheosis of solidity and reliability." But for women, or those men who, as Mathis would say, possess a woman's sensibility, "the truly regenerated self was a sincere and transparent self, whose outward conduct corresponded perfectly with his [or her] inner experience of grace." This phrase defines a spiritual identity, one not associated with the "solid anchors" of hard work, ownership, and autonomy, but with the possession of higher values of compassion and justice, the ability to overcome boundaries, and thus the discovery of identity through diffusion and giving rather than gathering and holding. T. J. Jackson Lears argues that the "masculine ideals" stated above were deceptive: "Success was a slippery business. Titans of industry, who seemed the apotheosis of solidity and reliability, turned out at crucial moments to be confidence men."[111] In response, melodramas such as *Ben-Hur*, *The Four Horsemen*, and many others presented unbelievable spiritual elements, chance occurrences, and incredible coincidences. In doing so, they often revealed the instability, cruelty, and corruption of the temporal world.

Mathis's decision to end the film with Christ's triumphal entry into Jerusalem on Palm Sunday is a unique and significant feature of her adaptation. She states the explicit meaning of her references to light as she refers to the marchers "whose Leader put hope into the hearts of men as a new light to the world," superseding all previous lights. This light, originating in this shot from the center of the crowds surrounding Jesus, now grows to cover the screen.[112] The projector's beam sent out onto the screen at the start of the performance is reversed and sent back toward the audience. As the film ends, Mathis writes, "Malluch [Simonides's servant] arrives with Esther [Simonides's daughter]. [Everyone] turn[s] and kneel[s] as the light, similar to the effect of the Star of Bethlehem, moves towards the camera." Mathis concludes with, "The joyous music swells and the picture ends."[113] Rather than neatly resolving all issues with the hero's physical return, Mathis keeps her focus on the idea of a spiritual triumph that individuals need to follow on their own. What will come next is uncertain, which means that the promise of spiritual growth remains open to everyone.

In its association with the projector's beam, the light that can enlighten the world is not just that of Christianity, but of the cinema. This is a broad vision, not a claim that the cinema is equal to Christianity, but that it can present great messages. It conveys the idea that Christ's message was one of spiritual enlightenment and not tied to possessions, family, or personal achievements. As in *The Willow Tree*, Mathis invites viewers to find alternatives to temporal conflicts in her film and in the cinema as an art.

Beyond shaping her adaptation to emphasize themes of forgiveness and spirituality, Mathis also includes ideas for saving time and money during the production. Certain passages reveal the knowledge of technology and filmmaking that she had grasped from the very start of her career. This knowledge helped her provide suggestions that could have skirted some of the problems with set constructions by filming more material at the studio. In fact, it is not hard to imagine that the entire production could have been planned for domestic completion right from the start. For example, for a galley scene, Mathis writes, "This is going to be very hard to break up as shooting arrangement of the actual galley is somewhat different from the stage set."[114] Later, for the start of the chariot race, she writes, "FADE IN FULL SHOT OF THE ARENA Shooting in the direction of the gateway, and taking in the area which is masked in the pillars, to form a composition which will give the effect of a huge arena, and yet at the same time not mean so much building."[115] For the first shot of the massive Joppa Gate, Mathis writes, "Worked if possible with glass or miniature top."[116] When new director Fred Niblo arrived to film the production for MGM, in May 1924, he wrote to studio chief Louis B. Mayer that a good glass man was urgently needed.[117]

For scene 34, introducing the wise man Melchior, Mathis instructs,

FADE IN LONG SHOT (TINT FOR NIGHT) A STOCK
SHOT OF THE LOFTY HIMALAYAS OR LOCATION SEEN
THROUGH GLASS OR BY WILLIAMS PROCESS SHOWING
HIMALAYAN MOUNTAINS.[118]

This material reveals Mathis's knowledge of several technical elements and
also the resources available. In scene 156 of the Sanhedrin facing Herod,
she notes, "(This shot can also be taken with an Akeley camera)."[119] Then,
in scene 1529, a fade-in of a long shot at the well in the leper colony, Mathis
notes, "It might be a very good thing to use the new lens shown us by
Gaudio, as this is just about the tone that would enable us to do this in the
daylight."[120]

Niblo apparently did not thoroughly read Mathis's script as he was
pressed for time. Neither, it seems, did Charles Brabin, as he never indicated a willingness to work with Mathis to get a shared vision of *Ben-Hur*
on the screen. Any potential collaborator who had read Mathis's script
carefully might have noticed her suggestions and responded constructively
as Herbert Brenon had on *The Spanish Dancer*. He might also have asked
questions about sets, props, costumes, and costs to make sure preparations
were completed or changed since Mathis indicates much of this work could
have been done in Hollywood.

Shooting in Italy created massive problems and expenses in terms of
working with the Fascist labor unions, building sets, and providing food
and water to the cast and crew. These should have been resolved before any
of the cast and crew arrived, but they were not. Goldwyn's men in Italy were
J. J. Cohn and Edward Bowes. Cohn was unimpressed with the available
resources, but Bowes was wined and dined into signing the necessary con-
tracts.[121] On February 9, 1924, *Motion Picture News* reported, "Work was
in progress on the big galleys which play so important a part in the story
when I left Rome."[122] Some slave galleys were built and the company did
film some battle scenes with them at Anzio as a picture of Brabin directing
aboard one of the ships shows.[123] But that picture and the magazine report
do not tell the whole story. Only two ships were actually built, the rest were
just false fronts mounted on rafts, and port authorities judged the full ships
unseaworthy and ordered that they remain anchored. The camera crew was
therefore faced with trying to make two ships stuck in a harbor appear to be
battling at sea. Furthermore, speedboats kept sailing into the shots, forcing
the company to hire a patrol to keep them away. Meanwhile, Brownlow

writes, "Art director Horace Jackson and technical director Colonel Braden were endeavoring to build the enormous Circus Maximus and the Joppa Gate sets outside the Porta San Giovanni, close to the Appian Way, but labor disputes were making progress impossible."[124]

Charles Brabin also caused major problems when he banned Mathis from the set and took control himself.[125] Instead of fostering collaboration, Brabin's action divided the production team and destroyed whatever efficiency plans Mathis had laid. On July 21, 1924, Fred Niblo wrote to the new Metro-Goldwyn president Louis B. Mayer, "Brabin and Mathis got at swords points the moment they both arrived here, with the result there were two factions, the Brabin crowd and the Mathis crowd, pulling against each other. From what I hear they both ran wild in extravagance."[126] Although Mathis had looked forward to working with Brabin as she had with Ingram, Karger, and others, he seemed to feel that the "feminine talent of noticing detail" was "a minor gift, appropriate [only] for clearing up after, and around, a male director."[127]

Brabin's refusal to undertake a serious collaborative effort with Mathis represents a significant episode in this story whose absence from film history is important. Mathis's celebrity due to her position at Goldwyn, their highly publicized insurance policy on her, and her notoriety for having picked the cast and director may have given her an increased sense of ownership of the production and incensed Brabin. Following her confrontation with Bayard Veiller in 1920 and Tod Browning's recalcitrance on *The Day of Faith*, her battles with Brabin continued a pattern of gender conflicts that would damage her influence. Mathis was still to face a dispute with First National producer John McCormick over the last two years of her life and career.

The dilution of female talent and influence in Hollywood at the time, which sometimes emerged in personal attacks and dismissive remarks such as Mathis experienced, might also have created an anti-female atmosphere in the studios that influenced Brabin. Hollywood's women writers provided Mathis a little support during her long, frustrating *Ben-Hur* ordeal. On June 3, 1922, an item in *The Script*, published by the Screen Writers' Guild, noted, "They do say June Mathis has already completed a fairly good first continuity of Ben-Hur. We have every confidence in this girl's [*sic*] future."[128] Success with *Ben-Hur* would have certainly helped increase her influence and may have bolstered the status of all women in the industry. As questions of "what happened" to women silent filmmakers linger, these episodes of battles fought and lost over both control and ideas must be remembered.

When Brabin decided to exile Mathis from the filming, he did so to his own detriment. Providing advice in the script and on the set were two of her strengths, and Brabin might have produced some useful footage for the production if he had exploited these. Instead, he seems to have wasted most of his time. When Niblo took over for Metro-Goldwyn in July 1924, he wrote to Louis B. Mayer that Brabin spent "weeks and weeks in North Africa making a few feet of desert stuff that took up thirty or forty reels of film that cannot be used."[129] Francis X. Bushman, whom Mathis cast as Messala, later recalled, "Charlie Brabin was a lovely fellow, and we were very dear friends. . . . He was the storyteller superb—he could describe the most marvelous picture in the most beautiful language, but he'd never do it. I was with him at Anzio for several days, and all the time he was telling stories and drinking wine. I didn't realize that out on the beach he had hundreds of extras roasting and doing nothing."[130] It's no wonder that Brabin never got to the close-ups Mathis was counting on. During his time on the job, Brabin shot over 300,000 feet of film. But it was almost completely worthless. On September 10, 1924, Mayer cabled Niblo, "Saw Brabin stuff tonight certainly congratulate you on wisdom discarding every inch."[131]

Niblo had a negative opinion of Mathis's cast as well. He may have been referring to Bushman when he wrote to Mayer, "The cast to me, with perhaps one exception, is the most uninteresting and colorless that I have ever seen in a big picture." (Ironically, Kevin Brownlow's comments about the cast of *The Four Horsemen of the Apocalypse* at the gala premiere of the restored film eighty years later strongly echoed this sentiment.) Niblo added that he believed *Ben-Hur* "should be recast almost entirely."[132] Yet, whether the Metro-Goldwyn staff disagreed, had no one else available, or no time or money to make the change, Mathis's choices for three major roles remained in place: Bushman as Messala, de Brulier as Simonides, and Carmel Myers as Iras (although her part was extremely shortened).

The most important cast member, of course, was George Walsh, who never got a chance to prove himself. Whether or not he could have handled the role with help from a talented director, Mathis's coaching, and an efficient production such as Valentino had received on *The Four Horsemen* can never be known. But what is certain is that despite whatever shortcomings he had, Walsh's treatment from everyone at Goldwyn and MGM was nothing short of humiliating. First, the Goldwyn staffers who created the sailing schedules kept him waiting for months and finally booked him a second-class passage. When he arrived, Brabin mainly ignored him. Then, when Metro-Goldwyn replaced him with Ramon Novarro, they did not bother to tell him. He had to learn it from costar Francis X. Bushman. Walsh later commented, "[MGM] had Novarro under contract, so they decided that he was their own boy. . . . I was the last to find it out. I was handled very, very cruel."[133]

Finally, Niblo criticized the Goldwyn company's cavalier attitude toward the Italians, writing in a July 21 letter to Mayer, "Another thing that got the [Italians] down on us was because [the Mathis/Brabin company] came in here boasting about the millions they were going to spend and then ordered all their costumes in Germany. . . . Going to Germany and spending nearly $100,000 for costumes made a very bad feeling among the high officials here." As a result, he added, "Speaking of costumes, they have been ordered by the hundred regardless of expense and material. There are still several hundred being made but not yet finished. I stopped about four hundred that we would never have used. . . . Some of those already here have been through hell. Some of them should have been."[134] In September, either Mayer or Thalberg further commented on Brabin's material: "It is almost beyond my conception . . . that June Mathis, in fact anyone over there, could have allowed to pass, for one single day, the ill-fitting costumes, the incongruous action, the almost silly and typical European movements of the people."[135]

Throughout his correspondence, Niblo interestingly always refers to "the Mathis company," seemingly assuming that she was in charge, not Brabin. Mathis built her status by taking big gambles on *The Four Horsemen* and winning, and a generous evaluation of her decisions on *Ben-Hur* was that she was repeating that pattern and may have been right. But to have chosen Walsh and Brabin when several more obviously accomplished talents were available for those positions raises questions. Then, to attempt to start production when sets and facilities were not ready, costumes were of poor quality, and ships needed for a major scene were unusable makes no sense. How could Mathis and Brabin possibly expect to produce a film that would meet the high expectations of the public? The Walsh selection might be the most defensible point because his career was on the rebound and he was an excellent physical match for Bushman. But the fact that his salary would be low, that he was given second-class passage, and that Brabin was hired for "$25,000 and boat fare" suggests that pressure to keep costs low may have been a major factor.[136] Once they reached Italy, Mathis seems to have had little influence and, giving some charitable consideration, Brabin tried to make the best of what he had. But that was clearly not going to be good enough. Mathis might have been attempting to deflect criticisms about delays in advance when she said before leaving, "It is very hard to make hard and fast rules about any portion of the making of pictures. For instance, you hear that a director should have a perfect script before he begins work to insure himself against excess footage. No director can gauge the number of feet or even reels that his picture will contain. It is impossible because the altering of a table, the lengthening of a set or some such seemingly trivial happening will put his calculations some hundreds of feet [off]."[137]

Niblo recognized Mathis's preparation and told Louis B. Mayer, "Mathis and her team did a great amount of research. What assurance do we have that we will have access to it?"[138] The answer to that question is unknown, but Mathis's *Ben-Hur* script shows how thoroughly involved she could become. Her research and attention to detail are clear in her description of a street scene in which she makes a note to herself about Egyptian costumes, carts, and water jars: "Look up this point. (Description in full to be written later.)"[139] A press report suggests that research on costumes and scenes began as early as November 1922.[140]

As Mathis's two years of work on *Ben-Hur* were rapidly turning to nought, her personal life took a positive turn as she met her future husband, cameraman Silvano Balboni. Their meeting was facilitated by director Clarence Brown, who had hired Balboni to work on his film *The Acquittal* (1923) and later told Kevin Brownlow, "He was a nice young lad, he was even designing lenses—he was that good." When Brown heard about the *Ben-Hur* company going to Italy, he said, "June, I have a cameraman that I think you ought to take . . .; he's a helluva cameraman and he'd be a good technician. . . . They had an interview and she hired him."[141]

Mathis's considerations about the production, however, almost prevented their union. She told the press, "I first chose John Boyle, because he had handled all the Theda Bara spectacles and was used to doing splendid work with mobs. I met Balboni and thought he would be useful to me, but I knew a man named Martinello who had photographed my first picture, and I thought he should have the privilege of going to Europe if he wished it. However, he refused and Mr. Balboni was chosen by me principally because he spoke Italian but naturally also because of his professional record." This last point is significant because Mathis then describes Balboni's talent and dedication to his craft: "What a struggle he had had to be sure. But I only found that out afterward. He had really directed in Italy, France and England, following the pictures wherever he found improvement in them and when America got to the top in film making he came here. But he had to make his first picture here for nothing [to have work] to show us!"[142]

Mathis first mentioned "Sylvano [*sic*] Balboni, the Italian cameraman" to stepsister Laura Mary in her letter from Rome when she related that he, "Abe [Mass, her secretary] and the laboratory man who came with us, all joined hands [and] went out to the various theatres, where they had almost nude women on display in the forms of chandeliers, statues, etc."[143] Mathis claimed that during the trip to Rome, "Bal" was tremendously helpful because he spoke Italian: "I got to a point where I didn't know what to do without him. When we reached Rome, he was still my guide, philosopher, and friend." She was also attracted by his temperament: "On the desert, I learned what a really capable man he was under all conditions and circumstances. Really any woman is in luck who finds for a husband a man who is always good-tempered under the conditions in which we found ourselves working. No wonder I kissed him for the first time down there! Then we had [a] little trip on the Mediterranean, and later in Rome I decided he was the one man in the world for me to marry."[144]

Mathis's letter to Balboni from Berlin's Continental Hotel as she headed back to the United States gives a better picture of their romance:

Just think a month ago tonight we were under the desert stars—
the new moon shedding its light and the cool night breeze
blowing across the wind creased sand doons [*sic*]. I would rather
be there now. The desert will always be recorded in my memory
as one of the most wonderful events in my life. To have lived there
so close to nature in all its barbaric splendor after the petted-
pampered life I have always led—I didn't say much to anyone but
I dreaded going out there, dreaded only to find out that I really
belonged to it, that [I] am really savage at heart belonging to it
and shall always feel its spell. What foolish things I write, when
you were there and lived through the same—only it was not new
to you—you seemed part of it—shall always be part of it to me.[145]

The three existing letters to him are addressed "My Dear Boy" and "Dear-heart" and two are signed "Babekatze," which must have been a pet name for her. Her *Ben-Hur* experience had been "a long weary and troublesome five months," but it also provided the romantic adventure offered in so many movies of the times. It seems fitting that she was able to have it in the midst of a very troubling time when all her professional achievements were starting to be whittled away. After more than twenty years of work when she was just thirty-seven, her judgment of her life as "petted-pampered" also sounds remarkable. But that was the impact of finally encountering cultures and lands that she had only experienced before through movies, books, and art.

Mathis's vision for *Ben-Hur* was to build on Wallace's work by incorporating her own themes, which would infuse it with relevance. Mathis's work repeatedly suggests that such order was a cause of war and the continued exploitation of workers and women. Lew Wallace's novel suggests that the man must reclaim a primary position in the family and society if justice is to come. Niblo and Metro-Goldwyn emphasized this idea. In the final shot, Ben-Hur stands on the balcony of his family home, reunited with his mother and sister. Like Odysseus, he has endured years of struggle in his journey back. In a reassuring gesture, with his arms protectively encompassing the women, he looks toward the three crosses of Calvary in the distance and says of Jesus, "He is not dead. He will live forever in the hearts of men."

To say that Mathis envisioned *Ben-Hur* as a culmination of the themes of female spiritual guidance for young men that she included in her Valentino scripts, the value of diversity present in *The Idle Rich*, the importance of art in *The Willow Tree*, and the battle of greed and spirituality in *The Day of Faith* might seem like overstatement. These themes were widely present in the culture. But Mathis's scripts reveal her personal focus on and skillful development of them over the course of her career. Without consideration of her entire oeuvre, it would be easy to dismiss the notion of giving serious consideration to her *Ben-Hur* script. Its strong similarities to its source and Abe Erlanger's suggestion that he had guided her work provide possible reasons to ignore Mathis's artistic efforts on the production, but they are minor. Seen within greater contexts, her efforts on *Ben-Hur* deserve serious recognition.

Mathis had arrived in Rome in March 1924 hoping to create a stunning masterpiece that would make the Goldwyn executives proud of her. Two months later, not only had she failed to complete the picture, but her career with Goldwyn, now a part of the newly formed Metro-Goldwyn, was over. Upon returning to the United States, she had to find a new position. A May 2 telegram to Loew from Joe Schenck, his top assistant, states, "Had a long talk with Mayer and his staff regarding Ben Hur . . . We have all come to unanimous conclusion that your present agreement with Mathis dominating entire production situation in Rome George Walsh leading man and even Brabin director will spell either absolute failure or at best tremendous waste of money running into at least half or three quarters of a million . . . Your scenario is seventeen hundred scenes which will make a picture of twenty-five reels and that is most conservative . . . You will no doubt encounter difficulties with Erlanger who is sold on June Mathis but you must be firm now before it's too late . . . I will call your attention to Greed which scenario Mathis approved under her own signature scenario consisting of thirteen hundred scenes and it is now twenty-four reels and cannot possibly be cut down . . . She also wrote scenario of Palace of King which was great story but her scenario made picture failure . . . She also wrote story Day of Faith which is another failure . . . Last two were biggest flops Goldwyn Company had for year . . . I am not trying to undermine Mathis but just to point out to you necessity of immediate action."[146] She did not go quietly however. On July 14, Bess Meredyth wrote Louis B. Mayer, "Miss Mathis leaves tomorrow and we'll all breathe more freely I think."[147] Whether Mathis had continued to push her ideas, tried to influence the script, or simply kept pestering people about what her new situation would be is unknown.

Mathis's private letter to her family ("Laura and folks") in July 1924 as she headed home from England aboard the S. S. Homeric, reveals her high aspirations for *Ben-Hur*, both artistically and commercially: "At last I am on my way home and it seems good to say it. . . . But strange to say I am not a bit upset over what has happened. I could not bring myself to write you regarding all the frightful things that for a while upset me. . . . But somehow when I kissed Ben Hur goodbye and had [a] talk with Loew I felt as though the burden of my soul had blown away." This message reveals a confusing mix of emotions Mathis was enduring after *Ben-Hur* had turned into a long ordeal for her. The dream of establishing her legacy as the creator of both *The Four Horsemen of the Apocalypse* and *Ben-Hur*, which had been so close and would have certainly elevated her position in film history, had ended. She expresses great relief, but there is also a tone of bitterness, which is to be expected. She writes, "They can't make the kind of picture I wanted to see made, why lend my name to it and be blamed."[148]

Sadly, in the midst of her struggles and frustrations, Mathis may have been blind to some of her own faults. To head for Rome with a script of 1,722 scenes was not likely to succeed, especially when it seems she had not gone over it with the director. The length may have been intentional as part of an effort to maintain control of the project. She planned to make further cuts, but some of her planning was intended not to work with Brabin but to manipulate him. These schisms were built into the project from the start, and Brabin recognized them. His reaction, while inappropriate, is understandable because Mathis was working just as hard as he to make the film her own.

Mathis's work on *Ben-Hur* still exists as a part of American film and culture, and it offers important lessons. The first lesson is that consideration of a script should not stop with a mere recognition of its length. Mathis's *Ben-Hur* work provides further support for identifying her as an artist. She had her own vision for the film, which she attempted to make at a time when her production methods were becoming outdated. The final lesson is that Mathis's failure with *Ben-Hur* marks not only the start of her decline but also that of influential women in Hollywood. Mathis recovered from the *Ben-Hur* fiasco. But she would not have another chance to reach the top levels of the industry again. In her last three years, Mathis created more notable work. But her battles with First National executive John McCormick would cause her to walk away from her final opportunity to become a producer and exemplify the struggles for all women filmmakers in the new Hollywood.

9

First National and Freelancing, 1924–1927

Mathis's last week in Europe did not allow her any rest. But she was able to catch up on some basic needs. From on board the S. S. Homeric in London, she wrote Balboni, "Yesterday before going to tea with Danny it was raining too hard to do the sights so had a shampoo as had not had one since Rome and who should I draw out of that big establishment but an Italian hairdresser from Rome who had been to America. Just can't keep away from Italy." There were also chances to shop and enjoy herself. One night "after eating and dancing arrived home at one-thirty then had to pack my evening things all pretty new Paris ones you haven't seen. . . . Had to be up at six to catch the boat train."[1] Her letters show how the American film industry had expanded and how this young woman from Leadville, Colorado, now had friends and acquaintances all over the world. On her way over, Mathis encountered a "strange circumstance—Rex [Ingram] and Ed Carewe were both in Paris when I was there. I saw Ed, but did not see Rex; of course."[2] She later wrote from London that "a friend of mine who is now a countess came and dragged me out to her very lovely home for tea." Later she told him, "Went to hear Gerald De Maurier [*sic*] [in London], with Mae [?] and her mother and afterwards we met Danny and a couple of prominent exhibitors I have known for a long time, as far back as when I was on the stage and used to play their theaters."[3]

Her letters also give insight into her constant career planning and ongoing family responsibilities. In a letter from Berlin, she tells Balboni, "I have had a frightful headache all day and do not feel very well tonight besides I had to reckon out accounts, plan my next two days figure out money and plan of action."[4] She considers one plan when she "receives word from Ivor Novello, he wants to see me about writing a picture for him and another English producer wants to get in touch with me. Who knows when contract is up may come back here."[5] To Laura and family, she writes,

"Cannot understand why you have not answered my cable asking you about solving deposites [sic]. Will straighten out all checks and everything when I get home." She adds, "I will stay in New York for about a week then go west to take up work at Culver. Special work—no grind. After all, I have my contract."[6] Perhaps she still felt her contract guaranteed her work at Metro-Goldwyn upon returning home.

At the end of August 1924, the Metro corporation issued a press release stating, "Miss June Mathis, having completed her work for Metro-Goldwyn Pictures, has terminated her services with that organization and will rest for a short time before undertaking the execution of plans which she has had in mind for some time."[7] The studio's suggestion that Mathis felt she could use a break but had been thinking about what to do next for some time may be fair. But Bess Meredyth's comment that the new *Ben-Hur* company would be happy to see her go suggests Mathis may not have been too quick to drop her efforts on the film. Her work over the next year would take a new direction as she signed with First National Pictures where Richard Rowland was now president.

Soon afterward, Mathis also signed with Valentino's independent Ritz-Carlton Pictures to write *The Scarlet Power* for him.[8] The role was that of a Spaniard as Valentino had played in *Blood and Sand* but also set in the more distant past like *The Spanish Dancer* or Goldwyn's canceled production of *The Spanish Cavalier*. Based on a story by Natacha Rambova, Valentino's wife, his role was that of a "young noble in the decadent court of the period of the Inquisition. . . . Accustomed to exercising the perquisites of his caste, he becomes involved with a mighty struggle of the soul when he finds himself in love with a beautiful Moorish princess, the flower of the beauty and culture of her race and civilization."[9] Valentino, Orientalism, a spiritual theme, interracial romance—many of Mathis's favorite elements. This script should have been easy for her, and maybe it was. But we will never know because Rambova did not like it and Valentino agreed. Their disapproval caused a split between Mathis and Valentino that lasted at least another year. *Motion Picture Magazine* reported, "June walked off the set where Rudolph is making *Cobra*, and ambassadors have been withdrawn."[10] Perhaps they could have worked together on revisions. But rather than talk to Mathis personally, the Valentinos distanced themselves from the situation and sent manager George Ullman to deliver the news.[11]

Rowland's assistance to Mathis when she returned from Europe makes sense. She had come through for him when he needed her on *The Four*

Horsemen, and now he did the same for her. But production at the new film corporations like Metro-Goldwyn-Mayer (MGM) and First National was very different from what she had experienced at Metro, Famous Players, and Goldwyn. In the new Hollywood where every aspect of a production— writing, cinematography, set design, makeup, costuming, props—was controlled by a separate department, Mathis's practice of total involvement in every area was no longer optimal. In addition, the studios had turned with the culture toward films that emphasized fun and safe adventures related to fulfilling personal desires. As the twenties progressed, American society became more pleasure-centered: "The decline in voting and the widespread indifference to reform . . . signaled a rejection of civic responsibility and a shift to the private and the personal." Prosperity was largely a white urban phenomenon, but "the flood of consumer goods, made more accessible by installment buying, did provide more Americans than ever with the delights and perils of conspicuous consumption." Within this context, "the increased importance of advertising and movies reflected and reinforced the thrust of the consumer culture towards leisure and consumption."[12] Concerns about the impacts of the war, the evils of greed, and gender identities began to fade. Instead, to profit off actors like Fairbanks and Valentino, the studios "emphasized charm, youth, and physical expressiveness, thus helping to set the tone for an updated version of masculinity, as well as for the new cultural emphasis on self-expression, leisure, and personality." Comedies fit the mold. In *Skinner's Dress Suit* (1925), a modern commuting office worker finds that constant effort only brings boredom. Luckily, his wife buys some dance lessons, and the skill they show at an office party brings him a promotion because his employer realizes "he has a personality that can sell goods. . . . In the age of cooperation, personality is a commodity that will advance one up the ladder."[13] Lynn Dumenil points out the films of Cecil B. DeMille from the start of the decade "suggest the trend toward privatization, with individuals looking for satisfaction increasingly in the personal sphere, and achieving it through consumption, leisure, and self-expression." Works like *Male and Female* (1919) and *Why Change Your Wife?* (1920) "portray women's identity as inseparable from the clothes and cosmetics that adorn them."[14]

Gloria Swanson used these productions to achieve top-level stardom and establish a woman's ability to use the consumer culture to obtain personal satisfaction while stuck in a boring marriage. Throughout the twenties, movies, fiction, and ads would encourage women to find happiness through fashion and cosmetics. But even as they learned to desire these products and master their usage, women would also receive criticism for doing so. On January 7, 1924, Mathis responded to sculptor Onorio Ruotolo who stated that luxury was killing "the dynamic force of the modern woman." Drawing on essentialist notions, Mathis argued that a woman is "a worshipper of beauty and down through the ages it has been beauty that has awakened the finer more noble instincts in women. It is when these instincts are full-flowered that she becomes most fully herself, and it is only then that she is truly dynamic." To this assertion, Mathis added, "Poverty crushes woman, stifles her and often destroys her. . . . Mr. Routolo [*sic*] need only look about him to find a thousand examples."[15]

Thus, women might be pushed toward using material consumption as a path to satisfaction and fulfillment but then condemned for their "softness" when they succeed. In the teens, when many women were combination actress/writer/director/editor, their gender did not draw criticism. But Karen Ward Mahar states, "as the definition of filmmaking shifted away from the feminine realm of art and toward the masculine realm of industry, . . . *all* women in the industry lost ground."[16] This redefining gained such momentum that "by mid-decade the primary argument put forward by the major studios to explain the exclusion of female directors centered on the physical demands of the job."[17]

In an article of superficial praise for Mathis, Ivan St. Johns applies this theory directly to her. He first claims that *The Young Rajah* was a picture "June made . . . by herself and it was terrible" although Philip Rosen actually directed it. Then, getting to his point, he asserts that women "stand head and shoulders above the men in writing for the screen. But they cannot stand the gaff—the hard, physical work, the tremendous weight of detail the necessity of executive organization. June Mathis, Frances Marion, Jane Murfin and Marion Fairfax are four great women writers who have had to admit defeat on that battlefield." St. Johns then claims that what Mathis is really seeking is "a director who would work with her as she and Ingram had worked together." Mathis actually gave this assertion some validity with her comment that ideal filmmaking involved a female writer and male director, and her search for a director of *Ben-Hur* lends the statement more credibility. She appears never to have considered a woman. But at the same time, St. Johns and all others who worked in and commented on the film industry, ignored the history of women not only directing but also performing multiple jobs simultaneously. St. Johns does so even as he states,

"June was made some impossibly important sort of supervisor and editorial chief and power-that-be at Goldwyn's, and she made a fortune, and some fine pictures."[18]

The second half of 1924 was not all misery and struggle for Mathis though. The December 1924 collection of gossip items in *Motion Picture Magazine* included news that "Hollywood was electrified last week by the unexpected marriage of June Mathis. . . . The bridegroom is Sylvano [*sic*] Balboni, a young Italian who has been a cameraman in Hollywood. . . . They were married in the St. Cecilia Chapel at the Mission Hotel in Riverside."[19] Laura served as a witness, and the bride and groom both stated they were thirty years old on the marriage license.[20] This was true for him, but she was thirty-seven. After the wedding, Mathis and Balboni returned to Hollywood and work.[21] Most likely, following the debacle of *Ben-Hur* and her conflict with the Valentinos, Mathis could now feel happy in her marriage, her new position at First National, and her reunion with Richard Rowland. In verification of Ivan St. Johns, her marriage also became a professional partnership as she and Balboni began working as a writer/director team.

Fortunately for Mathis, although she reportedly had the title of editorial director, Rowland assigned her to the Colleen Moore unit, which may have been surprising as Moore was a fast-rising star of "modern" comedies, not exactly Mathis's forte.[22] Perhaps Rowland felt that adding Mathis to Moore's team would provide this young talent with some security. It turned out that his decision was correct, at least for 1925. Moore's bobbed hair and acting in *Flaming Youth* (1923) made "flappers" popular movie figures, and the films she completed with Mathis helped make her the top female box office attraction in the country. These films, *Sally, The Desert Flower, We Moderns*, and *Irene*, were comic coming-of-age stories that offered little in the way of progressive roles for young women. Yet, Mathis's sudden transition into this genre was fortunate in that she now had to address young women's struggles to define themselves through material consumption. Moore's character was neither rebellious nor sensual: "She was cute and lively." Jeanine Basinger writes, "There was no real suggestion that she might ever do anything truly stupid or immoral. Her galoshes might be flapping, but she was pretty zipped-up otherwise."[23] These roles, as Emily Leider says, were "quite out of step with Mathis's mystical and somber bent." Leider dismisses these films by saying Mathis "took what work came her way."[24] In opposition to much of Mathis's earlier work, the young female protagonists headed into comic trouble and the male leads became the passive purveyors of stability as they waited for their counterparts to settle down. Nevertheless, "Moore's characters were very popular with women audiences, since she represented what women were hoping to accomplish: the discarding of the traditional burdens of femininity, the usual restricted female roles of mother, sexual partner, and romantic object."[25] Mathis also uses these films to emphasize women's resiliency while criticizing a young generation out of touch with the suffering of the recent past and its purpose.

In these films, Moore plays impulsive characters whose unorthodox choices might create trouble, opportunities, or both. But they never intend to be seriously disruptive. The openings to Moore's Mathis films emphasize her childishness and innocence. *Sally* begins with her living in an orphanage and getting into fights in the alley. Mathis introduces her with intertitles that sum up her character, which will be the basis for her eventual success:

> A little dash of deviltry—
> A little grain or two of humor—
> A pinch of temper—a half
> A pound of optimism—and
> A whole pound of sweetness—
> The Good Lord sure concocted
> A recipe when he created—
> Sally

At the start of *We Moderns*, Moore's character is thirteen, and *Irene* also starts with her living at home with her Ma and Pa. But her films downplay her characters' "struggles" as does Moore herself through her public image and commentary. Moore was often presented in boyish outfits (cowboy clothes for *The Desert Flower*, an English riding suit for *We Moderns*, as Uncle Sam for a publicity shot) and with the "toys" that a child would love (dolls, a huge Saint Bernard, her new Packard). All these costumes and props helped preserve Moore's and her characters' innocent persona and fit comfortably into the commercialized culture. Her January 1925 article, "The American Girl of Today," depicted a leisurely upper-class life in which "they play a round of tennis or golf or ride horseback . . . order a dinner for two or a brunch. Dance the latest dances all night without getting tired. Drive a car and be up-to-date on all the latest styles."[26]

Mathis had no argument with wealth or high society, but her work does not generally focus on such light girl-finds-boy material. Her influence therefore shines through with her adaptation of *The Desert Flower*. In this one, Moore plays Maggie Fortune, who lives in a boxcar with her father-in-law. Although she dresses in manly clothes and wears a derby, she is not all play. She must also tend a chicken, take care of a baby, and handle a gruff foreman. The plot involves her reforming a heavy-drinking New Yorker by staking him to a mine ownership in which he eventually succeeds. The film thus suggests an interesting contrast to the Fairbanks offerings of the previous decade in which the pampered easterner would be masculinized by the western wilderness. Here, a woman of toughness, patience, and virtue is required for his rejuvenation. Sumner Smith found that *Desert Flower*'s "chief value is in Miss Mathis' many clever touches affording Colleen chances to be funny, and Colleen is so funny that most of the time the audience will watch her and enjoy her without caring whether there is any story or not."[27] *Motion Picture Magazine* commented, "Had the director and adaptor treated this play seriously—had they followed the stage version in its entirety, it might have spelled old-fashioned hokum and failure. The screen version depicts the old plot being dressed up with humor."[28]

But John McCormick, First National producer and Moore's husband-manager, was unhappy. He telegrammed Rowland that "our last picture in spite of box office success was bad one."[29] Now, he, Mathis, and Moore were all enthusiastic about gaining the rights to the very popular play *Irene*, and Mathis was able to convince the other two that *We Moderns* would also work. But McCormick was upset with Mathis's first draft. He and First National executive Al Rockett wired Rowland: "We are of the opinion that first it is too long [typical of a Mathis first draft] second that it does not come anyway near theme of original play nor does it resemble word picture Verse [Mathis] painted to Model [Moore] myself when we agreed to do story." Jeff Cordori explains that Mathis's enthusiasm about the theme had sold McCormick and Moore on the play. But "Mathis had dropped the theme and so John felt it impossible to start shooting on July 20[, 1925]. Shooting would have to be postponed at least a week to get the story back to its original theme." McCormick and Moore were also upset with Mathis's method and did not feel she was focused enough on their projects: "Also get Verse personal attention to script which I understand has so far been lacking. . . . and Model asks me to tell you she does not intend start in on any more stories on promises of their being doctored."[30]

Unfortunately, what displeased McCormick about *Desert Flower* is impossible to know. Maybe he wanted a film with greater fidelity to the original. The film *We Moderns*, like the play, provides a serious moral of patriarchal instruction for a wayward younger generation rather than a more classic Mathis message of spirituality and social criticism. Whether or not this is the theme Mathis intended also cannot be known. But the prologue shows the older generation sacrificing all for the war effort, a history that always seems to have been on Mathis's mind. The film then focuses on the ingratitude of the young people who exploit their freedom and fall for the nonsense of falsely intellectual poets. In the opening scene, Mary Sundale (Moore) is sitting in her father's library during a wild party given by her brother. Mathis reveals Mary's budding desires by having her look over some books about women and sexuality, eventually selecting Elinor Glyn's famously scandalous *Three Weeks*, a scene used to suggest girls' emerging sexual interests in many films of the times.[31] Mary's parents want her attached to the hardworking conservative John Ashlar (Jack Mulhall), who calls her an innocent child. But Mary laughs at him, speaking with an ignorant Freudianism about her "suppressed desire to meet Oscar Pleat," the superficial avant-garde poet idolized by the youth. Eventually, Mary does meet him and goes to a party he hosts on a dirigible. When Pleat tries to sexually assault her, he causes a fire that leads to a crash. Mary escapes only slightly hurt and ends up crying happily in John's arms as he keeps calling her a child.

McCormick benefited in his interactions with Mathis from Hollywood's new production methods that put more men in charge and discouraged the Mathis approach of writing multiple drafts while overseeing most other aspects of the work as well. When Rowland hired Mathis as editorial director on August 25, 1924, his reference to her as a "dominant thinker, iconoclast of screen tradition, [and] woman of achievement" suggests she would have a high degree of control.[32] A year later, the story was quite different when Rowland promoted McCormick to First National's general manager of West Coast productions in July 1925. *Moving Picture World* stated, "Since the engagement of June Mathis as scenario editor on the Coast, Miss Mathis and Mr. McCormick have worked in the closest harmony, not only in the selection of story material, but in all phases of production. The present plan of operation, according to Mr. Rowland, is calculated to bring Mr. McCormick and Miss Mathis into even closer partnership in the development of First National product."[33] Actually, the opposite was true as McCormick began pushing Mathis out. For Mathis's final Colleen Moore production, *Irene*, she served as editorial director/continuity writer and Rex Taylor wrote the screenplay.

McCormick and Moore's complaints about Mathis's work habits reveal how practices she had been praised for a few years earlier now received the opposite reaction. Another example of this change is evident in director Al Santell's belated criticism of his work with her on *Classified*, Corrine Griffith's 1925 comedy hit. A 1920 press release that focused on Mathis's departure for a vacation at the train station stated that "at the last moment, after the Screen Classics, Inc., scenario chief had bought her ticket and made her Pullman reservations, she was called upon to revise a part of the last act of the Bert Lytell special 'The Right of Way,' adapted by her from Sir Gilbert Parker's famous novel of the same name. This Miss Mathis did, with the aid of her secretary, at the Santa Fe station in Los Angeles." The release concluded, "Hardly had she dictated the last line when the conductor's stentorian and long-drawn 'Board' sounded—and Miss Mathis's first real vacation in four years began."[34]

Her script for *Classified*, completed under similar circumstances, received a very different reaction from director Alfred Santell, who talked about the situation while viciously attacking Mathis's reputation in a 1972 interview. Based on a short story by Edna Ferber, *Classified* is an entertaining comedy and an insightful examination of young women's vulnerability in the workforce, where they are preyed upon and objectified by wealthy men who try to lure them with money, gifts, and false opportunities.

In his interview with William Dorward, Santell described a situation similar to the one at the train station in 1920 and claimed Mathis "had as much to do with [*Classified*] as Princess Margaret. She handed us the script when we went back to New York to do our location work." He then states that during the five-day train trip from Los Angeles to New York, "I sat in my drawing room with Corinne Griffith and my script girl and we took June Mathis' script, which was really a dramatic script—it was about as funny as an open grave. So we virtually ad-libbed a skeleton which we shot in New York with odds and bits of gags in it, [Mack] Sennett-like."[35] As an example of his contribution, Santell describes a series of incidents in which Griffith's character, who hitches a ride from the Bronx to her job in Times Square every day, always gets in the nicest-looking car she sees. The rich driver eventually puts his hand on her knee and draws her toward him until they reach her destination, and she jumps out. Santell's gag was to have the male lead, Jack Mulhall, playing a young mechanic and old friend who loves her, pull up one morning in an old Ford he has pieced together from "all sorts of parts from three different Fords, open and very [odd looking]."[36]

The gag, which Santell firmly asserts "was [his] gag, not June Mathis' gag," was that the camera then swung around to show a line of about fifty identical Fords, "all lined up like a damn regiment and she realized that Jack Mulhall's car might as well be the one she could take. So she got into that and Jack Mulhall never made a play for her."[37] Whether or not audiences would recognize a string of identical cars (could fifty fit on the screen?) and get the joke seems questionable. Even if they did, would it be that funny? Perhaps the joke was actually in having a line of wealthy drivers all awaiting their chance to pick up Griffith and make a play for her. Maybe Santell was not remembering it quite accurately, or it may have been missing from the incomplete Library of Congress print that I studied. In any case, Santell was not going to give Mathis any credit. Based on his experiences with Mathis, Santell stated, "from the standpoint of real ability, and I have worked with some pretty good writers. She comes way down among the high numbers— say up by No. 1 and drop her down to No. 60 on the charts."

Santell's opinions of Mathis are questionable because they are based more on prejudice rather than personal knowledge. He barely knew her. More of his thoughts about Mathis came out when Dorward, someone who obviously had some knowledge about Mathis's status, asked him, "What sort of a woman was she?" Santell asked if he meant "physically, mentally, or sexually," and Dorward said, "Let's have an amalgam of all three." Santell's answer shows that he knew very little about Mathis but was not shy about sharing his feelings. He used his opinion of her looks to make some very disparaging sexist remarks about her unknown personal life: "Well, first of all physically she was as broad as she was tall. In other words a true broad. And she looked like a three-quarter filled sack of wheat with a rope in the middle holding her together. She was very ugly. I think she was originally designed by the Maker just to bear children and sexually she could never be interested in me because her main desires were Italians." Santell's statement almost fifty years later that Mathis was not sexually interested in him suggests possible resentment of her status, perhaps because she treated him professionally rather than affectionately. A further basis for this resentment could be racism as he seems annoyed about her attention to Italians and not him. He expands on this racism while also diminishing her legacy: "I think she was the one that claimed to have found Rudy Valentino. And she eventually married an Italian cameraman. In other words, she went for the spaghetti."[38]

Santell also attacks what he believed to be her writing habits: "Mentally I think she had the hacks on Dick Rowland. For some reason she was his favorite writer, but I personally had very little contact with her because I had no admiration for her. I realized that she milked ideas from a person with whom she was talking and then cribbed them as her own."[39] Apparently, Santell did not realize that writers generally draw material from conversations with and observations of others.

To be fair, Santell was a talented director with a long, notable career who must be given his due. *Classified* clearly shows his ability, but the gag he describes is not the best evidence. Instead, his shot selections and scene constructions are especially admirable. The film opens with a sequence shot from inside the dumbwaiter of the tenement where Babs Comet (Griffith) and her family live. Whenever its door opens, one of the residents reaches in, takes her groceries, and calls up to the neighbors that theirs are on the way. The small-town values of trust and sharing apparently still operate within the building. Soon thereafter, Babs receives her daily ride to work from a strange man who picks her up at the bus stop. Santell uses three shots from behind the characters during their trip. Each shows a large billboard or marquee dominating the top half of the frame, representative of an oppressive consumer culture, while Babs fends off the overweight driver. The sequence thus establishes what Babs or any young female worker is up against: men and commercialism. It also more accurately describes a scene of Babs's typical ride to work rather than the ride from Mulhall that Santell claims to have created. This theme suggests the dramatic core of the work that Mathis would have been most interested in. Santell was an important contributor, but he claimed only to have added bits of gags.

As the story of a modern working girl, *Classified* presents the image of a woman whose "central and frivolous status as consumer (and the consumed) is essential for the pursuit of happiness and capitalism, yet she is guilty, somehow lacking. She is all and nothing, the problem and the cure."[40] As its title suggests, *Classified* (a reference to the ads) is saturated with situations involving buying and selling and personal transformation through consumer goods. In this modern urban world, Babs must leave her home to learn how to earn money and buy products, and she does quite well. Her job in a New York City newspaper's classified ads department gets her out of the house and helps her meet her future husband Whitey (Mulhall). At the end of the film, she finds the perfect house for them through the ads. Babs also negotiates consumer culture through her use of a payment plan to buy stylish clothes, her knowledge of clubs and restaurants, and her one-night job as a fashion model.

In her dual role as a consumer and an object for consumption, Babs needs to know how to continually change herself in order to survive. She must know how to please men who can provide her with mobility (a ride to work), stability (romance or marriage), or employment (at the newspaper or as a model) and also how to avoid their clutches because these same men (except for Whitey) constantly threaten her. When the man who gives her a ride tries to "get fresh" with her, a title says that she knew from experience that this would happen. The clothing merchants who hire Babs as a model (played by Bernard Randall and George Sidney) spy on her as she changes into their goods. Later, the wealthy Spencer Clark (Ward Crane) tries to steer her into a hotel room for a night after pretending he has run out of gas on a country road. Babs eludes him while he is in the hotel office by arranging some scarecrow clothes in the front seat of his car to resemble her.

In this narrative construction, without the spiritual element of melodrama, women had no alternatives to commodification, and society had no protection from its decadent secular culture. Babs is totally on her own in coping with the indignities she is subjected to daily. Mathis shows that her family and neighbors, formerly sources of strength in melodrama, are no help to her at all. Old Man Comet (Charles Murray), "Maw" (Edyth Chapman), and Babs's little sister (Jacqueline Wells), never leave their run-down tenement apartment. The older women in the building are quick to pounce on any evidence that a young woman has traded on her virtue to get ahead, which is a great irony since legitimate methods for self-progress are seemingly off-limits as well. The only contact Maw and her youngest daughter have with the outside world is when they spy on their neighbors through their apartment window. At one point, they get excited when one neighbor, "the Tiernan girl," emerges from a fancy car looking very well dressed. Apparently, several other women have been spying as well because they all stare accusingly at young Tiernan as she arrives at her mother's apartment. Mrs. Tiernan knows what they are thinking and gives them an angry look back.

Maw Comet, however, is not that willing to defend Babs and passes immediate judgment on her in a similar situation. When Babs escapes the lustful clothing merchants, she is still wearing their coat. They follow her to the Charleston Café, where she first meets Spencer Clark, and steal it back.

The next morning, Babs receives three new coats in return: one from the café, one from the apologetic merchants, and one from Clark. Her father is impressed, but her mother wonders what she did to get them. In the film's conclusion, Babs arrives home the morning after eluding Spencer Clark's attempt to spend the night with her. But her family does not buy her innocence until Whitey looks down forlornly and discovers that her shoes are, in fact, muddy from the night before when she had to run across fields in the dark. He then proposes and she accepts.

Thus, due to repeatedly spontaneous actions, Babs manages to escape various male schemes to trap her. Compared to the traditional melodramatic heroines in other Mathis films, however, Babs's skills are extremely limited. Whereas Princess Marya in *The Legion of Death*, Marguerite Laurier in *The Four Horsemen*, and Jane Maynard in *The Day of Faith* were able to transform men and societies, Babs Comet can only transform herself, and she must do so constantly to maintain her dignity and survive in the shallow world of consumerism. Within the modern world of consumer capitalism, Mathis is unable to draw upon the spiritual strengths of women as defined in melodrama. Additionally, the possibility that Babs might save her money to invest in an education or start her own business is never suggested. Instead, all of her changes aim at achieving a final change from a single working woman into a married woman and mother. Meanwhile, although the men in the film are lazy ("Old Man" Comet), lecherous (Spencer Clark), or poor (Whitey), they are not required to change at all. As Patricia Mellencamp wrote in 1992, within capitalist culture, "representations of men's bodies (and power) . . . remained relatively stable."[41]

Classified is not a feminist argument for equality or greater opportunities for women. But Mathis's adaptation shows more sympathy for Babs than does her source. In the original story, Edna Ferber blames Babs for being nothing more than an "imitation" of the kind of high-class girl she wants to be and puts her in her place as Whitey's fiancée.[42] The film, though, shows sympathy for Babs's attempts to maneuver through society and does not allow the audience to condemn her. It also repeatedly condemns how much women are objectified in modern culture and yet persecuted for doing what the culture encourages them to do—namely, transforming their bodies and trading on their appearance in order to succeed. But their vulnerability to male exploitation makes their chances for misery much higher.

The Babs Comet story without the happy ending was something like Mathis's over her last year and a half of life. Mathis maintained a heavy workload in all phases of production literally until her last breath. On June 15, 1925, production began of Mathis's *The Greater Glory*, another World War I epic that was slated to open in December. Journalist Tamar Lane defined the project as Mathis's attempt to restore her reputation, asking, "Will she redeem herself?" With great sympathy for Mathis's recent trials, Lane spoke encouragingly: "As director general of Goldwyn, June had what appeared to be the chance of a lifetime to show her real abilities . . . and met with disaster. But there are three men now at the Goldwyn studio trying to do what some expected one woman to do—and they are having their hands full. . . . As for me, I believe that June will come through with flying colors. Anyway, I'm rooting for her."[43]

In January 1926, Richard Rowland wrote in *Moving Picture World*, "To June Mathis, who has fairly lived with the story [of *The Viennese Medley/The Greater Glory*] for a year and who has seen it through from the beginning on into the cutting, editing, titling stages, goes great praise." Rowland further remarked, "Showing an atmosphere of Vienna, as it does, both before and after the war, and still not having a single war scene throughout the story is one of the many features of the film. The story preaches a lesson against war but does so without any propaganda—something decidedly unusual."[44]

Possibly in response to criticism about her alleged spendthrift ways on *Ben-Hur* and in reaction to the suggestion that she had insisted on filming overseas, Mathis reported, "I am not inclined to favor European film production when it can be done in America." She added, "Conditions in the foreign field are entirely different than here, first because of the lack of modern equipment and second, finances. Studios are not plentiful, sets are hard to obtain and props are scattered all over the land—quite a different situation than here in Hollywood."[45] Whether or not she had realized this before or after *Ben-Hur*, she did not say. But her plans for the production make clear that she earnestly desired to create a great drama as she believed she had with Valentino and Ingram and had hoped to achieve with von Stroheim and Brabin. The production scale of *The Greater Glory*, the fact that she again wrote the script and chose the director, and the focus on opulence and greed in the midst of widespread suffering all strongly suggest an attempt to recreate the success of *The Four Horsemen*. Mathis even included a shot of symbolic horsemen and told audiences, "In 'The Greater Glory' you will see an entirely new method in the use of symbols and symbolic characters to express . . . thought and the reaction of thought aroused by the action in a situation."[46] Mathis explained that one problem with symbolism "has been in the tendency to allow such symbolism to be extraneous to the dramatic action in the story, and to lay undue stress upon the symbolic character." Mathis's "new method" was to represent evil through "the figure of an old scissors grinder whose leering face and disreputable form appears in the background throughout the action. He is not dominant. He is not forced onto the attention of the spectator, but he is always there."[47]

Stroheim included symbolic inserts in *Greed*, and Mathis's work on *The Greater Glory* would become similar to his in other ways as well.[48] Stroheim's contract with Goldwyn in 1923 stated that his filming of any production could not last more than fourteen weeks. He doubled that in his work on *Greed*.[49] Production of *The Greater Glory* took six months, and it did not reach the theaters until three months after its originally scheduled release date. But while Stroheim came to be considered as an artist whose great effort was spoiled by commercialism, Mathis would not be. Instead, *The Greater Glory* (which, like *Greed*, also had a title change from that of the original novel's) is a forgotten film.

Even as she labored over *The Greater Glory* at the start of 1926, Mathis acquired her own production unit at First National, which she welcomed for its reduced workload. She told the press, "I have wanted to produce one picture at a time instead of the fifteen or twenty I have sometimes had to do. With my new arrangement, this is possible, and believe me I am mighty happy about it."[50] The first film from June Mathis Productions with Balboni directing was meant to be *Sinners in Paradise* from a novel by Clarence Budington Kelland. A romance with another "exotic" desert backdrop, First National announced it with a large ad saying, "Again June Mathis Scores with a Stupendous Special!" The ad continues, "It sweeps from the underworld alleys to the burnished East; from furtive dives to the throbbing purples of desert night. . . . Stirring, exotic, keyed to emotion's tensest pitch. . . . And the whole produced with the bigness and sureness of success that characterizes First National's Specials."[51] This synopsis, sounding like an enhanced version of Mathis's romance with Balboni, suggests why she was attracted to the story. In addition, the story includes "a wise old man [who tells the main couple that he is] the wandering Jew, a man condemned by Christ to wandering over the face of the earth until Christ comes again. He had the wisdom of the ages which he imparts to these young people."[52] An early report states that like *The Greater Glory*, *Sinners* would be produced "on a lavish scale."[53] Anna Q. Nilsson and Lewis Stone were signed to play the leads with Balboni directing. But a month later *Variety* announced that

Mathis had changed her mind and would now make *The Masked Woman* as her first production with Nilsson and Balboni.[54]

Mathis and Balboni's initial release in collaboration was *The Far Cry*, starring Blanche Sweet and Jack Mulhall. With a script by Katharine Kavanaugh and released in February 1926, the film was something of a dramatic version of *We Moderns*. Two young Americans, Sweet a divorcée, meet in Paris and then live together in Italy against their parents' wishes. Like Moore's comedy, the film is critical of the young generation, and the heroine is once again saved from a fire while at a party with the man who has tried to steal her away. This final scene was in color. A report from the manager of the National Theater in Graham, Texas, indicates the cultural/artistic goals of Mathis and Balboni in the film: "This picture was produced in a very lavish manner. The story is good; cast excellent. The technicolor sequences are really beautiful. It pleased the better class of my patrons; but the ordinary crowd just won't fall for [this] stuff—Paris divorce courts and Venetian water scenes. They seem to want home-brew here."[55] *Variety* found the film "flatly prosaic" where the stage play had been "far more subtle" but still called it "a good picture." However, that did not make it "an exceptional draw."[56]

As her work shifted more into producer, Mathis took every chance she could to capitalize on her success with Valentino by promoting her own star-making and casting abilities. She attributed these to some mysterious personal instinct: "I can tell at a glance how a player will look in any costume and I know at once whether or not he will do for a part," she bragged. As an example, she claimed, "A face with distinct American, modern characteristics will never successfully don old-world clothes or go back to the sixteenth century," a definition so indistinct that anyone could make it and sound like an expert without having any knowledge at all. But Mathis backs it up with two specific examples. First, she claims "everyone" told her John Sainpolis would not do for an important part in *The Viennese Medley* because he was not blond. Her response was, "'He can bleach his hair. He has the soul for the part'. . . . He did bleach his hair and was a success." She then claims, "Corliss Palmer is a new player who has that something and should do well on the screen. I selected her for a role in 'The Second Chance' because she seemed to me to have a certain wistfulness and appeal on the screen that ought to carry her far."[57]

Her Second Chance was another June Mathis Production, this one directed by Lambert Hillyer with a screenplay by Eve Unsell. "The Second

Chance" was the original title taken from the short story source. *Motion Picture News* reviewer Frank Elliott believed it would do well because of its entertainment value despite the unbelievably quick transformation of the main character from a "crude mountain girl into a brilliant, beautiful young lady." He added, "Corliss Palmer makes her debut in an unimportant bit."[58] Despite Mathis's high opinion of her, Palmer's career lasted only until 1931 and included just a few small roles in minor productions.[59] Also notable about the film's credits is a character referred to as "A darky stable boy."[60]

Mathis had been successful often enough with casting she probably believed in these statements about her ability. Claiming to have this talent also fit with her mystical beliefs; she chose actors whom she found had "soul" or "that something." Fan magazines helped with her self-promotion through pieces like "Aspiring Valentinos Seek Aid of June Mathis."[61] Following her angry split with the Valentinos, she may have confused some of these hopefuls by proclaiming she now believed the day of the Latin lover was over and predicted great success for Lloyd Hughes as the movies' next big romantic star. Hughes did have a twenty-year career, and Sainpolis's lasted thirty, though neither was featured in any notably great successes. Sometimes Mathis could go too far in her efforts to demonstrate her ability. Thus, Katherine Hoffman of Miami, Florida, suddenly found herself identified by Mathis as a new star one day while touring First National. Mathis simply looked at her and said, "Yes, she's got it," and offered her a contract. The picture accompanying the newspaper report of the incident shows Mathis standing on one side of Hoffman and Colleen Moore, looking uncomfortably off to the side, on the other. The young woman could only say that "she would have to ask her mother about what to do next."[62]

In spite of completing half of her required productions for the year, Mathis's new unit did not provide the relief she had hoped for. On March 16, 1926 as she was in New York's Fifth Avenue Hospital awaiting surgery to remove a large tumor from her abdomen, she produced a handwritten will and signed it "June Balboni." Mathis reveals her state of mind in the comment "not witnessed except by God in full solemnity."[63] She bequeathed her property to her grandmother "to revert in turn to my dearly beloved husband [Silvano Balboni] with this he is to provide faithfully for my step sister Laura Mary Mathis as long as she lives."[64] She then wrote a short letter to Laura Mary, to let her know "Bal will look out for you." She added, "Here too is a line for George telling him I love him and also Sam [her stepbrothers]— we have all been close."[65] Mathis sometimes sent George and Sam clothes that did not always fit their needs, so they would come up with creative uses. Sam, for example, once wore the tuxedo June gave him on his rural mail route in Minnesota.[66]

Mathis's primary affection was for her family, especially Laura Mary, twelve years her senior. The personal details in letters such as those written from Rome on March 3, 1924, provide the best personal insights on her. While writing about her efforts to meet a man there, she twice uses the catchphrase "you know me, Al," suggesting Laura understood a lot that was not written. Mathis signs her letter, "Oceans of love as ever, June."[67] Mathis's nephew, Philip Arthur Junio Balboni remembered Laura as "a very sweet person."[68] Laura followed June onto the stage in 1902, and while the length of her career, if she had one at all, is unknown, the experience probably added to their closeness.[69] It also seems likely that Laura shared Mathis's interests in literature, history, art, and beauty and maybe even inspired these.

Philip Balboni also met Silvano on his farm outside of Rome years later and remembered him as very nice. Occasionally, old friends from Hollywood stopped by. One time, it was Stan Laurel who entertained the kids with card tricks.[70] Balboni's artistic interests, wit, and great looks had to be attractive qualities. Perhaps his Italian looks reminded Mathis of Valentino, but their marriage, though brief, was happy.

Following her convalescence, Mathis again became flooded with work. In April 1926, the journal *Film Fun* wrote that "June Mathis, scenarist, has a lazy life. All she has to do just now, for instance, is to cut and edit 'The Viennese Medley,' editorially direct 'Irene,' Colleen Moore's new offering, . . . look after 'The Far Cry,' . . . see to the screen treatment and continuity of Corinne Griffith's new attraction, 'Mlle. Modiste,' and several other productions, meet and talk to forty persons a day, attend all the conferences held by the executive departments which have to do with production, write and prepare continuities herself and find time to run out on the sets to watch the work progress. Ho, hum, it's a dull life!"[71]

One problem for *The Greater Glory* may have been that Mathis chose Curt Rehfeld, a man with some unusual characteristics, to make his debut as a director with the film. Rehfeld was a former German military man who had been assistant director on *The Four Horsemen*. He was also a fitness enthusiast with a reputation for imposing strict fitness regimens on his cast, a trait that made enemies for him on the productions of both *Classified* and *The Greater Glory*.[72] These problems might also have caused delays, though the studio maintained an upbeat view of the production. On November 4, 1925, the *Los Angeles Times* reported that Mathis was cutting *The Greater Glory* and First National was negotiating with Richard Strauss to write a musical score for the film. Three months later Mathis said that waiting for color film for some episodes had caused "a short delay."[73]

The film was finally released on May 2. Viewing a print of "about 11 reels" in early May 1926, *Variety's* "Sisk." wrote that Rehfeld's effort was "adequate, [but] it cannot be said that he showed an inspired moment in the whole film."[74] The novel included twenty-one characters. Mathis cut that to twelve, but that was still too many. She produced a print of thirty reels, which was cut to nine. The *New York World* reported that this severe cutting left it episodic, incomplete, and loaded with titles that go by so fast only rapid readers can complete them.[75]

Finally, following its release, *Zit's* entertainment paper revealed some insights and pronounced their judgment: "First National makes no secret of the fact that they hauled in the reins at the last minute and realized their film was not quite so good. There followed months of frantic cutting and the picture came down to its present footage, which is about eight reels, or at least seven and a half too long."[76] Harriet Underhill of the *New York Herald Tribune* echoed this opinion: "The picture is the longest and dullest we ever hope not to sit through again. And aside from the money expended one realizes that the beautiful story is now lost to the screen forever."[77] Mathis reportedly began production with a script of a thousand scenes that she cut by a hundred; whether before the start of filming or after is not clear.[78]

However, the film also received many positive reviews. While several found the narrative too complicated, others praised the film's beauty and acting, particularly that of May Allison. *The Morning Telegraph* exclaimed, "It is not the principal thread of the story that makes 'The Greater Glory' an unusual and even remarkable picture, but the extraordinary amount of characterization crowded into it and the wealth of detail found in every scene." The last two points were traditional Mathis strengths. *The Evening World* commented, "June Mathis as adaptor and Curt Rehfeld as director attempted the almost impossible—and almost succeeded. The difficulties were enormous. No less than twenty-two players have parts entitling them to program credit. It is remarkable that the characters were as fully developed as they were. There is not a bad performance in the lot."[79]

The National Board of Review discussion of the film on April 23 mirrors this wide range of opinion and provides insights professional reviewers missed. A Mr. Paulding began with an appropriate observation: "It seems to me to bear some resemblance to 'The Four Horsemen of the Apocalypse.'" The film's detractors then felt confident enough to plunge right in. Mr. Kuttner: "The allegorical part is very poor—stupid movie stuff"; Mrs. Price: "I don't see why it should be on the list [for movies to be considered as meritorious] at all. It seems to me false, story full of loopholes, has no unity, jerky. Some of the acting is good"; Mrs. Patterson: "I think the characterization of the family pretty poor . . . and the ending, having Anna killed off in the riot, is very crude. . . . So much tawdriness."[80] (This comment is reminiscent of a board member's criticism of *Out of the Fog* in 1919 that films presenting a woman's struggles against misogyny should be banned for not being uplifting.)

The tone changes later, though, when a Mrs. Mencken courageously offers, "I liked the picture very much. Crude in spots but on the whole I liked it."[81] A Miss Hackney then goes into detail of how the film has actually attempted something new and important, which she believes it achieved: "In regard to the over elaboration of the last part, we in America have had very little stress laid on the contrast in Europe between poverty and luxury. I think this is the first attempt to drive home to us this tremendous social contrast in the metropolises. I think it quite remarkable in that it has brought in that new point in war psychology." Mrs. Hackney finds great depth in the film's depiction of civilian wartime struggles: "I think it as sincere as anything we have had referred to us lately. I think it a great deal better than 'The Four Horsemen.' That was very much more theatrical and photography worse, simply a surface attempt to depict war conditions. This digs down a little bit into the real emotions of the people living them."

Mr. Kuttner then jumps back in with an excellent insight: "What struck me was that it was delightfully free from the usual movie morality. Fanny [the main character] does not repent and become a war nurse, the man does not give her up because she has become a prostitute. It shows the utter subversion of morality which existed." Dr. Smith adds his agreement: "I would make the point that the fact that the woman sinking so low but nevertheless is permitted to achieve her love at the end, is out of the ordinary [in the] movie world and a great credit to the director." These viewers, in other words, looked past what others defined as the movie's drawbacks to find Mathis and Rehfeld breaking stereotypes in depicting their characters, especially the women, as humans. Miss Hackney at least also saw it as encouraging Americans to broaden their compassion.[82] *Photoplay's* reviewer admired the emphasis on character over spectacle: "No insincere attempt is made for the so-called 'punch' or 'thrill.' It is one of the most sincerely produced pictures ever presented to the American public, one of those rare pictures that you can stand seeing twice."[83]

Mathis seems not simply to have desired to adapt a Great War epic in order to relive her *Four Horsemen* triumph, but also to once again point out the great hidden suffering of the war and condemn those who profited from it. She furthermore had a feminist theme in the character of Fanny who is more reminiscent of Iras in *Ben-Hur* rather than Marguerite in *Four Horsemen*. Fanny is not condemned for selling her body to survive; she is instead understood. In the end, twelve National Board of Review members voted to give the film a minor mention of merit, while six voted against.[84] Of course, in 1921, the end of the war had been much more recent, and *The Four Horsemen* had not focused on women's struggles to survive; it had a heroine who could lead by exemplifying a traditional woman's role of service; and it had the intriguing new sexuality and talent of Rudolph Valentino. In *The Greater Glory*, Mathis offered a picture of hardship and struggle to a mass audience that had little interest in the topic. In 1939, *Gone with the Wind* offered heroic perseverance in the face of disaster, a perspective audiences could identify with in hindsight and in looking to the near future. Audiences in 1926, however, did not seem especially interested in either remembering or anticipating disasters.

Throughout that year, Mathis began to feel that "the details involved in production management and writing scenarios to meet a definite release schedule restricted her writing to a great extent."[85] In October, the American Motion Picture Association voted her the third most influential woman in movie history, finishing behind only Mary Pickford and Norma Talmadge.[86] But McCormick's criticism of her writing continued as she worked on the script for another comedy, *Here Y'Are Brother*, eventually filmed as *An Affair of the Follies* (Millard Webb, 1927), starring Billie Dove. It was meant to be another June Mathis Production, but her work seems to have come under McCormick's supervision as he was in charge of West Coast productions. Colleen Moore's biographer, Jeff Cordori, writes that McCormick felt great pressure because "if Colleen's career faltered, it would be a reflection on his abilities."[87] When First National later sued the Mathis estate for her failure to produce one last screenplay she owed them, the studio's Rob Allison wrote to Mathis estate attorney Karl E. Levy, "I remember very distinctly that Mr. McCormick was not satisfied with her work [for *An Affair of the Follies*—released in February 1927 and not a Colleen Moore film], and as a matter of fact, he had several people do it over and finally the supervision of the picture was placed in the hands of Mr. A. L. Rockett [chief of First National Story Department]."[88] But Mathis seems to have had a different viewpoint as she complained about McCormick's interference and ultimately asserted that she would use her script or the film would not be made.[89] She may have had the same opinion about her script for *We Moderns*. In any case, through illness and arguments, Mathis had experienced enough. On October 29, she wrote Rowland a letter of resignation, "Owing to conditions which have developed between the production office and myself, which in my opinion disregard the spirit of my letter-contract with First National."[90] She sent McCormick a copy. It was accepted on October 31.

In spite of her defense of her work, Mathis's subservience played a role in her departure from the studio. At one point, she wrote to company executives thanking them for having allowed her a leave of absence. On October 30, 1926, First National responded to her resignation of the day before with a letter expressing thanks that she had been "so gracious and appreciative of the treatment received by you from First National during your illness." They also asserted that she owed them one more continuity to be completed by November 1, 1927.[91] This claim would lead to the lawsuit following her death.

The Masked Woman, Balboni's second directorial effort, with a scenario by Mathis, and the third June Mathis Production for First National, was finally released in January 1927, eight months after *The Greater Glory*. For this film, Mathis appears to have completely changed her philosophy. She told the press that after careful study, she had decided that what the public wants is "the smart picture." These she defines as ones with "big production pieces with pretty ladies galore and gorgeous costumes." She explains, "It has been my experience that the simple story with but few sets is not nearly so likely to hit as the big spectacular production with a wealth of production material—provided, of course, that it is well done. The exhibitor likes his pictures dressed up."[92]

A *Variety* report on the production emphasized Balboni's great ability to make use of available space and technology. Mathis's and Clarence Brown's reports on Balboni's knowledge were not exaggerations. He started as an actor in 1910 and then became a director of photography and assistant director at the Actna Company of Sicily until the war interrupted his career. After working at Windsor Films and Broadhurst Films in England, he came to America and was lucky to have Brown recognize his talent and recommend him to Mathis for *Ben-Hur*.[93] *Variety* reported on his innovativeness in taking advantage of the spaciousness and technical capabilities of the First National studios. For *The Masked Woman*, he "had an elevator attachment connected to an aerial truck with a runway suspended from the rafters 40 feet above the stage itself. Sixteen cameras were trained on the set at various angles and the moving truck shooting the scene from one corner of the set to the opposite without so much as a break in the action. The first shots were long range with the distance gradually lessening and climaxing in close ups directly over the players." Balboni was also shooting "scenes from the rear with the camera stationed in the rafters and gradually brought closer and lower by means of another aerial truck. This type of camera work is made feasible at the new First National studio because of the extreme height of the stages."[94]

During filming, journalist Duvinelle Benthall chronicled a specific example of Mathis's activities as she watched Balboni direct a scene. In an incident that might very likely have been repeated hundreds of times in Mathis's career, Balboni asked, "'How did that look dear?' [She replied,] beautiful, except for one girl who 'tried to take a stellar walk.' Not for a second had her eyes left the scene while the cameras were grinding. Not the slightest detail escaped her. A remarkable woman. One of the names that we have known longest in pictures—June Mathis."[95]

On February 13, 1927, First National released their final film with a Mathis screenplay, *An Affair of the Follies*, starring Lewis Stone and Billie Dove and directed by Millard Webb. Comments from reviewers on this light production are generally positive and the film has some unique elements that go against the racy suggestiveness of its title. Dove quits dancing in the Follies to marry the poor clerk Stone. When he loses his job, she goes back to the stage to support him. Lloyd Hughes is a millionaire who falls in love with Dove. But rather than scheming to win her, he helps the couple, and the film ends happily. Webb's direction is praised, but how much of Mathis's script was used is unknowable, as copies of neither the script nor the film appear to exist.[96]

In early 1927, Joe Schenck, who (possibly unbeknownst to her) had been responsible for Mathis's removal from *Ben-Hur*, signed her to United Artists. She was first reported to be working on a script for a John Barrymore film and then on Corinne Griffith's *The Garden of Eden*, which she was later said to have completed.[97] But she is not credited as the film's screenwriter, so it seems possible that her work for this film was also rejected.

As a freelancer, Mathis wrote at least two drafts of a screenplay for MGM's *The Enemy* (Fred Niblo, 1927; script by Willis Goldbeck). Like *The Greater Glory*, this film was also about Viennese families who were shattered by the war and primarily focused on a young mother's struggle to feed her starving baby. In these scripts, Mathis continued her arguments against militarism and greed and for the values of spirituality and the concerns of women.

A first draft of Mathis's script based on a 1925 play by Channing Pollock is dated January 25, 1927.[98] Set again in Vienna just before the war, the film centers on a student named Carl Behrend who has written an antiwar play called *The Enemy*, which identifies hatred as the major nemesis of humanity. Carl is determined to get his work produced, become a writer, and marry Pauli Arndt, daughter of his favorite professor. When an important producer accepts his work, Carl and Pauli marry but he is soon caught up in patriotic fervor and goes off to war. The war turns Austria upside down. One especially interesting scene in this draft suggests the war's impact on civilian women and shows sympathy for a lonely Central Powers soldier. Carl, wandering the countryside and frustrated with the war, sits down on a fence to talk to a Russian "gypsy" girl. He is thinking about seducing her when he opens a letter from Pauli telling him about his new son. He walks away, and a few seconds later, she is killed by a rocket.[99] Very soon afterward, Mathis begins a scene with a close-up of the baby in Pauli's arms. She then calls for a "(Trick camera effect of the baby's features dissolving, as near as possible, into Carl's)."[100] These scenes suggest powerful realities of war: soldiers seeking sexual comfort, losing their sense of purpose, deaths of innocent civilians, and the separation of families. Perhaps the killing of the woman on-screen, which sounds quite graphic for the times, was too strong for the MGM executives and prompted the call for a rewrite.

Carl's father becomes a major profiteer, warehousing piles of food and cloth while his countrymen, including Pauli, her father, and her child (his grandchild) are starving and freezing. Behrend, formerly a great friend of Arndt and now grandfather to Pauli's child, does nothing to help. Pauli goes to his warehouse but is turned back by the guards. She buys a little milk, but someone steals it and a riot breaks out. In the end, Mathis draws on the scene of Pere Grandet suffocated by his gold in *The Conquering Power* to create a scene of Behrend trampled by a starving mob that breaks into his warehouse.[101] This conclusion may have been too repetitive of *The Greater Glory* and furthered the request for revision as that film also included a woman killed in a warehouse mob scene and a woman choosing prostitution, just as Pauli considers.[102]

Expressing a deep faith in art, Mathis prefaced her second draft of *The Enemy* with a statement only the production people would see:

> FORWARD [*sic*] Harriet Beecher Stowe's "Uncle Tom's Cabin"
> was directly responsible for the abolishment of slavery. And,
> unless the whole world is so blind it simply will not see, Channing
> Pollock's play, "The Enemy," is going to do more toward the
> realization of universal peace than Woodrow Wilson's Fourteen
> Points, the League of Nations, the World Court, and a dozen
> assorted Geneva Conferences.[103]

Whether or not Mathis believed that asserting a great theme would turn a standard production into a blockbuster, whether she was still trying to relive *The Four Horsemen* experience, or whether she believed the war had caused deep wounds that still needed to be addressed, this assertion that the movies, her art form, could help heal those wounds is present here as it had been throughout her career. She did not consider her films as an endpoint. Her goal was always to be one of the writers of "great artistic" works that would motivate movement toward a better world.

Mathis concluded *The Four Horsemen* with the Stranger warning that until love replaced hate in human hearts, the four horsemen would continue to spread misery. She opens her second draft of *The Enemy* with the intertitle

> EUROPE
> Battleground of the world. Through
> the ages the greedy spirit of Conquest
> has marked the ever-changing boundary
> lines of Nations with blood, sowing
> seeds of Hatred in the hearts of men.[104]

This message is not upbeat and probably not one the public wanted in 1927. While prosperity was the motto of the times, Mathis still warned about greed and hate. She tried to do so through a revised version of her greatest production, so the accusation that she was simply recycling a tried-and-true formula in another stab at greatness could be accurate. But the work might also suggest how she saw the world at that point. From her perspective, the industry had grown and offered wonderful new possibilities. But it was also more dominated by financial interests and women in the field were paying the price. That contrast with *The Four Horsemen* may be the most important element in her script for *The Enemy*. While Marguerite Laurier had been an angelic and inspirational figure without even intending to be, Pauli Arndt has to fight for survival.

In this draft, Mathis makes more use of montage than in any previous work. Following the opening title about hatred, she calls for a "montage starting with map of Europe and Roman feet trampling on it, Roman soldiers and repeated through to 1871."[105] Scene two calls for another including the Emperor's spring parade (if there was such a thing), marching troops, and an amusement park. Mathis hammers home the theme of war as destructive of culture and beauty and includes her usual details for authenticity. Scene sixteen includes a montage of news headlines over the month following the Archduke's assassination and leading up to Carl and Pauli's wedding and the start of the war.[106] A *Four Horseman* element in the script involves the parallels between the war fever in countries on both sides. As Carl leaves for the front, Pauli comforts him. Carl's prowar father offers the accurate comment, "And in St. Petersburg—in Paris—Berlin and London—women are doing the same."[107] In *Four Horsemen*, the Stranger uttered this line to emphasize the universal suffering of war. Carl's father is more likely thinking of how he can profit from the absence of social morality. As Carl marches off to war, Mathis calls for shots of a small bird retreating into a tree in Pauli's garden and her house emptied of art and beauty. In a time of hardship, these must be sacrificed for food.

Mathis still inserts references to artworks as models for specific scenes, writes intertitles in verse, and uses cultural details gained through research in an effort to raise the film to a lofty artistic level. For the opening scene, she suggests, "(Try to get an effect here similar to a painting by the great artist, Messonier, of the Franco-Prussian war)."[108] Soon after, Mathis notes that as he lies in bed one morning, Carl hears a band of street musicians playing outside his window. She informs the director, "It is usual to find one of a group of street musicians blind."[109] After a scene referencing the 1914 Christmas truce, Mathis writes, "Cut in this verse[:] The boom of guns gave way to a Christmas bell. And the world stood still like a halted hell."[110]

Another *Four Horsemen* reference is the character of Professor Arndt who parallels the Christlike figure of the Stranger in the earlier film. While war fever rages, Mathis refers to him lecturing his students "like a veritable Man of Sorrow."[111] She then calls for a shot of light shining in on him with a flag of Vienna, which includes a white cross, behind him. Later, Mathis includes a conversation in which Carl's father claims it's glorious to die for one's country. The Professor responds, "Yes, August—I've often heard it spoken of highly by men who don't do it!"[112] Mathis also includes more of the pro-American emphasis present in *The Four Horsemen* such as an intertitle that states, "Another year has passed and America came into the war, and after that the Armistice. America became the provider for starving Europe, and the first to send its relief trains into the stricken city of Vienna, under the supervision of the great American, Herbert Hoover."[113]

Mathis also builds on her depiction of greed by showing how Behrend's former servants Jan and Barushka manage to gain land, raise a few crops, and then grow very rich selling them at exorbitant prices. The theme of war's destruction of beauty and art continues as Pauli sells Carl's typewriter for food money and Professor Arndt sells his prized statue of Winged Victory for five eggs.[114]

Mathis's most harrowing depiction of this theme involves the figure of a young violinist who lives next door to the Behrends. In yet another borrowing from *Four Horsemen*, this character also parallels the Stranger but now in terms of appearance. Mathis introduces him by writing, "The young violinist is a spiritual-looking boy of about twenty-two—the artist-gypsy type. He plays as though his entire soul were in the music, as his long tapering fingers caress the violin."[115] This description defines the musician as an artist, and Mathis is calling for a performer who can communicate the spirituality of his music. But he is now unable to make his music rise above the conflict. As the Professor and Pauli are struggling with their hunger, they again hear the violinist who has returned from the war. But now the Professor complains about it, and a repeated close-up of the musician's hand shows why. He is trying but failing to play with two fingers missing. He stops and takes his life with a pistol.[116]

Later, Mathis reasserts her preference for staying with characters in present time. Jan has been in the fighting, returned mentally damaged, and is telling Pauli that Carl has been wounded and taken prisoner. This is at a point in the narrative parallel to the montage leading up to the war. But Mathis writes, "(NOTE: We can do a dissolve here of what happened, but I feel that it would break the straight action of the story—unless we can keep our characters in the drama on the screen at the same time)."[117] Others might feel that a montage of action from the war and Carl suffering in a prison camp would be preferable. But Mathis feels that the real drama is with Jan and Pauli; she shows that war's devastation now includes vast numbers of civilians. Jan begins acting wildly as some troops march by. Pauli, holding her baby who dies in her arms, yells at the passing soldiers, "Not my baby! He won't answer your trumpets—he'll never feel mud and agony—and bullets—I've nothing more to feed your guns. My baby is safe—my baby is dead—thank God—thank God—thank God!"[118]

Pauli represents the return of the woman with a moral message in Mathis's work. But these women are not the spiritually transcendental figures of her earlier films. They are strong but troubled. They fear for their husband's lives, care for the deranged and wounded who have returned, and watch their infants starve. They represent Mathis's main concern as expressed by Pauli's father who yells at Behrend, "All war is an outrage on women. All other outrages are as nothing to that. The supreme criminal is not the animal in the trenches—but the Statesman who declares war!"[119]

The script concludes not with the mob attacking Behrend and his warehouse as in the first draft. Instead, it follows Carl's best friend, the British Bruce, who has snuck back to the city to see Pauli because he believes she has been widowed. But as he was only a prisoner, Carl arrives just in time to save Bruce from the mob after it discovers him. The ending echoes the final pleading lines of *The Four Horsemen*. Professor Arndt says, "God give us Tolerance!" Carl adds, "God give us Love!" And Pauli ends the film with "God give us Peace!"[120] It is interesting that where Mathis sought to challenge viewers at the conclusion of *Four Horsemen*, the characters here ask for a better world as a gift from God. But the death of Pauli's baby, representing multitudes more, is a very dark vision that prayers for peace could not vanquish.

MGM must not have been satisfied and turned to another writer, Willis Goldbeck. He produced a treatment that condensed many of the plot elements Mathis had into fewer scenes and included two significant intertwined motifs of marching men and calls for unity overwhelmed by military music. He also includes Pauli rejoicing that her baby has died and will not grow to know the suffering of war. What Goldbeck provided that the studio probably wanted most, however, was a happy ending. While

Mathis had Carl return in the midst of turmoil and ended with the three main characters offering prayers for peace, Goldbeck cuts from the death of Pauli's baby to some unspecified later time. The Behrends and Arndts have mended their differences and are relaxing together at a cottage. A group of children playing soldiers shows that peace is not secure. New generations will always be ready to go to war. But for now reunion has overcome strife. Pauli believes Carl is dead. Bruce proposes to her but Pauli says no. Goldbeck then finishes somewhat caustically: "Then Carl reveals himself. Bruce is happy to see Pauli's happiness again. There is the happy end."[121] The clipped tone of those lines suggests Goldbeck had a very practical attitude toward this work. Give the studio and the audiences what they want and get on to the next screenplay. He treats the material with great respect throughout and gets the emotions across with a combination of concise dramatic scenes and montage. But Mathis would never finish a dramatic screenplay with a comment that suggested she was merely delivering what the studio executives wanted. When she had written one per request for *The Four Horsemen*, she sincerely hoped that it would not be used.

In her last seven months, Mathis was very aware of how Hollywood filmmaking had changed and seemed frustrated that her success would now depend on many others. In an article with the upbeat title of "Mathis Sees Day of Movie Co-operation," she comments, "We have had many instances of stars or directors who demonstrated striking ability in one or several pictures, and then, given every facility that money, skill or experience could bring to bear to make them repeat their successes, failed to do so. Perhaps the failure was their own—perhaps it was that of one or several of the other vital elements. The most responsible individual in production today, and one whose power is to grow, is the unit producer, editor, chief or supervisor—whatever his title may be—who acts as coach and manager of all the elements of the film team, and co-ordinates their efforts."[122] No longer claiming success with making directors see things her way, Mathis now related, "I can not, as a fiction writer often does, live on my name. I must fight as hard today to get points over with the director as I did when I was completely unknown. Movies need new writers with new ideas, but on those writers the struggle for survival picture by picture, is merciless."[123]

On June 27 or 28, Mathis headed to New York to tend to her ailing grandmother.[124] On July 4 or 5, Balboni received a message stating that

Mrs. Hawkes was "on the road to recovery."[125] On July 27, Balboni sent his own telegram to Sam Mathis in Milano, Minnesota: "George got news from the associated press that June died in a New York Theatre overcome by the heat am leaving for New York leaving Laura at home courage."[126] Balboni and Laura were in Los Angeles at the time. Mathis's cause of death is recorded as "chronic valvular heart disease" brought on by breaking her diet with "an unrestrained meal" before attending the theater that day.[127] Funeral services took place at both the Campbell Funeral Church on Broadway and Sixty-Sixth Street in New York where Valentino's body had lain in state just eleven months earlier and at the W. M. Strother funeral parlor in Hollywood a week later. First National, Charles Chaplin, Tom Moore, Colleen Moore, George Ullman, Valentino's manager, "and the Fan Club of New York" sent floral tributes to Campbell's. Attendees included Richard Rowland, Florence Strauss, head of First National's scenario department, Mabel Taliaferro, and Arthur James, editor of *Motion Picture World*.[128] Balboni and Mrs. Hawkes then accompanied the body by train to Los Angeles where Ullman made the arrangements and according to *Exhibitors Herald*, thousands passed by her body as it lay in state for two hours.[129]

First National's floral tribute was something of an empty gesture, probably urged by Rowland. The studio's actual final gesture was to sue her estate for about $15,004 still outstanding from $22,500 they had paid her toward the one final script she owed them. A letter to First National vice president Watterson Rothacker from the Los Angeles law firm of Loeb, Walker and Loeb, dated June 5, 1928, asked if he would sign the claim against the estate because Rowland had refused to "in view of the personal friendship which existed between [him] and Miss Mathis."[130] In a telegram a week later, Rothacker stated he would rather have one of two other vice presidents, A. L. Rockett or [Mr.] Marin, sign.[131] The lawyer's letter had asked that the claim be signed and returned "with all reasonable speed" as the deadline for filing was coming soon. Nevertheless, the case dragged on. Perhaps the estate lawyers got an extension.

On September 6, 1928, Mathis's longtime associate Katharine Kavanaugh submitted a story titled "Her Boy Friend" as evidence of work on the final script she owed.[132] On December 10, a Doris Malloy summarized and evaluated the work for Vice President Rockett: "This is a very obvious and artificial 'Cinderella' story. . . . However in the hands of a clever writer this might be brought up to date. Story evidently written for Colleen Moore."[133]

Another reader Pauline Forney had already suggested three months earlier that although the story was "slight" with "stuff" Moore had already done in another picture, she found it "a very sympathetic little story with a promising angle of development." She believed, "It should furnish Miss Moore an opportunity for a new and unique characterization, and a chance to build production values in the way of exotic stage settings." In closing, she wrote, "If this story was completed, it might be well worth considering as alternate compensation" for the work Mathis owed the company.[134] That First National rejected this advice and then gave the story to Malloy raises the possibility that they did not want to find a suitable property that would deny them the money. They then asked Malloy's opinion on another Mathis story, "A Child of the Sun," this one about a wild young Mexican girl who falls in love with the son of a wealthy and oppressive mine owner, "Told against a background of revolution, strikes, and stealthy intrigue." Malloy again does not seem impressed and refers to the script as "rambling [and] loosely-constructed."[135]

On January 31, 1929, Rockett wrote a communiqué rejecting Mathis's script of *The Scarlet Power*, written for Valentino in 1923.[136] Finally, on February 8, First National attorneys received a letter from Mathis estate attorneys Andreani and Haines, asking if they would like to consider a continuity of the novel *The Fortieth Door*; they did not.[137] Whether First National succeeded in their suit is not clear.

On August 14, 1927, United Artists released *The Magic Flame*, the final film with a June Mathis screenplay. Ironically, Bess Meredyth, who expressed such relief at Mathis's departure from Italy, received credit for the adaptation. *The Film Spectator* claimed it would help maintain her status, though *Variety* gave complete credit for its success to director Henry King and leads Ronald Colman and Vilma Bánky.[138]

In December 1927, Adela Rogers St. Johns paid high tribute to Mathis, calling her "beyond dispute one of the two greatest [screenwriters] who have yet lived."[139] In later years, occasional praise would also come from historians like Benjamin Hampton and Lewis Jacobs. But the most appropriate statement came soon after her death from *Hollywood Vagabond*, which proclaimed,

> If we are a people who recognize the immortality of great achievements, as we claim to do, and, further pledge ourselves to

perpetuate the memories of their creators, then the name of June Mathis must live among us for many years to come.

For June Mathis brought fame, honor and progress to the motion picture and in justice to our own consciences we cannot permit time to dim her memory nor the sacrilege of forgetfulness to mar her legacy of attainment.

June Mathis . . . honor to her name![140]

Acknowledgments

Learning so much about June Mathis would not have been possible without the help of people who told me where to look and what to look for. It started with my doctoral adviser, Peter C. Rollins, at Oklahoma State, who introduced me to Mathis in 1984. Others have included Kevin Brownlow who shared material from his files, his personal copy of Mathis's unfilmed screenplay for *Ben-Hur*, copies of photos from his collection, and answers to numerous other email questions over the past twenty-five years. Ned Comstock at the University of Southern California Cinema and Television Library has also been tremendously helpful in guiding me to resources and making them available. Brett Service and Sandra Garcia-Myers were also very helpful with providing copies of rare documents and scripts as have been the staff of the Special Collections Department at the Academy of Motion Picture Arts and Sciences' Margaret Herrick Library.

Over the years, I have benefited from providential meetings with very special helpful people. I must give a very special thank-you to Ruth Barton, author of *Rex Ingram: Visionary Director of the Silent Screen*, for providing copies of relevant pages from Ingram's unpublished memoir, "A Long Way from Tipperary," held at the Trinity College Dublin archives. Another was Constance McCormick, whose personal collection of materials is at the University of Southern California but who told me about the Louise Boyer letters in the Special Collections room at Georgetown University. I was also fortunate to interview the late actress Patsy Ruth Miller and late screenwriter Frederica Sagor Maas, who provided bits of information about Mathis, Valentino, and Nazimova. Scholar and author David Stenn helped me contact Miller and also locate a copy of the court records for the battle over Mathis's will. Other study centers used have been the Library of Congress Moving Picture Research Center and Manuscript Division, the

Acknowledgments

University of California Los Angeles Film Collection and UCLA Library Special Collections, the New York Public Library for Performance Arts, the NYPL Archives, and the George Eastman Center for Film Studies in Rochester, New York. Thank you also to David Catlin, curator of the Edwin Carewe Legacy Archive and website, who provided a copy of the *Her Great Price* poster. I hope Carewe's full story also gets told soon.

Other very special people who have helped have been Donna Hill, curator of the Rudolph Valentino website, producer of several beautiful Valentino books and calendars, and supplier of many pictures from her personal collection. She helped me contact Diane Mathis Madsen, who provided copies of personal letters by her great-aunt June and several pictures from her personal collection, and put me in touch with Mathis's nephew, who told me about meeting Mathis's husband Silvano Balboni and her stepsister, Laura Mary Mathis. Diane Madsen's sister, the late Barbara Mathis Bacich, also provided an important personal letter from June Mathis to her stepsister, Laura. Donna Hill also put me in touch with Rebecca Eash, private researcher and genealogist extraordinaire, who found literally everything about June Mathis's early life and family history for me and only asked for thanks. Thank you, Rebecca. You provided an amazing part of this story. Valentino expert Jim Craig offered tremendous resources early on, including a treasured picture of June Mathis on the cover of *Motion Picture Director*. Thanks to Tracy Terhune who included me in the ninety-fourth Valentino Memorial Service, which he does a tremendous job of organizing each year.

At the school where I taught from 1990 to 2020, Indiana University of Pennsylvania, I am thankful for the support of several Humanities and Social Sciences Deans over the years and the support of various faculty committees for providing grants and sabbaticals. I also need to thank a number of graduate research assistants including Vasanthi Mariadass, Celeste Calderon, Bryce Lucas, Julia Galm, Theo Sery, Sultan Alqutami, Kalie Zamierowski, and Caroline Speller. They all did great, often tedious, work. IUP reference librarian Teresa McDevitt has also been invaluable in tracking down resources, especially after I retired and lost access to the databases.

I am deeply indebted to an anonymous reader for the University Press of Kentucky who provided copious notes and suggestions for improvement

Acknowledgments

on an earlier draft and editors Ashley Runyon and Natalie O'Neal Clausen who guided me step by step. Finally, supreme thanks must go to my wife, Mary Ann, for her love, support, and invaluable editing skills. She improved the quality of my writing immensely. My beautiful daughters, Gretchen and Alli, are also due unending gratitude. Their importance is beyond what can be said in all the words I can offer here or anywhere else.

Notes

Introduction: The Importance of June Mathis

1. "Studio News and Gossip," *Photoplay*, April 1923, 76.

2. "Ben-Hur Titles," memorandum, December 15, 1925, *Ben-Hur* production file 1, Cinema Arts Library, University of Southern California.

3. "June Mathis Is Named Director of Goldwyn's Editorial Department," *Exhibitors Herald*, December 9, 1922, 35.

4. "W. R. Hearst Speaks at Goldwyn-Cosmopolitan Big Sales Meeting," *Moving Picture World*, June 2, 1923, 381.

5. "June Mathis Now in Field of Free Lance," *Moving Picture World*, November 13, 1926, 85.

6. Alison McMahan, "Alice Guy Blaché," in *Women Film Pioneers Project*, eds. Jane Gaines, Radha Vatsal, and Monica Dall'Asta (New York: Columbia University Libraries, 2013), https://doi.org/10.7916/d8-5a4c-yq24.

7. Christel Schmidt, "Mary Pickford," in Gaines, Vatsal, and Dall'Asta, *Women Film Pioneers Project*, https://doi.org/10.7916/d8-nkzz-e525; Shelley Stamp, "Lois Weber," in Gaines, Vatsal, and Dall'Asta, *Women Film Pioneers Project*, https://doi .org/10.7916/d8-zsv8-nf69.

8. Tom Trusky, "Nell Shipman," in Gaines, Vatsal, and Dall'Asta, *Women Film Pioneers Project*, https://doi.org/10.7916/d8-ymha-rg65; Gavin Lambert, *Nazimova* (New York: Alfred A. Knopf, 1997), 213–214, 225–229.

9. Antonia Lant and Ingrid Periz, "Part Five: Introduction," in *Red Velvet Seat: Women's Writing on the First Fifty Years of Cinema*, eds. comp. Lant and Periz (London: Verso, 2006), 562.

10. Patricia Mellencamp, "Female Bodies and Women's Past-Times, 1890–1920," *East-West Film Journal* 6, no. 1 (1992): 19.

11. Cari Beauchamp, *Without Lying Down: Frances Marion and the Powerful Women of Early Hollywood* (New York: Lisa Drew/Scribner, 1997).

12. Kay Armatage, *The Girl from God's Country: Nell Shipman and the Silent Screen* (Toronto: University of Toronto Press, 2003), 33.

13. Armatage, *The Girl*, 22.

14. Shelley Stamp, *Lois Weber in Early Hollywood* (Berkeley: University of California Press, 2015), 6.

15. Stamp, *Lois Weber*, 8.

16. Armatage, *The Girl*, 22.

17. Karen Ward Mahar, *Women Filmmakers in Early Hollywood* (Baltimore: The Johns Hopkins University Press, 2006), 4.

18. Mahar, *Women Filmmakers*, 5.

19. Virginia Wright Wexman, "June Mathis," in Gaines, Vatsal, and Dall'Asta, *Women Film Pioneers Project*, https://doi.org/10.7916/d8-npcm-5927.

20. Wendy Holliday, "Hollywood's Modern Women: Screenwriting, Work Culture, and Feminism, 1910–1940" (PhD diss., New York University, 1995), 67–68.

21. Mahar, *Women Filmmakers*, 79–80.

22. Lant and Periz, "Part Five: Introduction," 570. The authors cite Rebecca West's argument that the difference in men's and women's artistry "lay in men being 'on the side of death, women on the side of life'; where men cut through life with a knife, women carried a box 'in which to shut up things and preserve them.'"

23. Christine Gledhill, "The Melodramatic Field: An Investigation," in *Home Is Where the Heart Is: Studies in Melodrama and the Woman's Film*, ed. Gledhill (London: British Film Institute, 1987), 21.

24. Gledhill, "The Melodramatic Field," 21.

25. Matthew Buckley, "Unbinding Melodrama," in *Melodrama Unbound: Across History, Media, and National Cultures*, eds. Christine Gledhill and Linda Williams (New York: Columbia University Press, 2018), 28.

26. Helen Day-Mayer and David Mayer, "Performing/Acting Melodrama," in Gledhill and Williams, *Melodrama Unbound*, 101.

27. Ann Douglas, *Terrible Honesty: Mongrel Manhattan in the 1920s* (New York: Farrar, Straus and Giroux, 1995), 7.

28. June Mathis, "The Feminine Mind in Picture Making," *Film Daily*, June 7, 1925, 115; rpt. in Lant and Periz, *Red Velvet Seat*, 663–665; qtd. in Jane Gaines, *Pink-Slipped: What Happened to Women in the Silent Film Industries?* (Urbana: University of Illinois Press, 2018), 158.

29. Commentary on Mathis and her work has been mixed. A series of reference works on film in general and women filmmakers in particular published between 1972 and 1991 did not do Mathis any favors. The first, Georges Sadoul's *Dictionary of Film Makers*, chiefly asserted that she was an editorial "pork butcher" who had chopped Erich von Stroheim's *Greed* (1925) to pieces. Rosemary Ribich Kowalski's *Women and Film: A Bibliography* (1976) repeats Sadoul's criticism. Ally Acker's *Reel Women* (1991) gives Mathis credit for her actual achievements but also contains errors (e.g., she devotes two pages to Mathis but mistakenly credits her with writing *The Sheik* [1921], with continuing to develop epics for Valentino after *Blood and Sand*, and with commencing work on *Ben-Hur* in 1925, not 1922). A detailed discussion of her work, especially on *Ben-Hur*, is present in Kevin Brownlow's *The Parade's Gone By* (1968), while Richard Koszarski's *An Evening's Entertainment* provides a good, though brief, discussion of Mathis's importance and

influence. Gavin Lambert's *Nazimova: A Biography* and Emily Leider's *Dark Lover: The Life and Death of Rudolph Valentino* add to our knowledge about her work with each of those stars. More recently, Hilary Hallett's *Go West, Young Women,* Karen Ward Mahar's *Women Filmmakers in Early Hollywood,* and the edited collection *Silent Women: Pioneers of Hollywood* offer useful short passages on Mathis. Besides this author's essays, Lauren Elizabeth Smith provides a detailed critical analysis in the anthology *When Women Wrote Hollywood* (2018).

1. June Mathis's Journey from Acting to Writing, 1897–1915

1. Blanche Yurka, *Bohemian Girl: Blanche Yurka's Theatrical Life* (Athens: Ohio University Press, 1970), 122.

2. *The Squall,* Internet Broadway Database, accessed August 8, 2018, https://www.ibdb.com/broadway-production/the-squall-8370.

3. Yurka, *Bohemian Girl,* 123–124.

4. "Famed Author Succumbs at 48th St. Show," July 27, 1927, June Mathis clippings file, Film Study Center, Museum of Modern Art.

5. "June Mathis Dies While at Theatre," *New York Times,* July 27, 1927, 1.

6. "Audience Sees June Mathis Die in Theater," *New York Herald Tribune,* July 27, 1927, 1.

7. "Audience Sees," 1; "June Mathis Dies While at Theatre," 1; "June Mathis in Dramatic Exit," publication unknown, July 27, 1927, Robinson Locke Collection, New York Public Library for the Performing Arts (NYPLPA-RLC); "June Mathis Dies Seated in Theater," publication unknown, July 27, 1927, NYPLPA-RLC; "Famed Author Succumbs at 48th St. Show," reported that she attended the play alone.

8. Yurka, *Bohemian Girl,* 124.

9. "Audience Sees," 1.

10. Untitled articles, *La Plata Home Press* (La Plata, MO), June 17, 1876, 2; March 3, 1877, 4; July 10, 1880, 4.

11. 1881 and 1882 Leadville City Directories, Leadville, CO; Untitled article, *Leadville Daily Chronicle,* September 3, 1889, 1.

12. "Town Topics," *Colorado Transcript,* August 17, 1881, n.p.

13. 1883 Minneapolis City Directory, Minneapolis, MN.

14. "A Card Party," *Leadville Daily Herald,* April 1, 1883, 3.

15. *Buena Vista Democrat* (Chaffee County, CO), February 19, 1885, n.p.

16. Evergreen Cemetery, Leadville, CO, Findagrave.com; *Herald Democrat* (Leadville, CO), March 18, 1886.

17. "Across the River Styx," *Herald Democrat,* November 13, 1887, 4.

18. "Adjudged Insane," *Denver Rocky Mountain News,* July 22, 1891, 2.

19. "The Hughes Liquor Cure a Success," *Minneapolis Tribune,* December 20, 1891, 10.

20. "The Liquor Traffic, and How to Regulate It," *Minneapolis Tribune,* February 18, 1892, 8; "Hughes' System," *Minneapolis Tribune,* February 21, 1892,

10; "An O'er True Tale," *Minneapolis Tribune*, March 6, 1892, 15; "Another Cure for Dipsomania," *The Pantagraph*, December 30, 1892, 7.

21. Untitled articles, *Minneapolis Tribune*, April 22, 1892, 5; April 26, 1892, 2.

22. "Drugs in the System," *Minneapolis Tribune*, December 28, 1893, 8.

23. "The Hughes Institute," *Minneapolis Tribune*, December 31, 1893, 5.

24. Untitled article, *Herald Democrat* (Leadville, CO), February 18, 1894, 3.

25. Summons, *Salt Lake Herald*, February 2, 1896, 3.

26. Untitled article, *Salt Lake Herald*, April 23, 1896, 10.

27. Marriage of Virginia Hughes and William Mathis, May 16, 1896, in Salt Lake City, no. 429056, Family History Library.

28. "Death of Dr. Hughes," *Herald Democrat*, June 2, 1896, 2.

29. Goldwyn Production Corporation, Biographical Information, November 29, 1922, Core Collection, June Mathis Biography File, Academy of Motion Picture Arts and Sciences.

30. "Success at Sixteen," *Deseret* (Salt Lake City) *Evening News*, December 27, 1902, 8.

31. Metro Fan letter, *Photoplay*, November 1919, n.p., NYPLPA-RLC.

32. "Start for California," *Salt Lake Tribune*, June 14, 1899, 5.

33. "June Wished Herself Back to Health," *Motion Picture Classic*, February 1927, n.p., NYPLPA-RLC.

34. Crocker-Langley San Francisco Directory, 1900, 1049, 1131, Internet Archive, accessed December 29, 2020, https://archive.org/details/crockerlangleysa 1900sanf/page/1100/mode/2up. Mathis listed as William D. although he did not live there.

35. "Salt Lake Girl Winning Stage Fame," *Salt Lake Telegram*, April 21, 1902, 3; "Society Events," *The Denver News-Letter*, April 18, 1891, 5; "Plays and Players: Sarah Bernhardt Great Attraction Wednesday and Thursday Evenings," *Star Tribune* (Minneapolis), September 27, 1891, 11. Bernhardt was in Denver when Mathis was three and in Minneapolis later that year after she turned four, which means that June may have seen her either time.

36. Nell Shipman, *The Silent Screen and My Talking Heart* (Boise, ID: Boise State University, 1987), 5.

37. Hilary Hallett, *Go West, Young Women!: The Rise of Early Hollywood* (Berkeley: University of California Press, 2013), 40.

38. Eileen Whitfield, *Pickford: The Woman Who Made Hollywood* (Lexington: University Press of Kentucky, 1997), 19, 22–23.

39. Shipman, *The Silent Screen*, 6–9.

40. "Talented Young Lady," *Sterling Standard*, November 5, 1901, 5; "Teachers' Institute," *Tampico Tornado*, April 27, 1877, 2. Entertainment at this gathering of the Whiteside County Teachers' Institute at the Prophetstown, Illinois M. E. Church on Saturday, April 21, included recitation by Jennie Wilcox. Mathis began her career with many such performances.

41. Jeanne Klein, "Without Distinction of Age: The Pivotal Roles of Child Actors and Their Spectators in Nineteenth-Century Theatre," *The Lion and the Unicorn* 36, no. 2 (2012): 120.

42. Katherine Lipke, "Most Responsible Job Ever Held by a Woman," *Los Angeles Times*, June 3, 1923, III:16.

43. "The Maori Association," *Salt Lake Herald*, October 8, 1898, 5.

44. "Dinner and Music at the Pen," *Salt Lake Herald*, November 25, 1898, 8.

45. "Home Forum," *Salt Lake Tribune*, February 6, 1899, 5.

46. "Little Miss June Mathis Is Achieving Fame," *Salt Lake Herald*, July 14, 1901, 3.

47. "Amusements," *Salt Lake Herald-Republican*, April 1, 1897, 5; "Success at Sixteen," 8.

48. Ann Douglas, *Terrible Honesty: Mongrel Manhattan in the 1920s* (New York: Farrar, Straus and Giroux, 1995), 241.

49. Ben Singer, *Melodrama and Modernity: Early Sensational Cinema and Its Contexts* (New York: Columbia University Press, 2001), 262.

50. Untitled article, *Cleveland Plain Dealer*, October 15, 1909, n.p., NYPLPA-RLC.

51. Crocker-Langley San Francisco Directory, 1900, 1049, 1131.

52. "Clever Salt Lake Child," *Salt Lake Tribune*, July 14, 1901, 14.

53. "Little Miss June Mathis," 3.

54. "Drama and Music," *Salt Lake Herald-Republican*, July 21, 1901, 16.

55. "At the Theaters," *Salt Lake Herald*, January 11, 1903, 22.

56. "Amusements," *Salt Lake Herald*, January 6, 1903, 8.

57. Qtd. in "At the Theaters," *Salt Lake Herald*, March 6, 1904. 3:5.

58. "With the Theaters," *Salt Lake Tribune*, January 3, 1908, 20.

59. "Play Gives Satisfaction," *The Anaconda Standard*, March 1, 1909, 5.

60. "'Going Some' Scores Big Success at Majestic," *Brooklyn Daily Eagle*, December 14, 1909, n.p., NYPLPA-RLC.

61. C. H. C., No Title, *Philadelphia Telegraph*, June 16, 1907, n.p., NYPLPA-RLC.

62. Photographs provided by Diane Mathis Madsen, grandniece of June Mathis.

63. Untitled article, *Vanity Fair*, July 6, 1912, n.p., NYPLPA-RLC.

64. Charles Burnetts, *Improving Passions: Sentimental Aesthetics and American Film* (Edinburgh, UK: Edinburgh University Press, 2017), 15.

65. David Mayer, *Stagestruck Filmmaker: D. W. Griffith and the American Theatre* (Iowa City: University of Iowa Press, 2009), 23; "June Mathis Is Now Screen Classics Chief Scenarist," *Motion Picture World*, August 9, 1919, 816.

66. "Career of June Mathis, Former Salt Lake Girl, High Light in Filmdom," *Salt Lake Tribune*, October 10, 1926, 10.

67. "W. D. Mathis Makes Home in California," *Salt Lake Tribune*, June 2, 1919, 18.

68. "Career of June Mathis," 10.

69. "Dead Broke," *Photoplay*, February 1927, 27.

70. "Triumph of Salt Lake Girl," *The Inter-Mountain Republican* (Salt Lake City), May 19, 1907, 6.

71. Lipke, "Most Responsible Job," 13.

72. "College Students Pack Theatre and Give June Mathis Ovation," *Salt Lake Herald-Republican*, November 30, 1908, 10.

73. "Salt Lake Girl Winning Stage Fame," 3; James L. Hoff, "Greater New York News," *The Billboard*, April 27, 1907, 48.

74. "Woman Forming Chain of Hotels for Stage Folk," *St. Louis Post-Dispatch*, November 7, 1909, 6.

75. "Group of Stage Stars Plans to Build Hotels," *The Billboard*, October 16, 1909, 5.

76. "June Mathis Goes In For Musical Comedy," *Salt Lake Herald-Republican*, October 30, 1910, 3.

77. A. H. Giebler, "News of Los Angeles and Vicinity," *Moving Picture World*, December 14, 1918, 1195.

78. "Eltinge Road Show Opens," *Variety*, January 3, 1919, 5.

79. Anthony Slide, *The Vaudevillians: A Dictionary of Vaudeville Performers* (Westport, CT: Arlington House, 1981), 47.

80. Mark Berger, email message to author, "Eltinge/June Mathis connection," November 14, 2003; Laurence Senelick, "Lady and the Tramp: Drag Differentials in the Progressive Era," in *Gender in Performance: The Presentation of Difference in the Performing Arts*, ed. Senelick (Hanover, NH: University Press of New England, 1992), 30, 43 (no. 15).

81. Robert C. Hart, "Black-White Literary Relations in the Harlem Renaissance," *American Literature* 44, no. 4 (January 1973): 613.

82. Christine Gledhill, "Prologue: The Reach of Melodrama," in *Melodrama Unbound: Across History, Media, and National Cultures*, eds. Christine Gledhill and Linda Williams (New York: Columbia University Press, 2018), xxii.

83. Emory B. Calvert, "In the New York Theatres," *The Ogden* (Utah) *Examiner*, April 12, 1914, 11.

84. Carl Van Vechten, "Beginnings of a Negro Drama," *The Literary Digest* 48, no. 19 (May 9, 1914): 1114.

85. James Weldon Johnson, *Black Manhattan* (New York: Alfred A. Knopf, 1930), 175.

86. Van Vechten, "Beginnings," 1114.

87. Michael Rogin, *Black Face, White Noise: Jewish Immigrants in the Hollywood Melting Pot* (Berkeley: University of California Press, 1996), 5.

88. Douglas, *Terrible Honesty*, 75.

89. Gledhill, "Prologue," xxii.

90. Gledhill, "Prologue," xxiii.

91. June Mathis, *A Trip to Paradise*, screenplay, scene 152X1, MPD file 016879-2839, New York State Education Department Archives; June Mathis,

Ben-Hur, screenplay, sc. 94. Screenplay provided to the author by Kevin Brownlow. For the *Trip to Paradise* scene of an old man having his picture taken, Mathis specifies he should be "a very wizened old man, with a silk hat. A distinct type (whom I have in mind)." For the crowd scene in *Ben-Hur*, Mathis instructs the cinematographer, "note scene carefully for opportunity to close-up various types of humanity for telling characterization effects."

92. "Sifted from the Studios," *Motography* XVI, no. 11 (1916): 620.

93. Lucille Erskine, "Vision and Service," *Camera!*, January 19, 1924, 13.

94. William J. Mann, *Behind the Screen: How Gays and Lesbians Shaped Hollywood, 1910–1969* (New York: Penguin Books, 2001), 12.

95. Susan A. Glenn, *Female Spectacle: The Theatrical Roots of Modern Feminism* (Cambridge, MA: Harvard University Press, 2000), 3; qtd. in Victoria Duckett, "Theater Actresses and the Transition to Silent Film," in *Women Film Pioneers Project*, eds. Jane Gaines, Radha Vatsal, and Monica Dall'Asta (New York: Columbia University Libraries, 2022), 4, https://doi.org/10.7916/b2jj-8714.

96. "A New Playwright," *Morning Telegraph* (New York), June 9, 1913, n.p., NYPLPA-RLC.

97. Hariett C. Klesilag, "Persistence, Preparation, Prosperity," *Dunkirk Evening Observer*, July 24, 1922, n.p.

98. "The 'Million Dollar Girl,'" *Photoplay*, October 1923, 63.

99. Joseph Jackson, "Growing Rich on Dreams," *Oakland Tribune Magazine*, February 4, 1922, 10.

100. Steven Maras, *Screenwriting: History, Theory and Practice* (London: Wallflower Press, 2009), 137–139.

101. "Salt Lake Actress Leaves Legitimate for 'Movie' Realm," *Salt Lake Telegram*, January 20, 1915, 16.

102. *The Fairy and the Waif* (1915), Full Cast and Crew, Imdb.com, accessed February 2, 2021, https://www.imdb.com/title/tt0005298/fullcredits?ref_=tt_cl_sm#cast.

103. "Career of June Mathis," 10.

104. Alice Tildesley, "The Road to Fame," *Motion Picture Magazine*, April 1926, 94.

105. Singer, *Melodrama*, 238.

106. "Salt Lake Actress," 16.

107. Cari Beauchamp, *Without Lying Down: Frances Marion and the Powerful Women of Early Hollywood* (New York: Lisa Drew/Scribner, 1997), 42.

108. Wendy Holliday, "Hollywood's Modern Women: Screenwriting, Work Culture, and Feminism, 1910–1940" (PhD diss., New York University, 1995), 65.

109. Holliday, "Hollywood's Modern Women," 44.

110. Bide Dudley, "About Plays and Players," *New York Evening World*, October 1, 1914, 20; "Women Find in Universal Plays Women Gowned in Fashion's Latest Modes," *Leavenworth Post*, December 26, 1914, 6.

111. Jackson Schmidt, "On the Road to MGM: A History of Metro Pictures Corporation, 1915–1920," *The Velvet Light Trap*, no. 19 (1982): 47–49.

112. Edward Azlant, "The Theory, History, and Practice of Screenwriting, 1897–1920" (PhD diss., University of Wisconsin-Madison, 1980), 122–123, 127–138; Maras, *Screenwriting*, 137–141.

113. Maras, *Screenwriting*, 138.

114. Tildesley, "The Road," 94.

115. "June Mathis Scores Success," 1; Tildesley, "The Road," 94.

2. Success at Metro, 1915–1921

1. Chip Rhodes, *Structures of the Jazz Age: Mass Culture, Progressive Education, and Racial Disclosures in American Modernism* (London: Verso, 1998), 46.

2. Peter Brooks, *The Melodramatic Imagination: Balzac, Henry James, Melodrama, and the Mode of Excess* (1976; repr., New Haven, CT: Yale University Press, 1995), 2.

3. Rhodes, *Structures of the Jazz Age*, 50.

4. June Mathis, "Scenario Writers Must Find Theme," *New York Times*, April 15, 1923, 3:1.

5. Lucille Erskine, "Vision and Service," *Camera!*, January 19, 1924, 13.

6. Hariett C. Klesilag, "Persistence, Preparation, Prosperity," *Dunkirk Evening Observer*, July 24, 1922, n.p.; Katherine Lipke, "Most Responsible Job Ever Held by a Woman," *Los Angeles Times*, June 3, 1923, III:16.

7. Lipke, "Most Responsible Job," 16.

8. June Mathis, "The Original Screen Story," *Story World and Photodramatist* 5, no. 2 (August 1923): 23.

9. Lipke, "Most Responsible Job," 13.

10. Charles Burnetts, *Improving Passions: Sentimental Aesthetics and American Film* (Edinburgh, UK: Edinburgh University Press, 2017), 37–38.

11. Lipke, "Most Responsible Job," 13.

12. Lipke, "Most Responsible Job," 16.

13. Burnetts, *Improving Passions*, 39.

14. Burnetts, *Improving Passions*, 41.

15. "Edwin Carewe to Direct June Mathis," *Moving Picture World*, December 18, 1915, 2163; "'The Scheme' Vehicle for Bushman-Bayne," *Motion Picture News*, June 1, 1918, 3278; "Metro Engages Thompson," *Motography* 19, no. 22 (June 1, 1918): 1054; "Metro Announces Releases for June," *Motography* 19, no. 22 (June 1, 1918): 1049. These articles all mention screenplays written by Mathis that apparently were never filmed, although *Motography* claims *The Scheme* was set for release on June 28, 1918. The others were *The Sheriff of God's Land* and *For Revenue Only*.

16. Edward Azlant, "The Theory, History, and Practice of Screenwriting, 1897–1920" (PhD diss., University of Wisconsin-Madison, 1980), 158–159.

17. Margaret I. MacDonald, Review of *God's Half Acre*, *Moving Picture World*, August 26, 1916, 1394.

18. "Manufacturers' Advance Notes," *Moving Picture World*, November 18, 1916, 1035.

19. "Mabel Taliaferro's Vigil," *Vaudeville News*, August 13, 1927, 12. Taliaferro is mistaken about the film she refers to. *The Snowbird* (Carewe, 1916) was written by May Rider.

20. Mathis, "Scenario Writers," 1.

21. Mathis, "The Original," 23.

22. Edwin Carewe, "Directorial Training," in *Breaking into the Movies*, ed. Charles Reed Jones (New York: Unicorn Press, 1927), 152; "Edwin Carewe," accessed August 28, 2024, https://edwincarewe.com. Edwin Carewe was the first American Indian (Chickasaw) director in Hollywood. His birth name was Jay John Fox, and his brothers Finis and Wallace were also producers, directors, and writers. Finis worked with Mathis on four projects. He wrote the stories for *The Jury of Fate* and *The Voice of Conscience* (both 1917), cowrote the script for *The Way of the Strong*, and wrote the script for *The Parisian Tigress* (story by Mathis and Albert Capellani) (both 1919).

23. Erskine, "Vision," 13.

24. "Edwin Carew [*sic*] Discourses on Art of Picture Making," 1916 (no further information available).

25. Lipke, "Most Responsible Job," 16.

26. "Edwin Carew [*sic*] Discourses."

27. Lipke, "Most Responsible Job," 16.

28. Erskine, "Vision," 13.

29. Cari Beauchamp, *Without Lying Down: Frances Marion and the Powerful Women of Early Hollywood* (New York: Lisa Drew/Scribner, 1997), 42.

30. Frederica Sagor Maas, *The Shocking Miss Pilgrim: A Writer in Early Hollywood* (Lexington: University Press of Kentucky, 1999), 62.

31. E. M. Wickes, "Photoplay News," *The Writer's Monthly* 7, no. 6 (June 1916): 250.

32. Louise Boyer to "Hoffie" (college friend) (unsent), February 24, 1918.

33. Ian W. MacDonald, "The Silent Screenwriter: The Re-discovered Scripts of Eliot Stannard," *Comparative Critical Studies* 6, no. 3 (October 2009): 396.

34. Ruth Mayer, "Unique Doubles: Ornamental Sisters and Dual Roles in the Transitional Era Cinema," *JCMS* 60, no. 5 (2020–2021): 18.

35. Mayer, "Unique Doubles," 19.

36. Mayer, "Unique Doubles," 20.

37. Joan Vale, "Tintype Ambitions: Three Vaudevillians in Search of Hollywood Fame" (Master's thesis, University of San Diego, 1986), 71–72.

38. Hazel Simpson Naylor, "As Others See You," *Motion Picture Magazine* 6, no. 3 (April 1916): 182.

39. *The Woman in the Window* (Fritz Lang, 1944), script by Nunnally Johnson, uses the same plot structure with Edward G. Robinson as the apparent suicide at the start who is awakened at the end.

40. Review of *The Sunbeam, Moving Picture World*, December 2, 1916, 1383.

41. Ben H. Grimm, Review of *The Barricade, Moving Picture World*, March 17, 1917, 1761.

42. Review of *The Trail of the Shadow, Wid's*, July 12, 1917, 437; Peter Milne, Review of *The Trail of the Shadow, Motion Picture News* 16, no. 5 (August 4, 1917): 866; "Carewe Uses Family Relics for Atmosphere," *Moving Picture World*, June 23, 1917, 1967. Carewe's contributions as an American Indian in his attention to details were especially notable in this film. When he learned his son was making a western, Carewe's father, F. M. Fox, brought "handsome specimens of Navajo rugs, Indian basketry and beadwork" from his home in Corpus Christi, Texas, to authenticate the interiors.

43. Carewe, "Directorial Training," 153.

44. "'Voodoo' in Metro Picture," *Moving Picture World*, November 10, 1917, 889.

45. C. S. Sewell, Review of *The Voice of Conscience, Moving Picture World*, December 8, 1917, 1481.

46. "'Voodoo,'" 889.

47. "Two Directors for Bushman and Bayne," *Moving Picture World*, September 29, 1917, 2012.

48. Jack Lodge, "John Hancock Collins," in *Sulla vie di Hollywood, 1911–1920 (The Path to Hollywood, 1911–1920)*, eds. Paolo Cherchi Usai and Lorenzo Codilli (Pordenone, Italy: Le Giornate del Cinema Muto, 1988), 194–195, 216, 229.

49. Lodge, "John Hancock Collins," 218.

50. Edward Weitzel, Review of *Lady Barnacle, Moving Picture World*, July 21, 1917, 474.

51. Peter Milne, Review of *Aladdin's Other Lamp, Motion Picture News*, July 21, 1917, 435.

52. Randolph Bartlett, "A Melody for the Viola," *Photoplay*, October 1917, 72.

53. "Viola Dana to Star in 'Blue Jeans,'" *Moving Picture World*, September 8, 1917, 1546.

54. Christine Gledhill and Linda Williams, "Introduction," in *Melodrama Unbound: Across History, Media, and National Cultures*, eds. Christine Gledhill and Linda Williams (New York: Columbia University Press, 2018), 10.

55. William K. Everson, *American Silent Film* (New York: Oxford University Press, 1978), 116.

56. T. J. Jackson Lears, *No Place of Grace: Antimodernism and the Transformation of American Culture, 1880–1920* (Chicago: University of Chicago Press, 1981), 24.

57. Lears, *No Place of Grace*, 25.

58. All references to the film are from the copy held by the Eastman House in Rochester, NY.

59. Lears, *No Place of Grace*, xi.

60. Sarah Cooper, *The Soul of Film Theory* (London: Palgrave Macmillan, 2013), 84.

61. Cooper, *The Soul of Film Theory*, 85.

62. Everson, *American Silent Film*, 116.

63. Paul Schrader, *Transcendental Style in Film: Ozu, Bresson, Dreyer* (Berkeley: University of California Press, 2018), 3.

64. Schrader, *Transcendental Style in Film*, 67.

65. Burnetts, *Improving Passions*, 41.

66. Burnetts, *Improving Passions*, 36.

67. "June Mathis—The Child Actress and the Diamond Locket Owned by the King of Belgium," *San Francisco Examiner*, July 28, 1901, 31; "'Hoodoo Ring' Brings Fortune to June Mathis," *Telegraph* (New York), June 17, 1917, n.p., Robinson Locke Collection, New York Public Library for the Performing Arts (NYPLPA-RLC).

68. June Mathis, "Tapping the Thought Wireless," *Moving Picture World*, July 21, 1917, 409.

69. Natacha Rambova, *Rudolph Valentino: A Wife's Memories of an Icon* (Hollywood, CA: 1921 PVG Publishing, [1926] 2009), 73; "On the Camera Coast," *Motion Picture Magazine*, August 19, 1923, 66; "Sir Arthur Conan Doyle, world-famous author of detective stories. . . ." First line of undated, untitled, and unsigned press release in June Mathis File at the NYPLPA-RLC, copy owned by the author.

70. William Kalush and Larry Sloman, *The Secret Life of Houdini: The Making of America's First Superhero* (New York: Atria Bks., 2006), 50.

71. "Sir Arthur," unsigned press release.

72. Erskine, "Vision," 13.

73. "Theosophy," Britannica, accessed March 18, 2021, https://www.britannica.com/topic/theosophy.

74. John Limon, *Writing After War: American War Fiction from Realism to Postmodernism* (Oxford, UK: Oxford University Press, 1994), 206.

75. William J. Mann, *Behind the Screen: How Gays and Lesbians Shaped Hollywood, 1910–1969* (New York: Penguin Books, 2001), 15.

76. Franklin Lane, Secretary of the Interior, to Richard Rowland, August 4, 1917, RG 53, box 45, Records of the Bureau of Public Trust, Records of the War Savings Division, Library of Congress Manuscript Division.

77. "Forceful Details in 'Draft 258,'" *Pittsburgh Moving Picture Bulletin*, December 1917, 22.

78. "Jolo.," Review of *To Hell with the Kaiser*, *Variety*, July 5, 1918, 30.

79. Ben Singer, *Melodrama and Modernity: Early Sensational Cinema and Its Contexts* (New York: Columbia University Press, 2001), 224.

80. Singer, *Melodrama*, 232.

81. "Song of the Shirt," *New York Tribune*, August 25, 1918, n.p., NYPLPA-RLC.

82. "Navy Convalescents Send Thanks to Metro," *Motion Picture News*, May 4, 1918, 2656.

83. "'The Legion of Death': Women Soldiers on the Firing-Line," excerpts of articles from the *New York Times, New York American, Salt Lake Tribune, New York World, London Daily Telegraph*, and United Press, accessed November 27, 2006, www.greatwardifferent.com/Great_War/Women_Warriors (no longer existent); "Metro Claims Attention to Detail," *Motion Picture News*, February 2, 1918, 717.

84. Richard Rowland to Louise Boyer, January 23, 1918, box 5, folder 64, Helen King Boyer Collection, Booth Family Center for Special Collections, Georgetown University Library (GUL-SC-HKBC).

85. June Mathis, *The Legion of Death*, screenplay, sc. 71, Cinema Arts Library, University of Southern California.

86. Mathis, *The Legion*, sc. 115.

87. Mathis, *The Legion*, sc. 157.

88. Mathis, *The Legion*, sc. 132.

89. "'The Legion of Death,'" 10.

90. Mathis, *The Legion*, sc. 350 (approx.).

91. Mathis, *The Legion*, sc. 240 (approx.).

92. Richard Stites, *The Women's Liberation Movement in Russia: Feminism, Nihilism, and Bolshevism, 1860–1930* (New Haven, CT: Princeton University Press, 1991), 296.

93. Stites, *The Women's Liberation Movement in Russia*, 296.

94. Mathis, *The Legion*, sc. 17.

95. Mathis, *The Legion*, sc. 138.

96. G. J. Meyer, *A World Undone: The Story of the Great War, 1914 to 1918* (New York: Delacorte Press, 2006), 454.

97. Stites, *The Women's Liberation Movement in Russia*, 295.

98. Geoffrey Charles Klingsporn, "Consuming War, 1890–1920" (PhD diss., University of Chicago, 2000), 159–160.

99. Robin Blaetz, "Joan of Arc and the War," in *Film and the First World War*, eds. Karel Dibbets and Bert Hogenkamp (Amsterdam: Amsterdam University Press, 1995), 120.

100. Blaetz, "Joan of Arc and the War," 116.

101. Blaetz, "Joan of Arc and the War," 118.

102. Mathis, *The Legion*, sc. 71.

103. Mathis, *The Legion*, sc. 465.

104. Mathis, *The Legion*, sc. 246.

105. Mathis, *The Legion*, sc. 392.

106. Mathis, *The Legion*, sc. 490.

107. Gaylyn Studlar, *This Mad Masquerade: Stardom and Masculinity in the Jazz Age* (New York: Columbia University Press, 1996), 22–41.

108. Singer, *Melodrama*, 222.

109. Dorothy Goldman, "Introduction," in *Women and World War I: The Written Response*, ed. Goldman (New York: St. Martin's, 1993), 8.

3. Metro's Women Writers, 1917–1921

1. Wendy Holliday, "Hollywood's Modern Women: Screenwriting, Work Culture, and Feminism, 1910–1940" (PhD diss., New York University, 1995), 4–6.

2. "The Boyer Family: Pittsburgh Printmakers," Georgetown University Library, accessed August 30, 2024, https://www.library.georgetown.edu/exhibition

/boyer-family-pittsburgh-printmakers. Louise became a renowned artist whose work is present in many museums and galleries. Her husband Ernest was a prominent architect, and their daughter Helen surpassed both with the success of her drawings.

3. Louise Boyer to Ernest Boyer, February 8, 1918, box 5, folder 42, Helen King Boyer Collection, Booth Family Center for Special Collections, Georgetown University Library (GUL-SC-HKBC).

4. Boyer, February 8, 1918.

5. Louise Boyer to Ernest Boyer, February 19, 1918, box 5, folder 58, GUL-SC-HKBC.

6. Boyer, February 19, 1918.

7. Louise Boyer to Ernest Boyer, February 15, 1918, box 5, folder 32, GUL-SC-HKBC.

8. Louise Boyer to Ernest Boyer, February 17, 1918, box 5, folder 57, GUL-SC-HKBC.

9. Boyer, February 19, 1918.

10. Boyer, February 8, 1918.

11. Louise Boyer to Ernest Boyer, April 5, 1918, box 5, folder 46, GUL-SC-HKBC.

12. Louise Boyer to Katharine Kavanaugh, April 23, 1920, box 5, folder 60, GUL-SC-HKBC.

13. June Mathis to Louise Boyer, January 25, 1923, box 5, folder 67, GUL-SC-HKBC.

14. "Up-to-Date Songs," *Baltimore Sun*, January 1, 1898, 10.

15. "Katharine Kavanaugh, Who Does Jones Family Series, Sells Anything She Writes," *Los Angeles Times*, April 19, 1936, 50; "Miss Kavanaugh to Wed," *Baltimore Sun*, September 22, 1910, 4.

16. Irene Cook, "A Baltimore Woman Live Wire," *Baltimore Sun*, November 16, 1919, 34. Kavanaugh took a nine-year break from 1926 to 1935 from the movies.

17. "Metro Engages Three New Scenario Writers," *Motion Picture News*, December 9, 1916, 3617.

18. "The Winners of the Contest," *Photoplay* XIII, no. 2 (January 1918): 104. Metro released *Betty Takes a Hand*, directed by John Francis Dillon, in January 1918.

19. "Jolo.," Review of *The House of Gold, Variety*, June 28, 1918, 29.

20. "'The Scheme' Vehicle for Bushman-Bayne," *Motion Picture News*, June 1, 1918, 3278; "Hugh Thompson Supports Miss Wehlen," *Moving Picture World*, June 1, 1918, 1296.

21. "How a Clever Baltimore Girl Has Won Her Way to the Front as a Playwright," *Baltimore Sun*, July 26, 1908, 14.

22. Boyer, February 19, 1918; Cook, "A Baltimore Woman," 34. Cook's article gives a more complete picture of Kavanaugh.

23. Classified ad, *Baltimore Sun*, November 7, 1920, 29.

24. "Katharine Kavanaugh," 50.

25. "Says Woman's Big Field Is Motion Picture World," *Baltimore Sun*, December 29, 1922, 4.

26. "Katharine Kavanaugh," 50.

27. https://archive.org/search?query=katharine+kavanaugh. Accessed August 30, 2024.

28. Roy Obringer to Al Rockett, memorandum, September 6, 1928, Mathis legal folder 1, 2727A_F027546, Warner Bros. Archives, University of Southern California.

29. Carolyn Lowrey, *The First One Hundred Noted Men and Women of the Screen* (New York: Moffat, Yard, and Co., 1920), 92.

30. Boyer, February 17, 1918.

31. Boyer, February 19, 1918.

32. Boyer, February 19, 1918.

33. Boyer, February 17, 1918.

34. Channing Pollock, *Harvest of My Years: An Autobiography* (Indianapolis: Bobbs-Merrill, 1943), 230.

35. Ferdinand Earle to Louise Boyer, July 21, 1918, box 5, folder 65, GUL-SC-HKBC.

4. The Nazimova Films, 1917–1921

1. "Newsy Items from the Studios," *Motion Picture News*, June 8, 1918, 3449.

2. "That Metro Parrot," *Camera!*, November 15, 1919, 4.

3. "Where to Find People You Know," *Camera!*, August 2, 1919, 6.

4. "Hollywood Hokum," *Motion Picture News*, April 26, 1919, 2720.

5. "Atlantic Coast Notes," *Motography*, March 24, 1917, 650.

6. June Mathis, "The Original Screen Story," *Story World and Photodramatist* 5, no. 2 (August 1923): 22.

7. "Woman to Adapt Screen Classics," *Motion Picture News*, August 9, 1919, 1265.

8. Adela Rogers St. Johns, "Laughter and Tears: The Hollywood Story," *San Antonio Light*, November 12, 1950, 7.

9. Jackson Schmidt, "On the Road to MGM: A History of Metro Pictures Corporation, 1915–1920," *The Velvet Light Trap*, no. 19 (1982): 47.

10. Louise Boyer, letter to Ernest Boyer, February 3, 1918, box 5, folder 56.

11. Alan Dale, "Alan Dale Says Alla Nazimova Scores Veritable Triumph in English," *New York Times*, November 1906, Nazimova Papers, Library of Congress Manuscript Division.

12. Gavin Lambert, *Nazimova: A Biography* (New York: Alfred A. Knopf, 1997), 4.

13. Jack Lodge, "The Career of Herbert Brenon," *Griffithiana* 19, no. 57/58 (October 1996): 35.

14. Lambert, *Nazimova*, 192.

15. Boyer, February 19, 1918.

16. Schmidt, "On the Road to MGM," 49–50.

17. Edward Said, *Orientalism* (New York: Vintage, 1979).

18. Matthew Bernstein, "Introduction," in *Visions of the East: Orientalism in Film*, eds. Bernstein and Gaylyn Studlar (New Brunswick, NJ: Rutgers University Press, 1997), 2.

19. Gaylyn Studlar, "Theda Bara: Orientalism, Sexual Anarchy, and the Jewish Star," in *Flickers of Desire: Movie Stars of the 1910s*, ed. Jennifer M. Bean (New Brunswick, NJ: Rutgers University Press, 2011), 118.

20. Studlar, "Theda Bara," 123.

21. Mari Yoshihara, *Embracing the East: White Women and American Orientalism* (New York: Oxford University Press, 2003), 78.

22. Gaylyn Studlar, "'Out-Salomeing Salome': Dance, the New Woman, and Fan Magazine Orientalism," in Bernstein and Studlar, *Visions of the East*, 123.

23. Studlar, "'Out-Salomeing,'" 119.

24. Studlar, "'Out-Salomeing,'" 122.

25. Lambert, *Nazimova*, 192–193, 199.

26. Edward Weitzel, Review of *Toys of Fate*, *Moving Picture World*, June 1, 1918, 1330.

27. Kristin Thompson, "Observations on Film Art: 'Capelloni trionfonte,'" David Bordwell's website on cinema, July 14, 2011, http://www.davidbordwell.net/blog/category/directors-capellani/.

28. Studlar, "'Out-Salomeing,'" 124.

29. Studlar, "'Out-Salomeing,'" 125.

30. Henry Kistemaekers, *L'Occident* (Paris: Imprimerie de L'Illustration, 1913).

31. Christine Leteux, *Albert Capellani: Pioneer of the Silent Screen* (2013; Lexington: University Press of Kentucky, 2015), 33–41, 102.

32. Kistemaekers, *L'Occident*, Act 1, sc. 12.

33. Lambert, *Nazimova*, 182.

34. Larry Wayne Ward, *The Motion Picture Goes to War: The U.S. Government Film Effort during World War I* (Ann Arbor: UMI Research Press, 1985), 25.

35. Julian Johnson, "The Shadow Stage," Review of *Eye for Eye*, *Photoplay*, February 1919, 68.

36. Kistemaekers, *L'Occident*, Act 1, sc. 4.

37. Kistemaekers, *L'Occident*, Act 1, sc. 4.

38. June Mathis, *Eye for Eye*, screenplay, sc. 2, Nazimova Productions.

39. Mathis, *Eye for Eye*, sc. 77.

40. Mathis, *Eye for Eye*, sc. 124–125, 159.

41. Kistemaekers, *L'Occident*, Act 1, sc. 4.

42. Mathis, *Eye for Eye*, sc. 2.

43. Ella Shohat, "Gender and Culture of Empire: Toward a Feminist Ethnography of the Cinema," in Bernstein and Studlar, *Visions of the East*, 32–33.

44. Mathis, *Eye for Eye*, sc. 33.

45. Mathis, *Eye for Eye*, sc. 170.

46. Mathis, *Eye for Eye*, sc. 156.

47. Mathis, *Eye for Eye*, sc. 157.

48. Mathis, *Eye for Eye*, sc. 164.

49. Mathis, *Eye for Eye*, sc. 170.

50. Johnson, Review of *Eye for Eye*.

51. Mathis, *Eye for Eye*, sc. 170.

52. Leteux, *Albert Capellani*, 104.

53. Leteux, *Albert Capellani*, 109.

54. "Crowd Sees Nazimova 'Shooting,'" *Motion Picture News*, March 22, 1919, 1804.

55. Edith Wherry, *Journal of Edith Margaret Wherry*, Peking, China, 1891, University of Oregon Libraries, East Asia Collection (Beijing, n.n., 1891). MS Reader version.

56. Arthur H. Smith, *China in Convulsion*, vol. 1 (New York: F. H. Revell, 1901), 33–34.

57. June Mathis, *The Red Lantern*, screenplay, sc. 28, Academy of Motion Picture Arts and Sciences.

58. Mathis, *The Red Lantern*, sc. 2.

59. Mathis, *The Red Lantern*, sc. 36.

60. Mathis, *The Red Lantern*, sc. 2.

61. Mathis, *The Red Lantern*, sc. 12.

62. Mathis, *The Red Lantern*, sc. 18.

63. Mathis, *The Red Lantern*, sc. 21.

64. Mathis, *The Red Lantern*, sc. 18.

65. Nick Browne, "The Undoing of the Other Woman: Madame Butterfly in the Discourse of American Orientalism," in *The Birth of Whiteness: Race and the Emergence of U.S. Cinema*, ed. Daniel Bernardi (New Brunswick, NJ: Rutgers University Press, 1996), 240–241.

66. Mathis, *The Red Lantern*, sc. 23.

67. Mathis, *The Red Lantern*, sc. 108.

68. Mathis, *The Red Lantern*, sc. 18.

69. Mathis, *The Red Lantern*, sc. 114.

70. Mathis, *The Red Lantern*, sc. 100.

71. Giorgio Bertellini, "George Beban: Character of the Picturesque," in Bean, *Flickers of Desire*, 166–167.

72. Alla Nazimova to Nina Lewton, January 28, 1919.

73. Mathis, *The Red Lantern*, sc. 197, 200.

74. Mathis, *The Red Lantern*, sc. 201, 266.

75. This line is not in the script in any form.

76. Mathis, *The Red Lantern*, sc. 203. The film version is a slight variation on Mathis's original, which reads, "Take care! You have severed the last link that binds me to the white race. I am yellow—all yellow—and their cause is my cause." The

crucial difference here is that the film allows Sir Philip to deny his biracial connection, but Mahlee cannot deny her biracial identity.

77. Mathis, *The Red Lantern*, sc. 203.

78. Mathis, *The Red Lantern*, sc. 268.

79. Mathis, *The Red Lantern*, sc. 270.

80. Jane Gaines, *Pink-Slipped: What Happened to Women in the Silent Film Industries?* (Urbana: University of Illinois Press, 2018), 185.

81. Gaines, *Pink-Slipped*, 186.

82. Leteux, *Albert Capellani*, 112.

83. Leteux, *Albert Capellani*, 112; Henri Menessier interview, 1946–1948, Commission de Recherche Historique (Historical Research Committee), BiFi (Bibliotheque du Film, Paris).

84. *Film Daily*, February 6, 1919, 3; Leteux, *Albert Capellani*, 105.

85. Kay Sloan, *The Loud Silents: Origins of the Social Problem Film* (Urbana: University of Illinois Press, 1988), 86–87.

86. Shelley Stamp, *Lois Weber in Early Hollywood* (Berkeley: University of California Press, 2015), 138.

87. Heywood Broun, "Megaphones and Sex Education," *New York Tribune*, January 29, 1917, 14.

88. Lambert, *Nazimova*, 70, 72–75.

89. June Mathis, *Out of the Fog*, screenplay, sc. 15, Cinema Arts Library, University of Southern California.

90. National Board of Review, minutes of discussion of *Out of the Fog*, Special Collections Archives, New York Public Library.

91. Katherine Lipke, "Most Responsible Job Ever Held by a Woman," *Los Angeles Times*, June 3, 1923, III:16.

92. National Board of Review, minutes of *Out of the Fog*.

93. National Board of Review, minutes of *Out of the Fog*.

94. "National Board Honors Nazimova Production," *Motion Picture News*, March 15, 1919, 1645.

95. DeWitt Bodeen, *More from Hollywood: The Careers of 15 Great American Stars* (New York: A. S. Barnes and Co., 1977), 178.

96. "Nazimova, as Adaptor and Star, Spent Five Months on 'The Brat'; Six Weeks Devoted to Filming," *Moving Picture World*, August 23, 1919, 1134.

97. Lambert, *Nazimova*, 225.

98. Lucius Beebe, "Nazimova Regrets Her Vamping Days," *New York Herald Tribune*, March 20, 1932.

99. Lambert, *Nazimova*, 217.

100. Lambert, *Nazimova*, 237.

101. Lambert, *Nazimova*, 237–239.

102. June Mathis, *Camille*, screenplay, sc. 9–12, Academy of Motion Picture Arts and Sciences.

103. Lambert, *Nazimova*, 246.

104. Mathis, *Camille*, sc. 50.

105. Mathis, *Camille*, sc. 80.

106. Mathis, *Camille*, sc. 197.

107. "June Mathis with Nazimova," press release, Alla Nazimova file, Film Study Center, Museum of Modern Art.

5. The Valentino Films, 1921

1. Benjamin Hampton, *A History of the Movies* (New York: Covici-Friede, 1931), 310.

2. Jackson Schmidt, "On the Road to MGM: A History of Metro Pictures Corporation, 1915–1920," *The Velvet Light Trap*, no. 19 (1982): 46.

3. Ruth Barton, *Rex Ingram: Visionary Director of the Silent Screen* (Lexington: University Press of Kentucky, 2014), 74; Terry Ramsaye, *A Million and One Nights* (New York: Simon & Schuster, 1926; First Touchstone Ed., 1986), 798.

4. Ramsaye, *A Million*, 799.

5. Leslie Midkiff DeBauche, *Reel Patriotism: The Movies and World War I* (Madison: University of Wisconsin Press, 1997), 159, 166.

6. "Marcus Loew Announces Enlarged Program for Metro Corp. This Year," *Exhibitors Herald*, March 20, 1920, 85.

7. "June Mathis Begins Adaptation of Blasco Ibanez Masterpiece," *Exhibitors Herald*, January 17, 1920, 71.

8. "June Mathis Adapted 'Four Horsemen,'" *Motion Picture News*, March 26, 1921, 2220.

9. Ramsaye, *A Million*, 799; Barton, *Rex Ingram*, 74.

10. Barton, *Rex Ingram*, 95.

11. Barton, *Rex Ingram*, 65–66.

12. Rudolph Valentino, "The Woman Who 'Discovered' Me," *Ideas*, January 30, 1926, 7.

13. Rex Ingram, "A Long Way from Tipperary" (unpublished memoirs), 475. Trinity College Dublin archives. Excerpts provided by Ruth Barton.

14. Emily W. Leider, *Dark Lover: The Life and Death of Rudolph Valentino* (New York: Farrar, Straus and Giroux, 2003), 113.

15. Gladys Hall and Adele Whitely Fletcher, "We Discover Who Discovered Valentino," *Motion Picture Magazine*, June 1923, 93.

16. Giorgio Bertellini, "George Beban: Character of the Picturesque," in *Flickers of Desire: Movie Stars of the 1910s*, ed. Jennifer M. Bean (New Brunswick, NJ: Rutgers University Press, 2011), 158–162.

17. Bertellini, "George Beban," 172.

18. Ramsaye, *A Million*, 799.

19. Leider, *Dark Lover*, 117.

20. Vanda Krefft, *The Man Who Made the Movies: The Meteoric Rise and Tragic Fall of William Fox* (New York: HarperCollins, 2017), 335.

21. Gaylyn Studlar, *This Mad Masquerade: Stardom and Masculinity in the Jazz Age* (New York: Columbia University Press, 1996), 10–89.

22. Miriam Hansen, *Babel & Babylon: Spectatorship in American Silent Film* (Cambridge, MA: Harvard University Press, 1991), 264. Hansen provides a valuable discussion of female-driven fan culture as the basis for Valentino's success and male anger against him (264–268).

23. June Mathis, "How I Write a Screen Story," *Story World and Photodramatist*, September 1923, 54.

24. June Mathis, "Scenario Writers Must Find Theme," *New York Times*, April 15, 1923, 3:1.

25. Alfred Santell, interview by William Dorward, 1972, 3a/4, Special Collections, Academy of Motion Picture Arts and Sciences.

26. "June Mathis Confers with Ibanez on 'Four Horsemen of the Apocalypse,'" *Motion Picture World*, January 17, 1920, 431.

27. "June Mathis Begins," 71.

28. Ingram, "A Long Way," 468 (approx.).

29. June Mathis, *The Four Horsemen of the Apocalypse*, screenplay, sc. 76–78. Museo Nazionale del Cinema di Torino.

30. Barton, *Rex Ingram*, 81.

31. Hall and Fletcher, "We Discover," 94.

32. Studlar, *This Mad Masquerade*, 197.

33. Phil Powrie, Bruce Babbington, and Ann Davies, "Turning the Male Inside Out," in *The Trouble with Men: Masculinities in European and Hollywood Cinema*, eds. Powrie, Babbington, and Davies (New York: Wallflower Press, 2004), 12.

34. Stephen O'Shea, *Back to the Front: An Accidental Historian Walks the Trenches of World War I* (New York: Walker & Co., 1996), 186; "World War I," Britannica, accessed August 8, 2023, https://www.britannica.com/event/World-War-I/Killed-wounded-and-missing. This source provides a table of the numbers of casualties by country. In total, it states that 8.5 million soldiers were killed. But the numbers are uncertain as other sources place the count at 10 million or more.

35. Pat Kirkham, qtd. in Powrie et al., "Turning the Male," in *The Trouble with Men*, 13.

36. Powrie et al., "Turning the Male," 14.

37. Powrie et al., "Turning the Male," 12.

38. Mathis, *The Four Horsemen*, sc. 102, 705, 711–714. Julio's pet monkey is always dressed like him and imitates his attitudes, thus diminishing their sincerity. When Julio sits wallowing in self-pity after hearing his grandfather's will, the monkey sits with him, placing a sympathetic paw on his knee. Even more derisive is the monkey's marching back and forth with a paintbrush over his shoulder like a rifle after Julio has decided to enlist. The script I have studied does not include these scenes, but it is likely Mathis either wrote them independently or worked them out with Ingram. The script does refer to an earlier draft that included the monkey consoling Julio after the reading of the will.

39. Mathis, *The Four Horsemen*, sc. 68.

40. Mathis, *The Four Horsemen*, sc. 29.

41. Katherine Lipke, "Most Responsible Job Ever Held by a Woman," *Los Angeles Times*, June 3, 1923, 13.

42. William J. Mann, *Behind the Screen: How Gays and Lesbians Shaped Hollywood, 1910–1969* (New York: Penguin Books, 2001), 23.

43. Review of *The Four Horsemen of the Apocalypse*, no further information, Alice Terry microfiche, Academy of Motion Picture Arts and Sciences.

44. Vicente Blasco Ibáñez, *The Four Horsemen of the Apocalypse* (New York: Carol & Graf, 1946), 451–452. First published 1918.

45. Mathis, *The Four Horsemen*, sc. 453.

46. Mathis, *The Four Horsemen*, sc. 727.

47. Ibáñez, *The Four Horsemen*, 480.

48. Mathis, *The Four Horsemen* "(Happy Ending)," sc. 11–X12 (the numbering of scenes in this sequence is unique, beginning with 11, going to 15, and then going from X8 to X12 for the last five scenes).

49. Mathis, *The Four Horsemen*, sc. 738.

50. Mathis, *The Four Horsemen*, sc. 738. Mathis's emphasis on the audience's responsibility is important here. The effort to obtain peace and security through brutality and power will always lead to violence and death. Humanity must end its love of such actions and look inward instead. It must understand the vision of life that comes through women and male spiritual figures, one that includes recognition of the eternal realm.

51. Mathis, *The Four Horsemen*, sc. 738.

52. Honore de Balzac, *Eugenie Grandet* (Paris: Larousse, 1936), 169.

53. John F. Seitz, interview by James Ursini, transcript, oral history, American Film Institute Los Angeles.

54. Leider, *Dark Lover*, 143.

55. Qtd. by Barton, *Rex Ingram*, 89, from Robert Florey, *La lanterne magique* (Lausanne: Cinematheque suisse, 1966), 162.

56. Leider, *Dark Lover*, 143.

57. Barton, *Rex Ingram*, 93.

58. June Mathis, *The Conquering Power*, screenplay, sc. 1–7, Cinema Arts Library, University of Southern California.

59. Mathis, *The Conquering Power*, sc. 10.

60. Mathis, *The Conquering Power*, sc. 10.

61. Mathis, *The Conquering Power*, sc. 10.

62. Mathis, *The Conquering Power*, sc. 25.

63. Mathis, The Conquering Power, sc. 51.

64. Mathis, *The Conquering Power*, sc. 55.

65. Ture Dahlin, "My Interview with Rudolph Valentino Nonetheless," November 1923. Draft of interview from the files of Kevin Brownlow.

66. Mathis, *The Conquering Power*, sc. 207.

67. Mathis, *The Conquering Power*, sc. 501.

68. Mathis, *The Conquering Power*, sc. 508.

69. Mathis, *The Conquering Power*, sc. 311.

70. Mathis, *The Conquering Power*, sc. 312.

71. Mathis, *The Conquering Power*, sc. 361.

72. Mathis, *The Conquering Power*, sc. 294.

73. Mathis, *The Conquering Power*, sc. 122.

74. Mathis, *The Conquering Power*, sc. 408.

75. Mathis, *The Conquering Power*, sc. 298.

76. Mathis, *The Conquering Power*, sc. 383.

77. Ingram, "A Long Way," n.p.

78. Liam O'Leary, *Rex Ingram: Master of the Silent Screen* (London: British Film Institute, 1993), 94.

79. Barton, *Rex Ingram*, 94–95.

80. Leider, *Dark Lover*, 150–152.

6. The Valentino Films, 1922

1. Emily W. Leider, *Dark Lover: The Life and Death of Rudolph Valentino* (New York: Farrar, Straus and Giroux, 2003), 154.

2. Roger Horrocks, qtd. in Phil Powrie, Bruce Babbington, and Ann Davies, "Turning the Male Inside Out," in *The Trouble with Men: Masculinities in European and Hollywood Cinema*, eds. Powrie, Babbington, and Davies (New York: Wallflower Press, 2004), 14.

3. Gaylyn Studlar, *This Mad Masquerade: Stardom and Masculinity in the Jazz Age* (New York: Columbia University Press, 1996), 172–173.

4. Studlar, *This Mad Masquerade*, 173.

5. Studlar, *This Mad Masquerade*, 173.

6. Powrie et al., "Turning the Male," in *The Trouble with Men*, 14.

7. Studlar, *This Mad Masquerade*, 173.

8. Miriam Hansen, *Babel & Babylon: Spectatorship in American Silent Film* (Cambridge, MA: Harvard University Press, 1991), 271–273.

9. June Mathis, *Blood and Sand*, screenplay, sc. 385, Academy of Motion Picture Arts and Sciences.

10. Jeanine Basinger, *Silent Stars* (Hanover, UK: Wesleyan University Press, University Press of New England, 1999), 285.

11. Mathis, *Blood and Sand*, sc. 653. In the extant script, Don Joselito says, "There is the real beast. The one and only beast."

12. Basinger, *Silent Stars*, 285.

13. Leider, *Dark Lover*, 204.

14. Ture Dahlin, "My Interview with Rudolph Valentino Nonetheless," November 1923. Draft of interview from the files of Kevin Brownlow.

15. "Theosophy," Britannica, accessed March 18, 2021, https://www.britannica.com/topic/theosophy.

16. Alan Arnold, *Valentino* (New York: Library Publishers, 1954), 81.

17. "Not Much to the Story but It Will Please Star's Following," *Film Daily*, November 12, 1922, 7.

18. Review of *The Young Rajah*, *Exhibitors Herald*, November 25, 1922, 62.

19. Arnold, *Valentino*, 81.

20. Leider, *Dark Lover*, 211–216.

21. Leider, *Dark Lover*, 216.

22. "Rush," Review of *The Young Rajah, Variety*, November 10, 1922, 42.

23. Basinger, *Silent Stars*, 285.

24. Mary Kelly, Review of *The Young Rajah, Motion Picture World*, November 18, 1922, 288.

25. "Not Much," 7.

26. Leider, *Dark Lover*, 217.

27. Arnold, *Valentino*, 82–83.

28. Adela Rogers St. Johns, *The Honeycomb* (New York: Doubleday, 1969), 199.

29. Leider, *Dark Lover*, 217.

30. "Not Much," 7.

31. Review of *The Young Rajah, Exhibitors Herald*.

32. "'Don Cesar de Bazan' after 'The Cheat,'" *Paramount Pep*, February 28, 1923, 2.

33. "Valentino Injunction," *Variety*, October 6, 1922, 46.

34. Kevin Brownlow, *Hollywood, The Pioneers* (New York: Knopf, 1979), 185.

35. Leider, *Dark Lover*, 313–314, 323–324.

36. Leider, *Dark Lover*, 407.

37. "Aspiring Valentinos Seek Aid of June Mathis," *New York Telegraph*, January 23, 1927, n.p., Robinson Locke Collection, New York Public Library for the Performing Arts.

38. Frances Marion, *Off with Their Heads: A Serio-Comic Tale of Hollywood* (New York: Macmillan, 1972), 142.

39. Leider, *Dark Lover*, 389.

40. Leider, *Dark Lover*, 114.

41. Marion, *Off with Their Heads*, 142.

42. Leider, *Dark Lover*, 389.

7. Crucial Films and Transitions, 1920–1923

1. Ann Douglas, *Terrible Honesty: Mongrel Manhattan in the 1920s* (New York: Farrar, Straus and Giroux, 1995), 4.

2. Douglas, *Terrible Honesty*, 8.

3. Gaylyn Studlar, *This Mad Masquerade: Stardom and Masculinity in the Jazz Age* (New York: Columbia University Press, 1996), 20.

4. Lea Jacobs, *The Decline of Sentiment: American Film in the 1920s* (Berkeley: University of California Press, 2008), 128.

5. "Jolo.," Review of *The Sheik, Variety*, November 11, 1921, 37; Qtd. in Jacobs, *The Decline*, 228.

6. Review of *Blood and Sand, New York Times*, August 13, 1922, 2; Qtd. in Jacobs, *The Decline*, 229.

7. Jacobs, *The Decline*, 125–126.

8. Jacobs, *The Decline*, 137.

9. Jacobs, *The Decline*, 124.

10. Jacobs, *The Decline*, 171.

11. Studlar, *This Mad Masquerade*, 164.

12. June Mathis, "The Feminine Mind in Picture Making," *Film Daily* (New York), June 7, 1925.

13. Michelle Su-Mei Liu, "Acting Out: Images of Asians and the Performance of American Identities, 1898–1945" (PhD diss., Yale, 2003), 166.

14. Kevin Brownlow, *Behind the Mask of Innocence* (New York: Alfred A. Knopf, 1990), 486.

15. Kevin Brownlow, "The Making," official program for showings of the restored *The Four Horsemen of the Apocalypse*, London Film Festival (1992).

16. Studlar, *This Mad Masquerade*, 20; Jacobs, *The Decline*.

17. Studlar, *This Mad Masquerade*, 104.

18. Studlar, *This Mad Masquerade*, 105.

19. Studlar, *This Mad Masquerade*, 93.

20. Studlar, *This Mad Masquerade*, 120.

21. "June Mathis Speedy Writer," *Motion Picture News*, May 8, 1920, 4010.

22. Nora B. Giebler, "Rubbernecking in Filmland," *Moving Picture World*, Jun 18, 1921, 719. Other Mathis credits for 1920–1921, besides those already discussed, included *The Willow Tree, Old Lady 31, The Walk-Offs, The Price of Redemption, Polly With a Past, The Man Who, The Hole in the Wall, The Idle Rich, The Golden Gift, Turn to the Right, Kisses,* and *Hate.*

23. Other adaptations, all titled *Liliom*, have been by Frank Borzage, 1930; Fritz Lang, 1934; Otto Schenk, 1971; and Lubomír Vajdicka, 2014. Adaptations of *Carousel* have been filmed by Henry King, 1956; Paul Bogart, 1967; and Joseph Morgan, 2017.

24. "On Her Two Pet Stories," *Morning Telegraph* (New York), April 1923, n.p., Robinson Locke Collection, New York Public Library for the Performing Arts. The article states, "She is working overtime to adapt them herself rather than assign them to others."

25. Elaine Showalter, "Introduction," in *These Modern Women: Autobiographical Essays from the Twenties*, ed. Showalter (New York: The Feminist Press at the City University of New York, 1979, 1989), 4.

26. Showalter, "Introduction," 23.

27. Cari Beauchamp, *Without Lying Down: Frances Marion and the Powerful Women of Early Hollywood* (New York: Lisa Drew/Scribner, 1997), 356.

28. Jane Gaines, *Pink Slipped: What Happened to Women in the Silent Film Industries?* (Urbana: University of Illinois Press, 2018), 171.

29. Edward Weitzel, "Bayard Veiller Takes Part in Metro Two and a Half Million Shopping Tour," *Moving Picture World*, May 22, 1920, 1061.

30. Rex Ingram, "A Long Way from Tipperary" (unpublished memoirs), 468. It's possible that Ingram is making Mathis sound overly childish.

31. Ingram, "A Long Way," 468.

32. Ingram, "A Long Way," 468.

33. Thomas Schatz, *The Genius of the System: Hollywood Filmmaking in the Studio Era* (New York: Pantheon Books, 1988), 36.

34. June Mathis, "The 'Wave Length' of Success," *Motion Picture Director*, February 1927, 22.

35. June Mathis, "Harmony in Picture-Making," *Film Daily* (New York), May 6, 1923, rpt. in *Red Velvet Seat: Women's Writing on the First Fifty Years of Cinema*, eds. Antonia Lant and Ingrid Periz (London: Verso, 2006).

36. "Marcus Loew Announces Enlarged Program for Metro Corp. This Year," *Exhibitors Herald*, March 20, 1920, 85.

37. Sumiko Higashi, "Touring the Orient with Lafcadio Hearn and Cecil B. DeMille: Highbrow versus Lowbrow in a Consumer Culture," in *The Birth of Whiteness: Race and the Emergence of U.S. Cinema*, ed. Daniel Bernardi (New Brunswick, NJ: Rutgers University Press, 1996), 330.

38. Higashi, "Touring the Orient," 331.

39. Ann Cvetkovich, *Mixed Feelings: Feminism, Mass Culture, and Victorian Sensationalism* (New Brunswick, NJ: Rutgers University Press, 1992), 22–23.

40. Cvetkovich, *Mixed Feelings*, 42.

41. "Chickasaw Indian Heritage," Biography, Edwin Carewe Heritage Archive, accessed August 14, 2018, http://edwincarewe.com/biography.php.

42. First National Pictures Inc., "June Mathis Tells Scenario Secrets: 'Audience Are Real Actors,' Says Noted Adaptor of Colleen Moore's 'Sally,'" press release, Colleen Moore "Production Clippings from 'Affinities' to 'The Desert Flower,'" Academy of Motion Picture Arts and Sciences.

43. The Shirt, "Among the Women," *Variety*, March 9, 1917, 8.

44. All references to *The Willow Tree* are from the copy archived at the Eastman House, Rochester, NY.

45. "Leed.," Review of *The Willow Tree*, *Variety*, January 24, 1920, 61.

46. Gina Marchetti, "Tragic and Transcendent Love in The Forbidden City," in Bernardi, *The Birth of Whiteness*, 260.

47. Marchetti, "Tragic and Transcendent," 262.

48. Dana's only previous Orientalist role was in 1917's *Lady Barnacle*, scripted by Mathis and directed by John Collins, which has a similar narrative. She plays an Indian named Lakshima, who flees a marriage arranged by her father, who believes she has drowned, so she can marry the man she loves.

49. "What the Picture Did for Me," *Exhibitors Herald*, May 15, 1920, 79.

50. "What the Picture Did for Me," *Exhibitors Herald*, December 4, 1920, 95.

51. "Leed.," Review of *The Willow Tree*.

52. Review of *The Willow Tree*, *Wid's Daily*, January 3, 1920, 3.

53. J. S. Dickerson, Review of *The Willow Tree*, *Motion Picture News*, January 17, 1920, 913.

54. Review of *The Willow Tree*, *Exhibitors Herald*, January 17, 1920, 75.

55. Brownlow, *Behind the Mask*, 486.

56. Kay Sloan, *The Loud Silents: Origins of the Social Problem Film* (Urbana: University of Illinois Press, 1988), 75–76.

57. Glazer was a prolific and talented writer who would go on to win two Oscars for his efforts, one at the original ceremony in 1928. He is credited with the adaptation of *A Trip to Paradise*. Mathis, however, is given scenario credits, and the work seems most likely to be hers due to its heavy revision of the original and references that clearly come from her.

58. June Mathis, *A Trip to Paradise*, screenplay (New York State Education Department Archives, MPD file 016879-2839), sc. 3. In November 1992, Roger E. Ritzmann, senior archivist at the New York State Education Department in Albany, responded to a request I had placed in the *New York Review of Books* for materials relating to June Mathis by informing me that they held a copy of the script for *A Trip to Paradise*. Thanks to his assistance, I was able to purchase a copy for myself.

59. Mathis, *A Trip*, sc. 14.

60. Mathis, *A Trip*, sc. 60.

61. Mathis, *A Trip*, sc. 18½.

62. Mathis, *A Trip*, sc. 20–21.

63. Mathis, *A Trip*, sc. 62.

64. Mathis, *A Trip*, sc. 76.

65. Mathis, *A Trip*, sc. 82.

66. Another example of Curly's sexual desires comes in scene 119X3, where Mathis called for a "CLOSEUP OF CURLY As he realizes how easy it would be for him to have his own way." This lustful suggestion occurs even after he has declared his love for Nora.

67. Mathis, *A Trip*, sc. 84–85.

68. Mathis, *A Trip*, sc. 126.

69. Mathis, *A Trip*, sc. 152X1.

70. Mathis, *A Trip*, sc. 196–196X1.

71. Franz [Ferenc] Molnár, *Liliom: A Legend in Seven Scenes and a Prologue* (New York: Liveright, 1921), 184.

72. Mathis, *A Trip*, sc. 331.

73. Mathis, *A Trip*, sc. 339.

74. Mathis, *A Trip*, sc. 181–184.

75. Mathis, *A Trip*, sc. 344X1.

76. Mathis, *A Trip*, sc. 350.

77. The Karger/Mathis films were *The Man Who*, *A Trip to Paradise*, *The Hole in the Wall*, *The Idle Rich*, *Kisses*, and *Hate*.

78. Lawrence Reid, Review of *The Idle Rich*, *Motion Picture News*, November 12, 1921, 2610; "Attractive Story Makes Amusing Comedy Production," *Wid's Daily*, November 6, 1921, 8; George T. Pardy, Review of *The Idle Rich*, *Exhibitors Trade Review*, November 19, 1921, 1761; Review of *The Idle Rich*, *Exhibitors Herald*, December 17, 1921, 63.

79. June Mathis, *The Idle Rich*, screenplay, sc. 10, Cinema Arts Library, University of Southern California.

80. Agata Frymus, *Damsels and Divas: European Stardom in Silent Hollywood* (New Brunswick, NJ: Rutgers University Press, 2020), 7.

81. Mathis, *The Idle Rich*, screenplay, sc.17.

82. Mathis, *The Idle Rich*, sc. 47–49.

83. Mathis, *The Idle Rich*, sc. 52–53.

84. Mathis, *The Idle Rich*, sc. 72.

85. Mathis, *The Idle Rich*, sc. 247–265. These scenes include the entire exchange between Sam and Dill over finding value in discarded items and people.

86. The original story includes the O'Reillys and their unnamed Portuguese neighbors, the line comparing beans and bricks, and a few other basic narrative points. But the other ethnicities and the ideological criticism are absent. In fact, Sam's business does so well in the story that he opens additional locations and thinks about going international.

87. Mathis, *The Idle Rich*, sc. 167.

88. Starting with scene 167, two versions of the scene in which Sam bargains with the Jewish tailor and his son appear. Scenes 185–221 have been x-ed out by Karger, indicating which material he wants to keep. In scenes 241–243, Karger makes notes about cuts, adding transition shots and rearranging material.

89. Mathis, *The Idle Rich*, sc. 12.

90. Mathis, *The Idle Rich*, sc. 17.

91. Sarah Churchwell, *Careless People: Murder, Mayhem, and the Invention of The Great Gatsby* (New York: Penguin Bks, 2013), 14.

92. Mary Kelly, Review of *Kisses, Moving Picture World*, March 25, 1922, 402.

93. "Complicated and Unconvincing Story Hampers Star and Direction," Review of *Hate, Film Daily*, May 7, 1922, 7.

94. Mary Kelly, Review of *Hate, Moving Picture World*, May 13, 1922, 197.

95. Review of *Hate, Film Daily*, May 7, 1922, 7; "Abel.," Review of *Hate, Variety*, June 30, 1922, 32; Laurence Reid, Review of *Hate, Motion Picture News*, May 13, 1922, 2706.

96. Kelly, Review of *Hate*.

97. "Ben-Hur Titles," memorandum, December 15, 1925, *Ben-Hur* production file 1, Cinema Arts Library, University of Southern California.

98. "Erlanger to Confer on 'Ben Hur' Picture," *Moving Picture World*, December 16, 1922, 644; "Bowes Returns from Conference at Goldwyn Studio," *Exhibitors Trade Review*, January 6, 1923, 301; "In Honor of June Mathis," *Morning Telegraph* (New York), December 24, 1922, n.p., Robinson Locke Collection, New York Public Library for the Performing Arts.

99. June Mathis, "What the Pictures Are Striving For," Jim Tully Papers, box 115, folder 22, Special Collections, University of California Los Angeles.

100. Victor Sjöström to his wife, March 30, 1923, Swedish Film Institute Archives.

101. Victor Sjöström to his wife, April 8, 1923.

102. Victor Sjöström to his wife, March 11, 1923.

103. Bengt Forslund, *Victor Sjöström: His Life and His Work* (New York: Zoetrope, 1988), 183.

104. Emily W. Leider, *Dark Lover: The Life and Death of Rudolph Valentino* (New York: Farrar, Straus and Giroux, 2003), 227–228; "With the Producers," *Photodramatist*, September 1922, 29. *Photodramatist* announced that Alan Dwan was to direct and Nita Naldi play the female lead for Valentino in *The Spanish Cavalier*.

105. Herbert Brenon, annotations on the June Mathis screenplay of *The Spanish Dancer*, 6, Cinema Arts Library, University of Southern California.

106. Brenon, annotations, 1.

107. Brenon, annotations, 77.

108. Brenon, annotations, 78.

109. Frymus, *Damsels*, 52.

110. Frymus, *Damsels*, 49.

111. Frymus, *Damsels*, 52.

112. Margaret Eggleston, summary of the novel *The Day of Faith*, December 11, 1922, *Day of Faith* file, Cinema Arts Library, University of Southern California.

113. Brownlow, *Behind the Mask*, 457.

114. David J. Skal and Elias Savada, *Dark Carnival: The Secret World of Tod Browning, Hollywood's Master of the Macabre* (New York: Anchor Books, 1995), 80–81.

115. June Mathis, *The Day of Faith*, screenplay, sc. 601–604. Goldwyn Pictures.

116. Mathis, *The Day*, sc. 610.

117. "What the Picture Did for Me," *Exhibitors Herald*, March 22, 1924, 73.

118. "Newspaper Opinions on New Pictures," *Moving Picture News*, December 8, 1923, 2689.

119. George T. Pardy, Review of *The Day of Faith*, *Exhibitors Trade Review*, December 15, 1923, 23.

120. Laurence Reid, Review of *The Day of Faith*, *Motion Picture News*, December 8, 1923, 2693.

121. Qtd. in Skal and Savada, *Dark Carnival*, 81.

122. Skal and Savada, *Dark Carnival*, 82.

8. June Mathis's *Ben-Hur*, 1922–1924

1. "Ben-Hur Titles," memorandum, December 15, 1925, *Ben-Hur* production file 1, Cinema Arts Library, University of Southern California (USC-CAL).

2. "Goldwyn Signs June Mathis as Editorial Director," *Motion Picture News*, December 2, 1922, 2775.

3. "The 'Million Dollar Girl,'" *Photoplay*, October 1923, 63.

4. "Hollywood Homes," *Motion Picture Classic*, February 1924, 52–53.

5. *The Blue Book of the Screen* (Hollywood, CA: Gravure Publishing Co., 1923), 328.

6. Katherine Lipke, "Most Responsible Job Ever Held by a Woman," *Los Angeles Times*, June 3, 1923, III:13, 16.

7. Rupert Hughes, dir., *Souls for Sale*, Goldwyn Pictures, 1923. Mathis appears in a brief shot of several studio celebrities having lunch.

8. Emily W. Leider, *Dark Lover: The Life and Death of Rudolph Valentino* (New York: Farrar, Straus and Giroux, 2003), 211.

9. "Mother of Scenario Writer Dies in East," *Deseret News*, September 18, 1922, 5.

10. "Former Utah Druggist Dies," *Salt Lake Tribune*, September 14, 1923, 20.

11. Lucille Erskine, "Vision and Service," *Camera!*, January 19, 1924, 13; "Daughter of Utah's Pride Again Visits Home Town," *Salt Lake Tribune*, October 18, 1926, 24.

12. Goldwyn Production Corporation, Biographical Information, November 29, 1922, Core Collection, June Mathis Biography File, Academy of Motion Picture Arts and Sciences.

13. Thomas Schatz, *The Genius of the System: Hollywood Filmmaking in the Studio Era* (New York: Pantheon Books, 1988), 35–36.

14. Karen Ward Mahar, *Women Filmmakers in Early Hollywood* (Baltimore: The Johns Hopkins University Press, 2006), 191.

15. "Before June Mathis Sailed," *Morning Telegraph* (New York), February 10, 1924, n.p., Robinson Locke Collection, New York Public Library for the Performing Arts.

16. Benjamin Hampton, *A History of the Movies* (New York: Covici-Friede, 1931), 311.

17. "Valentino Injunction," *Variety*, October 6, 1922, 46.

18. Abe Mass, "Descriptive Matter: Ben-Hur," *Ben-Hur* Files, Academy of Motion Picture Arts and Sciences, Margaret Herrick Library, Beverly Hills, CA. Mass also offered that "Madame Sarah Adler, the famous Jewish tragedienne, would be a marvelous type . . . to play the Mother in this story."

19. "Working on 'Ben Hur,'" *Film Daily*, September 8, 1922, 1.

20. "Our Travelog," *Camera!*, November 18, 1922, 17.

21. "June Mathis Heads Goldwyn Department," *Moving Picture World*, December 2, 1922, 420.

22. Frederick Van Vranken, "Women's Work in Motion Pictures," *Motion Picture Magazine*, August 1923, 28.

23. Richard Koszarski, *An Evening's Entertainment: The Age of the Silent Feature Picture, 1915–1928* (Berkeley: University of California Press, 1990), 81–82.

24. Hampton, *A History*, 311.

25. Antonia Lant and Ingrid Periz, "Part Five: Introduction," in *Red Velvet Seat: Women's Writing on the First Fifty Years of Cinema*, eds. comp. Lant and Periz (London: Verso, 2006), 561.

26. Hampton, *A History*, 312.

27. Hampton, *A History*, 312.

28. Mark A. Vieira, *Irving Thalberg: Boy Wonder to Producer Prince* (Berkeley: University of California Press, 2010), 44.

29. Richard Koszarski, *The Man You Loved to Hate: Erich von Stroheim and Hollywood* (New York: Oxford University Press, 1983), 115.

30. *Blue Book*, 328.

31. "Before June Mathis Sailed."

32. Lewis Jacobs, *The Rise of the American Film* (New York: Harcourt, Brace and Co., 1939), 346.

33. "Before June Mathis Sailed."

34. Koszarski, *The Man*, 141.

35. Jacobs, *The Rise*, 349–350.

36. Bosley Crowther, *Hollywood Rajah: The Life and Times of Louis B. Mayer* (New York: Holt, Rinehart, and Winston, 1960), 103.

37. Roger Manvell, *The Film and the Public* (Baltimore: Penguin Books, 1955), 109.

38. Georges Sadoul, *Dictionary of Filmmakers*, translated, edited, and updated by Peter Morris (Berkeley: University of California Press, 1972), 244.

39. Koszarski, *The Man*, 144.

40. Ruth Barton, *Rex Ingram: Visionary Director of the Silent Screen* (Lexington: University Press of Kentucky, 2014), 135.

41. "Stroheim Writes about the Making of *Greed*," *Greed: Erich von Stroheim* (London: Faber and Faber, 1972), 28.

42. "Before June Mathis Sailed."

43. June Mathis, noting changes in her cutting continuity of *Greed*, memorandum, January 29, 1923, USC-CAL.

44. "'Greed Cutting Continuity #179,' Miss Mathis' version, January 24, 1924," Special Collections, University of Illinois Library.

45. Johnathan Rosenbaum, *Greed* (London: British Film Institute, 1993), 45–46; Philippe Garnier, "The Titular Bishops of Hollywood Silent Pictures," *Cineaste* 49, no. 1 (Winter 2023): 38. Garnier writes that Farnham, the only person ever to win an Oscar for titling, probably wrote the infamous "sewer" title "as a parody of the Stroheim style, if not an outright sabotage of the great man."

46. Koszarski, *The Man*, 145.

47. Vieira, *Irving Thalberg*, 48.

48. "Long Contest for Rights to 'Ben-Hur' Ends With Complete Victory for Goldwyn Company," *Moving Picture World*, June 24, 1922, 703.

49. Paul Bern to R. B. McIntyre, Goldwyn casting director, memorandum, November 3, 1922, *Ben-Hur* production file 2, USC-CAL.

50. "Elaborate 'Ben-Hur' Plans," *Motion Picture News*, July 1, 1922, 64.

51. Kevin Brownlow, *The Parade's Gone By* (New York: Ballantine Books, 1968), 445.

52. Carey Wilson to June Mathis, memorandum, January 20, 1923, *Ben-Hur* production file 3, USC-CAL.

53. "Goldwyn Will Film 'Ben Hur' in Europe; Charles Brabin to Direct Picture," *Moving Picture World*, October 13, 1923, 595.

54. George Kleine to himself, private memorandum, February 1, 1923, George Kleine papers, Manuscript Division, Library of Congress.

55. June Mathis, *Ben-Hur*, unproduced screenplay, sc. 139. Copy provided from the private collection of Kevin Brownlow.

56. Mathis, *Ben-Hur*, sc. 297.

57. Kleine, memo.

58. "Brabin Selected to Direct 'Ben-Hur,'" *Exhibitors Trade Review*, October 13, 1923, 899.

59. "'Driven' Acclaimed by Critics," *Motion Picture News*, February 24, 1923, 955.

60. "Goldwyn Will Film," 595.

61. June Mathis to Goldwyn Studios vice president Abraham Lehr, "Cutting Notes on 'Ben-Hur,'" memorandum, January 26, 1924, *Ben-Hur* production file 4, USC-CAL.

62. "James Kirkwood Becomes Contender for 'Ben Hur' Role," *Exhibitors Trade Review*, April 21, 1923, 1034.

63. Brownlow, *The Parade's*, 444.

64. Herbert Howe, "Close Ups & Long Shots," *Photoplay*, May 1923, 57.

65. Harry Carr, "The Only Bashful Actor in the World," *Motion Picture Magazine*, December 1923, 25.

66. Tamar Lane, "That's Out," *Motion Picture Magazine*, December 1923, 46.

67. "The Final Choice," *Motion Picture Classic*, April 1924, 34.

68. Lucille Larrimer, "When Screen Stars Get Together," *Screenland*, September 1924, 49; Grace Kingsley and G. W. Marion, "Gossip from Screenland," *Screenland*, November 1924, 67; Cal York, "Studio News and Gossip East and West," *Photoplay*, November 1924, 92.

69. Eunice Marshall, "What Will Happen to Ben Hur?," *Screenland*, April 1924, 25, 93.

70. Alice Tildesley, "The Road to Fame," *Motion Picture Magazine*, April 1926, 43.

71. Marshall, "What," 93.

72. Marshall, "What," 94.

73. June Mathis to Abraham Lehr, memorandum, January 5, 1924; Lehr to R. B. McIntyre, memorandum, January 7, 1924; R. B. McIntyre to Lehr, memorandum, January 9, 1924, *Ben-Hur* production file 2, USC-CAL.

74. Abraham Lehr to June Mathis, memorandum, January 9, 1924, *Ben-Hur* production file 4, USC-CAL.

75. R. B. McIntyre to Abraham Lehr, memorandum, January 23, 1924, *Ben-Hur* production file 4, USC-CAL.

76. R. B. McIntyre to Abraham Lehr, memorandum, February 29, 1924, *Ben-Hur* production file 5, USC-CAL.

77. June Mathis to Abraham Lehr, telegram, February 7, 1924, *Ben-Hur* production file 5, USC-CAL.

78. June Mathis to Laura Mary Mathis, March 3, 1924. Provided to the author by Mathis grandniece Barbara Mathis Bacich.

79. "'Ben Hur' Company Busy with Pre-Shooting Arrangements," *American Cinematographer*, May 1924, 7.

80. Brownlow, *The Parade's*, 442–474; Scott Eyman, *Lion of Hollywood: The Life and Legend of Louis B. Mayer* (New York: Simon & Schuster, 2005), 99–101; Andre Soares, *Beyond Paradise: The Life of Ramon Novarro* (Jackson: University Press of Mississippi, 2002), 69–102.

81. King Vidor Collection, memoir file, box 1:3, USC-CAL.

82. Fred Niblo to Metro-Goldwyn president Louis B. Mayer, May 20, 1924.

83. Mathis, "Cutting Notes."

84. Edward Bowes, telegram, January 30, 1924, *Ben-Hur* production file 3, USC-CAL.

85. Mathis, "Cutting Notes."

86. Erskine, "Vision."

87. David Mayer, "Challenging a Default Ben-Hur: A Wish List," in *Bigger Than Ben-Hur: The Book, Its Adaptations, and Their Audiences*, eds. Barbara Ryan and Milette Shamir (Syracuse, NY: Syracuse University Press, 2016), 179–180.

88. Mathis, *Ben-Hur*, epigraph.

89. Mathis, *Ben-Hur*, sc. 1722.

90. Mathis, *Ben-Hur*, sc. 1–60.

91. Mathis, *Ben-Hur*, sc. 137–138.

92. "Experiences with 'Ben-Hur,'" *New York Times*, January 31, 1926, X5.

93. David Mayer, introduction to the William Young stage version of *Ben-Hur*, in *Playing Out the Empire: Ben-Hur and Other Toga Plays and Films, 1883–1908. A Critical Anthology*, ed. Mayer (Oxford: Clarendon Press, 1994), 190. Mayer writes, "Wallace perceives the Romans as a temporary phenomenon before the rise of Christianity, which is to arrive 'without following, without armies, without cities or castles, a kingdom to set up, and Rome reduced and blotted out.' The Romans, meanwhile, cannot halt the local rites of Eros and Daphne; they cannot contain the exuberant naturalness of Sheik Elderim. *Ben-Hur*, play and novel, may therefore be, unintentionally, a further representation of America—as well as of the New Mexican territory—as a land where disparate cultures rub shoulders; it is a new Holy Land where the solution to harmony is not contention and rebellion (another civil war), but tolerance, democracy, or Christianity."

94. "To Begin on 'Ben-Hur' By March 1," *Exhibitors Trade Review*, February 16, 1924, 12.

95. Mathis, *Ben-Hur*, sc. 8–22.

96. Mathis, *Ben-Hur*, sc. 34, 49–51.

97. Mathis, *Ben-Hur*, sc. 42.

98. "To Begin," 12.

99. Lew Wallace, *Ben-Hur: A Tale of the Christ* (Oxford: Oxford University Press, 1998), 235–236.

100. Mathis, *Ben-Hur*, sc. 1023.

101. Mathis, *Ben-Hur*, sc. 1160.
102. Mathis, *Ben-Hur*, sc. 1173.
103. Mathis, *Ben-Hur*, sc. 1196.
104. Mayer, "Challenging," 188.
105. Wallace, *Ben-Hur*, 517–518.
106. Mayer, "Challenging," 189. The 2016 adaptation of *Ben-Hur* also eliminates Iras and blends her seductive characteristics into Esther.
107. Mayer, "Challenging," 189.
108. Mathis, *Ben-Hur*, sc. 1625.
109. T. J. Jackson Lears, *Rebirth of a Nation: The Making of Modern America, 1877–1920* (New York: HarperCollins, 2009), 273.
110. Lears, *Rebirth*, 1.
111. Lears, *Rebirth*, 57.
112. Mathis, *Ben-Hur*, sc. 1642–1643.
113. Mathis, *Ben-Hur*, sc. 1722.
114. Mathis, *Ben-Hur*, sc. 385.
115. Mathis, *Ben-Hur*, sc. 1080.
116. Mathis, *Ben-Hur*, sc. 92.
117. Niblo to Louis B. Mayer, May 24, 1924.
118. The Williams Process was a matte process such as that used in the MGM-completed film to show the destruction of the temple following the death of Christ. Thank you to Kevin Brownlow for information about the technology.
119. The Akeley camera was a handheld camera containing a gyroscope to improve steadiness. Information provided by Kevin Brownlow.
120. Antonio Gaudio was a cameraman with whom Mathis had worked for several years. He later won Oscars for Best Cinematography in 1937, 1940, 1941, and 1944. Information provided by Kevin Brownlow.
121. Brownlow, *The Parade's*, 445–446.
122. "Begin Filming 'Ben-Hur' March 1," *Motion Picture News*, February 9, 1924, 623.
123. Brownlow, *The Parade's*, 443.
124. Brownlow, *The Parade's*, 450–451.
125. Brownlow, *The Parade's*, 450.
126. Niblo to Mayer, July 21, 1924, *Ben-Hur* production file 10, USC-CAL.
127. Lant and Periz, "Part Five: Introduction," in *Red Velvet Seat*, 569.
128. "Goldwyn Gleanings," *The Script*, "A Weekly Bulletin for the Screen Writers' Guild of the Authors League of America and 'The Writers' Club,'" 1, no. 28 (June 3, 1922): 4, Special Collections, Academy of Motion Picture Arts and Sciences, Margaret Herrick Library, Beverly Hills, CA.
129. Niblo to Mayer, May 24, 1924.
130. Brownlow, *The Parade's*, 393.
131. Louis B. Mayer to Fred Niblo, telegram, September 10, 1924, *Ben-Hur* production file 8, USC-CAL.

132. Niblo to Mayer, May 20, 1924.

133. George Walsh, interview by Anthony Slide, June 13, 1972, box 2:13, Anthony Slide Collection, USC-CAL.

134. Niblo to Mayer, July 21, 1924.

135. Unknown writer (Louis B. Mayer or Irving Thalberg) to Fred Niblo, September 23, 1924, *Ben-Hur* production file 12, USC-CAL.

136. Eyman, *Lion of Hollywood,* 99.

137. "Before June Mathis Sailed."

138. Niblo to Mayer, May 20, 1924.

139. Mathis, *Ben-Hur,* sc. 8.

140. "Much Research Work Being Done for 'Ben Hur,'" *Motion Picture News,* December 2, 1922, 2781.

141. Clarence Brown, interview by Kevin Brownlow, Kevin Brownlow personal files.

142. Grace Kingsley, "Disprove Ancient Theory," *Los Angeles Times,* September 26, 1926, C19.

143. Mathis to Laura Mary Mathis, March 3, 1924. Provided to the author by Barbara Mathis Bacich. While Mathis has spelled Sylvano's first name with a "y," as is often seen, Diane Mathis Madsen told me he strongly preferred to spell it with an "i."

144. Kingsley, "Disprove," C19.

145. June Mathis to Silvano Balboni, undated. Written and sent on about July 20, 1924. Copy given to author by Diane Mathis Madsen.

146. Joseph Schenck to Marcus Loew, telegram, May 2, 1924, *Ben-Hur* production file 8, USC-CAL.

147. Bess Meredyth to Louis B. Mayer, July 20, 1924 (approx.), *Ben-Hur* production file 5, USC-CAL.

148. June Mathis to Laura Mathis and family, late July 1924. Provided to the author by Diane Mathis Madsen.

9. First National and Freelancing, 1924–1927

1. June Mathis to Silvano Balboni, undated. Written and sent on about July 20, 1924 from onboard the S. S. Homeric. Copy given to author by Diane Mathis Madsen. Identity of Danny is unknown. A writer for *Film Daily* who used just that name might have been the person with her.

2. June Mathis to Laura Mary Mathis, March 3, 1924.

3. Mathis to Balboni.

4. June Mathis to Silvano Balboni, undated. Written from mid-July 1924 from the Continental Hotel, Berlin. Provided to the author by Diane Mathis Madsen.

5. June Mathis to Silvano Balboni, undated. Written around July 17–19, 1924, from the Ritz Hotel, Piccadilly, London. Provided to the author by Diane Mathis Madsen.

6. June Mathis to "Laura and folks," undated. From late July 1924 from onboard the S. S. Homeric. Provided to the author by Diane Mathis Madsen.

7. John S. Spargo, "J. D. Williams Signs June Mathis to Do Valentino Story," *Exhibitors Herald*, September 6, 1924, 50.

8. Spargo, "J. D. Williams," 50.

9. "Ritz Preparing for Valentino Picture," *Exhibitors Trade Review*, November 1, 1924, 22.

10. "On the Camera Coast," *Motion Picture Magazine*, April 1925, 104.

11. Emily W. Leider, *Dark Lover: The Life and Death of Rudolph Valentino* (New York: Farrar, Straus and Giroux, 2003), 323.

12. Lynn Dumenil, *Modern Temper: American Culture and Society in the 1920s* (New York: Hill and Wang, 1995), 86.

13. Dumenil, *Modern Temper*, 93.

14. Dumenil, *Modern Temper*, 94.

15. "Denies Luxury Is Killing Women's Force," *Salt Lake Tribune*, January 7, 1924, 11.

16. Karen Ward Mahar, *Women Filmmakers in Early Hollywood* (Baltimore: The Johns Hopkins University Press, 2006), 191.

17. Mahar, *Women Filmmakers*, 197.

18. Ivan St. Johns, "Fifty-Fifty," *Photoplay*, October 1926, 123.

19. "On the Camera Coast," *Motion Picture Magazine*, December 1924, 90.

20. Marriage License, State of California, book 33, p. 481, Marriage Certificates, Records of Riverside County.

21. "June Mathis Marries Silvanio [*sic*] Balboni," *Exhibitors Trade Review*, December 20, 1924, 16.

22. "First National Will Bring Two Production Units East," *Moving Picture World*, October 4, 1924, 416.

23. Jeanine Basinger, *Silent Stars* (Hanover, UK: Wesleyan University Press, University Press of New England, 1999), 421–422.

24. Leider, *Dark Lover*, 313.

25. Basinger, *Silent Stars*, 428.

26. Colleen Moore, "The American Girl of Today," ca. January 1925, Colleen Moore scrapbook 2, Academy of Motion Picture Arts and Sciences (AMPAS). Qtd. in Kristin Anderson Wagner, "'Ever on the Move': Silent Comediennes and the New Woman," in *Not So Silent: Women in Cinema Before Sound*, eds. Sofia Bull and Astrid Soderberg Widding (Stockholm, Sweden: US–AB, 2010), 312.

27. Sumner Smith, Review of *The Desert Flower*, *Moving Picture World*, June 13, 1925, 762.

28. Review of *The Desert Flower*, *Motion Picture Magazine*, September 1925, 65.

29. Jeff Cordori, *Colleen Moore: A Biography of the Silent Film Star* (Jefferson, NC: McFarland, 2012), 156.

30. Cordori, *Colleen Moore*, 56.

31. Hilary A. Hallett, *Inventing the It Girl: How Elinor Glyn Created the Modern Romance and Conquered Early Hollywood* (New York: Liveright, 2022), 3.

32. Grace Kingsley, "June Mathis Signs," *Los Angeles Times*, August 25, 1924, 9.

33. "McCormick General Manager of First National on Coast," *Moving Picture World*, August 1, 1925, 504.

34. J. E. D. Meador, "June Mathis Speeding East on Vacation after Doing 'Old Lady 31' Scenario," press release, undated, Robinson Locke Collection, New York Public Library for the Performing Arts. The reference to *The Right of Way* clearly places this item in 1920.

35. Alfred Santell, interview by William Dorward, 1972, 3a, Special Collections, AMPAS.

36. Santell, interview, 3a/2.

37. Santell, interview, 3a/3.

38. Santell, interview, 3a/4.

39. Santell, interview, 3a/4.

40. Patricia Mellencamp, "Female Bodies and Women's Past-times, 1890–1920," *East-West Film Journal* 6, no. 1 (1992): 40.

41. Mellencamp, "Female Bodies," 38.

42. Edna Ferber, "Classified," in *One Basket*, ed. Ferber (Chicago: People's Book Club, 1947), 215–231.

43. Tamar Lane, "June's Great Test," *Film Mercury*, June 19, 1925, 1–2.

44. Richard A. Rowland, "First National's Hollywood Plant Making Explosive Sales Ammunition," *Moving Picture World*, January 30, 1926, 436.

45. "Found No Need to Go Abroad for Screening," *Greater Glory* Original Studio Press book, AMPAS.

46. "Introduces a New Art to the Screen," *Greater Glory*, Original Studio Press book, AMPAS.

47. June Mathis, "Symbolism in the Silent Drama," *Motion Picture Director*, December 1925, 32.

48. Johnathan Rosenbaum, *Greed* (London: British Film Institute, 1993), 34.

49. Rosenbaum, *Greed*, 24, 37.

50. "Daughter of Utah's Pride Again Visits Home Town," *Salt Lake Tribune*, October 18, 1926, 24.

51. "Banner Group," First National advertising insert, *Exhibitors Herald*, May 1, 1926.

52. "52 Productions in Banner Group Announced by First National," *Motion Picture News*, May 1, 1926, 2090.

53. "Nine Stars Appear in Banner Group," *Exhibitors Herald*, April 24, 1926, 85.

54. "June Mathis Opening Studio," *Film Daily*, June 21, 1926, 4.

55. A. Van Buren Powell, ed., "Straight from the Shoulder Reports," *Moving Picture World*, November 13, 1926, 107.

56. "Sisk.," Review of *The Far Cry, Variety*, April 7, 1926, 38.

57. Alice Tildesley, "The Road to Fame," *Motion Picture Magazine*, April 1926, 94.

58. Frank Elliott, Review of *Her Second Chance, Motion Picture News*, May 8, 1926, 2286.

59. Corliss Palmer, IMDbPro, accessed April 15, 2023, https://pro.imdb.com/name/nm0658176/about.

60. "Casts of Current Photoplays," *Photoplay*, July 1926, 141.

61. "Aspiring Valentinos Seek Aid of June Mathis," *New York Telegraph*, January 23, 1927, New York Public Library for the Performing Arts-Robinson Locke Collection.

62. "Just Stumbles into Picture Offer; Florida Tourist Drafted on Sight During Visit to Studio," *Los Angeles Times*, September 2, 1925: n.p., Colleen Moore scrapbook 3, AMPAS.

63. June Mathis, will dated March 16, 1926, Estate case no. 90235, Los Angeles County, October 14, 1930. Handwritten, composed at Fifth Avenue Hospital, New York; Diane Mathis Madsen, email message to author, August 24, 2021. Madsen identified the purpose of Mathis's surgery. Thank you to David Stenn for advising me to look for court records on the dispute over Mathis's will at the Los Angeles County Courthouse.

64. Mathis, will dated March 16, 1926.

65. June Mathis to Laura Mary Mathis, n.d., most likely March 16, 1926. Copy provided to the author by Barbara Mathis Bacich.

66. Diane Mathis Madsen, email message to author, May 27, 2004.

67. Mathis to Laura Mary Mathis, March 3, 1924.

68. Philip Arthur Junio Balboni, personal conversation with the author, 2004.

69. "At the Theaters," *Salt Lake Herald*, January 11, 1903, 22.

70. Philip Balboni, personal conversation.

71. *Film Fun* (New York), April 1926: n.p., Colleen Moore scrapbook 5, AMPAS.

72. Santell, interview; "Row on Wives' Roles in Picture Splits Foote-Gardiner Firm," *Exhibitors Herald*, July 25, 1925, 34.

73. "First National Is Hoping for Strauss," *Los Angeles Times*, November 4, 1925, n.p.; "Several First National Pictures in the Making," Omaha, NE Movie Page (journal title unknown), February 15, 1926, Jean Hersholt scrapbook 4, 1922–1926, AMPAS.

74. "Sisk.," Review of *The Greater Glory, Variety*, May 5, 1926.

75. *New York World*, no further information available, Jean Hersholt scrapbook 4, 1922–1926, AMPAS.

76. Review of *The Greater Glory, Zit's* (New York), May 8, 1926, Jean Hersholt scrapbook 4, 1922–1926, AMPAS.

77. Harriet Underhill, "On the Screen," *New York Herald Tribune*, May 4, 1926, Jean Hersholt scrapbook 4, 1922–1926, AMPAS.

78. "Inside Stuff," *Variety*, July 14, 1926, 11.

79. "Newspaper Opinions," *Film Daily*, May 10, 1926, 8.

80. National Board of Review of Motion Pictures Records, box 6, File: Minutes, 1922–1926: April 23, 1926, on *The Greater Glory* (NYPL-SCA).

81. National Board of Review, discussion of *The Greater Glory.*
82. National Board of Review, discussion of *The Greater Glory.*
83. "The Shadow Stage," *Photoplay*, May 1926, 49.
84. National Board of Review, discussion of *The Greater Glory.*
85. "June Mathis Now in Field of Free Lance," *Moving Picture World*, November 13, 1926, 85.
86. John S. Spargo, "Pickford, Talmadge, Mathis Head New A.M.P.A. List," *Exhibitors Herald*, October 16, 1926, 44.
87. Cordori, *Colleen Moore*, 147.
88. Rob Allison (First National) to Karl E. Levy, Loeb, Walker and Loeb (attorneys), May 4, 1928, June Mathis Legal Folder 1, 2727A_F027546, Warner Bros. Archives, University of Southern California (USC-WBA).
89. "June Mathis Resigns; McCormick Battle," *Variety*, November 3, 1926, 5.
90. June Mathis to Richard Rowland, October 29, 1926, June Mathis Legal Folder 1, 2727A_F027546 (USC-WBA).
91. M. C. Levee, Secretary (First National) to June Mathis, October 30, 1926, June Mathis Legal Folder 1, 2727A_F027546 (USC-WBA).
92. "Mathis Finishes First Film to Be Made at New F. N. Burbank Plant," *Exhibitors Herald*, September 4, 1926, 54.
93. "Balboni a 'Plugger,' Not a 'Meteor,' Now Attaining Success," *Exhibitors Herald*, August 7, 1926, 44.
94. "Inside Stuff," 11.
95. Duvinelle Benthall, "Which Road Leads to Happiness?," *Motion Picture Magazine*, December 1926, 120–121.
96. Review of *An Affair of the Follies, Film Daily*, March 13, 1927, 8; Review of *An Affair of the Follies, Moving Picture World*, March 5, 1927, 59; Norbert Lusk, "The Screen in Review," *Picture-Play Magazine*, June 1927, 71; "A Guide for Those Who Wish to See the Good Films and Avoid the Bad Ones," *Motion Picture Magazine*, May 1927, 62.
97. "Signs June Mathis," *The Film Daily* (New York), February 24, 1927, 1; "United's Deal with Corinne Griffith Set," *The Film Daily*, February 27, 1927; "'Garden of Eden' to Start," *The Film Daily*, May 27, 1927, 2.
98. June Mathis, *The Enemy*, screenplay, January 25, 1927, AMPAS.
99. Mathis, *The Enemy*, January 25, 1927, sc. 246–249.
100. Mathis, *The Enemy*, January 25, 1927, sc. 254.
101. Mathis, *The Enemy*, January 25, 1927, sc. 410.
102. Mathis, *The Enemy*, January 25, 1927, sc. 384–385.
103. Mathis, *The Enemy*, February 17, 1927, Foreword; Pierre de Rohan, criticism of *The Enemy, The New Haven Register*, June 2, 1925 rpt. as "Foreword" in Channing Pollock, *The Enemy* (New York: Brentano's, 1925), 5.
104. Mathis, *The Enemy*, February 17, 1927, sc. 1.
105. Mathis, *The Enemy*, February 17, 1927, sc. 1.
106. Mathis, *The Enemy*, February 17, 1927, sc. 4, 16.

107. Mathis, *The Enemy*, February 17, 1927, sc. 27.

108. Mathis, *The Enemy*, February 17, 1927, sc. 1.

109. Mathis, *The Enemy*, February 17, 1927, sc. 7.

110. Mathis, *The Enemy*, February 17, 1927, sc. 33.

111. Mathis, *The Enemy*, February 17, 1927, sc. 205–210.

112. Mathis, *The Enemy*, February 17, 1927, sc. 131; Pollock, *The Enemy*, 94. Showing the Professor's loving students celebrating his birthday but later turning on him foreshadows the plot of another excellent antiwar film, Frank Borzage's *The Mortal Storm* (1940).

113. Mathis, *The Enemy*, February 17, 1927, sc. 51.

114. Mathis, *The Enemy*, February 17, 1927, sc. 42–44.

115. Mathis, *The Enemy*, February 17, 1927, sc. 11, 40.

116. Mathis, *The Enemy*, February 17, 1927, sc. 35.

117. Mathis, *The Enemy*, February 17, 1927, sc. 49.

118. Mathis, *The Enemy*, February 17, 1927, sc. 51.

119. Mathis, *The Enemy*, February 17, 1927, sc. 47; Pollock, *The Enemy*, 158.

120. Mathis, *The Enemy*, February 17, 1927, sc. 52–55.

121. Willis Goldbeck, *The Enemy*, screenplay, April 16, 1927, with changes on April 21, sc. 405–408, AMPAS.

122. "Mathis Sees Day of Movie Co-operation," *Hollywood Topics*, November 3, 1927, 3.

123. Ruth Waterbury, "Don't Go to Hollywood," *Photoplay*, March 1927, 127.

124. Nellie Revell, "Nellie Revell in Hollywood," *Variety*, June 29, 1927, 40.

125. Ray Murray, "Associated Artists Moving to San Fernando; Buys Tract," *Exhibitors Herald*, July 9, 1927, 22.

126. Silvano Balboni to Sam Mathis in Milano, Minnesota, telegram, July 27, 1927 (USC-WBA).

127. "June Mathis Heart Victim," *New York Times*, July 28, 1927, 19; "Breaking Diet Brought Death to June Mathis," *New York Times*, August 3, 1927, n.p.; Certificate of Death 18071, Bureau of Records, Department of Health of the City of New York.

128. "Funeral of June Mathis," *New York Times*, August 2, 1927, 21.

129. "Thousands Visit June Mathis' Bier to Pay Last Tribute," *Exhibitors Herald*, August 13, 1927, 20.

130. Karl R. Levy, attorney at Loeb, Walker, and Loeb, letter to First National Vice President Watterson Rothacker, June 5, 1928.

131. [Watterson] Rothacker to R. W. Perkins, telegram, June 12, 1928, June Mathis Legal Folder 1, 2727A_F027546.

132. Roy Obringer, First National Interoffice Communication to Al Rockett, September 6, 1928.

133. Doris Malloy (First National Story Department) to Al Rockett, memorandum, December 10, 1928, Mathis Legal Folder 1, 2727A_F027546.

134. Pauline Forney (First National Story Department) to Al Rockett, memorandum, September 6, 1928, Mathis Legal Folder 1, 2727A_F027546.

135. Malloy to Al Rockett, memorandum.

136. Al Rockett to Roy Obringer, memorandum, January 31, 1929, Mathis Legal Folder 1, 2727A_F027546.

137. Roy Obringer to Martin Gang (Loeb, Walker and Loeb attorneys), February 11, 1929.

138. Norman Webb, "Story of the Box Office," *Film Spectator*, October 1, 1927, 19; "Rush," Review of *The Magic Flame, Variety*, September 21, 1927.

139. Adela Rogers St. Johns, "The Haunted Studio," *Photoplay*, December 1927, 31.

140. "The Passing of June Mathis," *Hollywood Vagabond*, August 11, 1927, 6.

Selected Bibliography

Articles, Letters, Screenplays, and Other Writings of June Mathis

Mathis, June. *Blood and Sand*, screenplay. Famous Players-Lasky, 1922, Academy of Motion Picture Arts and Sciences (AMPAS).

———. *Camille*, screenplay. Nazimova Productions, 1921, AMPAS.

———. *The Conquering Power*, screenplay. Metro, 1921, Cinema Arts Library, University of Southern California (USC-CAL).

———. "Cutting Notes on 'Ben-Hur.'" June Mathis to Goldwyn Studios Vice President Abraham Lehr. Memorandum. January 26, 1924. *Ben-Hur* production file 4, USC-CAL.

———. *The Day of Faith*, screenplay. Goldwyn Pictures, 1923, USC-CAL.

———. *The Enemy*, screenplay. January 25, 1927, AMPAS.

———. *The Enemy*, screenplay. 2nd draft. February 17, 1927, AMPAS.

———. *Eye for Eye*, screenplay. Nazimova Productions, 1918, loaned to the author by Georgina Starr.

———. "The Feminine Mind in Picture Making." *Film Daily* (New York), June 7, 1925.

———. *The Four Horsemen of the Apocalypse*, screenplay. Metro, 1921, Museo Nazionale del Cinema di Torino.

———. "Harmony in Picture-Making." *Film Daily* (New York), May 6, 1923; rpt. in Lant, Antonia, and Ingrid Periz. "Part Five: Cinema as a Job." In *Red Velvet Seat: Women's Writing on the First Fifty Years of Cinema*, edited by Lant and Periz, 662–663. London: Verso, 2006.

———. "How I Write a Screen Story." *Story World and Photodramatist*, September 1923, 54–55.

———. *The Idle Rich*, screenplay. Metro, 1921, USC-CAL.

———. *The Legion of Death*, screenplay. Metro Special De Luxe, 1918, USC-CAL.

———. "Lincoln Who?" Poem. June 1915, copy provided by Diane Mathis Madsen, grandniece of June Mathis.

———. Mathis to Abraham Lehr. Memorandum. January 5, 1924. *Ben-Hur* production file 2, USC-CAL.

Selected Bibliography

———. Mathis to Laura Mary Mathis. March 3, 1924, March 16, 1926, provided by June Mathis's grandniece, Barbara Mathis Bacich.

———. Mathis to Laura Mathis and family. Late July 1924, provided to the author by Diane Mathis Madsen.

———. Mathis to Louise Boyer. January 25, 1923, Helen King Boyer Collection, Booth Family Center for Special Collections, Georgetown University Library, box 5, folder 67.

———. Mathis to Richard Rowland. October 29, 1926. June Mathis Legal Folder 1, 2727A_F027546 Warner Bros. Archives, University of Southern California.

———. Mathis to Silvano Balboni from onboard the S. S. Homeric. Undated but likely July 20, 1924; from the Continental Hotel, Berlin, undated but from mid-July 1924; from the Ritz Hotel, Piccadilly, London, undated but likely from July 17–19, 1924, provided to the author by Diane Mathis Madsen.

———. Noting Changes in Her Cutting Continuity of *Greed*. Memorandum. January 29, 1923, USC-CAL.

———. *Out of the Fog*, screenplay. Metro, 1919, USC-CAL.

———. *The Red Lantern*, screenplay. Metro, 1919, AMPAS.

———. "Scenario Writers Must Find Theme." *New York Times*, April 15, 1923, VII:3.

———. *The Spanish Dancer*, with annotations by Herbert Brenon from a treatment suggested by Beulah Marie Dix. Famous Players-Lasky, 1923, USC-CAL.

———. "Tapping the Thought Wireless." *Moving Picture World*, July 21, 1917.

———. *A Trip to Paradise*, screenplay. Metro, 1921, MPD file 016879-2839, New York State Education Department Archives.

———. "The 'Wave Length' of Success." *Motion Picture Director*, February 1927.

———. "What the Pictures are Striving For." Undated. Box 115, Folder 22. Jim Tully papers. University of California Los Angeles Library Special Collections.

———. Will dated March 16, 1927, handwritten and composed at Fifth Avenue Hospital (New York), copy provided by her grandniece Barbara Mathis Bacich.

———. *The Young Rajah*. "Title List." USC-CAL.

Books and Essays and Stories in Books

Allen, Richard. "The Passion of Christ and the Melodramatic Imagination." In *Melodrama Unbound: Across History, Media, and National Cultures*, edited by Christine Gledhill and Linda Williams, 31–48. New York: Columbia University Press, 2018.

Anderson, Mark Lynn. *Twilight of the Idols: Hollywood and the Human Sciences in 1920s America*. Berkeley: University of California Press, 2011.

Arnold, Alan. *Valentino*. New York: Library Publishers, 1954.

Balzac, Honore de. *Eugenie Grandet*. Paris: Larousse, 1936.

Barton, Ruth. *Rex Ingram: Visionary Director of the Silent Screen*. Lexington: University Press of Kentucky, 2014.

Selected Bibliography

Basinger, Jeanine. *Silent Stars*. Hanover, UK: Wesleyan University Press, University Press of New England, 1999.

Beauchamp, Cari. *Without Lying Down: Frances Marion and the Powerful Women of Early Hollywood*. New York: Lisa Drew/Scribner, 1997.

Bertellini, Giorgio. "George Beban: Character of the Picturesque." In *Flickers of Desire: Movie Stars of the 1910s*, edited by Jennifer M. Bean, 155–173. New Brunswick, NJ: Rutgers University Press, 2011.

Blaetz, Robin. "Joan of Arc and the War." In *Film and the First World War*, edited by Karel Dibbets and Bert Hogenkamp, 116–124. Amsterdam: Amsterdam University Press, 1995.

The Blue Book of the Screen. Hollywood, CA: Gravure Pub. Co., 1923.

Bodeen, DeWitt. *More from Hollywood: The Careers of 15 Great American Stars*. New York: A. S. Barnes & Co., 1977.

Brooks, Peter. *The Melodramatic Imagination: Balzac, Henry James, Melodrama, and the Mode of Excess*. New Haven, CT: Yale University Press, 1995. First published 1976.

Brownlow, Kevin. *Behind the Mask of Innocence*. New York: Alfred A. Knopf, 1990.

———. *Hollywood, The Pioneers*. New York: Knopf, 1979.

———. *The Parade's Gone By*. New York: Ballantine Books, 1968.

Buckley, Matthew. "Unbinding Melodrama." In Gledhill and Williams, 15–30.

Burnetts, Charles. *Improving Passions: Sentimental Aesthetics and American Film*. Edinburgh, UK: Edinburgh University Press, 2019.

Carewe, Edwin. "Directorial Training." In *Breaking into the Movies*, edited by Charles Reed Jones, 151–156. New York: Unicorn Press, 1927.

Cooper, Sarah. *The Soul of Film Theory*. London: Palgrave Macmillan, 2013.

Cordori, Jeff. *Colleen Moore: A Biography of the Silent Film Star*. Jefferson, NC: McFarland and Co., Inc., 2012.

Cvetkovich, Ann. *Mixed Feelings: Feminism, Mass Culture, and Victorian Sensationalism*. New Brunswick, NJ: Rutgers University Press, 1992.

Day-Mayer, Helen, and David Mayer. "Performing/Acting Melodrama." In Gledhill and Williams, 99–114.

DeBauche, Leslie Midkiff. *Reel Patriotism: The Movies and World War I*. Madison: University of Wisconsin Press, 1997.

Douglas, Ann. *Terrible Honesty: Mongrel Manhattan in the 1920s*. New York: Farrar, Straus and Giroux, 1995.

Dumenil, Lynn. *Modern Temper: American Culture and Society in the 1920s*. New York: Hill and Wang, 1995.

Everson, William K. *American Silent Film*. New York: Oxford University Press, 1978.

Ferber, Edna. "Classified." In *One Basket*, 215–231. Chicago: People's Book Club, 1947.

Forslund, Bengt. *Victor Sjöström: His Life and His Work*. New York: Zoetrope, 1988.

Selected Bibliography

Frymus, Agata. *Damsels and Divas: European Stardom in Silent Hollywood*. New Brunswick, NJ: Rutgers University Press, 2020.

Gaines, Jane. *Pink-Slipped: What Happened to Women in the Silent Film Industries?* Urbana: University of Illinois Press, 2018.

Glazer, Benjamin F. "Introduction." In *Liliom: A Legend in Seven Scenes and a Prologue*, by Franz Molnár, 9–14. New York: Liveright, 1921.

Gledhill, Christine. "The Melodramatic Field: An Investigation." In *Home Is Where the Heart Is: Studies in Melodrama and the Woman's Film*, edited by Gledhill, 5–39. London: British Film Institute Publications, 1987.

———. "Prologue: The Reach of Melodrama." In Gledhill and Williams, ix–xxvi.

Glenn, Susan A. *Female Spectacle: The Theatrical Roots of Modern Feminism*. Cambridge, MA: Harvard University Press, 2000.

Hallett, Hilary A. *Go West, Young Women!: The Rise of Early Hollywood*. Berkeley: University of California Press, 2013.

Hampton, Benjamin. *A History of the Movies*. New York: Covici-Friede, 1931.

Hansen, Miriam. *Babel & Babylon: Spectatorship in American Silent Film*. Cambridge, MA: Harvard University Press, 1991.

Higashi, Sumiko. "Touring the Orient with Lafcadio Hearn and Cecil B. DeMille: Highbrow versus Lowbrow in a Consumer Culture." In *The Birth of Whiteness: Race and the Emergence of U. S. Cinema*, edited by Daniel Bernardi, 329–353. New Brunswick, NJ: Rutgers University Press, 1996.

Ibáñez, Vicente Blasco. *The Four Horsemen of the Apocalypse*. Translated by Charlotte Brewster Jordan. New York: Carroll & Graf, 1946. First published 1918.

Jacobs, Lea. *The Decline of Sentiment: American Film in the 1920s*. Berkeley: University of California Press, 2008.

Jacobs, Lewis. *The Rise of the American Film*. New York: Harcourt, Brace and Co., 1939.

Kistemaekers, Henry. *L'Occident*. Paris: Imprimerie de L'Illustration, 1913.

Koszarski, Richard. *An Evening's Entertainment: The Age of the Silent Feature Picture, 1915–1928*. Berkeley: University of California Press, 1990.

———. *The Man You Loved to Hate*. New York: Oxford University Press, 1983.

Krefft, Vanda. *The Man Who Made the Movies: The Meteoric Rise and Tragic Fall of William Fox*. New York: HarperCollins, 2017.

Lambert, Gavin. *Nazimova: A Biography*. New York: Alfred A. Knopf, 1997.

Lant, Antonia, and Ingrid Periz. "Part Five: Introduction: Cinema as a Job." In Lant and Periz, 547–584.

Lears, T. J. Jackson. *No Place of Grace: Antimodernism and the Transformation of American Culture, 1880–1920*. Chicago: University of Chicago Press, 1981.

———. *Rebirth of a Nation: The Making of Modern America, 1877–1920*. New York: HarperCollins, 2009.

Leider, Emily W. *Dark Lover: The Life and Death of Rudolph Valentino*. New York: Farrar, Straus and Giroux, 2003.

Leteux, Christine. *Albert Capellani: Pioneer of the Silent Screen*. 2013. Lexington: University Press of Kentucky, 2015.

Limon, John. *Writing After War: American War Fiction from Realism to Postmodernism*. Oxford, UK: Oxford University Press, 1994.

Lindvall, Terry. *God on the Big Screen: A History of Hollywood Prayer from the Silent Era to Today*. New York: New York University Press, 2019.

Lodge, Jack. "John Hancock Collins." In *Sulla vie di Hollywood, 1911–1920 (The Path to Hollywood, 1911–1920)*, edited by Paolo Cherchi Usai and Lorenzo Codilli, 194–230. Pordenone, Italy: Le Giornate del Cinema Muto, 1988.

Lowrey, Carolyn. *The First One Hundred Noted Men and Women of the Screen*. New York: Moffat, Yard, and Co., 1920.

Mahar, Karen Ward. *Women Filmmakers in Early Hollywood*. Baltimore: The Johns Hopkins University Press, 2006.

Mann, William J. *Behind the Screen: How Gays and Lesbians Shaped Hollywood, 1910–1969*. New York: Penguin Books, 2001.

Manvell, Roger. *The Film and the Public*. Baltimore: Penguin Books, 1955.

Maras, Steven. *Screenwriting: History, Theory and Practice*. London: Wallflower Press, 2009.

Marchetti, Gina. "Tragic and Transcendent Love in The Forbidden City." In Bernardi, 257–270.

Marion, Frances. *Off with Their Heads: A Serio-Comic Tale of Hollywood*. New York: Macmillan, 1972.

Mayer, David. "Challenging a Default *Ben-Hur*: A Wish List." In *Bigger Than Ben-Hur: The Book, Its Adaptations, and Their Audiences*, edited by Barbara Ryan and Milette Shamir, 179–190. Syracuse, NY: Syracuse University Press, 2016.

———. "Introduction to the William Young Stage Version of Ben-Hur." In *Playing Out the Empire: Ben-Hur and Other Toga Plays and Films. A Critical Anthology*, edited by Mayer, 189–200. Oxford: Clarendon Press, 1994.

Miller, Patsy Ruth. *My Hollywood: When Both of Us Were Young*. Hollywood, CA: MagicImage Filmbooks, 1988.

O'Leary, Liam. *Rex Ingram: Master of the Silent Screen*. London: British Film Institute, 1993.

Pollock, Channing. *The Enemy*. New York: Brentano's, 1925.

———. *Harvest of My Years: An Autobiography*. Indianapolis: Bobbs-Merrill, 1943.

Powrie, Phil, Bruce Babbington, and Ann Davies. "Turning the Male Inside Out." In *The Trouble with Men: Masculinities in European and Hollywood Cinema*, edited by Powrie, Babbington, and Davies, 1–17. New York: Wallflower Press, 2004.

Rambova, Natacha. *Rudolph Valentino: A Wife's Memories of an Icon*. Hollywood, CA: 1921 PVG Publishing, 2009. First published 1926.

Ramsaye, Terry. *A Million and One Nights: A History of the Motion Picture Through 1925*. New York: Simon & Schuster, 1926.

Rhodes, Chip. *Structures of the Jazz Age: Mass Culture, Progressive Education, and Racial Disclosures in American Modernism*. London: Verso, 1998.

Selected Bibliography

Schatz, Thomas. *The Genius of the System: Hollywood Filmmaking in the Studio Era*. New York: Pantheon Books, 1988.

Schrader, Paul. *Transcendental Style in Film: Ozu, Bresson, Dreyer*. Berkeley: University of California Press, 2018.

Senelick, Laurence. "Lady and the Tramp: Drag Differentials in the Progressive Era." In *Gender in Performance: The Presentation of Difference in the Performing Arts*, edited by Senelick, 26–45. Hanover, NH: University Press of New England, 1992.

Shipman, Nell. *The Silent Screen and My Talking Heart*. Boise, ID: Boise State University, 1987.

Shohat, Ella. "Gender and Culture of Empire: Towards a Feminist Ethnography of the Cinema." In *Visions of the East: Orientalism in Film*, edited by Matthew Bernstein and Gaylyn Studlar, 19–67. New Brunswick, NJ: Rutgers University Press, 1997.

Skal, David J., and Elias Savada. *Dark Carnival: The Secret World of Tod Browning*. New York: Anchor Books/Doubleday, 1995.

Slide, Anthony. *The Vaudevillians: A Dictionary of Vaudeville Performers*. Westport, CT: Arlington House, 1981.

Sloan, Kay. *The Loud Silents: Origins of the Social Problem Film*. Urbana: University of Illinois Press, 1988.

Stamp, Shelley. *Lois Weber in Early Hollywood*. Berkeley: University of California Press, 2015.

Stites, Richard. *The Women's Liberation Movement in Russia: Feminism, Nihilism, and Bolshevism, 1860–1930*. New Haven, CT: Princeton University Press, 1991.

St. Johns, Adela Rogers. *The Honeycomb*. Garden City, NY: Doubleday, 1969.

"Stroheim Writes about the Making of *Greed*." In *Greed: Erich von Stroheim*, 27–30. London: Faber and Faber, 1972.

Studlar, Gaylyn. "'Out-Salomeing Salome': Dance, the New Woman, and Fan Magazine Orientalism." In Bernstein and Studlar, 99–129.

———. "Theda Bara: Orientalism, Sexual Anarchy, and the Jewish Star." In Bean, 113–136.

———. *This Mad Masquerade: Stardom and Masculinity in the Jazz Age*. New York: Columbia University Press, 1996.

Vieira, Mark A. *Irving Thalberg: Boy Wonder to Producer Prince*. Berkeley: University of California Press, 2010.

Wallace, Lew. *Ben-Hur: A Tale of the Christ*. Oxford, UK: Oxford University Press, 1998.

Wherry, Edith. *Journal of Edith Margaret Wherry*. Peking, China, 1891. University of Oregon Libraries, East Asia Collection (Beijing, n.n., 1891), MS Reader version.

Yoshihara, Mari. *Embracing the East: White Women and American Orientalism*. New York: Oxford University Press, 2003.

Yurka, Blanche. *Bohemian Girl: Blanche Yurka's Theatrical Life*. Athens: Ohio University Press, 1970.

Selected Bibliography

Dissertations

Azlant, Edward. "The Theory, History, and Practice of Screenwriting, 1897–1920." PhD diss., University of Wisconsin-Madison, 1980.

Holliday, Wendy. "Hollywood's Modern Women: Screenwriting, Work Culture, and Feminism, 1910–1940." PhD diss., New York University, 1995.

Klingsporn, Geoffrey Charles. "Consuming War, 1890–1920." PhD diss., University of Chicago, 2000.

Su-Mei Liu, Michelle. "Acting Out: Images of Asians and the Performance of American Identities, 1898–1945." PhD diss., Yale, 2003.

Essays from Academic Journals

Klein, Jeanne. "Without Distinction of Age: The Pivotal Roles of Child Actors and Their Spectators in Nineteenth-Century Theatre." *The Lion and the Unicorn* 36, no. 2 (2012): 117–135.

Mayer, Ruth. "Unique Doubles: Ornamental Sisters and Dual Roles in the Transitional Era Cinema." *JCMS* 60, no. 5 (2020–2021): 22–47.

Mellencamp, Patricia. "Female Bodies and Women's Past-Times, 1890–1920." *East-West Film Journal* 6, no. 1 (1992): 17–65.

Schmidt, Jackson. "On the Road to MGM: A History of Metro Pictures Corporation, 1915–1920." *The Velvet Light Trap*, no. 19 (1982): 46–52.

Slater, Thomas. "June Mathis's *The Legion of Death* (1918): Melodrama and the Realities of Women in World War I." *Women's Studies* 37, no. 7 (October–November 2008): 833–844.

Welter, Barbara. "The Cult of True Womanhood, 1820–1860." *American Quarterly* 18, no. 2 (Summer 1966): 151–174.

Materials Obtained Through Research of Rebecca Esch

Items from *Anaconda Standard* (Anaconda, MT), England and Wales. FreeBMD Birth Index, 1837–1915, Findagrave.com. Evergreen Cemetery. Leadville, Colorado, *La Plata Home Press* (La Plata, MO), *Leadville Daily/Evening Chronicle*, (Leadville) *Herald Democrat*, Minneapolis Directories, (Minneapolis) *Star Tribune*, *Minneapolis Tribune*, Salt Lake City marriage license records, *Salt Lake Herald*, *Salt Lake Telegram*, *Salt Lake Tribune*.

Materials from Lantern Digital Media History Website: https://lantern.mediahist.org/

Items from *American Cinematographer*, *The Billboard*, *Camera!*, *Exhibitors Herald*, *Exhibitors Trade Review*, *Film Daily*, *Film Mercury*, *Film Spectator*, *Hollywood Topics*, *Hollywood Vagabond*, *Motion Picture Director*, *Motion Picture Magazine*, *Motion Picture News*, *Motography*, *Moving Picture World*,

Selected Bibliography

Paramount Pep, Photoplay, Picture-Play Magazine, Screenland, Story World and Photodramatist, Variety, Wid's Daily, The Writer's Monthly.

Materials from the New York Public Library for the Performing Arts Robinson Locke Collection

Items from *Brooklyn Daily Eagle, Motion Picture Classic, New York Telegraph, New York Tribune, Philadelphia Telegraph, Photoplay, Toledo Times,* undated press release, *Vanity Fair.*

Materials from Utah Digital Newspapers Website: https://digitalnewspapers.org

Items from *Deseret Evening News, The Inter-Mountain Republican, The Ogden Examiner, Salt Lake Herald, Salt Lake Herald-Republican, Salt Lake Telegram, Salt Lake Tribune.*

Materials from Personal Letters, Interviews, Photos, and Emails

Interview with Philip Arthur Junio Balboni, copies of interview excerpts by Kevin Brownlow from his personal files, copies of personal letters and other writings by Mathis from Bacich and Madsen, emails from Mark Berger, Brownlow, and Diane Mathis Madsen, letters from Barbara Mathis Bacich, Brownlow, and Madsen, photos from Madsen, Brownlow, and Donna Hill, program of premiere for restored *Four Horsemen of the Apocalypse* from Brownlow.

Other Archives Used: American Film Institute Louis B. Mayer Library, Academy of Motion Picture Arts and Sciences Margaret Herrick Library general and special collections, George Eastman House Film Study Center (Rochester, NY), Georgetown University Library special collections, Heinz History Center Library (Pittsburgh, PA), Library of Congress Moving Picture Research Center and Manuscript Division, Los Angeles County Bureau of Records (thank you to David Stenn), Museo Nazionale del Cinema di Torino, Museum of Modern Art Film Study Center, New York Public Library Special Collections, Swedish Film Institute Archives, Trinity College Dublin archives (materials provided by Ruth Barton), University of Illinois special collections, University of California Los Angeles Library Special Collections, University of Southern California Cinema Arts Library (special thank you to Ned Comstock) and Warner Bros. Archives.

Other Internet Sources

American Film Institute Silent Film Catalog, https://catalog.afi.com/Catalog/persondetails.

Britannica.com, https://www.britannica.com.

Corliss Palmer, IMDbPro, https://pro.imdb.com/name/nm0658176/about.

Crocker-Langley San Francisco Directory, 1900. Internet Archive, https://archive
.org/details/crockerlangleysa1900sanf/page/1100/mode/2up.

David Bordwell's Website on Cinema, http://www.davidbordwell.net/blog
/category/directors-capellani.

Edwin Carewe Heritage Archive, http://edwincarewe.com/biography.php.

The Fairy and the Waif (1915), Full Cast and Crew, imdb.com, https://www.imdb
.com/title/tt0005298/fullcredits?ref_=tt_cl_sm#cast.

Fitch, Clyde. *The City*. Boston: Little, Brown, and Co., 1915, https://babel
.hathitrust.org/cgi/pt?id=loc.ark:/13960/t06w9xb6k&view=1up&seq=5.

Georgetown University Library, https://www.library.georgetown.edu/exhibition
/boyer-family-pittsburgh-printmakers.

Illinois Digital Newspaper Collections, https://idnc.library.illinois.edu.

Internet Broadway Database, Internet Movie Database, "June Mathis." *Women
Film Pioneers Project*, https://wfpp.cdrs.columbia.edu/pioneer/ccp-june
-mathis.

"'The Legion of Death': Women Soldiers on the Firing-Line," www.greatwar
different.com/Great War/Women_Warriors. No longer existent.

Newspaper Archives.com.

Newspapers.com.

Index

Adams, Maude, 13, 14

Arnold, John, 38, 133, 135

Balboni, Silvano, 55, 122, 178–80, 183, 187, 197, 198, 199, 200, 204–205, 211–12

Balzac, Honoré de, 12, 100, 101, 106

Barrymore, Ethel, 7, 54

Basinger, Jeanine, 114, 116, 119, 187

Bayne, Beverly, 37, 60, 161

Ben-Hur (film), 1, 3, 4, 5, 32, 64, 121, 128, 131, 132, 147, 149, 151, 152–82, 184, 186, 187, 196, 203, 205

Ben-Hur (novel), 4, 158, 164, 167, 168, 170, 171, 180, 249n93

Ben-Hur (play), 158, 170, 249n93

blackface, 19, 22, 36, 132

Blood and Sand (1922), 4, 27, 85, 87, 91, 92, 95, 96, 109–17, 118, 119, 122, 124, 127, 147, 164, 167, 184, 220n29

Blue Jeans (1917), 4, 26, 37–41, 45, 70

Bowes, Edward, 1, 165, 174

Boyer, Louise, 33, 44, 51–57, 60, 62

Brabin, Charles, 36, 160–61, 164, 174–78, 181, 182, 196

Brown, Clarence, 178, 204

Browning, Tod, 36, 44, 48, 49, 147, 149–50, 151, 155, 175

Brownlow, Kevin, 37, 126, 156, 159, 164, 174, 176, 178

Bryant, Charles, 64, 66, 86

Bushman, Francis X., 37, 60, 161, 176, 177

Camille (1921), 4, 21, 59, 64, 83–86, 87, 91, 92, 96, 100, 101, 131, 140

Capellani, Albert, 63, 64, 65, 69, 71, 78, 79, 82, 83, 89

Carewe, Edwin, 24, 25, 28, 29, 30, 31, 32, 33, 35, 36, 51, 59, 89, 132, 183, 227n22

'Ception Shoals (play), 61, 79, 80

Chaplin, Charlie, 116, 124, 212

City, The (play), 18, 21, 59

Classified (1925), 4, 191–96

Cobra (1925), 121, 184

Collins, John H., 37, 38, 39, 40, 41, 53, 59, 89

Conquering Power, The (1921), 4, 85, 87, 89, 91, 100–108, 110, 131, 144, 153, 206

Dana, Viola, 37, 38, 39, 60, 62, 133, 135, 136, 170

Day of Faith, The (1923), 21, 55, 128, 147, 149, 150, 152, 159, 167, 175, 180, 181, 195

DeMille, Cecile B., 49, 185

Desert Flower, The (1925), 187, 188–89

Dorward, William, 191, 192

Douglas, Ann, 5, 13, 123, 152

Doyle, Sir Arthur Conan, 42, 229n69

Draft 258 (1917), 43, 44, 49

Eltinge, Julian, 18–19, 98

Enemy, The (1927), 3, 4, 206–11

Erlanger, Abraham, 154, 158, 159, 160, 161, 165, 180, 181

essentialism, 4, 5, 81, 186

Eye for Eye (1918), 4, 59, 64, 65–69, 73, 78, 118, 136

Fairbanks, Douglas, 91, 95, 123, 126, 127, 142, 185, 189

Index

Famous Players(-Lasky), 1, 24, 86, 108, 109, 116, 118, 119, 127, 147, 152, 154, 185

Far Cry, The (1926), 55, 198, 200

First National Pictures, 1, 8, 55, 64, 127, 133, 175, 183, 187, 189, 190, 197, 199, 201, 203–4, 205, 212–13

Four Horsemen of the Apocalypse, The (1921), 1, 3, 4, 5, 57, 83, 84, 86, 87–100, 101, 102, 105, 106, 108, 109, 110, 111, 112, 116, 118, 120, 121, 123, 126, 127, 140, 154, 156, 159, 160, 167, 168, 169, 172, 176, 177, 181, 195, 196, 200, 202, 203, 207, 208, 209, 237n38

Fox, Finis, 36, 227n22

Gaines, Jane, 78, 129

Gledhill, Christine, 5, 21, 38, 126

Godsol, Joseph, 1, 147, 154, 155, 159

Goldbeck, Willis, 206, 210, 211

Goldwyn Studios, 1, 10, 55, 86, 127, 147, 148, 149, 152, 153, 154, 155, 156, 158, 159, 162, 163, 165, 174, 175, 177, 181, 184, 185, 187, 196, 197

Granny Maumee (play), 19–21, 36, 59

Greater Glory, The (1926), 3, 196–97, 200–203, 204, 206, 207

Great Victory, The (1919), 43, 44

Greed (Erich von Stroheim, 1925), 128, 156–58, 163, 165, 166, 181, 197

Griffith, Corinne, 191, 192, 193, 200, 205

Griffith, D. W. (David Wark), 36, 41, 47, 79, 125, 157

Hawkes, Emily (grandmother), 8, 212

Her Great Price (1916), 26, 34–35

homosexuality, 19, 98, 168–69

Hughes, Lloyd, 199, 205

Hughes, Philip (father), 8–10, 153

Ibáñez, Vicente Blasco, 92–93

Idle Rich, The (1921), 4, 128, 131, 132, 142–46, 167, 180, 241

Ingram, Rex, 1, 84, 85, 88, 89, 93, 94, 99, 101–2, 103, 105, 107–8, 120, 125, 129–30, 153, 157, 160, 175, 183, 186, 196, 237n38, 241n30

In the Palace of the King (1923) 128, 152, 159, 181

Irene (1925), 187, 188, 189, 190

Jacobs, Lea, 124, 126, 152

Jacobs, Lewis, 156, 157, 213

Karger, Maxwell, 36, 52, 53, 54, 55–56, 59, 61, 71, 83, 90, 93, 127, 128, 132, 137, 141, 142, 143, 144, 145, 146, 175, 243n77, 244n88

Kleine, George, 160

Lady Barnacle (1917), 37, 242n48

Lasky, Jesse, 108, 116, 118, 119, 153

Leadville, Colorado, 8, 9, 10, 183

Legion of Death, The (1918), 4, 41, 44–50, 195

Lehr, Abraham, 147, 148, 154, 155, 156, 157, 162, 163

Leider, Emily, 91, 109, 119, 187, 230

Levy, Archie, 14

Liliom (play), 128, 137, 141, 241n23

L'Occident (play), 65, 66, 67

Loew, Marcus, 87, 88, 90, 127, 129, 131, 181

Lytell, Bert, 137, 142, 143, 191

Mahar, Karen Ward, 3, 153, 186

Marion, Frances, 2, 23, 186

Masked Woman, The (1927), 198, 204–5

Mathis, June: as actress (film), 22–23; as actress (stage), 12–22, 59, 81, 183; articles by, 32, 58, 130; artistry of, 3–4, 59, 121, 133–36, 165, 166, 173, 180, 196–97, 209–10; art references in films/scripts, 39, 79, 138, 208–9; birth of, 9; career in film industry, 3, 24–25, 108, 128–31, 152–56, 159–60, 177–78, 180–82, 187, 189, 190–91, 196, 208, 211–13; challenges to dominant masculinity in the films of, 3, 6, 69, 70, 72–73, 76–78, 85–86, 91, 96–97; childhood of, 7–14; collaborative efforts, 29–31, 35, 36–37, 53–54, 59, 64, 65, 71, 73–74, 79, 84, 88–89, 90, 92–93, 101, 105–6, 107–8, 116–17, 121, 127–28, 142, 145, 149–51,

160–61, 175–76, 177–78, 182, 191, 193; criticism of greed/violence/war, 6, 94, 95, 100–101, 107–8, 109–16, 172, 180, 201–3, 206, 208–10; critiques of capitalism/materialism, 5, 6, 40, 81, 103–4, 137–46, 193–95, 209; death of, 1, 7–8, 212; as Editorial Director (editor general), 152, 155, 196–99; emphasis on details, 26, 27–29, 32, 45, 58, 201, 203; at Famous Players-Lasky, 108, 116, 147; father (Philip Hughes), 8–10, 153; filmmaking knowledge of, 3, 23, 52, 139, 156, 157–58, 161, 164–65, 173–74, 177–78; filmmaking tasks of, 147–49, 152–53, 156, 159–62, 178, 196, 200, 205; at First National Studios, 187, 189, 190, 201, 203–4, 205, 212–13; as freelancer, 205–6, 211; gender attitudes of, 5–6, 19, 76, 103–4, 107, 121–22, 130, 134, 186; goals for her work, 23–24, 27, 28, 32, 58, 165, 168, 181–82; at Goldwyn Studios, 1, 86, 127, 147, 148, 149, 152, 154, 155, 156, 159, 162, 163, 165, 175, 184, 185, 187, 196; grandmother (Emily Hawkes), 8, 212; health problems, 10–11, 153, 199; inclusivity in screenplays of, 131–32, 143–44, 167–69; June Mathis Productions, 197–98; marriage of, 187; at Metro Pictures, 1, 8, 24, 30, 36, 37, 44, 51, 52, 53, 57, 58, 59, 60, 65, 66, 82, 86, 88, 90, 92, 99, 108, 127, 129, 131; mother (Virginia [Jennie] Wilcox), 8–12, 13–14, 16–17, 21, 34, 122, 153, 222n40; movement and expression in work of, 14–16, 28–29; orientalism in the films of, 59, 62–64, 65, 67–68, 70, 73, 133–134; plan to build vaudeville hotels, 18, 19; playwright ambitions of, 52; poetry by, 22, 132; preference for drama, 18, 19, 21, 22, 59; promotion of alternative feminine values, 6, 39–40, 59, 65, 66–67, 92, 93, 95, 98–100, 126–27, 139–41, 146, 172, 206; racial attitudes of, 21, 36, 75–76, 102–3, 106, 125, 128, 132, 134, 135, 138, 144, 164;

recitations by, 12–13; relationship with Julian Eltinge, 18–19; at Rolfe Studios, 24–25; screenwriting techniques of, 26, 45, 59, 92, 140–41; screenwriting training of, 23, 27–29; sexuality in films of, 80–81, 90–91, 97–98, 102–3, 113, 168–70; spiritual beliefs of, 42; spirituality in the films of, 4, 26–27, 39–41, 47, 59, 66–67, 70–72, 75, 78–79, 92, 95–96, 98–100, 117–18, 138–42, 144, 146, 152, 162, 166–70, 171–73, 197, 206; stepfather (William D. Mathis), 8–12, 13–14, 16–17, 21, 34, 122, 153; stepsiblings (Laura Mary, George & Sam Mathis), 10, 14, 163, 179, 181, 183, 187, 199, 200, 212; stories for films by, 25, 212–213, 227n22; theatrical writing of ("His Night at the Club"), 19; thoughts on realism in film, 26, 31–32, 41, 81, 91; use of melodrama, 5–6, 26, 28, 37–38, 45, 76, 80, 96, 97, 141, 152, 166, 170; on women's roles in the film industry, 5, 130; as workaholic, 29, 51, 52, 58, 127
–Screenplays by or contributed to: *An Affair of the Follies* [*Here Y'Are Brother*] (1927), 203–4, 205; *Aladdin's Other* Lamp (1917), 37; *The Barricade* (1917), 35; *Blood and Sand* (1922), 4, 27, 85, 87, 91, 92, 95, 96, 109–17, 118, 119, 122, 124, 127, 147, 164, 167, 184, 220n29; *Blue Jeans* (1917), 4, 26, 37–41, 45, 70; *The Brat* (1919), 83; *Camille* (1921), 4, 21, 59, 64, 83–86, 87, 91, 92, 96, 100, 101, 131, 140; *Classified* (1925), 4, 191–96; *The Conquering Power* (1921), 4, 100–108; *The Dawn of Love* (1916), 56; *The Day of Faith* (1923), 21, 55, 128, 147, 149, 150, 152, 159, 167, 175, 180, 181, 195; *The Desert Flower* (1925), 187, 188–89; *The Divorcee* (1919-with Katharine Kavanaugh), 54; *Draft* 258 (1917), 43, 44, 49; *Eye for Eye* (1918), 4, 59, 64, 65–69, 73, 78, 118, 136; *The Far Cry* (1926-editorial director), 55, 198, 200; *The Four*

Index

Horsemen of the Apocalypse (1921), 1, 3, 4, 5, 57, 83, 84, 86, 87–100, 101, 102, 105, 106, 108, 109, 110, 111, 112, 116, 118, 120, 121, 123, 126, 127, 140, 154, 156, 159, 160, 167, 168, 169, 172, 176, 177, 181, 195, 196, 200, 202, 203, 207, 208, 209, 237n38; *God's Half Acre* (1916), 30; *The Greater Glory* [*The Viennese Medley*] (1926), 3, 196–97, 200–203, 204, 206, 207; *The Great Victory* (1919), 43, 44; *Greed* (1925-producer/editor), 128, 156–58, 163, 165, 166, 181, 197; *Hearts Are Trumps* (1920), 125; *Her Great Price* (1916), 26, 34–35; *His Bonded Wife* (1918), 161; *His Father's Son* (1917), 56; *The House of Gold* (1918-with Kavanaugh), 54; *The Idle Rich*, 4, 128, 131, 132, 142–46, 167, 180, 241n22; *In the Palace of the King* (1923) 128, 152, 159, 181; *Irene* (1925-editorial director/continuity), 187, 188, 189, 190; *The Jury of Fate* (1918), 227n22; *Lady Barnacle* (1917), 37, 242n48; *The Legion of Death* (1918), 4, 41, 44–50, 195; *The Magic Flame* (1927), 213; *The Man Who* (1921), 137; *The Masked Woman* (1927), 198, 204–5; *Name the Man* (1924-editorial director), 147, 148, 149; *The Parisian Tigress* (1919-story only with Albert Capellani), 227n22; *Red, White, and Blue Blood* (1917), 36, 161; *The Red Lantern* (1919), 4, 47, 59, 65, 69–79, 118, 125, 134, 234–35n76; *The Right of Way* (1920), 127, 129, 191; *Sally* (1925), 187, 188; *The Silent Woman* (1918), 54; *Social Quicksands* (1918-with Kavanaugh), 54; *Somewhere In America* (1917), 43; *The Spanish Dancer* (1923), 121, 128, 147, 148–49, 152, 174, 184; *A Successful Adventure* (1918), 54; *The Sunbeam* (1916), 30, 35; *To Hell with the Kaiser* (1918), 43, 44, 49, 93; *The Trail of the Shadow* (1917), 35; *A Trip to Paradise* (1922), 4, 5, 21, 128, 131, 136–42, 224n91, 243n57, 243n58, 243n77; *The Voice of Conscience* (1917), 37, 227n22; *Way of the Strong* (1919-with Finis Fox), 227n22; *We Moderns* (1925), 187, 188, 189, 190, 198, 204; *Wife by Proxy, A* (1917), 37; *The Willow Tree* (1921), 127, 133–36, 173, 180, 241n22; *The Winding Trail* (1918-with Kavanaugh), 53; *The Winning of Beatrice* (1918), 54; *The Young Rajah* (1922), 40, 87, 109, 110, 117–20, 122, 127, 167, 186

–Screenplays by (unproduced): *Ben-Hur* (1922–1924), 1, 3, 4, 5, 32, 64, 121, 128, 131, 132, 147, 149, 151, 152–82, 184, 186, 187, 196, 203, 205; *The Enemy* (1927), 3, 4, 206–11; *The Fascinating Widower* (1918), 18; *The Scarlet Power/The Hooded Falcon* (1923), 121, 184, 213; *The Scheme* (1918), 52; *Sinners in Paradise* (1926), 197–98; *A Terrible Silence* (ca. 1915), 25

Mathis, Laura Mary (stepsister), 10, 14, 163, 179, 181, 183, 187, 199, 200, 212

Mathis, Virginia (Jennie) Wilcox (mother), 8–12, 13–14, 16–17, 21, 34, 122, 153, 222n40

Mathis, William D. (stepfather), 8–10, 12, 14, 16, 17–18, 42, 153

Mayer, David, 5, 166, 170, 171

Mayer, Louis B., 24, 158, 173, 175, 176, 177, 178, 181

McCormick, John, 64, 175, 189, 190, 191, 203–4

McIntyre, R. B., 159, 162, 163

melodrama, 5, 16, 19, 21, 22, 26, 28–29, 34, 35, 37, 38, 41, 43, 44, 45, 48, 54, 55, 63, 70, 76, 80, 86, 94, 96, 97, 100, 104, 112, 113, 117, 126, 132, 137, 138, 141, 142, 145, 146, 149, 151, 152, 156, 166, 170, 171, 194, 195

Menessier, Henri, 69, 79

Meredyth, Bess, 23, 159, 181, 184, 213

Metro-Goldwyn, 154, 158, 164, 175, 176, 177, 180, 181, 184

Metro-Goldwyn-Mayer (MGM), 32, 37, 38, 87, 128, 157, 159, 164, 169, 172, 177, 185, 206, 210, 250n118

Index

Metro Pictures, 1, 2, 8, 24, 30, 33, 36, 37, 44, 51, 52, 53, 55, 56, 57, 58, 59, 60, 62, 63, 64, 65, 66, 69, 79, 80, 82, 83, 86, 87, 88, 90, 91, 92, 99, 102, 108, 110, 127, 129, 131, 136, 141, 142, 146, 152, 160, 161, 184, 185

modernity (and gender), 4, 5, 6, 13, 26, 29, 39, 40, 61, 65, 96, 123, 124, 128, 134, 136, 138, 146, 156, 171, 185, 186, 193, 195

Moore, Colleen, 121, 187, 188, 189, 190, 191, 198, 199, 200, 203, 204, 212, 213

Naldi, Nita, 113, 122, 245n104
Name the Man (1924), 147, 148, 149
National Board of Review of Motion Pictures, 80, 82, 201–3
Nazimova, Alla, 2, 4, 42, 47, 57, 58–86, 98, 120, 130, 132, 133, 153, 170
Negri, Pola, 121, 128, 148, 149
Niblo, Fred, 114, 116, 164, 165, 171, 173, 175, 176, 177, 178, 180, 206

orientalism, 59, 62–63, 65, 66, 67, 69, 70, 73, 74, 76, 78, 102, 118, 125, 127–28, 149, 184, 242n48
Otto, Henry, 89, 127, 133, 134, 135

Pollock, Channing, 30, 56, 206, 207

Rambova, Natacha, 83, 118–19, 121, 184
Red Lantern, The (1919), 4, 47, 59, 65, 69–79, 118, 125, 134, 234n76
Rehfeld, Curt, 200, 201, 202
Right of Way, The (1920), 127, 129, 191
Rockett, Al (A. L.), 189, 204, 212, 213
Rolfe, B. A. (Benjamin Al)/Rolfe Photoplays, 24, 25, 33, 36
Rosen, Philip, 120, 186
Rowland, Richard, 8, 24, 36, 37, 43, 44, 51, 52, 55, 56, 59, 60, 61, 62, 65, 87, 88, 90, 92, 108, 184, 187, 189, 190, 193, 196, 204, 212

Sally (1925), 187, 188
Salt Lake City, Utah, 9, 10, 12, 13, 17, 23
Santell, Al, 92, 191–93
Schenck, Joe, 181, 205

Seitz, John, 89, 93, 101
Sheik, The (1921)/*The Son of the Sheik* (1926), 86, 90, 109, 110, 114, 116, 123, 124, 220n29
Shipman, Nell, 2, 11
Sjostrom, Victor, 147–49
Spanish Dancer, The (1923), 121, 128, 147, 148–49, 152, 174, 184
spirituality, 3, 4, 5–6, 21, 22, 26–27, 35, 39, 40, 41, 42, 43, 44, 48, 57, 59, 63, 65, 66, 67, 69, 70, 71, 75, 76, 81, 85, 86, 92, 94, 96, 99, 102, 105, 109–10, 111, 113, 118, 121, 123, 127, 128, 132, 136, 137, 138, 139, 141, 146, 149, 152, 162, 165, 166, 167, 169–73, 180, 184, 190, 194, 195, 206, 209, 210
Stevens, Emily, 33, 34, 53
St. Johns, Adela Rogers, 60, 120, 213
St. Johns, Ivan, 186, 187
Studlar, Gaylyn, 49, 62, 63, 65, 91, 94, 110, 111, 112, 113, 124–25, 126, 128, 152
Sunbeam, The (1916), 30, 35

Taliaferro, Mabel, 30, 34, 35, 44, 212
Terry, Alice, 90, 104
theosophy, 42
To Hell with the Kaiser (1918), 43, 44, 49, 93
Torrence, Ridgely, 19–20
transcendental theme in film, 41
Trip to Paradise, A (1922), 4, 5, 21, 128, 131, 136–42, 224n91, 243n57–58, 243n77

Ullman, George, 184, 212

Valentino, Rudolph, 1, 7, 8, 27, 40, 42, 83, 84, 85, 86, 87–122, 123, 124, 125, 126, 127, 132, 139, 148, 153, 154, 161, 176, 184, 187, 192, 196, 198, 199, 200, 213
Valli, Virginia, 137, 142, 143
Veiller, Bayard, 129, 131, 175
von Stroheim, Erich, 91, 128, 130, 153, 156, 157, 158, 165, 166, 196, 197, 220n29, 247n45

Wallace, Lew, 158, 164, 167, 168, 170, 171, 180, 249n93

Index

Walsh, George, 161–62, 176–77, 181
War Brides (1916), 61, 66
Weber, Lois, 1, 2, 23, 79, 88, 130, 153–54
We Moderns (1925), 187, 188, 189, 190, 198, 204
Whose Baby Are You? (play), 14, 15, 18
Willow Tree, The (1921), 127, 133–36, 173, 180, 241n22

women and the Great War, 42–50, 201–3
women in silent film, 23–24, 51–57, 131, 153, 155, 175, 182, 186

Young Rajah, The (1922), 40, 87, 109, 110, 117–20, 122, 127, 167, 186
Yurka, Blanche, 7–8

Screen Classics

Screen Classics is a series of critical biographies, film histories, and analytical studies focusing on neglected filmmakers and important screen artists and subjects, from the era of silent cinema through the golden age of Hollywood to the international generation of today. Books in the Screen Classics series are intended for scholars and general readers alike. The contributing authors are established figures in their respective fields. This series also serves the purpose of advancing scholarship on film personalities and themes with ties to Kentucky.

Series Editor   Patrick McGilligan

Books in the Series

Olivia de Havilland: Lady Triumphant
    Victoria Amador
Mae Murray: The Girl with the Bee-Stung Lips
    Michael G. Ankerich
Harry Dean Stanton: Hollywood's Zen Rebel
    Joseph B. Atkins
Hedy Lamarr: The Most Beautiful Woman in Film
    Ruth Barton
Rex Ingram: Visionary Director of the Silent Screen
    Ruth Barton
Conversations with Classic Film Stars: Interviews from Hollywood's Golden Era
    James Bawden and Ron Miller
Conversations with Legendary Television Stars: Interviews from the First Fifty Years
    James Bawden and Ron Miller
They Made the Movies: Conversations with Great Filmmakers
    James Bawden and Ron Miller
You Ain't Heard Nothin' Yet: Interviews with Stars from Hollywood's Golden Era
    James Bawden and Ron Miller
Charles Boyer: The French Lover
    John Baxter
Von Sternberg
    John Baxter
Hitchcock's Partner in Suspense: The Life of Screenwriter Charles Bennett
    Charles Bennett, edited by John Charles Bennett
Hitchcock and the Censors
    John Billheimer
The Magic Hours: The Films and Hidden Life of Terrence Malick
    John Bleasdale
A Uniquely American Epic: Intimacy and Action, Tenderness and Violence in Sam Peckinpah's The Wild Bunch
    Edited by Michael Bliss
My Life in Focus: A Photographer's Journey with Elizabeth Taylor and the Hollywood Jet Set
    Gianni Bozzacchi with Joey Tayler
Hollywood Divided: The 1950 Screen Directors Guild Meeting and the Impact of the Blacklist
    Kevin Brianton
He's Got Rhythm: The Life and Career of Gene Kelly
    Cynthia Brideson and Sara Brideson

Ziegfeld and His Follies: A Biography of Broadway's Greatest Producer
    Cynthia Brideson and Sara Brideson
Eleanor Powell: Born to Dance
    Paula Broussard and Lisa Royère
The Marxist and the Movies: A Biography of Paul Jarrico
    Larry Ceplair
Dalton Trumbo: Blacklisted Hollywood Radical
    Larry Ceplair and Christopher Trumbo
Warren Oates: A Wild Life
    Susan Compo
Helen Morgan: The Original Torch Singer and Ziegfeld's Last Star
    Christopher S. Connelly
Improvising Out Loud: My Life Teaching Hollywood How to Act
    Jeff Corey with Emily Corey
Crane: Sex, Celebrity, and My Father's Unsolved Murder
    Robert Crane and Christopher Fryer
Jack Nicholson: The Early Years
    Robert Crane and Christopher Fryer
Anne Bancroft: A Life
    Douglass K. Daniel
Being Hal Ashby: Life of a Hollywood Rebel
    Nick Dawson
Bruce Dern: A Memoir
    Bruce Dern with Christopher Fryer and Robert Crane
Intrepid Laughter: Preston Sturges and the Movies
    Andrew Dickos
The Woman Who Dared: The Life and Times of Pearl White, Queen of the Serials
    William M. Drew
Miriam Hopkins: Life and Films of a Hollywood Rebel
    Allan R. Ellenberger
Vitagraph: America's First Great Motion Picture Studio
    Andrew A. Erish
Jayne Mansfield: The Girl Couldn't Help It
    Eve Golden
John Gilbert: The Last of the Silent Film Stars
    Eve Golden
Strictly Dynamite: The Sensational Life of Lupe Velez
    Eve Golden
Stuntwomen: The Untold Hollywood Story
    Mollie Gregory
Jean Gabin: The Actor Who Was France
    Joseph Harriss
Yves Montand: The Passionate Voice
    Joseph Harriss
The Herridge Style: The Life and Work of a Television Revolutionary
    Robert Herridge, edited and with an introduction by John Sorensen
Otto Preminger: The Man Who Would Be King, updated edition
    Foster Hirsch
Saul Bass: Anatomy of Film Design
    Jan-Christopher Horak
Lawrence Tierney: Hollywood's Real-Life Tough Guy
    Burt Kearns

Hitchcock Lost and Found: The Forgotten Films
    Alain Kerzoncuf and Charles Barr
Pola Negri: Hollywood's First Femme Fatale
    Mariusz Kotowski
Ernest Lehman: The Sweet Smell of Success
    Jon Krampner
Sidney J. Furie: Life and Films
    Daniel Kremer
Albert Capellani: Pioneer of the Silent Screen
    Christine Leteux
A Front Row Seat: An Intimate Look at Broadway, Hollywood, and the Age of Glamour
    Nancy Olson Livingston
Ridley Scott: A Biography
    Vincent LoBrutto
Mamoulian: Life on Stage and Screen
    David Luhrssen
Maureen O'Hara: The Biography
    Aubrey Malone
My Life as a Mankiewicz: An Insider's Journey through Hollywood
    Tom Mankiewicz and Robert Crane
Hawks on Hawks
    Joseph McBride
John Ford
    Joseph McBride and Michael Wilmington
Showman of the Screen: Joseph E. Levine and His Revolutions in Film Promotion
    A. T. McKenna
William Wyler: The Life and Films of Hollywood's Most Celebrated Director
    Gabriel Miller
Raoul Walsh: The True Adventures of Hollywood's Legendary Director
    Marilyn Ann Moss
Veit Harlan: The Life and Work of a Nazi Filmmaker
    Frank Noack
Harry Langdon: King of Silent Comedy
    Gabriella Oldham and Mabel Langdon
Mavericks: Interviews with the World's Iconoclast Filmmakers
    Gerald Peary
Charles Walters: The Director Who Made Hollywood Dance
    Brent Phillips
Some Like It Wilder: The Life and Controversial Films of Billy Wilder
    Gene D. Phillips
Ann Dvorak: Hollywood's Forgotten Rebel
    Christina Rice
Mean . . . Moody . . . Magnificent! Jane Russell and the Marketing of a Hollywood Legend
    Christina Rice
Fay Wray and Robert Riskin: A Hollywood Memoir
    Victoria Riskin
Lewis Milestone: Life and Films
    Harlow Robinson
Michael Curtiz: A Life in Film
    Alan K. Rode
Ryan's Daughter: The Making of an Irish Epic
    Paul Benedict Rowan

Arthur Penn: American Director
    Nat Segaloff
Film's First Family: The Untold Story of the Costellos
    Terry Chester Shulman
Claude Rains: An Actor's Voice
    David J. Skal with Jessica Rains
June Mathis: The Rise and Fall of a Silent Film Visionary
    Thomas J. Slater
Horses of Hollywood
    Roberta Smoodin
Barbara La Marr: The Girl Who Was Too Beautiful for Hollywood
    Sherri Snyder
Lionel Barrymore: Character and Endurance in Hollywood's Golden Age
    Kathleen Spaltro
Buzz: The Life and Art of Busby Berkeley
    Jeffrey Spivak
Victor Fleming: An American Movie Master
    Michael Sragow
Aline MacMahon: Hollywood, the Blacklist, and the Birth of Method Acting
    John Stangeland
My Place in the Sun: Life in the Golden Age of Hollywood and Washington
    George Stevens, Jr.
There's No Going Back: The Life and Work of Jonathan Demme
    David M. Stewart
Hollywood Presents Jules Verne: The Father of Science Fiction on Screen
    Brian Taves
Thomas Ince: Hollywood's Independent Pioneer
    Brian Taves
Picturing Peter Bogdanovich: My Conversations with the New Hollywood Director
    Peter Tonguette
Jessica Lange: An Adventurer's Heart
    Anthony Uzarowski
Carl Theodor Dreyer and Ordet: *My Summer with the Danish Filmmaker*
    Jan Wahl
Wild Bill Wellman: Hollywood Rebel
    William Wellman Jr.
Harvard, Hollywood, Hitmen, and Holy Men: A Memoir
    Paul W. Williams
The Warner Brothers
    Chris Yogerst
Clarence Brown: Hollywood's Forgotten Master
    Gwenda Young
The Queen of Technicolor: Maria Montez in Hollywood
    Tom Zimmerman